Plug & Transplant Production

A Grower's Guide

by Roger C. Styer, Ph.D.
and David S. Koranski, Ph.D.

Ball Publishing

Batavia, Illinois USA

Ball Publishing
335 North River Street
Batavia, Illinois 60510 USA

Library of Congress Cataloging-in-Publication Data

Styer, Roger C., 1952–
    Plug & transplant production : a grower's guide / by Roger C.
Styer and David S. Koranski.
        p.   cm.
    Includes bibliographical references and index.
    ISBN 1-883052-14-9
    1. Bedding plants—Propagation. 2. Vegetables—Propagation.
3. Plant plugs. I. Koranski, David S., 1941– . II. Title.
SB423.7.S88 1997   96-37957
635'.04531—dc21   CIP

Disclaimer of liabilities:
Reference in the publication to a trademark, proprietary product, or company name is
intended for explicit description only and does not imply approval or recommendation to the
exclusion of others that may be suitable.

While every effort has been made to ensure the accuracy and effectiveness of the information
in this book, the authors and Ball Publishing make no guarantee, express or implied, as to the
procedures contained here. Neither the authors or publisher will be liable for direct, indirect,
incidental, or consequential damages in connection with or arising from the furnishing, performance, or use of this book.

Cover photos by Chris Beytes, managing editor of *GrowerTalks* magazine.

ACKNOWLEDGMENTS

W e want to thank all the growers and researchers who have contributed in so many ways to the information in this book. Through their hard work, solutions to problems, and discussions of results with us over the years, we have been able to accumulate much of the volume of knowledge presented here.

Special thanks go to the staff at Ball Publishing Co., particularly Liza Sutherland and her corps of editors, for their encouragement, enthusiasm, and effort in making this book possible.

Finally, an extra special thanks to my mother, Vicky Styer, who, with her willingness to listen, her support, and her love, helped me through the many changes in my life in the past few years. With her help, this book has finally been born!

Contents

PREFACE

P lug and transplant production has become a worldwide business in the past 15 to 20 years. To successfully produce any seedling in the miniature container called a plug cell requires highly technical growing skills. Even though a grower may produce thousands or millions of seedlings, attention to detail is a must. Serious—and costly—mistakes can occur at any growing operation. How to avoid these mistakes, as well as how to improve the production process, are what growers around the world want to know.

Growers constantly ask us where they can find detailed information on nutrition, environment, germination, and other areas of plug growing, and many articles have been published in the past 10 years on growing plugs. But there has never been one published source for all the information needed to successfully produce all types of seedlings in a plug system. Now, for the first time, we have put together the concepts, procedures, and details for successfully growing plugs and transplants of many types of crops. Much of the information in this book comes from our own experiences, as well as published information.

This book can be used by advanced or beginning plug growers. Any grower currently involved with producing plugs or transplants, as well as anyone thinking about producing plugs or transplants, will find valuable information here. In addition, researchers, extension agents, students, and industry personnel involved with the production of bedding plants, cut flowers, vegetables, tobacco, pot crops, or any growing plants will greatly benefit from the basic and detailed information provided.

Key topics covered include germination, water and media quality, nutrition, environment, growth regulators, diseases and insects, scheduling, and more. A color section provides vivid diagnosis of problems involving nutrition, diseases, insects, and growth regulators. Finally, there are separate wall-size charts detailing information about growing different crops in a plug. Use these charts as handy references.

We hope you find this book of great benefit to your growing operation and knowledge base. Everyone needs to understand the key points in plug production, from getting started in plug production, to finding solutions to problems such as germination or nutrition. This book should help you understand the key growing concepts that apply to all plants, not just plugs. We hope that increasing your overall knowledge of growing seedlings and plants will help you become more profitable through better and more efficient plug and transplant production.

CHAPTER 1

INTRODUCTION

PART 1: INTRODUCTION TO PLUGS

What is a plug? To answer this question, let's first look at how seedlings were produced before plugs came about. The traditional method of growing seedlings involved sowing seed in rows or broadcast in seedling flats (fig. 1.1) or in a prepared ground bed. Once germination occurred and seedlings were big enough to transplant, they were dug up in clumps, separated by hand, and each transplanted by hand into a bigger container or into the field. This very labor-intensive method resulted in considerable losses after transplanting from root rot and in uneven growth due to loss of roots and transplant shock.

FIGURE 1.1 Seedling tray with seed sown in rows.

A *plug* is a containerized transplant. Seed is mechanically sown into individual cells in a plug tray. After germination the seedling grows in its own miniature container until ready to transplant. Each root system is totally self-enclosed (fig. 1.2), resulting in optimum root growth with plenty of root hairs. When transplanted, the plug is simply pushed or pulled out of the cell and placed intact into the larger container or the field. Little if any damage occurs to the root system, so losses from root rot are greatly reduced, and growth after transplanting is very even. The transplanting process is much faster and easier than with bare-rooted seedlings.

FIGURE 1.2 Plug seedling with intact root system.

ADVANTAGES OF USING PLUGS

There are many advantages, but also disadvantages, to using plugs compared to bare-rooted seedlings from a seedling flat or seedling bed. Plugs offer these advantages:

- Less time and labor to transplant
- Faster and more uniform growth after transplanting
- Reduced loss to root rot after transplanting
- Earlier and more uniform flowering and yields
- Increased production per ft² or m², with faster crop time
- Better use of seed and space
- Mechanization and labor reduction due to handling ease
- Can be held for delayed transplanting
- Less chance for disease to spread

Transplanted plugs keep more root hairs, which quickly absorb water and nutrients. This active root system allows more uniform and faster plant growth, with little or no transplant shock. There is little need to replace dead seedlings in the container or field because usually 100% of the seedlings survive and grow. Bare-rooted seedling roots, damaged by handling, must regenerate to allow the top growth to begin growing again. A damaged root system also allows entry of different soil fungi that cause root rots, principally *Pythium, Phytophthora, Fusarium,* and *Thielaviopsis.*

The plug's shoot and root growth means less time is needed to flower, set fruit, or whatever else may be the desired end product. This faster crop time results in more production in the same space in a season, which means more profits with less investment in land and greenhouses.

Plug production can be highly mechanized, and seed can be singulated resulting in better use of seed and space. Plugs can be transplanted by mechanical transplanters, thereby saving more on human labor for a very menial task.

Since each plug is in its own container, the plant can be held for a period of time with little loss of quality if transplanting is delayed for any reason. With seedling boxes or beds, you must transplant quickly, or the plants will stretch tremendously, and their root systems will be more intertwined.

DISADVANTAGES OF PLUGS

Even with all these advantages, plugs do have disadvantages:

- Grower required to change production method
- More difficult to produce plugs yourself, as opposed to buying them in
- High initial costs for equipment and greenhouse space
- Specially trained people needed to seed and grow the plugs
- Specialized techniques needed for growing plugs
- Four times more greenhouse space to propagate
- Longer time to produce plug than seedling flat
- Greater cost per seedling for plugs

The most important plug disadvantage to overcome is simply the idea of change. Growers have to totally change what they have been doing for the past 20 or more years. Seedling boxes and beds share water and nutrients easily, so growing seedlings is not difficult. In a plug tray, however, each cell is a container, so moisture and nutrients cannot be shared with its neighbors. The small size of each container allows rapid changes in soil pH, nutrient levels, and moisture availability, making mistakes more costly. However, germination percentages are easily determined visually.

Rapid changes in individual plugs mean more investment is needed in facilities, equipment, and people to grow good plugs. Any mechanical seeder requires a trained person to operate it. A plug grower must be dedicated to growing the plugs during the whole season and willing to adjust to changes between seasons. Inattention to plugs can result in plant death from such hazards as drying out and chemical burn.

Finally, since the plug tray occupies the same space as a seedling flat but with fewer seedlings, and since one transplants later with plugs, the cost per seedling is greater.

EARLY U.S. PLUG PRODUCTION

Despite the many advantages of plugs, their use did not develop overnight. Plug production began in the late 1960s and early 1970s in the United States. Four different individuals and their companies figured prominently in the development of plug technology. George Todd, Sr., at Speedling Inc., in Sun City, Florida, developed his own Styrofoam plug trays (fig. 1.3), seeder, and production system for growing veg-

FIGURE 1.3 Styrofoam trays for vegetable transplants originated by George Todd at Speedling Inc. Courtesy Speedling Inc.

etable plugs for field transplanting. Bill Swannekamp at Kube-Pak in Allentown, New Jersey, also developed his own seeder, hard plastic trays, and production system for growing bedding plant plugs. Ed Pinter, Sr., of Pinter Brothers Greenhouse, Ypsilanti, Michigan, along with Fred Blackmore, Blackmore Transplanter Co., Ypsilanti, developed an interesting plug production system for bedding plants. Using a shallow, waffle-type, hard plastic tray (fig. 1.4), the seedling could be punched out through the bottom into a finished container by a "mechanical transplanter." They also developed a seeder that could seed this type of plug tray accurately.

In 1979 there were about a half million bedding plant plugs produced in the United States. In 1994 the best guess was that there were more than 4 *billion* bedding plant plugs in the United States and Canada alone. More than 90% of all bedding crops are now produced from plugs. Adding vegetable plugs (about three to four times the number of bedding plants), along with pot crops, cut flowers, perennials, tissue-culture material, and trees, the current number of plugs used is easily more than 25 *billion* in the United States and Canada alone!

FIGURE 1.4   Original Blackmore plug tray (above), the 648-waffle, designed for seedlings to be pushed out through the bottom of the tray into the finished container by Blackmore mechanical transplanter (below).

PLUG PRODUCTION WORLDWIDE

In Europe most all the greenhouse vegetables are started from plugs. The percentage of bedding plants started from plugs is maybe 50%, far less than in the United States, but rapidly increasing. In Europe cut flowers started from seed are

almost 100% from plugs. In Japan there is major plug production in vegetables, cut flowers, and bedding crops. Australia also does a high percentage of its bedding crops from plugs. In Israel a large number of vegetable plugs are produced. Plug technology has now spread to Korea, Taiwan, mainland China, Colombia, Central America, Mexico, South Africa, and many other countries. The greatest usage of plugs is in producing trees, vegetables, bedding plants, and cut flowers. Worldwide plug production will continue to grow as more countries look to save labor, feed their people, and move new agricultural and horticultural businesses into the world market.

GROW YOUR OWN PLUGS OR BUY THEM?

There are a number of factors to consider thoroughly before choosing between producing your own plugs or buying them from a specialist. As with any major economic decision, the better you answer the questions, the better decision you make for your operation.

ADVANTAGES

Control. The most obvious advantage is *control.* When you grow your own plugs, you have a greater variety of cultivars from which to choose. You may have some old favorites that plug specialists don't produce. If you have a wide variety list for petunias, for example, you can grow just one or two trays of each whenever you need them. Plug suppliers, on the other hand, generally require that you order a minimum number of trays per variety and ship week.

In growing your own plugs, you also control all the production factors and the quality. Everyone has a different opinion on what a perfect plug is. Perhaps you want a softer or shorter plug than what is available from plug specialists. Many growers do not want to be victimized by a plug specialist's crop failures. There is a certain satisfaction that comes from overcoming the challenges of plug production yourself and growing a successful crop.

Cheaper cost. A large reason for growing your own plugs is a *cheaper cost* per plug. Many growers believe that buying plugs is too expensive and that they can produce their own for less. When buying plugs, you are paying for shipping, as well as a profit margin for the broker and plug specialist. Figure 1.5 illustrates the costs of producing finished bedding flats from your own plugs and from bought-in plugs [1]. Use your own figures to calculate what it would truly cost you to produce your own plugs.

Timing. *Timing* could be another reason to grow your own plugs, especially if you produce your crop somewhat differently from other growers.

No plug specialists. There may be *no plug specialists* or brokers in your area or country. This fact may leave you no choice but to produce plugs yourself.

QUESTIONS TO CONSIDER

Do you know how much investment will be needed to improve your facilities and equipment to grow plugs? Plug production requires special equipment,

FIGURE 1.5 With the example given, 1804 flats produced from plugs grown in-house with two turns yield plants that come in at 11 cents each. Compare that to 1804 flats produced from purchased plugs where plants are 10 cents each. Do you know where your costs fall?

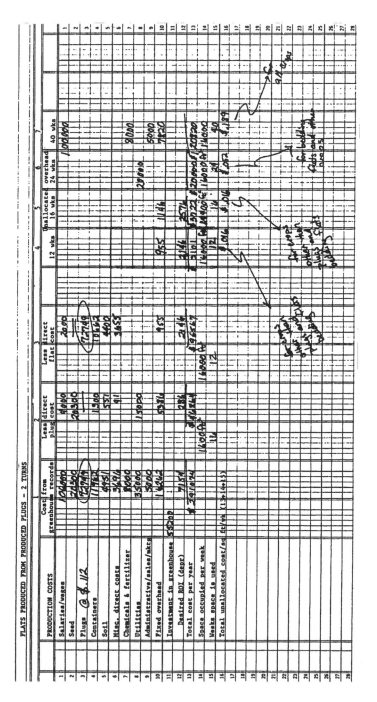

FIGURE 1.5 continued—Look at purchasing plugs. The average going price for a 406-cell plug is about 6 cents, including freight. Figure 1.5 illustrates how the expense will change by purchasing plugs rather than producing plugs. From Laffe, Styer and Szmurlo.

FLATS PRODUCED FROM PURCHASED PLUGS – 2 TURNS

	PRODUCTION COSTS	Expense from greenhouse records	Less direct flat cost	Unallocated overhead 28 wks	40 wks
1	Salaries/wages	102000	2000	100000	
2	Plugs @ $.06	54562	54562		
3	Containers	10662	10662		
4	Soil	4400	4400		
5	Misc. direct costs	3655	3655		
6	Chemicals & fertilizer	6000			6000
7	Utilities	33000			33000
8	Administrative/sales/mktg	5000			5000
9	Fixed overhead	10874	917	2138	7819
10	Investment in greenhouse	55200			
11	Desired ROI (depr)	7159	2147	5009	
12	Total cost per year	$257307	$73343	$71147	$50819
13	Space occupied per week	16000 ft	16000 ft	16000 ft	16000 ft
14	Weeks space is used		12	28	40
15	Total unallocated cost/sq ft/wk (12÷13÷14)			$.016	$.237
16					
17					
18					
19					
20					
21					
22					
23					
24					
25					
26					

such as a plug flat filler (for filling plug trays with media), a mechanical seeder (or more than one seeder), a covering machine (for covering with coarse vermiculite or other materials), and a watering tunnel (for watering in trays after seeding). Most of this equipment is specific for plugs and cannot be used for other production. Plug growing requires more precise control of the environment, watering, and fertilizing. You may need to either retrofit an existing greenhouse or build a new greenhouse specifically for plugs. Whether you use environmental computer control, fog or mist systems, root-zone heating, boom irrigators, movable benches, HID lights, shade curtains, HAF fans, monorails, or carts, you need to decide what facilities you need and how much to spend. One special facility to consider is a germination chamber, where you can precisely control temperature, moisture, and light for best germination. The result is an altogether much higher cost per ft^2 (m^2) for a plug growing area.

Do you have the space available to grow plugs? Plug growing space must be allocated throughout the growing season in order to have plugs ready when needed for transplanting. Will you have room during your busiest season, when your greenhouses are full of plants in larger containers?

Who will grow the plugs? Usually, if the operation is small, the owner will be growing the plugs. This takes away time from other responsibilities of running the business. When the season gets busy, plug quality can suffer from neglect. Do you have a grower you can designate to grow the plugs?

While we are discussing personnel, don't forget about training someone to run the seeder. Each type of mechanical seeder is different, but all depend on the skill and attention of the seeder operator. Think of the seeder operator as a pilot, who needs so many hours of flying to become properly trained and keep his or her skills sharp. A high plug germination rate is often made or shattered at the seeder!

Do you have high-quality water? *Do you even know your water quality?* The water that you use to grow plants in regular-sized containers may not be good enough to grow plugs. Factors such as alkalinity, soluble salts, and boron may require you to look at alternate water sources or at methods for cleaning up your water. Before you ever buy land for a plug operation, remember to test the quality of water available first!

Costs and profitability. Do plugs conflict with other crops for space and time? Could you be growing other crops and selling them during the time needed for growing plugs? You need to have space for plugs even during your busiest season, and you need to pay attention to them. Most growers make money by selling finished product, not plugs. Can you justify more investment of money, space, and time into growing plugs if plugs contribute only to your costs? Can you make more efficient use of greenhouse space by focusing on turns and finished product rather than growing your own plugs? To grow plugs, you need to start up your greenhouses earlier in the year, however, resulting in greater costs for heating, cooling, and electricity.

The learning curve. Growing plugs requires certain levels of knowledge. As you increase your knowledge, you also reach different economic thresholds, where you must make economic decisions based on space, time, and money. We have summarized these general knowledge levels and economic thresholds in fig. 1.6. Where do you fit on this curve?

BUYING PLUGS FROM A BROKER

If you have decided that growing your own plugs may be too much for you, then look at buying plugs from a specialist or broker. Why?

1. Less investment in greenhouses and equipment

2. Fewer of your own skilled personnel needed

FIGURE 1.6 Plug learning curve.

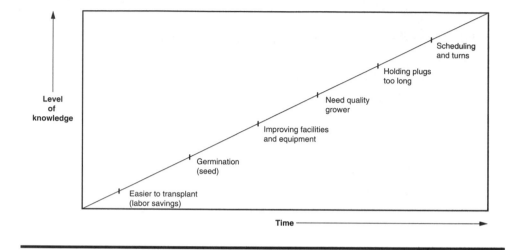

3. Less space and time

4. Easier and better production scheduling

5. Time of the year may be too hot or too cold for you to grow plugs

6. Greater choice of plug sizes

7. Last-minute needs satisfied

QUESTIONS TO ASK

Before you decide to buy plugs from a specialist or broker, ask yourself some questions. Are you willing to give up control and rely on the plug supplier to deliver your plugs when you need them? Does your plug supplier offer a wide range of varieties, deliver a quality product consistently, have a number of plug sizes to meet your needs, deliver the plugs by truck, and have extra plugs to meet your last-minute needs? Supplier reliability is the key to your dealings and success.

The cost of the purchased plug is always a big concern. To look at this issue, remember to compare plug cost to the selling price of your finished product. Generally, with bedding plants the cost of the plug should be no higher than 20 to 25% of your selling price. For other crops this cost relationship will be different but should still be looked at closely. Also, the cost relationship will be different for a wholesale grower compared to a retail grower. A wholesale grower needs to buy a cheaper-priced plug because of selling the finished product for less than a retail grower.

GROW SOME, BUY SOME

Some growers who have started growing their own plugs have problems growing certain crops. Instead of continuing to struggle with plug production of these crops, they decide on buying them from a specialist and grow only the plug crops that they do best. If you are just starting to grow plugs, grow the easy crops first. Buy the rest of your plugs from a reliable specialist. Many growers have difficulty growing plugs of begonia, vinca, or verbena but can easily do petunias, impatiens, or pansies. Do what you do best, and buy the rest! Sometimes growers produce their own plugs for the first turn in the season, then buy in the rest to optimize their space and time.

PART 2: THE FOUR STAGES OF PLUG PRODUCTION

In this book we frequently talk about the four stages of plug production. Much of our information defines the optimum conditions for different crops in each of the four stages and how to create and apply these conditions for best results.

STAGES 1 TO 4

To make plug production easier to understand and more specific for crop recommendations, it is divided into four different stages from the beginning of germination to the time of transplanting (fig. 1.7). In Stage 1, the primary root (or radicle) emerges from the seed. This period of growth requires high levels of moisture and oxygen around the seed. The seedlings enter Stage 2 after the radicles emerge. In Stage 2 the radicles penetrate the soil, and the stem (hypocotyl) and seed leaves (cotyledons) emerge. At this time the amount of oxygen needed by the root increases, so the amount of moisture applied should be decreased. Stages 1 and 2 comprise the **germination stages**, meaning that all germination should be finished by the end of Stage 2. During Stage 3, the true leaves grow and develop. In Stage 4, seedlings are ready for shipping, transplanting, or holding. Stages 3 and 4 make up the **growth stages** because most of the seedling growth occurs at this time.

We divide plug production into stages because different environmental and cultural conditions are needed for each developmental stage. The most critical time period for plugs is during Stages 1 and 2. The supply of optimal levels of moisture, oxygen, temperature, and light is critical and will

---

FIGURE 1.7 The four stages of plug production.

STAGE 1—From sowing to radicle emergence

STAGE 2—From radicle emergence to cotyledon expansion; germination is finished

STAGE 3—From cotyledon expansion to growth of all true leaves

STAGE 4—From growth of all true leaves to toning for shipping or holding; plug growth is finished

---

mean success or failure for the plug grower. Generally, the warmest temperatures are needed for Stage 1 to start the germination process; each succeeding stage means a reduction in temperature. Moisture levels are usually the highest for most crops in Stage 1 and are reduced in Stage 2 for best rooting in. Light is at the lowest level for germination and increases with seedling growth.

Nutrition is the lowest during Stage 1 because not many nutrients are needed for the seed to germinate. Nutrient levels increase with each stage until you reach Stage 4, which is the toning or holding stage. Here is a summary of the conditions needed for most plug crops:

Condition	Stage 1—> Stage 4
Temperature	High —> Low
Moisture	High —> Low
Light	Low —> High
Nutrition	Low —> High

Plug growers can use these stages in several ways. By defining optimum conditions for both the beginning and end of germination, growers can better optimize their plant stands. Growers can move crops to different environments or optimize the environment where the plug trays are at without moving the trays until shipping or transplanting.

REFERENCES

[1] Laffe, S.H., R. Styer, and G. Szmurlo. 1990. Plug Economics 101: Tackling the grow vs. buy issue. *GrowerTalks* 54(8):52–60.

CHAPTER 2

GREENHOUSE STRUCTURES AND EQUIPMENT

T o grow plugs, you first must have a greenhouse (or glasshouse, as it is called in Europe) designed as an enclosure for economically producing crops in optimum environmental conditions. The structure must withstand wind, rain, hail, snow, and the stress of hanging things from it. It must also allow sufficient photosynthetically active radiation (PAR) through the glazing or covering for plant growth. In certain climates a shadehouse can be used to grow and harden older plugs (Stages 3 and 4 of plug production).

The structure must also be designed so that a plug crop can be handled efficiently, with minimum labor and management. The cropping system, environmental control system, and material-handling features must be integrated into an effective greenhouse production facility. Considering one piece of the puzzle without the others can only lead to an ineffective and uneconomical operation.

In this chapter we will discuss the key parts of building or retrofitting a greenhouse for plug production, including types of greenhouses and the equipment that should go into them. For details about greenhouse construction beyond this chapter's scope, please refer to the excellent book *Greenhouse Engineering* by Aldrich and Bartok [1].

BUILD NEW OR RETROFIT EXISTING GREENHOUSE

Before building or retrofitting a greenhouse for plugs, there are several key points to consider:

- Greenhouse space needed
- Length of time devoted to plugs

- Existing greenhouse conversion
- Plug production for self or for selling
- Construction time
- Cost comparison
- Research of other operations

If you are growing other crops at the same time or throughout the year, how much room will you need just for plugs? Remember, this will be the most costly production space you will have! Should you share greenhouse space between plugs and other crops or have a dedicated greenhouse just for plugs? Most growers need greenhouse space for plugs only from January to April. What will you do with this space the rest of the year?

Retrofitting an existing greenhouse will involve compromises that could affect your plug quality. In most cases, when growers retrofit an existing greenhouse, they keep the frame and covering but replace benching, heating, and cooling. The height of the gutters will affect air movement, heating, and cooling. The type and age of covering will affect light transmission.

Are you producing plugs only for your own use, or are you planning on selling plugs? Generally, better greenhouse structures and equipment are needed for an operation that plans on selling plugs to other people. Plug quality is very dependent on the ability to control environment, nutrition, and water, and to move trays efficiently as needed. If you will produce only for yourself, retrofitting an existing greenhouse or a part of one might be all you would need.

When will the construction be done, and how long will it take? Will you still be producing crops while all this construction goes on? Nothing about greenhouse construction ever goes according to schedule, so make sure to put in a fudge factor. Our experience with growers and building greenhouses is to take the time period estimated by the greenhouse contractor and add one to two months to it. It will also take about a month to fully debug a new greenhouse, with all the equipment needed for plug production.

Make sure you can compare greenhouse construction costs properly. When asking for quotes from various greenhouse contractors, be specific about what you want included in the quote. If not specific enough, a grower may leave it up to the greenhouse contractor to figure out what is needed. Then a quote may include only certain items while leaving others out, giving an unrealistically low total.

Finally, before starting to build, make sure you travel around your area and other parts of the United States and Europe visiting other greenhouse plug operations, visiting trade shows, and asking a lot of questions. Do your research before it costs you money to build!

SITE SELECTION

A good building site and plan layout can make a big difference in the functional and environmental operation of a plug greenhouse. Let's consider the following key factors in site selection: (1) location, (2) high-quality water supply, (3) greenhouse orientation to sun, (4) headhouse location, and (5) electric power. Where you decide to build will depend on the amount of land available, slope and drainage, local zoning and tax laws, climate, accessibility for trucks, labor supply, and fuel source. Make sure you have enough room for expansion.

A dependable supply of high-quality water is needed for plug production. Many growing operations have failed because the water quality or quantity was not determined before the greenhouses were built. Test the available water source for alkalinity, soluble salts, sodium, chlorides, boron, and other key elements before buying the land. If the water source is not of good quality, then consider the costs of improving the water with acid injection, reverse osmosis, filtration, or other techniques. Is municipal water available, and at what price? What about pond water or collection areas for rainwater? You may need chlorination to remove disease organisms and algae from pond water. You need to know local laws related to water usage. Keep in mind how much water you will need and how many wells you may have to drill.

Greenhouse orientation depends on latitude, type of greenhouse (single or gutter-connected), and how much shading you are willing to tolerate during the winter. Generally, beyond 40 degrees north or south latitude, single greenhouses should be built with the ridge running east-west, whereas gutter-connected greenhouses should be oriented north-south. This latter orientation compensates for the shadow from the north roof and gutter of each adjacent greenhouse, permitting it to move across the floor during the day. Below 40 degrees north or south latitude, single greenhouses and gutter-connected greenhouses should both be oriented with ridges running north-south, since the angle of the sun is much higher [3, 4].

Locate the headhouse to the north of the growing area, if possible, so there will be less shading. A good headhouse layout will help the material flow smoothly and efficiently. On the average, the headhouse should be about 10% of the greenhouse growing area.

An adequate electric power supply and distribution system should be provided to serve the environmental-control and mechanization needs of the plug greenhouse. If you use HID lights, pad and fan cooling, HAF fans, and other heavy users of electricity, you will need more electricity than you might think. Make sure you have a big enough transformer available to your operation.

GREENHOUSE SIZE AND SHAPE

Many types of greenhouses are being used successfully for plug production throughout the world. While some may have advantages over others for particular reasons, there seems to be no one best plug greenhouse! Simply put, the structural design of a plug greenhouse must provide safety from wind, rain, hail, snow, and crop load damage while permitting maximum light transmission. And it must fit your budget!

Let's look at the different types of greenhouses used for plug production. Figure 2.1 shows the basic styles and roof designs. Greenhouses can be freestanding (A and B) or gutter-connected (C through F). Freestanding houses can have an arched or Quonset roof (A) or a peaked (gable) roof of even span (B).

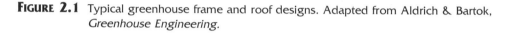

FIGURE 2.1   Typical greenhouse frame and roof designs. Adapted from Aldrich & Bartok, *Greenhouse Engineering.*

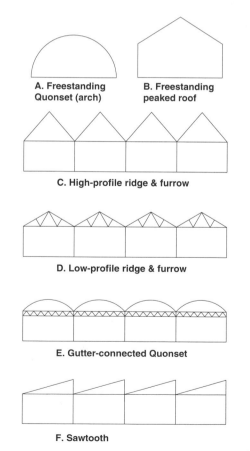

A ridge-and-furrow design consists of two or more A-frame greenhouses connected to one another along the length of the gutter (C, D). These greenhouses can have a high profile (C) or a low profile (D). The low-profile greenhouse (Venlo) is most popular in the Netherlands. The lower profile slightly reduces exposed surface area, thereby reducing the heating cost. However, these greenhouses are more expensive to cool in warm climates where fans are required. Single panes of glass or rigid plastic extend from gutter to ridge, making roof construction cheaper and faster.

High-profile greenhouses allow more air movement, due to more head space in the peak, making them easier to cool in warm climates. Since there is more surface area in the roof, heat loss is greater in cold climates. Construction is more difficult and costly due to more panels needed in the roof.

In North America both low-profile and high-profile greenhouses are currently used for plug production, with high-profile designs becoming more popular. Advantages of ridge-and-furrow design include: (1) elimination of side walls between greenhouses, resulting in a structure with a single, large interior; (2) reduction of labor; (3) lower cost of automation; (4) improved personnel management; and (5) reduced fuel consumption. The main disadvantage is snow cannot slide all the way off the roofs; therefore, snow loads must be taken into account in the load calculations for construction. Heating pipes are generally located beneath the gutters, or cables can be placed in the gutters, for the purpose of melting the snow away.

Ridge-and-furrow greenhouses are also commonly called *gutter-connected*. Another type of gutter-connected greenhouse does not have peaked roofs, but arched or Quonset roofs (fig. 2.1E). This shape is commonly used with double-polyethylene-inflatable roofs.

Finally, the sawtooth design is a gutter-connected greenhouse with peaked roofs but uneven spans (fig. 2.1F). This greenhouse has one roof vent per span and usually has sides that roll up or down. Sawtooth roofs are usually made out of rigid plastic or fiberglass. This design is not commonly used throughout North America but can be found in Florida (fig. 2.2) and California.

FIGURE 2.2 Sawtooth plug greenhouse in Florida with external retractable shade curtains. Courtesy Suncoast Greenhouses Inc.

Consider carefully whether you want a peaked roof or arched (Quonset) roof for your freestanding or gutter-connected plug greenhouse. Condensation collecting inside the roof covering can better run off to the sides without dripping on the plug trays (fig. 2.3) in a peaked roof design.

Many plug growers have had to spray Sun Clear, a liquid surfactant, on the inside of Quonset poly roofs to reduce condensation and prevent drips. Other growers set up a third layer of poly as a tent just under the roof to channel drips away to the sides. Still other plug growers have replaced their double-poly Quonset roofs with peaked roofs of glass or rigid plastic to reduce drips. Furthermore, an arched roof is difficult to ventilate, so heat builds up in the top.

If you live in an area subject to high winds or where snow is common, then you must calculate design loads carefully. Design loads include the weight of the structure (dead load), loads brought on because of building use (live loads), and loads from snow and wind. The National Greenhouse Manufacturers Association (NGMA) recommends a maximum live load of 15 lb/ft² (73 kg/m²) of ground area covered [1]. Greenhouses should also be

FIGURE 2.3 Drips on plug trays cause blow-out of cells.

designed to resist an 80-mph wind (129 km/h) from the direction that will produce the greatest wind load. For snow load, the NGMA has used a minimum value of 15 lb/ft² (73 kg/m²) of covered area. Figure 2.4 shows how loads act on greenhouse frames.

Gutter height is critical for good air movement, heating, cooling, and providing room to hang equipment such as boom irrigators, HID lights, shade curtains, and HAF fans. The best plug greenhouses have gutter heights of 12 to 14 feet (3.7 to 4.3 meters) or higher.

The type of floor will depend on your benching system. Most plug greenhouses have either a gravel floor with concrete traffic aisles or an all-concrete floor for drainage and weed and insect control. Porous concrete makes a good floor surface for greenhouses because it allows water to pass through, avoiding puddles or other standing water. Usually, the concrete

FIGURE 2.4 Loads on greenhouse frames. The arrow lengths and directions indicate relative sizes of loads and how the loads act on greenhouses.
A, gravity loads act downward and include dead load (the weight of the greenhouse itself), live loads (the weight of suspended crops, equipment, workers), and snow load; B, wind loads on similar frames. Adapted from Aldrich & Bartok, *Greenhouse Engineering.*

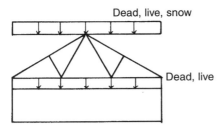

Arch

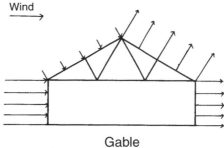

Arch

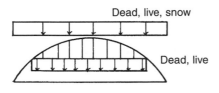

Gable

Gable

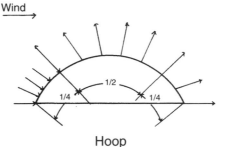

Hoop

Hoop

A

B

needs to be 4 inches (10.2 cm) thick to carry personnel and light vehicle traffic. However, concrete gets slippery with algae and hotter than gravel in the summer due to heat retention, and it costs more to install.

COVERINGS

Several glazings are used for greenhouses today. Glass is the original and most reliable from the standpoint of light transmission. Other rigid coverings include fiberglass reinforced panels (FRP), acrylic panels, polycarbonate panels, Plexiglas, and some forms of rigid polyvinyl chloride (PVC). Flexible coverings include polyethylene, polyvinyl chloride, and polyvinyl fluoride films. All these flexible coverings have been used in double-covering schemes to conserve energy by reducing heat loss from the greenhouse. However, the second layer will also reduce light transmission by about 10%. Table 2.1 outlines the different coverings, their advantages and disadvantages, light and thermal transmittance, estimated life, and estimated cost/ft^2.

Light transmission is the key factor for any greenhouse covering. Know how much photosynthetically active radiation (PAR), the light wavelengths that the plant needs for photosynthesis, is allowed through the coverings you are considering. This type of light is not exactly the same as the human eye can see. Remember, when a second layer of covering is added, light transmission is reduced 10%. Also, condensation on the inside of the covering significantly reduces light transmission; this problem is particularly acute with such flexible coverings as polyethylene films.

Heat transmission and retention vary between coverings (indicated in table 2.1 as "Thermal transmittance"). Heat comes through the covering into the greenhouse by higher light transmission, allowing mostly infrared (IR) light, which causes a buildup of heat. Heat can also come through a thinner covering, allowing a higher temperature outside to heat up the greenhouse inside. Heat can be lost to the outside on a clear, cold night by objects inside radiating IR heat to the outside. The heat transmission and retention can be improved by IR blockers in the covering and by using a double layer.

Combining the estimated life of the covering with the cost/ft^2 should give you a good idea of the cost of the covering per year of useful life. How often do you want to replace the covering? How easy is it to replace? What additional treatments can you look for to extend its life? Glass is more expensive than polyethylene film but will last much longer. You can get polyethylene film with an extended lifetime by getting film with UV inhibitors, but this may add only another year or so to the typical film's life. On the other hand, poly films are easy to replace and can save on heating costs.

TABLE 2.1 **GREENHOUSE COVERINGS CHARACTERISTICS**

Type, trade name	Light (PAR) transmittance [a] (%)	Thermal transmittance [b] (%)	Life (yrs)	$/ft^2 [c]
Glass				
Double strength	88	3	25+	0.75–2.00
Insulated unit	75–80	<3	25+	3.50–7.00
Solatex	91–94	<3	25+	1.25–3.50

Advantages Excellent transmittance; superior resistance to heat, UV, abrasion; low thermal expansion-contraction; readily available; transparent
Disadvantages Low impact resistance unless tempered, high cost, heavy

Acrylic				
Single-wall Plexiglass	93	<5	20+	1.50–2.00
Double-wall Exolite	87	<3	20+	2.00–3.50

Advantages Excellent transmittance; superior UV and weather resistance; will not yellow; lightweight; easy to fabricate on site
Disadvantages Easily scratched; high expansion-contraction; slight embrittlement with age; high cost; relatively low service temperatures; flammability

Polycarbonate				
Single wall Lexan Dynaglas	91–94	<3	10–15	1.25–1.50
Double wall Macrolux PolyGal Lexan	83	23	10–15	1.75–2.50

Advantages Excellent service temperatures; high-impact resistance; low flammability
Disadvantages Scratches easily; high expansion-contraction

Fiberglass reinforced polyester (FRP)				
Lascolite Filon Excelite	90	<3	10–15	0.85–1.25
Double-wall roof panels	60–80		7–12	5.00

Advantages Low cost; strong; easy to fabricate and install
Disadvantages Susceptible to UV, dust, and pollution degradation; yellows with age

TABLE 2.1   CONTINUED

Type, trade name	Light (PAR) transmittance [a] (%)	Thermal transmittance [b] (%)	Life (yrs)	$/ft² [c]
Polyethylene film (PE)				
Tufflite III 603 Standard UV	<85	50	3	0.06
Tufflite Dripless 703 Fog Bloc		50	3	0.07
Sun Saver Cloud 9 Tufflite Infrared Dura-Therm		<20	3	0.09

Advantages Inexpensive; easy to install; readily available in large sheets
Disadvantages Short life; low service temperature

Polyvinyl chloride (PVC) corrugated				
Bio 2	84	<25	10+	1.00–1.25

Advantages Durable; good fire rating; high-impact strength; IR inhibitor
Disadvantages Lower light transmittance; high expansion; yellows with age; only 4-ft. widths available

[a] Solar radiation wavelength from 0.38–2.5 microns; data are for glazing thickness used for greenhouse.

[b] Thermal radiation at approximately 10 microns, the wavelength at maximum radiation from surfaces at 70F; data are for glazing thicknesses used for greenhouses.

[c] Local prices may differ; cost includes support extrusions and attachments but not installation labor.

Notes: Adapted from manufacturers' data. No endorsement is implied where trade names are given. All plastics described will burn, so fire safety should be emphasized in greenhouses with such coverings.

Source: Adapted from Aldrich & Bartok, *Greenhouse Engineering.*

BENCHING

Raised benches are generally used for plug production. Benching can come in many forms, from simple concrete blocks with wood slatting to containerized benches that can be moved anywhere in the greenhouse. Some large growers in Holland and the United States grow plugs on concrete floors, either watering overhead or using ebb-and-flow irrigation. Many of these growers use Styrofoam plug trays.

Growing plug trays on a porous concrete floor requires careful grading and pouring of the concrete to achieve proper drainage. This system can be used in gutter-connected greenhouses with a large interior space (fig. 2.5).

Utilizing 90% of the floor area for grow-ing is the result. However, this method requires more extensive hand labor to put down and pick up the trays, thereby reduc-ing labor efficiency. Growers using this system generally combine it with ebb-and-flow irrigation. Recirculation of water and fertilizer is easily achieved. This system works best when crops and tray sizes having similar growing require-ments are grouped together, or when a large group of the same crop and age can be grown in one area (monoculture). Root growth coming out of the bottom of the trays is a problem. Heating pipes need to be located in the concrete, as well as above. Air movement is restricted below the trays, making it more difficult to man-age moisture.

FIGURE 2.5 Plug trays growing on concrete flood floors in Holland.

Fixed benches can be used for a small greenhouse operation. Space utilization can range from 59 to 80%, depending on the width of the aisles (fig. 2.6). Benches should generally be 32 to 36 inches (81 to 91 cm) high for working conve-nience. Width should not exceed 6 feet (1.83 m) to be accessible from both sides. Typical bench widths are 4 to 5 feet (1.22 to 1.52 m), and main aisle widths of 3 to 5 feet (0.91 to 1.52 m) or side aisle widths of 20 to 30 inches (51 to 76 cm) are common. Air circulation is best when benches are covered with wire mesh or expanded metal. To prevent sagging, uneven benches, the covering must be braced with piping underneath. For vegetable growers using Styrofoam trays, fixed benches may consist of rails on which the trays are suspended, with no bench covering.

Movable or rolling benches can increase production space 10 to 25% and can reduce labor. The bench tops are supported on pipe rollers and allowed to move sideways 18 to 24 inches (46 to 61 cm), the width needed for a work aisle. When there is a need to get to a particular bench, the other benches in the house are pushed together, leaving the open aisle at the desired bench (fig. 2.6). Only one side of the bench can be worked on at a

FIGURE 2.6 Greenhouse bench layouts. A, Longitudinal bench layout—59% growing area; B, Peninsula bench layout—69% growing area; C, Movable bench layout—81% growing area. From Aldrich & Bartok, *Greenhouse Engineering.* Reprinted by permission.

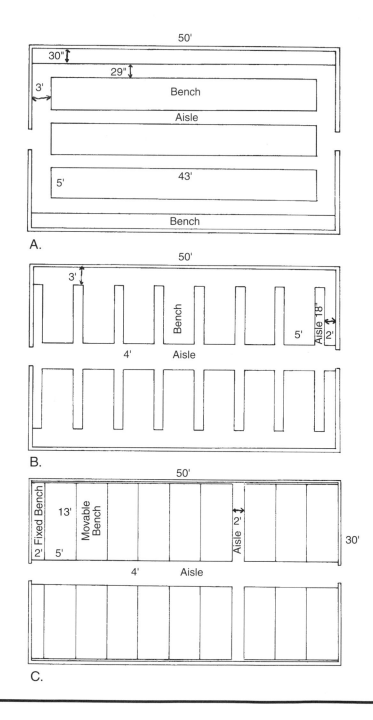

time. Because the benches move, connections for water, heat, and electrical systems that are attached to the bench are flexible. Benches as long as 200 feet (61 m) can be moved easily by turning one of the support rollers with a crank at the end of the bench [1]. Make sure that the edges of the benches are not sharp and the expanded metal covering is supported by piping to prevent unevenness. Difficulties with this benching system include dragging hoses for hand-watering, inability of having more than one worker in a section at a time, and frequently ripped clothes as greenhouse workers and growers walk among these benches.

Containerized benching is a movable system that utilizes pallet trays. These units, 4 to 6 feet (1.22 to 1.83 m) wide by 6 to 16 feet (1.83 to 4.88 m) long, are handled on roller conveyors or tracks (fig. 2.7). Greenhouse

space utilization is not as efficient with this system as with a rolling bench system, due to the fixed conveyor or track supports. However, moving trays is easy, with minimal labor from seeding to shipping. This system costs more than other benching, too.

FIGURE 2.7 Containerized bench system (above) with end aisles (below) for moving benches around a greenhouse in Japan.

The size of the greenhouse, the number of greenhouse zones, how many trays are produced of how many different crops and varieties, the availability of cheap labor, and the plug quality desired all enter into the decision about moving or not moving plug trays and how this moving should be accomplished. With vegetables, it is easy to

move the trays to the bench for germination and leave them there until time to ship. With many bedding plants, trays may need to be moved anywhere from two to five times to take advantage of different growing environments. If you do not want to move trays, you must consider making each greenhouse zone as flexible as possible for environmental and cultural control.

HEATING

A central boiler system is justified for the plug grower who starts out with a large range and expands in large increments. However, a boiler can be very inefficient, when it is operated at partial capacity. A central boiler system uses either steam or hot water. The advantages of a steam system are a smaller boiler, no circulating pumps, and less plumbing. However, the heat of steam is quickly dissipated, placing greater dependency on continual operation of the boiler. A hot water system uses water heated to either 180F or 203F (82C or 95C), with more pressure and thus greater heat capacity. Air temperatures in a hot-water-heated greenhouse remain more constant. The large volume of water in the system provides a reservoir of heat that could protect the greenhouse against frost for several hours after boiler failure.

FIGURE 2.8 Two types of under-bench hot-water heating pipes: BioTherm (above), Delta T (below). Courtesy BioTherm Hydronic Inc. and Delta T Sales.

The most common method of heating a large plug greenhouse is with hot water pipes or fin tubes under the benches (fig. 2.8). This location provides better root-zone heating, which is beneficial for plug growth, and does not waste so much heat on air above the crop. Fin tube is a conventional pipe with numerous thin metal plates radiating outward from it, increasing the effective conductive surface area of the pipe and thus the rate at which it transfers heat from the water inside to the surrounding air. Depending on the design, 1 foot (30 cm) of fin tube can be the heating equivalent of 4 or more feet (122 or more cm) of conventional pipe, so it should be remembered that heat released from fin tube is much more intense. Fin tubes need to be distributed evenly below the benches.

Root-zone heating can also be achieved with pipes buried in the floor or with flexible EPDM tubing (fig. 2.9) fastened just underneath the expanded metal bench. Buried pipes in a gravel or porous concrete floor are best for operations growing on the floor. Usually, you will need a supplemental heating system in addition to the pipes under the floor. The flexible EPDM tubes are usually spaced about two inches apart and must be located *under* the expanded metal for the best heat distribution and moisture control.

FIGURE 2.9 BioTherm flexible tubing root-zone heating system under expanded metal bench. Courtesy BioTherm Hydronic Inc.

Water is circulated through the tubes at temperatures up to 140F (60C). This type of system is best for the small grower who wants to provide root-zone heating for only a few benches. Installation costs are high, as are costs of materials.

A localized heating system can consist of either unit forced-air heaters or low-energy (infrared) radiant heaters. The localized system requires a small initial investment, which suits it to the greenhouse operation that starts small and expands steadily, purchasing heaters as needed. Make sure that forced-air heaters are vented to the outside, as carbon monoxide and other hazardous gases may be built up by incomplete combustion. These heaters are best used for plugs beyond the germination stages.

Low-energy radiant heaters, placed overhead in the greenhouse, emit infrared radiation, which travels in a straight path at the speed of light. However, radiant heaters are not widely used in plug growing, for several reasons. The capital costs are higher than with unit heaters. The metal piping covered by the reflector will eventually corrode in the humid environment of the greenhouse and have to be replaced. Coverage is not uniform enough for growing many plug crops, resulting in differences in drying out and plant growth.

Overall heat loss at night can be reduced with the use of a thermal blanket or curtain. This curtain can be combined with a shade curtain into one curtain for cooling, too. When a thermal curtain is pulled over the crop at night, heat loss can be reduced from 40 to 60%. The curtain can be computer-controlled and should be located above any other equipment hanging from the greenhouse trusses, such as HID lights and HAF fans.

Heating costs can be reduced and more uniform temperatures achieved in pipe-heated greenhouses by using a horizontal airflow (HAF) system, which utilizes small horizontal fans to move the air mass within the greenhouse. This movement stirs up the warmer air from the gable down to the plant height and helps to keep foliage dry, preventing disease. Minimum and maximum airflow velocities for this system are 40 and 200 ft/min (0.2 and 1.0 m/sec). Specifications for HAF systems for different greenhouse configurations are shown in figure 2.10.

Using tempered (heated) water to water plugs can also help heat the root zone. Generally, well water in northern areas during the winter can be from 40 to 50F (4.5 to 10C). Watering with this cold water quickly reduces the soil temperature, making the greenhouse heating system work harder or longer to raise the plug temperature. Look into installing a hot water heater to raise the temperature to 70F (20C) before watering.

COOLING

The need for cooling depends on the type of greenhouse, location, time of year, sunlight, outside temperature, crops grown, and inside temperature desired. Cooling equipment can include such items as vents, fans, shading, evaporative pads, and fog nozzles. The types of cooling systems commonly used include natural ventilation, fan-assist, pad and fan, and fog and fan systems.

Natural ventilation can consist of ridge or top vents, side vents, or roll-up or roll-down sides (fig. 2.11). This system depends on using the natural

Figure 2.10 Fan layout for horizontal airflow systems to provide uniform temperature distribution: 8 = fan; → = direction of airflow.

Note 1. Add a "vertical" row of fans for each additional 50 ft of "horizontal" greenhouse length. Note 2. For a greenhouse with three bays, air in the two outside bays should move in the same direction. For a greenhouse with an odd number of bays, air in the center three bays should flow in the same direction. Note 3. Total fan capacity in cubic feet per minute (cfm) should equal one-fourth the house volume. 16"-dia. circulating fans with 1/15 hp motors will generally be sufficient. From Aldrich & Bartok, *Greenhouse Engineering.* Reprinted by permission.

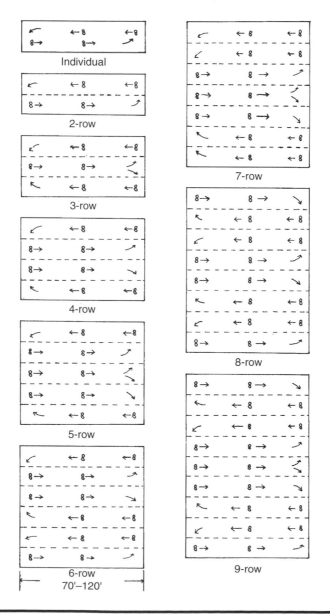

forces of wind and outside temperature. Growers located in northern geographic areas, cool coastal valleys, or in high elevation areas may need only natural ventilation, but everybody else will need to look at systems with more than natural ventilation for summer cooling.

FIGURE 2.11 Natural ventilation greenhouse with roll-down sides.

In areas where natural ventilation works for most of the year, some growers can use fans to improve the airflow across the plants, or fan-assisted ventilation. Fans can be located on one side of the greenhouse, while the other side is open. Top vents will not work well with this system, as uneven air circulation occurs. However, if the greenhouse is built with a large center aisle with its own twin roof vents, air can be pulled into the greenhouse equally by fans located on both sides (fig. 2.12). Again, if the outside air temperature gets too high, then this system will not provide enough cooling.

A pad-and-fan system utilizes evaporative cooling and large amounts of air movement to cool the greenhouse. This system features cellulose pads on one wall, through which water is circulated, and exhaust fans on the opposite wall. Air, cooled when entering through the pads, is drawn to the exhaust fans. Evaporative cooling can achieve temperatures within 3 to 4F (1.6 to 1.7C) of the wet-bulb temperature (the lowest cooling temperature possible), but it is affected by the outside air temperature and relative humidity (fig. 2.13). Cooling capability of this system also depends on width of greenhouse, surface area of pads, and airflow. Pad-and-fan cooling is more expensive than any natural ventilation system.

Fog cooling, also an evaporative cooling system, is an alternative to the pad-and-fan system. Water droplets 40 microns or smaller are generated under high pressure (1,000 psi, 6.9 MPa). Fog introduced into the incoming air, just inside the intake ventilators along one wall, cools the air as it evaporates (fig. 2.14). A second set of fog nozzles across the greenhouse counteracts any temperature rise as cooled air moves toward the exhaust fans opposite the intake ventilators. An air exhaust rate of 4 to 5 cfm/ft^2 (1.2 to 1.5 cmm/m^2) of floor area is used [3]. Fog cooling can also be used with natural ventilation or with fan-assisted natural ventilation. The fog system can essentially achieve the wet-bulb temperature inside the greenhouse. However, water quality is extremely important to keep these high-pressure fog nozzles from clogging. This system is expensive to install due to the high-pressure pump and lines needed. Controlling the amount of fog is also important. The high humidity that this system introduces into the greenhouse may cause excessive stretching of plugs.

FIGURE 2.12 Fan-assisted natural ventilation greenhouse. Center aisle with air intake (above) pulled by fans on either side (below). Courtesy X.S. Smith Inc.

SHADING

Generally, from late spring to early fall, light levels inside the greenhouse exceed levels desired for optimum plug growth from germination to shipping. These high light levels produce radiant heat within the greenhouse and place an impossible heat load on your cooling system. Shading will reflect some of this solar energy. Figure 2.15 illustrates the benefits of shading combined with air changes inside the greenhouse.

Shading can be achieved by one of the following methods: (1) whitewash sprayed on the outside of the greenhouse covering, (2) a screen fabric installed over the greenhouse or in the greenhouse above head height, or (3) a copper-colored plastic film used as greenhouse covering. The whitewash method is the least expensive but the most difficult to control. Once it is sprayed on, it remains until it wears off or is washed off.

FIGURE 2.13   Evaporative cooling effect as a function of relative humidity and temperature of outside air. Adapted from Aldrich & Bartok, *Greenhouse Engineering*.

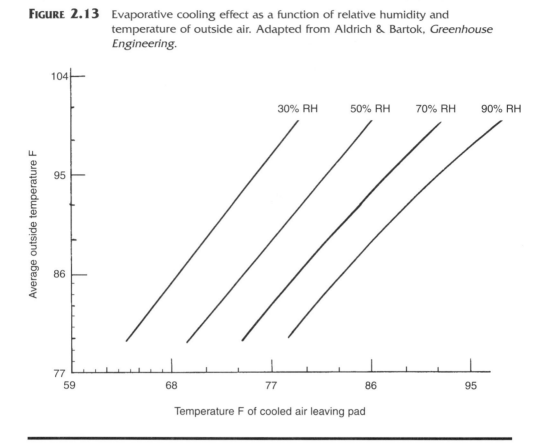

Sheets of screening can be made of various materials, with the ability to reduce light levels from 20 to 90%, although 50% is commonly used. Modern greenhouses have automated equipment to draw shade screens across the greenhouse in response to photocells (fig. 2.16). In this way, shading is applied only during the hours when needed. Retractable screening is available for above the greenhouse, as well as inside the greenhouse, in different configurations.

Copper-colored films have been tested in Spain, with growers reporting a 10 to 20F (5 to 11C) reduction in temperature during the day and a 7 to 15F (3.8 to 8C) temperature increase at night [2]. This type of film covering may offer potential for shading and light diffusion in other parts of the world, as well.

Insect screening will also affect the cooling capacity of your system. Keep in mind that up to 50% reduction in cooling can occur, depending on the screen size used to keep out insect pests. You need to increase your vent area, pad area, and fan capacity to account for the decreased airflow from insect screening.

LIGHTING

During the winter, light intensity is below optimum (less than 1,500 fc, 16,140 lux) for most plug crops in most greenhouse production areas of the world. Supplemental lighting can increase the rate of photosynthesis and thus plant growth. High-intensity-discharge (HID) lamps are the preferred lamps for growing plug crops in greenhouses today. The high-pressure sodium (HPS) type of HID lamp is the most commonly installed throughout the world (fig. 2.17). The HPS lamp is very efficient, converting 25% of the electrical input into visible radiation. These lamps are commonly offered in 400- and 1,000-watt sizes, with life expectancy as long as 24,000 hours.

FIGURE 2.14 High-pressure fog nozzle (above) for fog cooling in greenhouse (below). Courtesy Mee Industries Inc.

The various lamp manufacturers determine for growers the lamp height and spacing according to the desired light intensity and the configuration of the greenhouse. The 400W lamps are more commonly used because of better uniformity in light intensity (400 fc, 4,300 lux at plant height) with normal-height greenhouses. The 1,000W lamps can be used only with taller greenhouses. Appendix 4 lists some manufacturers and suppliers of HID lights.

FIGURE 2.15 Greenhouse temperature rise as a function of air exchange rate. Solar intensity is 280 Btu/hr-ft^2 on a horizontal surface at solar noon; the greenhouse is full of actively growing crops. From Aldrich & Bartok, *Greenhouse Engineering*. Reprinted by permission.

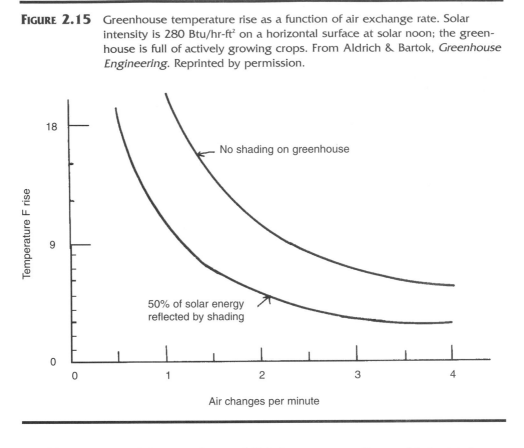

Plug crops receiving supplemental lighting are generally provided a total light period of 16 to 18 hours. This includes the time when lamps are on as well as the part of the day when it is bright enough to turn lamps off. Plant response to supplemental light is greatest in the young-plant stage, beginning with the first true leaves, and diminishes with time. Crops most responsive include geraniums, petunias, impatiens, vinca, and begonias. A big benefit is that plug crop

FIGURE 2.16 Retractable shade curtains located inside greenhouse.

times can be reduced during the winter, with better control of growth, when HID lighting is used.

Many plug crops respond to duration of light by either flowering or remaining vegetative, a response called *photoperiodism*. We can group plants into three categories: (1) short-day or long-night, (2) long-day or short-night, and (3)

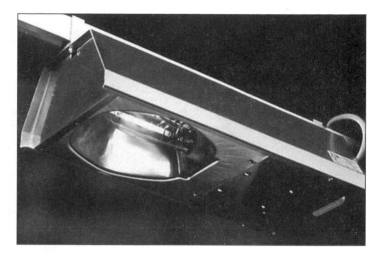

FIGURE 2.17 HID high-pressure sodium (HPS) light with reflector. Courtesy P.L. Light Systems.

day neutral plants. To control photoperiodism for short-day crops, you need an opaque screen to help make short days or long nights. This screening will be needed for a certain number of days or weeks, depending on the crop and time of year. To control photoperiodism for long-day crops, you can use night interruption with incandescent lights, or use HID lights to extend the day length. With incandescent lights, a minimum intensity of 10 fc (108 lux) should be provided. Use standard chrysanthemum lighting of 60W bulbs 4 feet (1.2 m) apart, not more than 5 feet (1.5 m) above the bench and 4 feet (1.2 m) wide. Turn the lights on for four hours between 10 P.M. to 2 A.M.

IRRIGATION

The complete system supplying water to the plug greenhouse consists of a water source, pump, pressure tank, piping, and a way to deliver the right amount of water to the plug trays. The water source could be a well, city water, rainwater, or a pond. Make sure you have enough high-quality water available to meet your plug growing needs.

There are four main ways of delivering the right amount of water to the plug trays: (1) hand-watering, (2) stationary mist nozzles, (3) watering booms with nozzles, and (4) ebb and flood on concrete floors. Hand-watering is straightforward and needs little equipment.

Stationary mist systems require mist lines either overhead or up through the benches. Nozzle size will depend on the area to cover and particle size desired. Solenoid valves and an electronic mist controller are mandatory.

Watering booms are supported on a track system suspended from the greenhouse truss (fig. 2.18). In selecting nozzles, check to see that total nozzle capacity does not exceed available water supply in gallons/minute (liters/minute). Most booms are motorized, with control over the rate of travel. Some new types of booms are even computerized for maximum flexibility in watering different plug trays.

Some large growers are using Styrofoam trays and an ebb-and-flood system to grow plugs on a concrete floor (fig. 2.5). The floor is paved with

FIGURE 2.18 Watering boom on rails in greenhouse. Courtesy ITS.

a lip around the edge and a drain in the center so that it can be flooded and drained. The floor, usually sloped from either side to the drain channel in the center, must be precisely laid out using a laser beam. The individual zones should not be made larger than can be flooded in 10 minutes, preferably five minutes. A key advantage with this system is the ability to recirculate water and nutrients.

To fertilize plug trays, it is best to have at least two separate water lines going into the greenhouse, one for clear water and one for fertilizer. Most greenhouse fertilizer is water-soluble and purchased in solid form, then dissolved in a concentrated stock tank. An injector or proportioner mixes precise volumes of concentrated fertilizer solution and water together and injects them into the water line (fig. 2.19).

There are a number of manufacturers of these types of injectors (appendix 4). Make sure you size the injector properly based on the water flow to be used. Also, a dual-head injector will allow you to inject more than one type of fertilizer at a time. Portable injectors may also be needed to give flexibility for spot-feeding or when there are many different types of crops being grown in plugs at the same time.

CARBON DIOXIDE ENRICHMENT

The normal atmosphere contains about 300 ppm CO_2. With CO_2 enrichment, plugs grow faster and flower earlier. Levels for plugs range from 700 to 1,500 ppm, but the optimum level depends on light intensity, temperature, nutrients, type of crop, and crop maturity.

Addition of CO_2 is effective only during the daylight hours when photosynthesis occurs, so it should be added from sunrise until one hour before sunset. Depending on the latitude of the greenhouse, the season for CO_2 enrichment begins between late October and early November and extends to April or early May. Addition of CO_2 can continue for plug crops even when ventilators are partly open during the day.

Two methods of CO_2 injection are used. Generators or burners that burn LP or natural gas are the cheaper method, but you must have high-purity gas to burn and must watch out for incomplete combustion and oxygen depletion. Liquid CO_2 in tanks is cleaner, more expensive, and

FIGURE 2.19 Single-head portable (above) and dual-head stationary (below) fertilizer injectors. Courtesy (above) Dosmatic USA Inc. and (below) H.E. Anderson Co.

needs to be applied on a larger scale. Various CO_2 control systems can maintain proper levels, with many of them being computerized. Internal air circulation is needed to provide sufficient distribution of CO_2.

CONTROL SYSTEMS

Factors to be controlled in plug growing include temperature, relative humidity, light intensity and photoperiod, watering, carbon dioxide levels, and fertilizing.

As you may already know and will see throughout this book, environmental factors need to be controlled more accurately for plug growing than for any other type of crop. Plugs are small plants in small containers grown at an extremely high density, with a resultant high value of product in a greenhouse. Any large variations in temperature, light levels, or other environmental factors can cause a loss of crop or quality.

A control system consists of a sensor (to detect a change and produce a signal related to the change), a signal receiver, a comparator, and an operator to respond to the change to bring about an increase or decrease in supply [1]. All control systems respond to the conditions represented by the sensor; therefore, sensor location is critical. Sensors should be as close to the crop as possible and in the center of the greenhouse zone. Sensors placed in an aspirated box will result in better control than those exposed directly to the greenhouse environment.

Temperature control can be improved by a system in which supply varies with demand. An example is a proportioning valve for hot water or a fan motor speed that varies with demand. Computer-operated control systems now have the ability, with proper programming and supply equipment, to maintain not only temperature but any other environmental parameter that the grower desires.

To be effective, the plug greenhouse should have systems with variable or proportional control, or at least equipment that can be staged. There is no need to use a computer to turn a single fan or heater on or off, when a thermostat can perform this just as effectively. However, simple controls cannot integrate temperature, light, humidity, CO_2, and fertilizer needs along with weather conditions. A computer can.

An alarm system is an inexpensive form of insurance that can protect your large investment in your plug greenhouse. Alarms can indicate that an environmental control system has failed, a power failure has occurred, a fire has started, or an intruder has entered the facility.

Power interruption can create serious problems for a plug grower at any time of the year. A standby electrical generator is essential to any greenhouse operation. The generator can be wired into the greenhouse circuit in such a way that it automatically turns on in the event of a power failure. Identify the electrical equipment that *must* be operated during an emergency.

Before purchasing a generator, go over the details of the installation with an electrician and your local power company. A situation where there is only one heater in a given greenhouse or only one central boiler requires that a backup heating system be available.

SOME FINAL THOUGHTS

By now you should be convinced that there is no one perfect plug greenhouse. Look around at other plug operations, ask questions of manufacturers and suppliers, visit trade shows, and look at the information contained in the appendices at the back of this book. Decide what fits your budget, your method of growing, your personnel, and your business philosophy. Be willing to upgrade your plug greenhouse facility and equipment in stages in order to spread out the capital costs. Depending on your location, you may need some of the equipment described but not others. Do some hard thinking before spending your hard-earned money!

KEY POINTS TO REMEMBER

- The greenhouse structure needs to provide the optimum environment for that tiny plant in that tiny plug cell. There is no one best plug greenhouse, but a high-profile greenhouse with high gutter height provides better air movement, optimizing heating and cooling.

- Decide on the type of greenhouse covering based on your needs, weather, and budget. Be aware of condensation forming inside and causing drips on your plug trays.

- A dependable supply of high-quality water is needed for plug production.

- Use a benching system that fits your budget and allows efficient movement and care of plug trays.

- Root-zone heating is the best system for controlling soil temperature. Use thermal curtains to reduce energy costs during winter.

- Any cooling system is greatly improved with retractable shade curtains. Natural ventilation can be used where temperatures are not extremely warm. Otherwise, fan-and-pad cooling may be needed. Cooling capacity is reduced with increasing width or length of the greenhouse.

- In low light areas, HID/HPS lights are beneficial for speeding up plug growth. Combine them with CO_2 injection for best results in winter and early spring.

- It is best to have at least two separate water lines going into the greenhouse, for clear water and fertilizer. Use a dual-head injector for greatest flexibility in using different fertilizers or concentrations.

- Automatic control systems are best for handling more than one task at a time and integrating other information in deciding how to control temperature, light, CO_2, relative humidity, and other factors needed for optimum plug growth.

REFERENCES

[1] Aldrich, R.A., and J.W. Bartok, Jr. 1994. *Greenhouse Engineering*. Ithaca, N.Y.: Northeast Regional Agricultural Engineering Service.

[2] Neal, K. 1993. Colored greenhouse plastics can speed up crops, improve quality. *Greenhouse Manager* 12(1): 92–93.

[3] Nelson, P.V. 1991. *Greenhouse operation and management.* 4th ed. Englewood Cliffs, N.J.: Prentice Hall.

[4] Roberts, W.J. 1994. Greenhouse structures. In *Bedding plants IV*. ed. E.J. Holecomb, 215–31. Batavia, Ill.: Ball Publishing.

CHAPTER 3

STAGE ZERO (0)— EQUIPMENT AND TECHNIQUES

I n the previous chapter, we discussed what kinds of greenhouse facilities you need to grow plugs. Now we will review what equipment and techniques you need to properly fill plug trays with media, seed accurately and quickly, and initially water the seeded trays, as well as what types of plug trays you need. We call this part Stage Zero (0) because everything starts here. What decisions you make, how you do things, the training of key personnel, and how much money you have to spend will all determine how successful you are in getting the seed into the plug cell. Stage 0 lays a foundation for the rest of the plug production stages. Your germination percentage will be greatly influenced by actions in Stage 0, as will moisture management and optimum root growth of your plug crops.

The basics of Stage 0 are:

1. Selecting the proper plug cell sizes for your needs

2. Filling the plug trays properly

3. Placing a seed into the center of each cell

4. Covering the seed uniformly, if necessary to cover

5. Watering in the trays properly

Sounds easy, doesn't it? However, Stage 0 is where many plug growers plan improperly, overspend, pay little attention, and lose more money than at any other plug stage. Use well-trained personnel in Stage 0. If you start off poorly in this stage, you will be just putting more money into solving problems later!

PLUG TRAYS

Plug production is characterized by specialized plug trays. Rather than seeds being sown and grown together in conventional bulk flats, they are separated into small cells. The North American standard plug tray for ornamentals is 11 × 22 inches (28 × 56 cm) and can hold 18 to 800 cells (see appendix 4 for list of manufacturers). Vegetable plug growers mainly use larger trays made of Styrofoam. In Europe plug trays can be larger than in North America. Some California growers use the California tray, which is 17 × 17 inches. Individual plug cells range from 2 inches square × 2½ inches deep, to ½ inch square × ½ inch deep (fig. 3.1). The more cells per tray, the smaller the cells. Though a variety of sizes of plug cells are available, you must choose the size adaptable to the type of mechanical seeder and robotic transplanter you are using, the crops grown, and the available greenhouse space or production scheme.

FIGURE 3.1 Different plug tray sizes from 648-waffle to 128. Courtesy Blackmore Company Inc.

The smaller the cell size, the more vulnerable the plug is to fluctuations in moisture, nutrients, oxygen, pH, and soluble salts in the soil. Generally, the deeper the plug cell, the more air space there is in the media, which improves drainage, leaching of salts, and aeration, resulting in more roots and root hairs. A 48-cell bedding flat containing peat moss and vermiculite has an air porosity of approximately 7 to 10% and, thus, excellent drainage. The same media in a 648-cell waffle plug tray would have an air porosity of approximately 0.3% (see table 7.5). The difference is the depth of the container. At least a 2-inch column is needed for gravity to have an effect, for water to drain out and air to move in (see table 7.6). The deeper the cell, the more oxygen there is.

Plug cells may be round, square, hexagonal, octagonal, or star-shaped. Cell design commands more and more attention in our search for faster turnover of the finished product. Parallel-sided cells have given way to those with sloping sides approaching an inverted pyramid (fig. 3.2). This development leads roots to grow in a vertical configuration, with less circling around the walls of the cell than when grown in a round or straight-sided cell. Square cells have 30% more soil volume than round cells (288

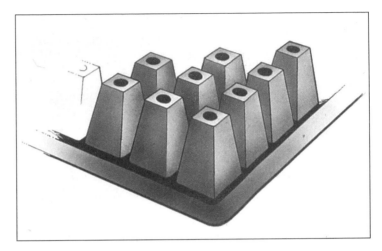

FIGURE 3.2 Inverted pyramid shape of plug cell. Courtesy TLC Polyform Inc.

round size versus 288 square). This additional soil translates into a greater surface area, where more roots and root hairs develop. Water distribution is more uniform on top of the tray with square cells, since there is little plastic between the cells. The hexagonal, octagonal, or star-shaped plug cells increase the soil volume and surface area of roots even more. Uniformly faster drying of the media also occurs.

Some trays also have ventilation holes between the plug cells, resulting in airflow between the plants (fig. 3.3). Drier foliage and less disease, more even drying, and more uniform height even in the middle of the tray (no mounding) are some of the benefits of ventilated plug trays.

The color of the plug tray affects root temperatures. Styrofoam trays are always white, reflecting more light, besides providing better temperature insulation due to Styrofoam's other pro-

FIGURE 3.3 Air holes between plug cells for ventilation. Courtesy TLC Polyform Inc.

perties. Rigid plastic trays are black, gray, or white. Most growers use black trays, especially during the winter and spring seasons, because they absorb more of the sun's light energy and translate that into more heat for the roots. However, during summer and early fall production, some plug growers switch to gray or white trays, which reflect more light and thus keep the root zone temperature from getting too hot. However, tests by plug growers have shown that roots do not grow toward light, which is transmitted into the soil more by the white trays, so some growers are now using gray plug trays year around.

Plug trays can be made out of Styrofoam, other polystyrene, polyethylene, or polypropylene and can be vacuum-formed or injection-molded. Styrofoam trays are commonly used in the United States and other parts of the world for vegetables (the Speedling tray) and in Europe for ornamentals. Styrofoam trays are reused within the vegetable industry many times, until they fall apart, then usually discarded via the landfill. In Europe the plug customer's Styrofoam trays can also be reused several times if collected back. Many European tray suppliers are required to take back used trays and recycle the Styrofoam for other purposes. In the United States there is no concerted effort to recycle Styrofoam, although some communities and landfills are starting to reject Styrofoam trays. The future of Styrofoam for plug trays remains uncertain throughout the industrialized world.

Polystyrene is commonly used for plug trays for ornamentals in the United States, Asia, Europe, and other parts of the world. Manufacturers make trays of different thicknesses. Thinner ones are not intended for reuse. Their edges will vary from manufacturer to manufacturer, thereby influencing movement through certain seeders. Most trays are fabricated with a flattened edge on one side for placing labels.

Before you decide on a tray manufacturer, obtain some samples of the tray sizes you are interested in and test their durability. This is particularly important if you are planning on reusing trays several times for your own production. High temperatures, bright sunlight, and chemicals gradually cause polystyrene to fade, crack, and become brittle. Also, the holes in the bottom of polystyrene trays may be punched, die-cut, or burned out. These holes should be uniform to provide the best drainage. Most growers prefer die-cut or punched holes for their uniformity.

New plug trays should be used for certain crops more prone to root rot diseases, particularly *Thielaviopsis*. These crops include vinca, pansy, and petunia. Some growers do not reuse Styrofoam trays for crops sensitive to algae, such as begonia and lisianthus.

Trays may be reused if thoroughly cleaned and soaked for 15 to 20 minutes with a special disinfectant, such as quaternary ammonium salts (Physan 20, Greenshield). Clorox or bleach solution is not recommended for disinfecting trays, since some types of plastic absorb chlorine, which forms toxic compounds with the polystyrene, adversely affecting germination and growth of the next crop, particularly begonia. Styrofoam trays may be sterilized with steam if the Styrofoam density will tolerate such high temperature without melting. It is important to allow the trays to dry thoroughly before using.

Plug trays should not be used more than two or three times because prolonged handling creates cracks in the trays, drainage holes become enlarged by mechanical plug dislodgers or transplanters, and the growing media may fall through the bottom of the cells. In most cases, it is more economical to use new plug trays rather than reuse old ones. By the time you wash, disinfect, stack, wrap, and store used trays, the labor cost of reusing a tray almost equals the 40- to 50-cent cost of a new one. In addition, side-by-side comparisons by growers tend to show better seedling growth in new plug trays.

The main decision about what type of plug trays to use is based on the size of the cell. Decisions about plug sizes are based on type of crop grown, size of finished container, and production time, space, or schedule. Many growers use more than one plug size for different times of the year, different crops, or different finished container sizes (fig. 3.4). Other growers make one size fit all their purposes.

What cell size best fits the crop? Succulent crops (begonia, impatiens) and crops that require a longer period of growth before transplanting (perennials, cut flowers, flowering pot crops) grow better in the larger cell sizes. Fast crops do well in smaller plug cells. Some crops, such as

FIGURE 3.4 Different plug sizes of begonia. From left to right— 800, 390, 220, 112.

anemone, delphinium, lisianthus, and certain vegetables, prefer a deeper cell because of their root systems (fig. 3.5). Other crops, such as geranium, gerbera, cyclamen, and perennials, are started in small cells, transplanted into larger plug cells, and then transplanted into the final container or ground bed.

Seed size is also a consideration. Marigolds are difficult to sow into an 800 tray, even with detailing. Large seeds just do not fit well into small plug cells.

What will be the final container for the plug? Smaller plugs finish well in cell-packs. Larger plugs produce attractive plants for pots, baskets, and planters. Larger plugs

FIGURE 3.5 Deep cell of 73-tray for best rooting of anemone.

also do well when transplanted into the field or ground bed (vegetables, cut flowers). In the United States the 800 and 512 trays are the two most popular plug tray sizes for cell-packs. A slightly larger plug (406 or 288) is more desirable for the deeper 36-cell-packs now being used more in the United States. Price is also a major consideration, as the smaller plugs cost less. For best performance in baskets and pots larger than 4 inches, a grower should use the 128 plug size. For 4-inch pots, the 288 or 338 plug is the best size.

How can production space and time be best scheduled? Larger plugs produce a quality finished plant in a shorter period of time (turnover) than smaller plugs. Larger plug cells are more tolerant of stress than smaller plug cells, allowing the plants to finish faster. A large percentage of the fall pansy plug crop is produced in northern areas and shipped to southern and southwestern states in the United States. A large volume of soil (288 plug) is generally believed desirable to ensure success following transplanting because of the high temperatures at that time of the year. Smaller plugs (512 or smaller), not as tolerant of shipping due to their small soil volume, need to be transplanted immediately.

Smaller plug cells pack a higher density in a given area (more plants per ft^2 or m^2) during peak production times, when space is limited. Some crops, though, such as begonia, can be almost impossible to handle in an 800 tray. Uniform watering is often more difficult with very small cells. Larger cells provide more space per plant, result in a larger seedling, and are a logical choice for late production times. However, many growers opt for a 288 plug size during the peak weeks of spring, counting on a faster turn for color during the so-called green period between Mother's Day and Memorial Day. Smaller-sized plugs (512 to 800) are often used in the north for the first crop of bedding plants. The plugs are transplanted in late winter and grown slowly for a spring crop, when space is not limiting. Larger plugs are then used for the next one or two turns for faster finished color.

FLAT FILLING

Plug trays may be filled by hand or by a mechanical flat filler. The number of trays grown will determine which method is used. Whichever method is used, some important considerations should be kept in mind: (1) media moistening before filling, (2) uniform filling, (3) particle size reduction possibility, (4) cell depression without compression, (5) deeper cell depression for large seeds, and (6) compaction avoidance.

Moisture should be added to dry media before filling. Compressed bales of plug mix should be fluffed up (completely broken apart) prior to filling trays, then moistened. A moistened mix will not fall through the drainage holes as readily as a dry mix. Add only enough moisture before filling so that when you squeeze a handful, no water drops come out. The squeezed handful of media retains its shape when you open your hand, but when you push your finger onto it, it will fall apart. If the media were too wet, then it would be difficult to get good filling of the trays without air pockets. If the media were too dry, then settling of the media would occur after filling, resulting in less aeration and less root volume.

Additionally, make sure enough of the media is getting into the plug tray. Press your finger slightly into several cells of a recently filled tray. Your finger should not be able to compress the media halfway down. Otherwise, the flat filler is not pushing enough media into each cell, and the media will settle after handling and watering.

Trays need to be filled uniformly for best germination and growth. All plug cells should contain the same amount of media, with the excess brushed off. If some cells in the plug tray have visibly less fill, then these cells will dry out early, making it too difficult to uniformly water all cells in the plug tray. Sometimes mechanical flat fillers are not adjusted properly, so the edges (or the middle) of the trays get less media than the rest.

Do not keep the same batch of media circulating continuously through the flat filler, as reduction of particle sizes will result. All mechanical flat fillers reduce particle sizes of peat, vermiculite, and perlite through friction, especially the tail end of the batch or the excess media. Reduced particle sizes result in increased water-holding capacity and reduced air porosity. You may notice that the trays filled at the end of a run do not dry out as fast as the trays filled at the beginning of the run.

Create a depression in the plug cell by brushing properly without compression. This depression without compression is called the *pillow effect.* Think of the seed landing on a soft surface like a pillow: no seed bounce occurs. When the surface is harder than a pillow, seed bounce increases. Even when the surface is wet but hard, seeds will bounce, particularly with certain seeds and seeders. Depression without compression will also give you more aeration in the plug medium. You do not want to start off with less than 1% air porosity.

Some crops need more depression in the plug cells for the seed to fit and still be covered. When using coarse vermiculite as your covering, you need to brush the trays a little more to get a deeper depression without compression. This gives more room for the seed and the vermiculite to sit on the surface without covering up the ribs of the tray. Crops such as marigolds, cosmos, geranium, zinnia, dahlia, cyclamen, and melons have large seeds. The bigger the seed, the more depression is needed. You can also dibble the trays to create the additional depression needed. Sometimes the dibbler is attached to the flat filler, but most times it is part of the seeder conveyor (fig. 3.6).

Avoid compaction of the media by cross-

FIGURE 3.6 Dibbler on Hamilton seeder. Courtesy BFG Supply Co.

stacking filled trays. Do not nest filled trays directly on top of each other, as the bottom trays would become more compacted than the top trays (fig. 3.7). Such compaction reduces air porosity severely! Try to fill trays no earlier than one day before seeding to minimize drying out. Many growers fill plug trays the actual day they are to be seeded. If you need to fill trays ahead of time, either wrap them in plastic or place them in your plug chamber until ready to be seeded. Trays that were filled with too moist media will turn to concrete when dry, resulting in more seed bounce and less air porosity for the roots.

When buying a mechanical flat filler, consider your purchase carefully. How many different plug sizes will you be filling? How easily adjustable is the filler when switching from one size to another? How well does it fill both plug trays and cell-packs? Models that also do pots and baskets may not be adjustable for plug sizes as small as 800 trays.

How big is the soil hopper? If you do only a limited number of trays a day, then you do not need a filler with a

FIGURE 3.7 Improper (above) compared to proper (below) stacking of filled plug trays.

big hopper. You will only have to take out the media each time, or risk contaminating the excess media in the hopper with soil-borne diseases such as *Thielaviopsis,* which can be spread by dust. Will your flat filler handle small-sized plug trays but not large-sized trays? Check out models that come with a vibrator to settle more media into the larger cells. Also, fillers with a larger soil chute will be able to deliver more media into the plug tray.

How fast do you want to run the machine? Some models have variable speed controls for the flat conveyor and the soil chute. How many people will be required to fill flats? Do not expect the flat filler to replace all of them. It will still take two or three people to load, operate, and unload the flat filler. However, it will not take as long to fill your daily require-

ment of plug trays, so these people can then work at other jobs in your greenhouse.

Many plug growers have more than one flat filler, depending on the number of trays needed and the types of trays filled (fig. 3.8). Check with other plug growers about the types of flat fillers they use and like. Go to trade shows and talk with the manufacturers (appendix 4). Make sure to ask about different voltages and total amp draw for the motor sizes used, since many countries have different electrical requirements. Manufacturers should be able to provide the necessary motors.

FIGURE 3.8 Mini Flat Filler™. Courtesy Bouldin & Lawson Inc.

SEEDING AND SEEDERS

A mechanical seeder is standard equipment for the plug producer. Many different types of seeders are available, each with special exclusive features. Prices range from less than $1,000 to more than $50,000 (appendix 4).

When choosing a seeder, a plug producer should take into consideration: (1) the size of the operation and number of flats being produced, (2) the grower's expertise in plug production, (3) the types and quantities of seed to be sown, and (4) how frequently the seeder will be used. All seeders can sow seed into a plug tray, but the accuracy of the seeder is related to the type and

size of seed, the person operating the seeder, and how many trays are to be sown in a day. Growers should choose the seeder that is right for their program and operation in order to get the most out of the initial investment.

For seeder manufacturers, the challenge has been to develop a seeder that

FIGURE 3.9 Vandana vacuum template seeder. Courtesy Growing Systems Inc.

picks up seed accurately, then delivers the seed into the plug tray accurately and at a rate of speed that permits the grower to make optimum use of time. Just as both the seed and the germination environment have improved, seeders have also become faster and more accurate. Sowing accuracy (exceeding 95% for single placement of raw seed) and seed placement (as close to the center of the plug cell as possible) are requirements. Today seeders handle a variety of seed, ranging from raw begonia to watermelon seed.

Mechanical seeders can be divided into four main types: (1) vacuum template, (2) manifold vacuum (tips or needles), (3) electric eye (similar to seed counters), and (4) vacuum cylinder or drum. The least expensive type is the vacuum template (fig. 3.9). The operator manually scatters seed over a template with small depressions (cavities) in it. The individual seeds are

held in the cavities by a vacuum, while excess seeds are knocked off. When the cavities are filled, the template is positioned over a pattern of tubes or directly over the tray. The vacuum is manually released, and the seeds fall through the tubes (or directly) into the plug cells. The entire flat is seeded at once. Typically, prices for template seeders range from less than $1,000 to $5,000, depending on the number of templates needed.

FIGURE 3.10 Vacuum manifold seeders with rubber tips (above) or needles (below). Courtesy Blackmore Company Inc. (above) and Flier USA Inc. (below).

The second type of seeder uses a manifold vacuum system. Seed is picked up from a seed tray or reservoir by a manifold, which has a row of nozzles or needles to which individual seeds become

attached by means of a vacuum (fig. 3.10). Each cycle of this system delivers one row of six to 18 seeds. Following delivery of one row of seeds, the plug flat is advanced one space, and the next row of seeds is delivered. A double-row attachment from Blackmore Company allows two rows (up to 24 seeds/cycle) to be sown at a time for tray sizes 84 to 288. Various manifolds with different sizes of nozzle tips or needles are needed for different seed sizes. Prices for vacuum manifold seeders range from $8,000 to $13,000, depending on the number of manifolds and options needed. There are now also available manual wand seeders that use the vacuum needle system to sow one row at a time. Designed for small growers, prices are less than $1,000.

The seed-counting seeder uses electric eye technology to count and deliver seeds into a tray. These electronic seed counters can accurately detect a seed as small as raw begonia as it passes through a chute and past an electric eye. The seed is then switched to a tube lined up with a plug cell and dropped into the cell via gates operated with compressed air. This type of seeder can handle a wide range of seed sizes and shapes with no changing of templates, mani-folds, or drums. However, it is slower than other seeders. Prices range from $10,000 to $13,000.

The final type of seeder delivers seed using a cylinder or drum with holes in it (fig. 3.11). Seeds are picked up from a hopper with a vacuum, then dropped into the plug tray with release of the vacuum and

FIGURE 3.11 Hamilton vacuum cylinder seeder. Courtesy BFG Supply Co.

either air or water expulsion. For most seeders in this group, different drums or cylinders are needed when using different sizes of seed, various numbers of seeds per cell, or different plug tray sizes. These seeders can be highly accurate if adjusted properly. The main advantage is their speed, exceeding 700 flats per hour. Prices range from $18,000 to more than $50,000. Every one of these seeders has its own conveyor system, along with other options, such as dibblers and top coaters.

Before choosing a mechanical plug seeder, you should first assess your needs and ask the various seeder manufacturers the following questions:

- **What type (size, shape) of seed does the machine handle most efficiently?** Does the machine have the ability to sow raw and pelleted seed, defuzzed seed, de-tailed seed, and coated seed?

- **What materials are used in the construction of the machine?** The seeder parts should be of durable material, such as steel and aluminum, to withstand wear and tear. These materials also reduce the problem of static electricity, which causes seeds to stick together or to the machine. Some machines contain static-resistant plastics. You should know what equipment (motor, pump, air compressor, table) comes with the seeder and what you must supply yourself.

- **How does the machine operate?** Seeder operations range from the simple vacuum techniques to complicated, automated processes involving electronic, optical, pneumatic, and mechanical operations. Some machines fill an entire flat at once; others sow one or two rows at a time. How much plug flat handling is involved? Are flats moved by hand, or do they pass through the seeder on a conveyor belt or other type of movable system? What other features are provided, such as dibblers or top coaters? How much room does the seeder require for operation, and is it mobile?

- **How much seed must be used at one time for the machine to function properly?** Some seeders require that the seed hopper remain full to ensure accurate seed pickup. This is not a problem when working with larger seeds, such as tomato or pepper, but can become very expensive if working with begonia or petunia seeds.

- **What types of plug trays can be used with the seeder?** Certain seeders can be adapted to sow into different types of plug trays, even into cell-packs. Additional templates, manifolds, or drums will need to be purchased, depending on the type of trays you use.

- **Is the seeder easily adaptable to different plug sizes and different seed shapes and sizes?** This may be as simple as dialing the proper combination for vibration, vacuum pressure, height, and speed, or it may require using tools to make the adjustment. The plug seeder should be adaptable for accurate single-, double-, and triple-seed pickup and placement. It is helpful if the seeder operator is able to stop the machine for visual inspection for proper seed pickup.

- **How fast (seeds/hour, trays/hour) does the seeder operate?** Is speed important for your operation? What will your average seeding run be per variety? The speed of even the simplest machine largely depends on the skill of the operator, but several seeders have variable speed control. The faster the seeder, the higher the price tag.

- **What maintenance is required of the machine?** Does the machine have a self-cleaning mechanism that automatically dislodges any trapped seed or foreign material from the assembly during operation? Check regularly for clogged holes. Learn how frequently filters, tubes, and other parts must be replaced and about their availability.

  In a greenhouse environment, dust, dirt, and moisture abound. Therefore, operate the seeder in a room away from blowing dust particles. Air movement should be minimal, though well-circulated and maintained at a comfortable 70 to 75F (21 to 24C). Ample light is necessary for the operator to check accuracy. Humidity should be kept at approximately 50 to 55% to reduce the problem of seeds clinging to each other or to the machine because of either static electricity or too much moisture. Remember, keep it clean and keep it dry!

- **Is the manufacturer willing to modify an older machine to meet the capabilities of new plug technology?** If an older machine cannot be upgraded, check for trade-in possibilities. Most machines have parts and accessories for adapting to the different seed types. Learn what the availability of these parts is, especially for an older seeder model.

- **How much technical support can you expect from the manufacturer or distributor when your seeder does not work properly?** This point becomes more critical the greater the distance you are from the technical support. Equipment failure occurs even with well-made units. Before purchasing the seeder, establish a parts and service agreement with the manufacturer or distributor to prevent costly downtime during the sowing season. Locate the nearest supplier for parts that can be easily replaced by the operator. Know the life expectancy of the seeder and whether any warranties accompany the purchase agreement.

No matter how simple or complicated the seeder, accuracy depends on the seeder operator. For every seeder, you need a trained operator. Do you have people who can handle this equipment and not be scared to make adjustments as needed? One person can serve as the captain or leader of this group of operators, who need many hours of training on the seeder. At the beginning of the season, speed and accuracy will not be as great, due to lack of training and practice since the past year. Also, you need to have a backup operator for each seeder. Otherwise, what happens when your main seeder operator gets sick or leaves the company? You cannot just take any person off the street and quickly train him or her to be an accurate and efficient seeder operator.

For a grower who is just entering into plug production, it is advisable to consider a simple and inexpensive seeder. A small grower who sows small batches of seed may choose a basic, simple machine that handles the seed of easy-to-grow plug crops, such as peppers and defuzzed tomato seeds. Once the grower becomes familiar with the methods of plug production, a more sophisticated machine may be purchased. It is important to choose a machine that fits the operation's production needs. A large, experienced plug grower who grows a diversity of crops may consider having more than one type of seeder, one which handles small seeds well and another suited more for larger seeds. Speed, accuracy, and flexibility are crucial in a large, progressive operation.

COVERING

Many seed crops benefit greatly from being covered with media, some other component, or plastic to improve germination and rooting in (table 3.1). There are several reasons why we cover certain types of seed. First, large seeds need to be covered in order to maintain moisture levels around the seed for germination. Crops such as geranium, marigold, zinnia, dahlia, aster, and most vegetables are examples of large-seeded crops that should be covered.

TABLE 3.1   SEEDS TO COVER

Aster	Pepper
Calendula	Phlox
Carnation	Primula
Cosmos	Ranunculus
Dahlia	Salvia
Dianthus	Tomato
Flowering kale/cabbage	Verbena
Gazania	Vinca
Geranium	Viola
Marigold	Zinnia
Pansy	

Some seeds need darkness to germinate better. A covering of plug media, coarse vermiculite, or some other component will provide enough darkness to promote germination. If not, these plug trays can be put in the dark. Crops that need darkness include cyclamen, phlox, and vinca.

Although a covering keeps humidity high immediately around the seed, it should allow oxygen to the seed. Both are needed in certain amounts for best germination. Generally benefiting the most are large seeds, such as pansy, viola, verbena, and New Guinea impatiens.

Finally, some crops need a covering to promote the initial roots to penetrate the plug medium. Roots can be very sensitive to light, losing their desired orientation downward into the plug cell. Examples include pansy, marigold, and geranium.

Problems can occur when you try to cover plug trays. It is easy to get too little, too much, or uneven covering, especially if doing it by hand. If too little is applied, the benefits of covering are lost. If too much, then seed gets buried and will likely either die from suffocation or come up very erratically. If trays are covered unevenly, then germination will be uneven, and uniform watering will be impossible.

For these reasons, most plug growers use a covering unit or top coater to apply a covering to their plug trays. Most top coaters come with the cylinder or drum seeders, but some can be ordered separately (see appendix 4). These units operate with either electric eyes or contact wheels. If you are using several different plug tray sizes, then get a unit with an electric eye, as it is more easily adjustable.

The material you use to cover the plug trays is very important. The most common ones include the plug medium itself, coarse vermiculite, sand, or plastic. There are advantages and disadvantages to each material. Covering with the same media is simple, as availability is not an issue. The plug grower can easily tell by color when the covering is getting dry. However, uniform covering with plug media is difficult. In addition, a fine plug media tends

FIGURE 3.12 Plug trays covered with white plastic for germination.

to form a wet blanket over the seed after watering a few times, thereby suffocating the seed or promoting mold.

Coarse vermiculite is the covering of choice for many growers. It retains humidity well around the seed but allows oxygen to penetrate. Difficulties arise in reading coarse vermiculite for watering. Also, you need uniformly coarse vermiculite, as fine particles will smother the seed. Availability of uniform size in certain parts of North America and the world can be a problem.

Sand or perlite can be applied and are very difficult to overwater. However, retaining humidity can be a problem. Be aware of what type of sand is used and how sterile it is (i.e., no algae, disease).

Some growers who germinate their plug trays on the bench use solid plastic or porous plastic as their covering. Solid plastic is draped over all trays in Stage 1, retaining high humidity and temperature for germination (fig. 3.12). However, when the sun comes out, clear plastic heats up the plug too much. Be careful of applying too much water initially when using solid plastic coverings, as moisture is not lost from the surface. Use white plastic during sunny periods. Black plastic can be used for crops that want darkness, but not during sunny weather without also covering with white plastic.

Porous plastic, such as Vispore or some of the frost-protection materials (Agricloth), can also be pulled over all trays in Stage 1

FIGURE 3.13 Plug trays covered with Vispore (above) and frost cover (below) for germination.

(fig. 3.13). The advantage of this plastic is that you can easily water through it to trays when needed. Humidity is kept high, temperature does not get as high as with solid polyethylene, and oxygen gets to the seed.

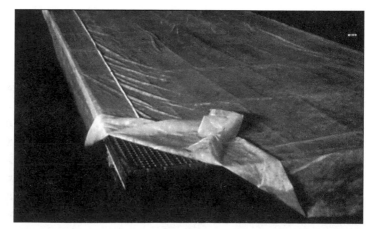

Once germination is finished, all plastic should be pulled off carefully, and the plug trays grown on. Plastic can be washed and reused many times. Difficulties arise with the labor needed to apply and remove, possible disease problems in reusing plastic, and in monitoring germination rates of different crops.

INITIAL WATERING OF SEEDED PLUG TRAYS

Once plug trays have been properly seeded—and covered, if needed—they are ready for their first watering. There are two basic approaches to this initial watering: (1) bench germination requires light watering, followed by transportation and the rest of the watering later; or (2) chamber germination requires complete watering before loading into the chamber. If you are a plug grower who germinates trays on the bench, you will do most of your initial watering there. First, though, you can lightly water the trays as they come off the seeder line, either by hand or watering tunnel (fig. 3.14). This

light watering will prevent the seed and media from being jostled out of the trays as they are moved to the greenhouse bench. Use care in transporting these trays. Once on the bench, a complete watering can be done with either booms, mist nozzles, or by hand. Make sure not to overwater, bury the seed, or blow the seed out of the tray.

FIGURE 3.14 Watering tunnel. Courtesy Gleason Equipment.

If you use germination chambers instead of germinating on the bench, then you must water the trays completely before loading them up on carts, racks, or movable benches, which are then placed inside the chamber. The germination chamber is designed to maintain the level of moisture you initially give the tray, not add to or subtract from it. Complete watering is best done by watering tunnels located at the end of your seeding lines (see appendix 4). A watering tunnel can come with an electric eye to turn on water once a tray comes by. Make sure you run the tunnel at the same speed as the conveyor for

TABLE 3.2   PLUG MOISTURE LEVELS

Crop	Stage 1 Wet	Stage 1 Medium	Stage 1 Dry	Stage 2 Wet	Stage 2 Medium	Stage 2 Dry
Ageratum		M			M	
Alyssum		M			M	
Aster			D			D
Begonia	W			W		
Browallia		M			M	
Calendula			D			D
Carnation		M			M	
Celosia		M			M	
Coleus		M			M	
Coreopsis			D			D
Cosmos			D			D
Dahlberg daisy		M			M	
Dahlia			D			D
Dianthus		M			M	
Dusty miller		M			M	
Flowerlng kale/ cabbage		M				D
Gazania			D			D
Geranium		M			M	
Gomphrena		M				D
Hypoestes		M			M	
Impatiens	W				M	
Lisianthus		M			M	
Lobelia		M			M	
Marigold		M				D
Nicotiana		M			M	
Pansy	W				M	
Pepper		M				D
Petunia		M			M	
Phlox			D			D
Poppy		M			M	
Portulaca		M				D
Primula		M			M	
Ranunculus	W			W		
Salvia	W				M	
Snapdragon		M				D
Stock		M			M	
Tomato		M				D
Verbena			D			D
Vinca	W				M	
Viola	W				M	
Zinnia			D			D

your seeding line. Some growers make their own watering tunnels. Others modify existing tunnels to make them longer or add more nozzles for watering different plug tray sizes. An 800 plug tray can easily be flooded, whereas a 128 tray may not get enough water. You can alternate fine and coarser nozzles with additional shutoff valves to control how much water you give different tray sizes and different crops.

How much water to add for a certain crop for best germination can be a problem. Generally, small seeds need less water than large seeds. Covered seeds have a moisture buffer, meaning they will not dry out as fast as seeds sitting on the surface of the plug medium. In addition, some crops like it moist (wet) for imbibition and initial radicle emergence, whereas other crops like it on the dry side. Many a plug grower has had poor germination with verbena by giving it too much water. We have put together early moisture requirements for some crops in table 3.2. Refer to the plug charts included with this book for more complete information on other crops. "Wet" means you can see glistening of the media, and when you touch the surface, free water is evident. "Medium" means the medium is moist to the touch, but no free water can be seen. "Dry" medium does not feel moist, and the tray is light, but the medium is not bone dry. Crops that like it dry in Stage 1 are always covered, providing some moisture reservoir. Maintain a crop's proper moisture levels to achieve the best germination from the seed you buy.

KEY POINTS TO REMEMBER

- Match up plug tray types and sizes with the crops you grow, finished container sizes, and growing schedule.

- No matter how you fill plug trays, do it uniformly! Get the pillow effect with good brushing. Avoid compaction of the media and drying out. Dibble trays for best placement of large seeds that are covered with coarse vermiculite.

- Ask a lot of questions before buying a mechanical seeder. Know the advantages and disadvantages of each type of seeder. Never believe manufacturers' claims as to how fast their seeders will go: you will never achieve this speed, due to short seeding runs! Train your seeder operators well; they can save you a lot of money!

- Cover seeds properly and for the right reasons. Many a mistake has been made here that cost a grower money!

- Initially you can water plug trays based on crop requirements and tray size. If you use germination chambers, pay closer attention.

CHAPTER 4

SEED PHYSIOLOGY

S eed germination involves many different processes, some apparent and some hidden. To many plug growers, germination should occur quickly and at 100% if they sow the seed into plug cells and provide reasonable moisture, temperature, and light. If this rate does not occur, it must be the seed's fault. However, many things go into a seed's ability to germinate, even given optimum conditions.

Seed quality is one of the most talked-about subjects with plug growers everywhere. Yet, few growers really understand what seed quality is, what seed companies are doing to improve it, and what the plug grower can do to get the most out of this high seed quality. Producing a seed involves a few distinct steps, each equally important in the determination of seed quality. These steps are like the links in a chain: if one link is weak, then the chain will break.

FACTORS AFFECTING SEED QUALITY

GENETICS

The first step in seed production is the genetic development of parental lines. The true genetic potential for seed quality is developed by the breeders. Evaluation of breeding lines for germination and vigor needs to be conducted routinely. Many seed companies now have tests developed for breeders to evaluate potential vegetable and flower varieties for higher germination and vigor and for germination performance under specific adverse conditions.

SEED PRODUCTION

The second step, producing the seed for sale from the breeder's parental lines, involves three main factors, each of which influences seed quality:

1. Pollination, seed set, and seed development
2. Production culture and growing environment of mother plants (disease, watering, nutrition, temperature, and light)
3. Harvest stage and method

The development of a seed begins with pollination, a process where pollen, germinating on a stigma from the same (self-pollination) or different flower (cross-pollination), eventually penetrates into an ovule and sexually fuses with an egg. After fusion there is rapid cell division; by the end of this stage, the embryo is almost fully formed. However, the flower may contain more than one ovule, and incomplete pollination could occur, resulting in seed set in some but not all ovules.

Nutrients and hormones are flowing into the developing seed from the mother plant on a priority basis. The seed acts as a nutrient sink, accumulating food reserves from the green parts of the plant. The seed gains weight rapidly, and the moisture content falls to about 50%. No further cell division occurs in the embryo. At the end of this stage, the seed is structurally complete.

During the final phase of seed maturation, the seed may dry down to as low as 10 to 20% moisture content. No additional food reserves are added, and dry weight remains constant. Finally, a layer of cork is laid down at the base of the seed, severing its lifeline with the mother plant. The seed is now ready to be harvested.

If seeds are harvested before the maturation phase is completed, then they will tend to be undersized, immature, and of lower vigor. If harvesting is delayed and the seeds are left on the plant after ripening, then some may be lost due to shedding, lodging, or birds and insects. They may deteriorate in vigor due to weathering.

Some seeds are hand-harvested, such as impatiens, petunia, pansy, and snapdragon. Other crops are field-harvested, dried in the field and combined to extract the seed. Examples include dry-seeded vegetables, such as broccoli and onion; many cut flowers, such as delphinium and larkspur; and other flowers, such as vinca, verbena, aster, and alyssum. Some crops are vacuum-harvested, such as marigold, and others are hand-shaken off the mother plant, as with lettuce. Regardless of the harvest method, mature seeds must be separated from immature seeds and trash, providing the plug grower a uniform-sized product to sow with mechanical seeders.

Healthy mother plants grown under proper environmental and cultural conditions have the best chance of producing healthy, high-quality seeds. The development of buds into flowers and of fertilized ovules into seeds depends on the supply of water, mineral nutrients, and light; for these, there is always competition between plants and between different parts of the same plant. Mother plants grown under nutrient or water stress will not have enough sugars and other food reserves to supply the developing seeds. Plants grown with excess water and nutrients may not produce enough flowers to supply the seed yields needed.

Temperature, rainfall, and light have a great effect on the health of mother plants, length of crop season, viability and vigor of seed, and where the seed can be produced. Cool growing temperatures may prevent pollination or proper seed development. Low light levels will not allow the mother plants to provide enough storage reserves via photosynthesis to the developing seeds, resulting in small, lower vigor seeds. Rainfall at the harvest stage will cause problems with disease.

POSTHARVEST

After the seed is harvested, the third link in the seed-quality chain begins, including everything that then happens to the seed before it is sown by the plug grower. This postharvest period includes cleaning, storage, dormancy, and enhancements. The cleaning process separates trash and most immature seeds from the mature seeds. Often, immature seeds are physically indistinguishable from mature seeds—the same size, weight, shape, and specific gravity. Additional separations may then be needed to provide seeds with uniform vigor (refined or graded seed).

Germination occurs after the seed is sown. The seed producer has controlled the genetic potential of germination through breeding and tried to maintain this potential through seed production and postharvest, thereby delivering a high-quality seed to the plug grower. The actual germination phase, though, is controlled entirely by the plug grower. If poor-quality seed is delivered, the grower cannot achieve high germination. However, many plug growers have sown high-quality seed and achieved less than desired stands due to a failure to understand the germination process.

THE GERMINATION PROCESS

According to seed physiologists, germination begins with water uptake by the seed (imbibition) and ends with the start of elongation of the embryonic axis, usually as the radicle (fig. 4.1). To everybody else, germination begins with water uptake by the seed and ends with seedling establishment. The embryo within the seed is a plant in miniature. In the dry seed, the embryo has stopped growing but is alive and respiring very slowly. When a dry seed is placed on a wet medium or subjected to a moisture source, the most

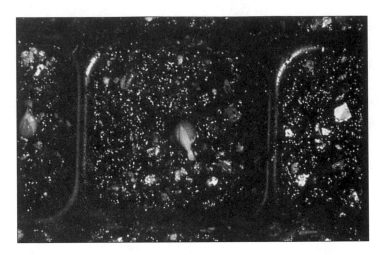

FIGURE 4.1 Radicle emergence of germinating pansy seed.

obvious event is a rapid uptake of water. The driving force behind this rapid uptake is the difference in water potential between the seed and the surrounding atmosphere. A dry seed has moisture content around 5 to 8% by weight. For the radicle to grow, the moisture content of the embryo must increase to around 80 to 90%, whereas the rest of the seed may only have less than 50% moisture content.

WATER UPTAKE

Under optimal conditions of supply, the seed's uptake of water occurs in three phases (fig. 4.2). Phase 1, imbibition, is the physical process of water uptake from the wet surroundings into the dry seed, causing the seed to swell. This process occurs regardless of whether the seed is dormant or nondormant, alive or dead. Within four to eight hours, most seeds have absorbed most of the water necessary to germinate completely.

After this initial uptake, a lag phase, Phase 2, in water uptake occurs, lasting from hours to days. During this phase major metabolic events take place in preparation for radicle emergence from the nondormant seed. These events include enzyme activation, membrane reorganization, sugar metabolism, protein synthesis, storage reserve breakdown, and RNA synthesis [1]. Dormant seeds are also metabolically active at this time. During the lag phase, little additional water accumulates in the seed, but the water balance is critical.

Viable seeds, whether dormant or nondormant, have similar water uptake patterns to this point. However, only nondormant seeds will show another period of water uptake (Phase 3). This increase in water uptake is initially related to the changes that cells of the radicle undergo as they extend, marking the completion of germination.

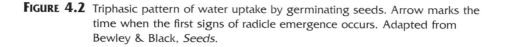

FIGURE 4.2 Triphasic pattern of water uptake by germinating seeds. Arrow marks the time when the first signs of radicle emergence occurs. Adapted from Bewley & Black, *Seeds.*

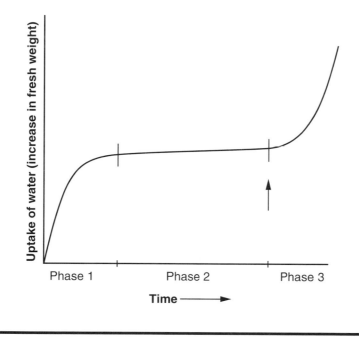

The duration of each of these phases depends on certain properties of the seed (seed coat permeability, seed size, oxygen uptake) and on the conditions during hydration (temperature, moisture level, composition of media). How the plug grower understands the characteristics of the seed and controls the conditions during hydration will determine how well the germination process can be completed in a timely manner.

FACTORS AFFECTING GERMINATION

Four key factors influence the germination process: temperature, moisture, oxygen, and light. Temperature affects both the capacity for germination and the rate of germination by controlling the rate of water uptake through membrane reorganization, enzyme synthesis, respiration, and many other biochemical reactions going on within the seed [1]. For germination events to occur in a timely, coordinated manner, it is essential to provide the optimum temperature. Most seeds will germinate over a range of temperatures, but for plug production, temperatures too far from the optimum are not acceptable because they result in slow, irregular germination or low germination percentages.

High temperatures may prevent some seeds from germinating by impos-ing a secondary dormancy called *thermodormancy*. Crops affected by ther-modormancy include geranium (>75F, 24C), impatiens (>78F, 25C), and let-tuce (>85F, 30C). Low temperatures will not only slow down the rate of ger-mination but may actually reduce total germination. For example, vinca seeds will germinate at a higher percentage as temperature increases between 70 to 90F (21 to 32C).

Equally important are uniform, reproducible, and controllable moisture conditions. Insufficient moisture can reduce both the speed and percentage of germination. The smaller the seed, the less water it needs to germinate. In gen-eral, even moderately moist media will provide enough water for germination.

The water balance in the seed is most important. Most of the water used in germination actually goes to maintaining the high humidity necessary to ensure the optimum seed water balance [6]. With decreasing seed size, water loss to a dry atmosphere will occur more quickly, with the seed becoming des-iccated during the germination process. The timing and coordination of meta-bolic events is thus disrupted, resulting in poor and irregular germination.

In plug production it is often necessary to cover seeds during germina-tion with plug media, coarse vermiculite, sand, perlite, or plastic coverings of various types in order to maintain high humidity around the seed. Generally, the larger the seed, the more it needs to be covered to keep mois-ture in contact all around it. In addition to covering, some seeds require more moisture than others. Seeds that need wet conditions include impatiens, begonia, pansy, ranunculus, and cyclamen. Examples of seeds that need dry conditions (meaning high humidity around the seed but no squeezable water) include delphinium, verbena, seedless watermelon, aster, and zinnia. Crops such as pepper need to be covered but do not need as much water as tomato to germinate.

A further complication in the moisture picture is too much wetness, resulting in a lack of oxygen to the seed. Generally, there is enough oxygen available to the seed in the air or soil for germination. However, when too much covering is applied, or when fine vermiculite is used instead of coarse vermiculite, the seed stays too wet too long, oxygen is reduced, and mold growth increases. The seed becomes smothered with a wet blanket and can-not breathe. Net result is reduced germination and erratic plant stands. For instance, impatiens seeds buried in the plug media have little chance of becoming quality seedlings. Seeds germinating on the surface of the plug media, though, are not affected by wet conditions [6]. Pepper seeds covered with moist coarse vermiculite instead of moist fine vermiculite will germi-nate better because more oxygen is available to the seed. However, it is still possible to provide too much water even to these pepper seeds, causing a reduction in plant stands.

Continuous exposure to high levels of white light during germination may inhibit radicle extension and growth, thereby causing nonuniform seedling growth [2]. This inhibition may not totally prevent germination, but only reduce its percentage. Some crops affected include vinca, cyclamen, phlox, and lettuce. Some varieties of vinca will germinate 15 to 20% higher when kept in darkness than when germinated in continuous light. Secondary dormancy can be initiated by exposure to short periods of far-red light when the seed requires darkness to germinate. This happens in seeds of certain cultivars of tomato, lettuce, and cucumber. Some crops, though, such as certain cultivars of impatiens and petunia, may actually need exposure to light to germinate. Generally, most crops grown in plugs do not need light to germinate but will need light for early seedling growth.

DORMANCY

When viable seeds are placed in optimum conditions but do not germinate, they are said to be dormant. Dormancy is basically the inability of the embryo to germinate fully because of some inherent inadequacy. Primary dormancy can be controlled genetically; it also occurs while the seed is still on the mother plant. Secondary dormancy can also be controlled genetically but is mainly due to unfavorable conditions for germination.

There are two basic types of primary dormancy: coat-imposed or embryo. With coat-imposed dormancy, the seed coat and related structures exert constraints that the embryo cannot overcome. These constraints can include the seed coat being impervious to water or oxygen, containing growth inhibitors, or providing a mechanical restraint to the germinating embryo. Embryo dormancy is generally caused by immature embryos or growth inhibitors.

Some dormant seeds, when dry, slowly lose their dormancy by the process of *afterripening,* perhaps requiring as little time as a few weeks or as long as five years. Afterripening may be dependent on temperature, moisture, and oxygen for its success. No one knows what really happens during afterripening, although immature embryos may develop to mature embryos, and growth inhibitors may break down or growth promoters build up. With cut snapdragon seeds, an afterripening period of three months to one year may be needed.

Chilling temperatures, or *stratification,* usually done in moist conditions, can break dormancy in delphinium, larkspur, moluccella and many types of perennials. Alternating temperatures between cool and warm can also bring delphinium and *Ammi majus* out of dormancy. These treatments need to be administered after the seed has been sown and the plug media moistened.

Light can help to break dormancy in lettuce and campanula. Chemicals such as gibberellic acid (GA), cytokinins, ethylene, or potassium nitrate (KNO₃) can alleviate dormancy in delphinium and petunia. Hard seed coats can be scarified by acid, mechanical means, or microbial activity in the soil, as with geranium and lupine. Soaking in water can leach out inhibitors and increase seed coat permeability in cyclamen, freesia, and primula.

For most bedding plant seed sold, dormancy is not a problem to the plug grower. Hard seeds are already scarified by the seed companies, afterripening has already finished during storage, and breeders have genetically removed other dormancies. The seed sold to growers could not meet the germination requirements of the seed companies if still dormant.

However, if proper conditions for germination are not provided by the grower, then secondary dormancy can be induced. This dormancy can easily occur with high temperature in geranium, lettuce, and impatiens, or with light in vinca, cyclamen, phlox, and lettuce.

VIABILITY AND VIGOR

The ability of a live seed to germinate under optimum conditions is called *viability*. The ability of a live seed to germinate under a range of conditions and still produce a usable seedling is called *vigor*. These two terms are not the same! Viability is usually determined in a seed-testing laboratory under optimum, very controlled conditions. This result determines the *true germination potential*.

What the plug grower actually gets once the seed is sown may not be the same. Plug germination depends on temperature, moisture, light, and oxygen. The ability of a plug grower to optimally control these four factors will determine how close actual germination comes to the true germination potential. However, as you may already know, getting close is easier said than done.

Thus, a plug grower needs to know how vigorous a seed lot is, in order to know what plug stands (usable seedlings) to expect when conditions are not quite optimal. Many plug growers are now testing seed lots in plug tests at their own locations before seeding for production.

Other methods currently being used by various seed companies to determine vigor include:

■ Accelerated aging

■ Peak germination counts

- Cool and warm germination stress tests
- Conductivity of seed leachate
- Soil or plug tests
- Seedling growth tests (root length, seedling height)
- Image analyses of cotyledon expansion (fig. 4.3) or root length

Vigor tests allow the seed company to determine which are the strongest seed lots, predict how long they will store, and under what conditions they will still germinate well. A grower who purchases this seed can then be sure to be getting not only the most viable but also the most vigorous seed. Vigor determines the uniformity of germination and early seedling growth, how fast the germination will occur, and how much germination will be achieved under less than optimum conditions.

FIGURE 4.3 Example of cotyledon expansion using a computer vision system to determine seedling vigor. Courtesy Ball Seed Co.

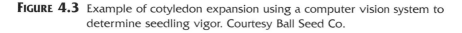

Germination: 99%
BALL VIGOR INDEX   800

Total cells measured: 126
Total germinated cells: 125

How long that seed stays vigorous is a function of its genetics, storage conditions, and time. The relationship between viability and vigor during storage can be seen in fig. 4.4. Over time, vigor will decrease before viability, meaning that germination will not be the best indicator for how the seed is holding up in storage. Two lots of the same variety can both have 90% germination in the lab, but one lot may already be declining on the vigor curve while the other lot still has great vigor. Once a seed starts moving down the vigor or viability curve, the decline cannot be reversed, only slowed down. All seeds eventually decline and die during storage. It is only a matter of time!

FIGURE 4.4 Decline of seed quality with time.

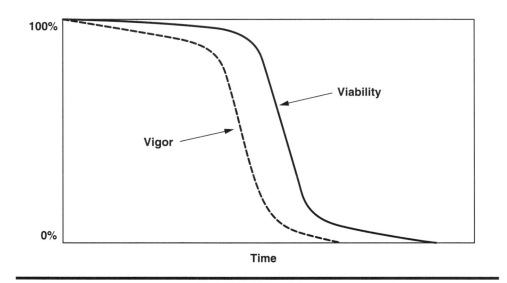

STORAGE AND HANDLING

The two most important factors in seed storage are moisture (measured as % relative humidity [RH] or seed moisture content) and temperature, with seed moisture content being more important. In 1960 Harrington [4] determined the following rules of thumb for seed storage:

- Every 1% decrease in seed moisture content (to a point) doubles the storage life.

- Every 10F (5C) decrease in seed storage temperature doubles the storage life.

- The sum of degrees F and % RH should be less than 100 for good storage conditions.

Proper storage conditions maintain % RH between 20 and 40% and seed moisture content of 5 to 8%, the optimal storage moisture content for most seeds. When seed moisture content drops too low (less than 5%), storage life and seed vigor may decline. When seed moisture content goes above 12%, fungi and insects can adversely affect viability, and aging of the seed will speed up. Most all seed is stored and shipped in hermetically sealed foil packets and bags or vacuum-packed cans (fig. 4.5). These containers provide excellent barriers against moisture moving in or out. Therefore, seed must have the proper moisture content before being packed, and the air in the containers should be at low % RH.

Storage temperatures should stay between 40 and 70F (5 and 21C), with special attention paid to the % RH and the "100 Rule." In fact, the "100 Rule" should be revised to be the "80 Rule." Most seeds can be stored below freezing if their moisture

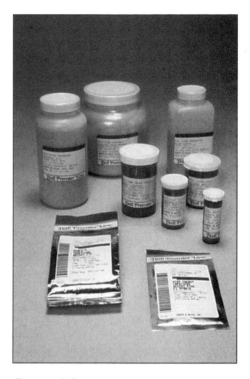

FIGURE 4.5 Various protective containers for flower seeds. Courtesy Ball Seed Co.

content is low enough (5 to 8%). Some seeds, such as delphinium, primula, and cyclamen, must be stored at cool temperatures (42F, 5C) for best storage life. Other seeds, such as impatiens, will store longer at this lower temperature and relative humidity (fig. 4.6).

A plug grower can use a frost-free refrigerator or climate-controlled room set at 42F (5C) to store all seed (fig. 4.7). The foil packets and metal cans will protect against moisture as long as they are sealed. Once opened, care must be taken to prevent seeds from taking up moisture from the air. Relative humidity in a seeding area can easily exceed 80%, with all the moisture from the filled plug trays, seeders, and watering tunnels. Many times opened seed packets are left out all day in the seeding area while the seeder operator uses them to seed the day's production. Exposed seed can easily increase its moisture content 2% in two hours under such conditions. If this process continues with the same seed lots over several weeks, significant deterioration and reduction of seed vigor can occur, especially in such sensitive crops as impatiens.

FIGURE 4.6 Changes in impatiens seed quality after storage for one year at various temperatures and relative humidities. Courtesy of PanAmerican Seed Co.

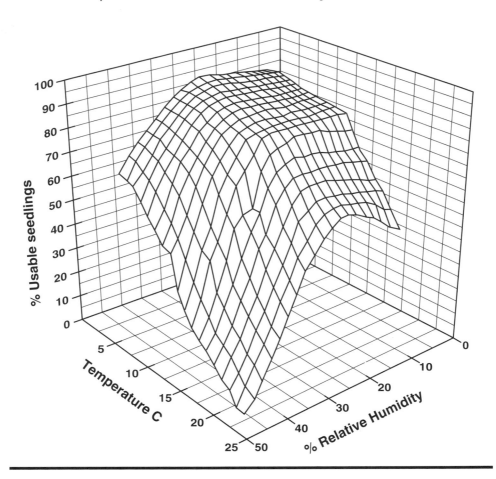

Simply closing the foil packet later and placing it in a refrigerator will not remove the extra moisture the seed has absorbed from the air. The grower should place the seed in a water vapor-proof container that can be sealed (Tupperware, Mason jar), with a thin layer (a quarter of an inch) of silica gel desiccant in the bottom, and store it in a refrigerator. Silica gel desiccant with a color indicator can be purchased from Sigma Chemical Co. (800/325-3010) or other distributors of scientific supplies. When the color of the desiccant changes from blue to pink, the silica gel can be regenerated by being placed in an oven at 230 to 360F (110 to 180C) until the color changes back to blue. A microwave oven can also be used for this purpose.

If a refrigerator is too small to store all of your seed, then look into building a climate-controlled room or buying a walk-in cooler. This room should be very well insulated (R = 30) and vapor-sealed, with a thermostat and a humidistat for controlling the conditions at 42F (5C) and 25 to 30% RH. Make sure that the fans on the cooling unit are set on continuous operation to eliminate temperature fluctuations in the room. Humidity can be controlled with a commercial desiccant dryer, available from Bry Air (614/965-2974) or Cargoaire (800/843-5360).

Dehumidifiers for home use are not suitable for controlling RH in a seed storage area because they can only reduce the RH to 35% and they generate heat. Consult your local heating and cooling company for industrial coolers. An alarm system should be installed, due to the large amount of money tied up in the seed inventory. Continuous recording of temperature and RH is worthwhile [3].

Different crops will generally store for lengths of time determined by their genetics. Table 4.1 lists the major vegetable and flower crops and their relative storage lives. When seeds have been refined, enhanced, or otherwise altered—which includes pelleted, coated, primed, de-tailed, defuzzed, dewinged, or scarified seed of many flowers and vegetables—their storage life will be shortened. Many plug growers order seed for only one season and by seed count so as not to carry over inventory. If storing seed from one year to the next, however, test it first before putting it into production.

FIGURE 4.7 Refrigerated seed storage area.

Seed cleaning and purity are important aspects of quality. Mechanical seeders used in plug production require uniform seed for good sowing. If seed is a hand-pollinated, hand-harvested hybrid such as impatiens, it is unlikely that any weed seed would be in the lot. With field-grown seed, however, the potential for weed seed contamination exists, and seed must be cleaned thoroughly. Seed companies have done a much better job with seed cleaning in the past five to 10 years and continue to focus on seed cleaning and separations to provide the most uniform type of seed.

Besides weed seeds, other particles in a seed packet may clog a seeder. Even flower seeds that are small can be very fragile. Plug growers need to be aware of this and *handle with care*. For example, impatiens seed packets may have some white seed and other particles showing. The particles are

TABLE 4.1   Relative storage life of seeds

Short	Medium	Long
Anemone	Ageratum	Amaranthus
Asparagus fern	Alyssum	Daisy, Shasta
Aster	Cauliflower	Stocks
Begonia	Celery	Sweet pea
Browallia	Celosia	Tomato
Delphinium	Coleus	Zinnia
Herbs	Cyclamen	
Impatiens	Dahlia	
Lettuce	Dianthus	
New Guinea impatiens	Dusty miller	
Onion	Eggplant	
Pansy	Geranium	
Pepper	Lisianthus	
Phlox	Lobelia	
Salvia	Marigold	
Vinca	Petunia	
Viola	Portulaca	
	Snapdragon	
	Verbena	
	Watermelon	

Source: Adapted from Justice & Bass, *Seed storage.*

often seed coats that have been rubbed off, and the white seed is the naked seed, resulting from mechanical damage. White petunia is another seed sensitive to mechanical damage. Begonia seed is easily crushed, but it is difficult to tell with the naked eye. At present, begonia seed is shipped in special vials to protect it. Some crops, such as dahlia, zinnia, and aster, always seem to have some trash in their packets from handling. Keep a set of small screens by the seeder to quickly take the trash out of the seed you want to sow.

Fungicide seed treatments have become important for many types of seed, particularly vegetables. Fungicide treatments protect the seed and seedling once it is planted. It is not hazardous for people to handle seed treated with fungicides such as Captan or Thiram, if a grower uses common sense. These fungicides are not as toxic as most other chemicals used in a normal growing operation. For example, Captan is nontoxic. Although Thiram is more toxic, it still requires about 2 to 3 ounces taken orally for a 180-pound man to obtain a lethal dose.

Yet, problems can occur with these materials. Thiram causes an allergic skin reaction in some people, while others do not suffer at all. It is important to identify sensitive people and not have them handle treated seed. People that do handle treated seed should wear protective equipment (gloves and mask), use common sanitation procedures, and avoid rubbing their eyes with the chemical on their fingers. New fungicide treatments are being applied to seed with a protective coating (for example, Safecoat) to make them safer to handle by seeder operators.

KEY POINTS TO REMEMBER

■ The key factors affecting seed quality are genetics, seed production, postharvest techniques, and germination conditions.

■ Water uptake in a seed occurs in three phases: rapid physical imbibition, a lag phase, and another rapid uptake when the seedling comes out. Only live, nondormant seeds go through all three phases. Uniform moisture availability is essential to the germination of small flower seeds.

■ The four key factors that influence the germination process are temperature, moisture, oxygen, and light. Separate sets of environmental conditions are needed for optimum germination of different seeds.

■ Monitor and control your soil temperature during germination, whether in a chamber or on a bench. All seeds have upper and lower temperature limits for best germination.

■ When covering or watering seeds in a plug tray, make sure that oxygen is available to the seed and emerging seedling.

■ Light is needed by some seeds to germinate, whereas other seeds prefer darkness.

■ Viability and vigor are not the same! Over time, vigor will decrease before viability, meaning that germination percentage will not be the best indicator of vigor.

■ Storage conditions are the key to prolonging seed vigor! Seed moisture content and temperature are the most important factors in storage. Maintain storage conditions of 42F (5C) and 25 to 35% RH for all seeds.

REFERENCES

[1] Bewley, J.D., and M. Black. 1994. *Seeds: Physiology of development and germination.* 2nd ed. New York: Plenum Press.

[2] Carpenter, W.J., E.R. Ostmark, and J.A. Cornell. 1994. Light governs the germination of *Impatiens wallerana* Hook. f. seed. *HortScience* 29(8):854–857.

[3] Cross, D., and R.C. Styer. 1996. Store your seed the right way. *GrowerTalks* 59(11):41, 46.

[4] Harrington, J.F. 1960. Thumb rules for drying seed. *Crops and Soils* 13:16–17.

[5] Justice, O.L., and L.N. Bass. 1978. *Principles and practices of seed storage.* USDA Agric. Handbook #506. Washington, D.C.: U.S. Department of Agriculture.

[6] Karlovich, P., and D. Koranski. 1989. Quality seed and Stage 1—Your best start toward turning a profit with plugs. *GrowerTalks* 53(8):62, 64.

CHAPTER 5

SEED TYPES

Years ago, the vegetable industry recognized the need to change the labor-intensive thinning processes required to space seedlings in field production. Technology was developed to refine and enhance seed in order to better adapt seeds to mechanical seeders and in other ways increase the number of transplantable seedlings. The improvements began with seed production and postharvest handling. The refinement process has involved cleaning and physically altering the seed for better seeder handling, such as defuzzing tomato seeds and pelleting light-sensitive seeds, such as lettuce. Fungicides have been applied in some cases to improve disease resistance. Physiological enhancements have altered the seed for faster germination and tolerance of a broader range of environmental conditions under which it will still germinate.

Plug performance demands have forced the flower seed industry to improve seed quality, using the same concepts as in the vegetable seed industry. A dramatic improvement in standard seed quality has occurred, along with the introduction of many different seed types. Presently, a plug grower can order seed that has been refined, de-tailed, defuzzed, dewinged, primed, pelleted, coated, or any combination of these. Also, pregerminated seeds, where the radicle is already visible, are now available for several crops, nearly achieving the goal of 100% germination. With all these choices, how is a grower to decide?

REFINED SEED

All seed lots are cleaned of dirt, pollen, and chaff after they are harvested. Some sizing may also occur as seeds are run over a set of screens to remove debris. Most seeds can be further separated by physical characteristics such as size, shape, weight, color, and density to increase the uniformity of seed vigor and thereby the yield of uniform seedlings. Equipment may include screens, gravity tables, air columns, indent cylinders, electrostatic separators, and liquid density separators. A particular seed lot may be separated into two, three, or more fractions, with each fraction then being tested for germination and vigor. Fractions that meet certain criteria are then sold as separate lots of refined seed.

This process increases total germination percentage and speed and uniformity of germination, resulting in increased seed performance in the plug tray. However, the amount of improvement differs between crops and varieties. Side-by-side trials should be run to determine how much difference there will be in your plug production system.

Commercial names of refined seed include High Tech, High Energy, High-Vi, and Unifrax. Refined seed is available for salvia, impatiens, some vegetables, and many other types of flower seeds where priming is still not practical, but pelleting and coating is.

THE "D" SEEDS—DEFUZZED, DEWINGED, DE-TAILED

Modern mechanical seeders can range from simple template models to high-speed drum models. Most all seeders operate with a vacuum pickup. Seeders work best with round, uniformly sized seeds. However, many types of seeds are thin, long, curly, or flat and have sharp edges, fuzz or wings. Such nonround seeds are harder to sow accurately with most seeders. For this reason, seed companies have been offering to defuzz tomato seed (fig. 5.1) and

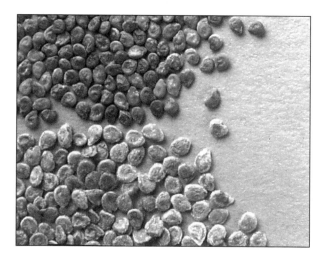

FIGURE 5.1 Defuzzed (upper) compared to untreated (lower) tomato seeds. Courtesy Ball Seed Co.

anemone seed, dewing ageratum and ranunculus seed, and de-tail marigold seed (fig. 5.2). After these processes, the seeds are easier to pick up with a vacuum seeder, flow through the seeder better, fit into the plug tray better, or are easier to pellet or coat for faster and more accurate seeding.

Remember, the defuzzing, dewinging, and de-tailing processes mechanically damage the seed coats, thereby reducing the storage life of these seeds. Broken seeds can be removed by mechanical separations, but the scraping of the seed coat removes some of the protective coating of even an otherwise intact seed. These seeds should be used during the season they were bought and not carried over in inventory.

PRIMED SEED

FIGURE 5.2 De-tailed and untreated marigold seeds.

After mechanically refined seed, enhancing seed performance physiologically was the next logical step. *Priming,* or *osmoconditioning*, is defined as controlled hydration of seeds that permits pregerminative metabolic activity, but prevents subsequent radicle emergence. Seed is soaked in an osmotic solution to activate the metabolic processes of germination, but the osmotic solution also prevents complete germination from occurring. Before the radicle (root) emerges, the seed is dried back to its presolution moisture content, packaged, and handled like raw seed. When it is sown and rehydrated by watering, germination occurs quickly because many of the metabolic processes have already been completed. The result is an increase in the speed of germination and total germination percentage, greater uniformity, and enhanced seedling vigor over a wide range of environmental conditions.

Each crop has its own priming treatment. Variables to control include treatment duration, osmotic or matric potential, temperature, light, and oxygen availability. Not all seed lots of the same crop behave the same way during priming, so before and after priming, they must be tested for germination and vigor. Storage life is reduced for primed or enhanced seed compared to raw seed, and primed seed generally has a "sow by" date for best performance.

Commercial names of primed seed include Protech, PRE-PREP, Peto Plus, Genesis, and Primex. Primed vegetable seed commonly sown in plugs include tomato, pepper, lettuce, and celery. Primed flower crops include pansy, vinca, verbena, tuberous begonia, dusty miller, dianthus, dahlia, and impatiens.

Sometimes priming also overcomes seed dormancy, such as in thermo- and photodormancy. Research at Texas A & M University showed primed coreopsis seed had 34% higher germination, reached 50% germination three days earlier, and had more vigor than standard seed [2]. If a plug grower cannot exactly control the germination temperature, moisture, or light, then primed seed will give better results than raw seed. Primed pansy seed had a higher germination speed and percentage compared to standard seed at all temperatures [1]. Plug growers in the southern United States have much better success with primed than raw pansy seed when sowing in the hot months of July to September. Furthermore, when production schedules are tight, primed seed can cut off a week of crop time, and give more uniform plant stands than raw seed.

PELLETED AND COATED SEED

As mentioned, seeds that aren't round make it more difficult for vacuum seeders to sow accurately at high speeds. If a drum seeder has to be run slowly in order to seed more accurately, then its efficiency is lost. Also, many sown seeds are small or difficult to see in the plug tray, making it hard to determine if the seeding was done properly.

Many seeds can be pelleted or coated for faster, more accurate seeding and allowing better visual inspection. The pelleting process increases size and uniformity of small seed, whereas coating increases the flowability of odd-shaped seed. Another reason to pellet or coat seeds is to provide a safe and efficient carrier for seed-based treatments (fungicides, insecticides, biocontrol agents, growth regulators).

Pelleting usually consists of adding layers of a clay-type material with a binder to build up small or irregular-shaped seeds (fig. 5.3), such as tomato, pepper, lettuce, celery, begonia, petunia, lisianthus, and dusty miller. Coating provides a thinner layer sprayed onto the seed, usually containing a dye, to make the seed more flowable in the seeder. Coating does not change the overall shape of the seed (fig. 5.4), whereas pelleting does. Examples of coated seed include marigold, dahlia, zinnia, ranunculus, anemone, and impatiens.

The fluorescent dyes used in pelleting and coating allow the seed to be more visible in the plug tray after seeding. Pelleted or coated seed does not store as long as raw seed. However, a plug grower can order by seed count, making seed inventory control much easier.

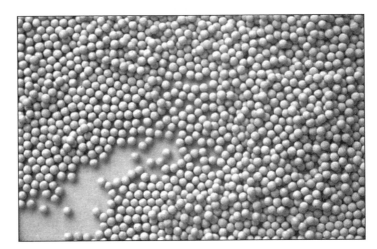

FIGURE 5.3 Pelleted petunia seeds. Courtesy Ball Seed Co.

Once pelleted seed is sown, the initial watering starts to break down the pellet. Depending on the amount of water applied during the first few days, the pellet may partially or completely break down. Pellets from different seed companies are not the same! To test how pellets break down, drop a few into a glass of water and observe their meltability. Some pellets split apart, some explode from oxygen generation, others melt away, and still others may not melt at all. For best germination of pelleted seed, keep moisture availability uniform throughout Stage 1 and early Stage 2. Once pellets dry out, the seed will die! On the other hand, if kept too moist because of your trying to wash away the pellet, the seed will drown!

FIGURE 5.4 Coated de-tailed marigold seeds. Courtesy Ball Seed Co.

Coated seed, in contrast, will not lose its coat after watering. The coat color will diffuse into the media, but the coat itself will not dissolve away. It will not interfere with germination, so do not try to rinse it off!

The benefits of pelleted and coated seed are in the easier and more accurate seeding, not in germination. Generally, pelleting or coating slows down the germination rate, usually by a day. However, more seed companies are using refined or primed seed along with pelleting or coating to overcome this delay and provide the highest germination and uniformity possible.

PREGERMINATED SEED

The next logical step beyond primed seed, which starts the germination process but stops it before the radicle emerges, is to continue the process through radicle emergence, separate the live seed from the dead, and sow quickly. This is the concept behind pregerminated seed, which got started in the 1970s with the advent of fluid drilling. This technique sowed pregerminated seed into a field by means of some type of gel-extrusion seeder. The goal was to allow the farmer to germinate his or her own seed in the fluid, then quickly sow into the field, thus getting a faster start on stand establishment. However, fluid drilling never became popular, mainly due to the large burden placed on the farmer for germinating and mixing the seed and to a lack of equipment for singulation seeding. There still is a company in England making seeders that sow pregerminated seed bubbling in a water bath into plug trays, but the cost is high and the speed is slow.

Recently, pregerminated seed has become commercially available for impatiens, pansy, primula, and other crops, with more still being developed. Availability is limited to a few series of each crop, but this product is expected to expand greatly in coming years. Commercial names include Pre-Magic and PowerBall.

The seed needs to have special handling (store at 42F, 5C) and be sown quickly (within two to four weeks) using normal seeding equipment. Since the radicle has already emerged, however, the germinated and nongerminated seed can be separated with liquid density separations. Also, there is little or no need for Stage 1. A plug grower can realize a week shorter crop time with higher germination (up to 100%), faster germination, and better uniformity.

WORKSHEETS FOR CALCULATING ECONOMICS OF SEED TYPES

This section presents two tables—table 5.1 is for growing plugs for yourself and finishing in a cell-pack. Table 5.2 is for growing plugs and then selling the plug flat to someone else. The figures that are underlined are hypothetical but common values we filled in for the examples. You can fill in your own specific numbers in your individual calculations. We are comparing pansy standard (raw) seed with primed seed in these examples, but the tables can be used for any crop or seed type.

TABLE 5.1 Pansy finished flat

Assumptions	Options[a]	Standard	Genesis
Standard seed (M)	$15.90		
Genesis seed (M)	$20.30		
Percentage sown in doubles	0	0	0
Percentage sown in misses	0	0	0
1. Transplantable plugs (%)	70	70	85
2. Seed units ordered	1,000,000	1,000,000	1,000,000
Seeds germinated		700,000	850,000
3. Tray size	512	512	512
4. Seed cost/1,000		$15.90	$20.30
5. Ft^2/tray	1.75	1.75	1.75
6. No. of weeks tray grown	6	6	5
7. Fixed cost/tray	$1.00	$1.00	$1.00
8. Bench cost/ft^2/week	$0.20	$0.20	$0.20
9. No. of trays needed		1,953	1,953
Seed cost = 2/1000 × 4		$15,900.00	$20,300.00
Fixed cost = 7 × 9		$1,953.13	$1,953.13
Bench cost = 9 × 6 × 8		$2,343.75	$1,953.13
Total cost		**$20,196.88**	**$24,206.25**
Cost/transplantable plug		$0.03271	$0.03026
Selling price/flat	$6.50		
Selling price/plant		$0.18056	$0.18056
Flat size (density)	36		
No. of marketable flats		19,444	23,611
Total sales		$126,386	$153,472
Total cost		$20,197	$24,206
Total profit		**$106,189**	**$129,266**

[a] These are hypothetical values used for this example. Growers can enter their own numbers and then do the calculations.

Worksheet courtesy Ball Seed Co.

TABLE 5.2   Pansy plug tray: 406

Assumptions	Options[a]	Standard	Genesis
Standard seed (M)	$15.90		
Genesis seed (M)	$20.30		
Percentage sown in doubles	0	0	0
Percentage sown in misses	0	0	0
1. Germination (%)	70	70	85
2. Seed units ordered	406,000	406,000	406,000
Seeds germinated		284,200	345,100
3. Tray size	406	406	406
4. Seed cost/1,000		$15.90	$20.30
5. Ft^2/tray	1.75	1.75	1.75
6. No. of weeks tray grown	6	6	5
7. Fixed cost/tray	$1.00	$1.00	$1.00
8. Bench cost/ft^2/week	$0.20	$0.20	$0.20
9. No. of trays needed		1,000	1,000
Seed cost = 2/1000 × 4		$6,455.40	$8,241.80
Fixed cost = 7 × 9		$1,000.00	$1,000.00
Bench cost = 9 × 6 × 8		$1,200.00	$1,000.00
Total cost		**$8,655.40**	**$10,241.80**
Cost/transplantable plug		$0.03045	$0.02968
Selling price/flat		$14.85	$18.15
Selling price/plant		$0.05500	$0.05500
Flat size (density)		284	345
Sold as (flat size)		270	330
No. of marketable flats		1,000	1,000
Total sales		$14,850	$18,150
Total cost		$8,655	$10,242
Total profit		**$6,195**	**$7,908**

[a] These are hypothetical values used for this example. Growers can enter their own numbers and then do the calculations.

Worksheet courtesy Ball Seed Co.

REFERENCES

[1] Koranski, D.S. 1988. Primed seed—A step beyond refined seed. *GrowerTalks* 51(9):24–29.

[2] Samfield, D.M., J.M. Zajicek, and B.G. Cobb. 1988. Priming perennial seed. *GrowerTalks* 52(8):66–67.

CHAPTER 6

WATER QUALITY

Many people consider water the most important factor in plug production. Understanding water quality is essential. Sphagnum peat moss-based media have made the issue even more important, since they are more susceptible to chemical changes in the water.

Poor water quality can:

- destroy soil structure, hence prevent aeration and water infiltration

- cause direct salt damage to leaves and roots

- cause individual ion toxicities (for example, from high boron or fluoride)

- cause individual ion deficiencies (for example, low calcium or magnesium)

- change media pH and decrease fertilizer uptake, thereby causing mild to severe nutrient deficiencies

- introduce and spread fungal and bacterial diseases, such as *Pythium, Phytophthora,* and *Xanthomonas*

- cause stunting, chlorosis, and poor flower development

Water quality varies greatly between different regions of the United States and the world. Within each region, water can also vary significantly from location to location, depending on the water source. Water obtained from wells may contain a high nitrate (NO_3) or iron (Fe) content. Municipal sources may contain too much sodium (Na), chlorides (Cl), or fluorides (F). Run-off collected in retention ponds may contain fertilizers, pesticides, and salts from surrounding fields and roads. Any environmental change causing a fluctuation in the groundwater table, such as drought, heavy rain, and snow melt, creates a change in water quality. Water tests taken two or three times per year, or whenever any major environmental change occurs, can reveal potential problems.

Issues relating to water quality seem to fall into three categories: pH and alkalinity, toxicity, and chemical content requiring compensation in fertility programs. Most plug growers do not test their water quality, test it too infrequently, or do not know how to interpret the results they get from a laboratory. In this chapter we cover the major factors in water quality and how to measure and control them, outline methods for treating your water if you have problems, and provide water quality guidelines for plug production.

WATER pH AND ALKALINITY

Water pH refers to whether the water is acid or alkaline. The pH measure is a negative logarithm of hydrogen ion (H^+) concentration. A pH of 7.0 is neutral, below 7.0 is acid, and above 7.0 is alkaline. Since pH is measured logarithmically, a pH of 8.0 is 10 times as alkaline as a pH of 7.0. The pH of your water should be between 5.0 and 6.5 because most elements and other chemicals, such as growth regulators, fungicides, and pesticides, are soluble at that pH. High water pH may reduce the efficacy of chemicals, such as Truban, Florel, and various pesticides.

Water pH does not directly affect the pH of growing media. Water alkalinity, however, does directly affect growing media pH and, therefore, the availability of nutrients to plants. Water pH and alkalinity are not directly related! You can have two water sources, each with a pH of 8.0, but one could have 400 ppm alkalinity while the other could have just 80 ppm. Their effect on raising media pH would be vastly different. Using the alkalinity measurement, a grower can predict water's potential to cause an increase or decrease in growing media pH.

Alkalinity can be defined as the capacity of water to neutralize acids (H^+), the buffer capacity. The alkalinity level is determined by the total amount of dissolved bicarbonates (HCO_3^-), carbonates (CO_3^{-2}), and hydroxides (OH^-). An alkalinity measurement is conducted by slowly adding a standard sulfuric acid solution to a water sample of known volume to achieve a pH end point of 4.5. The amount of acid used is directly proportional to the alkalinity reading and is expressed as milligrams of calcium carbonate per liter of water (mg $CaCO_3$/l) or parts per million calcium carbonate (ppm $CaCO_3$). A plug grower can measure alkalinity with a simple test kit from Hach (800/227-4224), Cole-Parmer Instrument (800/323-4340), or Thomas

Scientific (800/345-2103) for about $20 to test 50 samples, or by sending a water sample to a testing laboratory (see appendix 4 for listing of laboratories).

Another way of thinking about alkalinity is that it is like lime in the water. The higher the alkalinity level, the more rapidly the media pH rises (becomes basic). When media pH gets above 6.5 for most crops, uptake of most minor elements, such as Fe and boron (B), is reduced, resulting in minor element deficiencies.

Table 6.1 illustrates the effect of water alkalinity on plug media pH. Here we compare two different water sources.

TABLE 6.1 Effect of water alkalinity on media pH

Water characteristics		Plug soil pH	
pH	Alkalinity	Start	One week
5.5	60 ppm	5.5	5.8
5.5	280 ppm	5.5	7.8

This reaction occurs quickly in a plug cell but much slower in a larger container. Do not underestimate the influence of high-alkalinity water on plug media pH. Over time, the effect of irrigation water alkalinity on plug media pH far exceeds that of initial lime charge in the media (table 6.2) [1].

Sometimes water alkalinity can be too low, and the water has no buffering capacity and is too pure. Low levels of calcium (Ca), magnesium (Mg), and Na may signal low alkalinity. If the alkalinity is too low (less than 50 ppm), then the media pH will fluctuate more widely, depending on whether acid or basic fertilizers are used. Generally, the media pH will decrease, as many fertilizers are acid. When media pH goes below 6.0 for some crops and 5.5 for most crops, micronutrient toxicities can occur, along with Ca deficiency. Sensitive crops include marigold, geranium, impatiens, and New Guinea impatiens. Alkalinity may need to be introduced into the soil by adding hydrated lime [$Ca(OH)_2$] at 1 lb per 100 gal of water or by adding potassium bicarbonate at 0.1 lb per 100 gal [2]. The main thing is to increase Ca and Mg to offset the water's low buffering capacity.

SOLUBLE SALTS

After alkalinity, total soluble salts is the most important water quality factor in plug production. The total soluble salts concentration is the quantity of all soluble ions, including fertilizers, per unit of solution. Total soluble salts are

TABLE 6.2   **Media pH change in cell packs of Pretty in Rose vinca due to initial liming charge and water alkalinity**

Water alkalinity (meq/l)[a]	Media pH		
	Day 1[b]	28	49
6.4 lb/yd³ lime addition[c]			
0	5.1	4.9	6.0
4	5.2	6.0	7.1
5.4	5.2	6.5	7.4
10.5 lb/yd³ lime addition			
0	5.3	5.1	6.3
4	5.3	6.2	7.1
5.4	5.3	6.8	7.4
16.9 lb/yd³ lime addition			
0	5.4	5.3	6.6
4	5.4	6.2	7.1
5.4	5.5	6.8	7.6

[a] 50 ppm calcium carbonate = 1 meq; 61 ppm bicarbonate = 1 meq.
[b] Beginning of plug Stage 2.
[c] Dolomitic limestone.
Source: Adapted from Bailey et al., Plug pH, *GrowerTalks.*

measured with a conductivity meter, expressed as electroconductivity (EC) and quantified as millimhos per centimeter (mmhos/cm) or millisiemens/cm (mS/cm), which are equal measurements. Generally, we want the soluble salt level in irrigation water (without fertilizer) to be less than 1.0 mmhos/cm. Remember, the total soluble salt level is cumulative, between the irrigation water, growing media, and fertilizer.

A high concentration of soluble salts can decrease germination, damage roots and root hairs, and burn leaves (fig. 6.1). Salt sensitivity is based not only on the plant species being grown but also on the individual elements that make up the solution. If your water test shows high soluble salts, then make sure you know what salts are involved—most commonly Na, Cl, B, F, and sulfates (SO_4). It has been demonstrated by many plug growers that numerous plug crops can be sensitive to high levels of soluble salts in the growing media, coming from poor-quality irrigation water. High soluble-salt levels in plugs may be managed by using coarse, well-drained media and applying 5 to 10% excess irrigation water to trays to facilitate leaching. Do not allow growing media to dry too much, which would concentrate soluble salts three or four times around the roots.

SODIUM
ABSORPTION RATIO

Another major factor of concern in water is the sodium absorption ratio (SAR). This value quantifies the Na level

FIGURE 6.1 Effect of high soluble salts in water on petunia root growth. Normal (left), high salts (right).

in relation to Ca and Mg levels. It evaluates the potential for soil permeability problems after long-term use of the irrigation water in question. SAR values are calculated using the following formula:

$$SAR = \frac{Na}{\sqrt{\dfrac{Ca + Mg}{2}}}$$

In this formula, Ca, Mg, and Na values must be expressed in milliequivalents (meq). To calculate milliequivalent values for these elements when results are originally expressed in milligrams per liter (mg/l) or parts per million (ppm), divide the Ca value by 20, the Mg value by 12.15, and the Na value by 23.

If the SAR is less than 2.0 and the Na level is less than 40 ppm (mg/l), the ratio should be adequate. Ca and Mg compete against Na. High levels of Na will cause the soil to tighten up, holding more water and less air and reducing root growth significantly. If Na levels are more than 40 ppm but the SAR value is less than 4.0, extra Ca and Mg can be added into the media with dolomitic limestone, gypsum, or magnesium sulfate. Use fertilizers containing more Ca, Mg, and potassium (K), starting early in the plug crop cycle. Avoid using 15-16-17 or any other fertilizer containing nitrate of soda (sodium nitrate), as this will only increase Na levels. Make sure to leach 5 to 10% with every watering to remove excess Na.

OTHER NUTRIENTS

When present in irrigation water at elevated levels, B, F, Cl, and SO_4 not only reduce plug quality in specific ways but may influence soluble salt levels in water and growing media. Boron levels greater than 0.5 ppm (mg/l) can be toxic to certain plants and cause tip abortion or burning. Chloride levels greater than 80 ppm (mg/l) may cause root tip burning, root rot, and lower leaf necrosis. Elevated levels of B and F can be managed in some situations by maintaining higher media pH levels of 6.5 to 6.8, which would reduce the solubility of these elements and make them unavailable to the plants. High B and F can also be controlled with more Ca. However, be careful with high-pH-sensitive crops, such as vinca, snapdragons, petunia, pansy, and primula, as Fe deficiency and *Thielaviopsis* will be promoted if media pH is too high.

Agricultural runoff can be a problem in certain countries and areas. Make sure you account for any extra NO_3, phosphorus (P), and K in your well or pond water due to agricultural runoff. Herbicides and pesticides may also leach into your water source.

High levels of Fe may cause discoloration of leaves, clog up mist nozzles, promote algae growth, and tie up competing nutrients, such as manganese (Mn), Ca, and Mg. Usually, you can add enough of the competing nutrients in the media and fertilizer program to avoid Fe tie-up. However, in some situations, a water filtration program may be needed to remove the excess Fe from the irrigation water.

Good water quality and a thorough understanding of what to look for in water gets you off to a good start in plug production. Table 6.3 recommends water quality guidelines for plug production. If you have poor water quality, you need to know how to correct it, or you decrease your chances of producing healthy plugs.

WATER TREATMENTS

Most water-quality problems involve high or low alkalinity, high soluble salts, high Na, high or low Ca and Mg, high Cl, or high B. If you have one or more of these problems, you need to know how to correct them. Correcting less than desirable water quality can involve using certain fertilizers, adding acid to irrigation water, switching water sources, or cleaning up the water by reverse osmosis (R/O).

TABLE 6.3   Water quality guidelines for plug production

pH	5.5–6.5
Alkalinity	60–80 ppm (mg/l) $CaCO_3$
Soluble salts (EC)	< 1.0 mmhos/cm
Sodium absorption ratio (SAR)	< 2
Nitrates (NO_3)	< 5 ppm (mg/l)
Phosphorus (P)	< 5 ppm (mg/l)
Potassium (K)	< 10 ppm (mg/l)
Calcium (Ca)	40–120 ppm (mg/l)
Magnesium (Mg)	6–25 ppm (mg/l)
Sodium (Na)	< 40 ppm (mg/l)
Chlorides (Cl)	< 80 ppm (mg/l)
Sulfates (SO_4)	24–240 ppm (mg/l)
Boron (B)	< 0.5 ppm (mg/l)
Fluoride (F)	< 1 ppm (mg/l)
Iron (Fe)	< 5 ppm (mg/l)
Manganese (Mn)	< 2 ppm (mg/l)
Zinc (Zn)	< 5 ppm (mg/l)
Copper (Cu)	< 0.2 ppm (mg/l)
Molybdenum (Mo)	< 0.02 ppm (mg/l)

Source: Adapted from Curtice & Templeton, *Water quality reference guide.*

FERTILIZERS

Moderately high alkalinity levels (100 to 200 ppm) can be managed with acid-forming fertilizers, which can include 21-7-7, 20-20-20, 20-10-20, or the Excel line of fertilizers from Scotts. The difficulties of using acid-forming fertilizers for alkalinity control are the need to continually use these fertilizers (constant feeding) and the amount of ammonium nitrogen (NH_4) in these fertilizers. Controlling plug growth relies on controlling fertility levels. Constant feeding is neither needed nor desired for plugs. Fertilizers containing high NH_4 promote shoot growth but not root growth. Soft, stretched plugs are the result! The need to use acid-forming fertilizers should be balanced with the desire to control plug growth and the type of plant.

Fertilizers containing some Ca and Mg can be beneficial by adding some buffering capacity to low-alkalinity water (less than 50 ppm), which has naturally low levels of Ca and Mg. Remember, however, that fertilizers containing Ca tend to raise media pH, as calcium nitrate is basic. When using low-alkalinity water, be careful about how much fertilizer and what type you use, as this water will tend to cause quick pH swings in your plug media.

If you have moderate to high levels of B in your water, you should use a fertilizer with no B added, or B toxicity could become a problem. Most fertilizers do add enough for plug growth in low-B water.

ACID INJECTION

For high-alkalinity water (up to 350 to 400 ppm), injection of inorganic (mineral) acids are needed to neutralize alkalinity to the 60 to 80 ppm range for good plug growth. The primary inorganic acids used are sulfuric, phosphoric, and nitric acid. Recently, organic acids (Seplex-L, from GreenCare) have been used to neutralize alkalinity due to their safety, assurance of complete nutrient availability to the plant roots, and no leaf spotting. However, organic acids are weaker, thereby requiring more to be used and increasing the cost.

Acids are available in various strengths and degrees of purity. Look for technical-grade purity to avoid any contaminants that may damage young seedlings. Sulfuric acid is commonly available in fairly pure form, 93% by weight. This is a dangerous acid to handle since it produces substantial heat when added to water. If water is added to the acid, in fact, an explosion can occur! All acids are highly corrosive in concentrated form. Wear protective clothing, including eyeguards, when handling acids. Phosphoric acid, usually available as 75 or 85% grade, is the least corrosive of the three acids. Nitric acid, available in some areas at 61% grade, is quite corrosive and must be handled with great care.

Let's run through a simple example of correcting alkalinity with acid (fig. 6.2):

Step 1: You have determined that your water contains 250 ppm $CaCO_3$. You need to reduce the alkalinity to 80 ppm for optimum plug growth. Therefore, you subtract 80 ppm from 250 ppm and find out you need to neutralize 170 ppm.

Step 2: To convert this to meq/l, divide by 61, and you get 2.79 meq $CaCO_3$ per liter of water. Each type of acid has its own capacity to neutralize bicarbonates.

Step 3: To neutralize 1 meq $CaCO_3$ per liter requires different amounts of the three acids, as fig. 6.2 shows.

Step 4: Now multiply by the total meq $CaCO_3$ per liter needed to neutralize to determine how much acid to add. This gives us 43.5 fl oz nitric acid per 1,000 gal water, or 20.9 fl oz phosphoric acid per 1,000 gal water, or 10.4 fl oz sulfuric acid per 1,000 gal water. Table 6.4 is a quick reference guide

---

FIGURE 6.2 Acid injection calculation

Step 1

Your water alkalinity　　=　250 ppm[a]

Desired alkalinity　　　=　　80 ppm

Alkalinity to neutralize =　170 ppm

Step 2

Convert 170 ppm alkalinity ($CaCO_3$) to meq/l:

$$\frac{170 \text{ (ppm bicarbonates to neutralize)}}{61 \text{ (ppm bicarbonates/meq)}} = 2.79 \text{ meq } CaCO_3/l$$

Step 3

To neutralize 1 meq $CaCO_3$/l use:

Sulfuric acid	Phosphoric acid	Nitric acid
3.72 fl oz/1,000 gal[b]	7.5 fl oz/1,000 gal	15.6 fl oz/1,000 gal

Step 4

To determine how much acid to use in your water, multiply by 2.79 (meq $CaCO_3$/l):

Sulfuric	Phosphoric	Nitric
2.79	2.79	2.79
× 3.72	× 7.5	× 15.6
10.4 fl oz/1,000 gal	20.9 fl oz/1,000 gal	43.5 fl oz/1,000 gal

[a] ppm = mg/l

[b] To convert oz/gal to ml/l, multiply by 7.812

---

for how much acid to use for various levels of bicarbonates. We generally round off phosphoric acid to 7.0 fl oz per 1,000 gal needed to neutralize 1 meq/l, and sulfuric acid to 3.5 fl oz per 1,000 gal to neutralize 1 meq/l.

Some important points to remember about acid injection:

- Do not exceed 14 fl oz phosphoric acid per 1,000 gal, as it may tie up Fe, or 14 fl oz sulfuric acid per 1,000 gal, as it will tie up Ca.

- All acids are caustic, particularly sulfuric and nitric. You may need plastic (PVC) pipes and fittings to prevent corrosion.

- Always inject acid *before* fertilizer and *do not mix concentrates*.

- Test the water alkalinity and pH after acid injection at the end of the hose to make sure you are at the proper levels.

When choosing which acid to use, the grower should carefully consider how much acid is required to neutralize the alkalinity, and the acids' characteristics. Sulfuric acid can tie up Ca, will give a hard type of growth to the

TABLE 6.4   Neutralizing water alkalinity with acid

| Alkalinity | Fl oz acid / 1,000 gal water | |
(meq/l HCO₃)ᵃ	85% phosphoric	93% sulfuric
0.5	3.5	1.75
1.0	7.0	3.5
1.5	10.5	5.25
2.0	14.0	7.0
2.5	17.5	8.75
3.0	21.0	10.5
3.5	—	12.25
4.0	—	14.0
4.5	—	15.75
5.0	—	17.5

ᵃ May be expressed as $CaCO_3$ equivalent.

plant, and can increase the solubility of Fe, Mn, and zinc (Zn). Often sulfuric acid is combined with phosphoric acid to reduce the degree of trace element solubility [5]. Phosphoric acid can supply P (10 fl oz of 85% acid per 1,000 gal of water will provide 33 ppm P) but can tie up micronutrients (Fe, Zn, and Mn). Generally, a grower uses a combination of sulfuric and phosphoric acids to reduce high alkalinity levels without providing too much P. Nitric acid supplies N but is very caustic. It is less beneficial in neutralizing alkalinity because it takes so much acid per meq/l bicarbonates. Nitric acid may increase Ca and Na uptake, resulting in hard growth of the plant. Nitric acid will *not* leave an unsightly foliar residue, but in water with low levels of Ca and Mg, it has been known to contribute to Fe deficiency.

When injecting concentrated acid into your water line, make sure you use an acid-head injector (fig. 6.3). Regular fertilizer injectors and heads will not last long, due to the caustic nature of inorganic acids. Insist on acid-compatible heads for your acid injector (appendix 4 lists some manufacturers).

Base the amount of acid you inject on a water analysis for alkalinity, not pH. If the pH fluctuates a bit, this should not be a major problem. Periodically test for alkalinity at the end of the hose to make sure it is staying low enough. Measure pH routinely as a quality control. If the pH gradually creeps up, it probably means that your water alkalinity has increased since your last test. Use an in-line pH sensor to sound an alarm if the injector is malfunctioning or you incorrectly add too much acid.

SWITCHING WATER SOURCES

Another option when water quality is very poor is to switch to a different water source, such as city or municipal water, pond water, rainwater, or another well on the property located away from the previous well. If your current well-water quality is very high in alkalinity, soluble salts, B, Na, or Cl, then test the water from these alternate sources.

FIGURE 6.3 Portable dual-head injector for acid and fertilizer.

City or municipal water test results are usually available from your water district office. However, these results may not have all the information you need. City water usually has some chlorine (Cl_2), F, and other chemicals added for purification. Also, the sources of this water may change during the year, and the city or municipality does not need to tell you. Examples of city water sources include aquifers (tapped by wells), reservoirs, rivers, lakes, snow melt, and springs. Several sources could be blended together. Check with your city or municipality to see what sources it uses throughout the year—cost of the water may be the determining factor.

A retention or collection pond catches rainwater or used water. Lining the pond with plastic keeps the water from being lost through the soil. Difficulties with this method include (1) high salt level from reusing water, (2) algae buildup, due to nutrients from reusing water or stagnant water, (3) low water or high evaporation levels at certain times of the year, and (4) guaranteeing the water does not contain disease organisms, such as bacteria and fungi, hazardous to the young plants you are growing. If you use pond water, make sure to test not only salts and nutrients but also for *Phytophthora* and other disease organisms. You can use a low amount (1 to 2 ppm) of chlorine injection in your main water line to avoid disease problems from the water.

Catching rainwater off the greenhouse roofs and into a collection pond or tanks is an environmentally sound practice. In Holland, where much of the well water has high soluble salts, it is common to see large, covered tanks, where rainwater is stored, next to greenhouses (fig. 6.4). Generally, there are no problems with the quality of rainwater. However, many areas of the world do not have sufficient rainfall throughout the year to make this method work. Rainwater could be used to dilute well water of poor quality and not be relied on as a sole source of high-quality water.

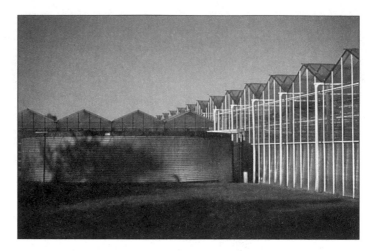

FIGURE 6.4 Rainwater collection tank. Courtesy Debbie Hamrick, *GrowerTalks.*

If your property is large, then there may be an opportunity to drill another well at a different site. Many times, especially in parts of California, well water can substantially differ in quality between wells only a mile apart or even just across the road from each other. Only by test-drilling and sending a water sample to a qualified laboratory for analysis will you know if this is an option. Remember, many a greenhouse grower has bought property without ever testing the well-water quality, and ended up with big growing problems!

REVERSE OSMOSIS

Reverse osmosis (R/O) filtration should be considered for plug production when water quality is very high in alkalinity, soluble salts, Na, or Cl and when switching to a different water source is not an option. However, R/O will not sufficiently remove high B from the water [4]. Reverse osmosis separates dissolved salts and organics from water by means of pressures exerted on a semipermeable membrane (fig. 6.5). Normally, water moves from the less salty side to the more salty side of the membrane (osmosis) until both sides reach equilibrium. The process of R/O takes place under pressure. With R/O the incoming solution passes over a membrane, and pressure forces a percentage of the water through the membrane (not allowing any salts to pass through), while as much as 20 to 50% of the initial solution, enriched in solutes, remains to be carried away [2].

There are three basic parts to a R/O system for greenhouse use: pretreatment of the water, the R/O unit itself, and a storage tank. Pretreatment is necessary to protect the membranes in the R/O system from contamination with bacteria, Ca, Mg, and Fe. These membranes are delicate and expensive, and the efficiency of the system depends on their condition. A

FIGURE 6.5 Reverse osmosis filtration compared to osmosis. *Osmosis:* water moves across the membrane toward the high-salt solution; salts do not move through. *Reverse osmosis:* when pressure is applied to the high-salt solution, the water moves through the membrane, leaving the salts behind. ■ = high-salt solution; □ = low-salt solution. Adapted from Biernbaum, Treat your water right, *Greenhouse Grower.*

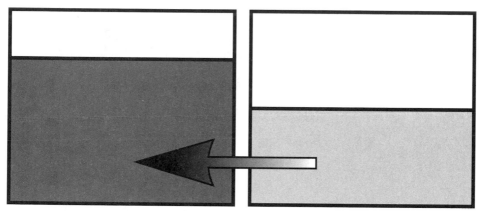

Osmosis

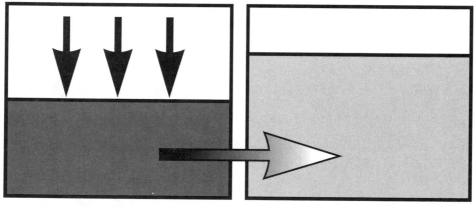

Reverse Osmosis

typical pretreatment may consist of chlorinating the water to remove bacteria, if needed; an acid injector to lower pH and neutralize alkalinity, or a water softener, either of which will take out Ca and Mg; and a dual-media sediment filter to remove Fe and some other suspended materials.

R/O units come in a capacity range from 215 to 10,800 gal/day (35 to 1,700 l/hr). The size of the unit, which will depend on your water needs, should be sized for your heaviest water usage (fig. 6.6). Additional membranes and a larger pump can be added to increase the unit's capacity.

A storage tank is needed to collect the clean water and pressurize it for use in the greenhouse. The R/O unit alone cannot keep up with your water usage in the greenhouse during the day. It will catch up during the night, however, by filling up the storage tank. To cut down on the cost and water usage, many growers blend some of their original water with the R/O water as it

FIGURE 6.6 Reverse osmosis system. Pretreatment tanks (left), columns containing semipermeable membranes (center), and storage tank (right).

leaves the storage tank and goes to the greenhouse. This blending decreases the demand on the tank and reduces the overall water cost. It also adds some buffering back into the water, for R/O water can be as low as 10 ppm alkalinity before blending.

Remember, R/O is more costly than acid injection or filtration, but it will take out high salts, high Na, high Cl, high alkalinity, and other ions. Test your water thoroughly and explore other water sources and options before buying a R/O system.

KEY POINTS TO REMEMBER

- Water alkalinity directly affects the growing media pH and, thus, nutrient availability to plants. Keep alkalinity to 60 to 80 ppm for plugs.

- Soluble salts in the water should be less than 1.0 mmhos/cm. Know what salts are involved if levels are higher than recommended.

- Sodium competes with Ca and Mg, which can be expressed by the SAR. Keep Na less than 40 ppm and SAR less than 2.

- Boron can be excessive in some parts of the United States. Levels should be less than 0.5 ppm to avoid toxicity.

- The need for acid-forming fertilizers should be weighed with the desire to control plug growth and with the type of plant.

- Using fertilizers high in Ca and Mg can add buffering capacity to low-alkalinity water (less than 50 ppm).

- Use acid injection to control moderate to high alkalinity (150 to 400 ppm). Consider carefully which acid to use and how much. Test alkalinity regularly at the end of the hose.

- Consider switching to a different water source if your well water is of poor quality.

- Use a R/O system when your well water is of poor quality and a different water source is not an option.

REFERENCES

[1] Bailey, D.A., P.V. Nelson, W.C. Fonteno, J.W. Lee, and J.S. Huang. 1995. Plug pH—The make or break factor in nutrition. *GrowerTalks* 59(9):6–13.

[2] Biernbaum, J. 1994. Treat your water right. *Greenhouse Grower* 12(2):31–35.

[3] Curtice, G.M., and A.R. Templeton. 1987. *Water quality reference guide for horticulture.* Pennsauken, NJ: Aquatrols Corporation of America.

[4] *Osmonics engineering memo #13.* 1993. Minnetonka, MN: Osmonics, Inc.

[5] Vetanovetz, R., and J.F. Knauss. 1988. Injecting acid may change more than just alkalinity! *GrowerTalks* 52(6):137–138.

CHAPTER 7

MEDIA QUALITY

The growing media, which must support plug growth from the time of germination to the time of transplanting, is often a main source of problems for plug growers. All the water and minerals required for plant growth are absorbed from the growing media through the roots. To supply the plant adequately with nutrients, the growing media must retain these nutrients, have an acceptable pH for availability of these nutrients, and provide an environment in which the roots can grow and function.

Media quality can be broken down into two main areas: physical properties and chemical properties. These properties are very important in good plug media, regardless of the plug size. The small plug cell volume makes the media subject to rapid fluctuations in moisture content, aeration, pH, soluble salts, and nutrients. Nutrient deficiencies and toxicities, root rot diseases, poor root growth, stretched plants, and poor germination are all problems that can originate with media quality. Many plug growers have lost crops due to not understanding media quality and how to handle plug media!

Plug growers can buy commercial plug mixes or make their own. In this chapter we will cover the main physical and chemical properties of good plug media, show how to test the media, and provide guidelines for quality plug media for you. The overall goal is for each grower to develop his or her own specifications for high-quality plug media, then test the media for consistency every time.

PHYSICAL CHARACTERISTICS

The general suitability of plug media for water and mineral absorption is determined by the nature of the open spaces, or *pores,* between the solid particles of the media. It is in the soil matrix that the plant's roots grow and where water and air are stored and move. Both total pore volume (porosity) and pore size distribution are important. *Porosity,* or pore volume, determines the potential water-holding capacity, and *pore size distribution* determines the actual water retention and air space after irrigation and drainage. Suitable growing media must maintain a balance between water retention and aeration. Excess water retention means plants will suffer from poor soil aeration, and excess aeration means plants are likely to experience water deficit. Under conditions of rapid plant water use (low humidity, high light, relatively large size), less air porosity is generally required than under conditions of low water use (high humidity, low light, small size).

The main physical characteristics to know about plug media are water-holding capacity, air porosity, and cation exchange capacity. The *water-holding capacity* (WHC), or *container capacity,* of growing media is simply the ability to hold water. Water held in the media may be either available or unavailable to the plant. Unavailable water is so tightly held to particle surfaces, it cannot be removed by roots. In mineral soils very little of the water is unavailable to roots. The amount of unavailable water in organic media or commercial mixes is high and is influenced by the components making up the media. The WHC of the media affects the frequency of water application. Capillary pore space (very small pores between particles) holds water against gravity, thereby contributing to WHC. The higher the WHC, the less often the media needs to be watered [7].

Somewhat opposite to WHC is *air porosity* or *space* (AP), which is determined by the amount of noncapillary pore space in the media. Noncapillary pore spaces are the larger pores between particles from which water drains by gravity and into which air moves [7]. Normally, in a 6-inch pot, good soilless growing media should have 15 to 20% AP. In a plug cell, the AP may range from less than 1 to 10%. This reduced porosity is due to the finer particles making up plug media, the smaller container (plug cell), and the media handling.

The *cation exchange capacity* (CEC) of growing media measures the media's ability to prevent nutrients from leaching, thus retaining them for plant use. The CEC is generally expressed as millequivalents per 100 cm³ (meq/100 cc) of dry root-media component. A level of 6 to 15 meq/100 cc is considered desirable for greenhouse root media [9]. Peat-based plug mixes typically have a lower CEC compared to mineral soils, requiring more frequent fertilizer supplements.

MEDIA COMPONENTS

Most plug mixes contain 30 to 70% peat moss. There are different types of peat. *Peat moss,* light tan to brown in color, is the least decomposed and is formed from sphagnum or hypnum moss. It has the highest WHC of all the peats, holding up to 60% of its volume in water. *Sphagnum peat moss* is the most acid of the peats, with a pH level of 3.0 to 4.5, whereas *hypnum peat moss* has a pH level in the range of 5.2 to 5.5 [9]. Hypnum peat moss may have more problems with particle size consistency and with holding more nutrients initially than sphagnum peat moss. A large quantity of water is held on the extensive surface area of any moss, while good gas exchange occurs in the large pores between the peat moss chunks. Therefore, peat moss should not be finely ground down to the fiber level prior to use. How the peat moss is harvested (vacuum or block-cut) and from where it is harvested determine the particle size consistency even before any further handling.

Reed-sedge peat, brown to reddish brown, is formed from swamp plants, including reeds, sedges, marsh grasses, and cattails. It is generally more decomposed than peat moss. Therefore, more fine particles are present, giving a poorer structure. The WHC of reed-sedge peat is lower than that of peat moss. The pH level can vary from 4.0 to 7.5 [9].

Peat humus, dark brown to black, is the most highly decomposed of the peats. It is usually derived from hypnum peat moss or reed-sedge peat. Its WHC is less than that of other peats, and its pH level can range from 5.0 to 7.5. Peat humus has a moderately high nitrogen content, which makes it undesirable for plug media. Ammonium nitrogen released from the peat humus can build up to a level toxic to young seedlings [9].

The physical and chemical properties of peat need to be tested before using it in plug media. (Table 7.1 summarizes some peat characteristics for soilless mixes). Generally, sphagnum peat moss is preferred because its fiber structure has advantages over that of hypnum or reed-sedge peat, allowing for good aeration and drainage. However, not all sphagnum peat moss is the same. In table 7.2, we can see the air and water content of several media components in both 288 and 648 plug cells. The first three are all Canadian sphagnum peats (CS I, II, and III), yet they are different enough in container capacity, or WHC, and air space to perform differently in plugs on the same greenhouse bench.

TABLE 7.1 CHARACTERISTICS OF PEAT FOR SOILLESS MIXES

	Very light brown to yellow peat moss	Medium to brown peat moss	Dark humus peat
Organic matter	Usually sold at 50% moisture content. A 6 cu ft bale weighs 78 lbs, or 39 lbs of dry organic matter.	Usually sold at 40% moisture content. A 6 cu ft bale weighs 95 lbs, or 54 lbs of dry organic matter.	Only approx. 30% organic matter in a 6 cu ft bale on dry weight basis. Characteristic of native U.S. peat (mucklike).
Reaction in soilless mix	With the high level of aeration, may dry out too rapidly.	Proper aeration. Dries out slowly and uniformly.	Poor aeration. Will remain wet for a long time unless extra drainage material is added.
Chemical properties	Does not have the ability to hold plant nutrients. Poor buffering and low cation exchange capacity.	Able to hold nutrients and release them for plant growth. Good buffering and cation exchange capacity.	May hold nutrients in excess, causing plant injury. Buffering and cation exchange may be detrimental.
Reaction in soilless mix	Fertilizer has to be applied more frequently because it is not held by the peat moss.	Holds and releases fertilizers for efficient utilization by the plant.	Excessive level does not provide the flexibility for fertilizer error.
Drainage	Rapid drainage. Water passes through too quickly, carrying nutrients with it.	Medium drainage. Holds an adequate amount of water for plant growth.	Poor drainage. Plant nutrients may build and cause injury.
Reaction in soilless mix	More time and labor spent watering, especially during the late spring and summer months. Excessive leaching increases fertilizer costs.	All capillary water, which is available to the plant. Ideal for supplying nutrients. Normal fertilizer costs.	Excess fertilizers cannot be leached out due to poor drainage.
Texture	Light and hairy. Coarse, long fibers provide too high a level of aeration (more than 30%). Difficult to control water supply.	Optimum size of fibers, providing best level of aeration (20 to 30%). Good water control.	Compact, tiny fibers. Almost no aeration (less than 20%). Very low rewetting capabilities.
Reaction in soilless mix	Elastic, with very low density. Pots tend to fall over.	Higher density and perfect weight. Stabilizes pots.	High density. May be wet and heavy, which will limit root growth.
Fibrosity	Almost all fiber.	Proper proportions of fiber and decomposed organic matter.	Low fiber. Almost all decomposed organic matter. Dusty when dry. Muddy when wet.
Reaction in soilless mix	May be too loose to supply physical support for large plants.	Provides good support without compacting.	Compacts when planting, limiting plant growth.

TABLE 7.2   AIR AND WATER CONTENT OF MEDIA COMPONENTS

| Media | 288 plug | | 648 plug | |
	Container capacity (%)	Air space (%)	Container capacity (%)	Air space (%)
CS peat I	85	2.6	87	0.7
CS peat II	84	1.0	84	0.2
CS peat III	92	1.9	94	0.4
Vermiculite #2	64	8.8	69	4.1
Vermiculite #3	57	0.1	57	0.0
Perlite	53	10.6	59	4.2
Polystyrene	29	6.2	34	1.0

Source: From Fonteno, How to get 273 plugs, *GrowerTalks.*

Aggregates are generally added to peat moss to provide more rapid drainage and increase aeration. Most commonly, vermiculite, perlite, and calcined clay are added for plug mixes. *Vermiculite,* which may be used from 20 to 30% for plug mixes, consists of fine clay-type platelets that are popped at high (1,000F) temperature. This material is mined as an ore, principally in the United States and South Africa. Vermiculite comes in different sizes, or grades, and should be uniform. The WHC of expanded vermiculite is high because of the extensive surface area of each particle. Aeration and drainage properties are also good because of the large pores between particles [9].

In a plug mix, the main contribution of vermiculite is to WHC, not to AP, due to the fine size used (U.S. grade #3). The difference in WHC and air porosity between #2 (coarser grade) and #3 vermiculite is tremendous (table 7.2). Yet, most plug mixes use the finer #3 vermiculite, which allows the mix to flow more evenly into the trays at filling. The #3 vermiculite does not look popped; it contains flat-shaped particles that can easily stick together and prevent air from moving into the spaces between them. This increases the capillary pore spaces, which hold water, but decreases the noncapillary pore spaces, which drain water and bring in air. Many growers are now using less fine vermiculite and more perlite to increase AP and decrease WHC.

Not all vermiculite is chemically the same, either. The predominant nutrients in vermiculite are K, Mg, and Ca, with higher Mg content in African vermiculite. The pH of U.S. vermiculite is slightly alkaline, while African vermiculite tends to be very alkaline, with pH levels approaching 9.0 [9]. Particle size also varies greatly between suppliers and depends on screening, popping, and handling.

Perlite is a siliceous volcanic rock that, when crushed and heated to a high (1,800F, 982C) temperature, expands to form white particles with numerous closed, air-filled cells. Water adheres to the perlite surfaces, but it is not absorbed into the perlite aggregates. It is added to soilless mixes for aeration (see table 7.2). It is sterile, chemically inert, and nearly neutral in pH [9]. Sand-finished perlite comes in different meshes, with finer meshes being used for plug mixes. If the mesh is too fine, though, it looks like powder and will not improve the AP of the plug mix.

Calcined clay can also be added to plug mixes (up to 10 to 15%, depending on the CEC of the peat moss) for aeration and to increase particle size variation. When clay particle aggregates are heated to high temperatures, they form hardened particles that resist breakdown in growing media. These aggregates can be large and irregularly shaped. As a result, they fit together loosely in plug media, creating large pores for drainage and aeration. Within each calcined clay aggregate are numerous clay particles, forming a myriad of small water-holding pores [9]. Calcined clay increases the plug media CEC and may increase the Na level. Test the calcined clay before using.

These are the main questions to ask about any type of plug medium:

■ What's in it?

■ How much water does it hold?

■ How much air space does it have?

■ Is it consistent?

■ Does it meet my specifications?

Table 7.3 summarizes the attributes of individual components that may make up greenhouse growing media, not all of which are commonly used in plug media. In some areas, key components such as sphagnum peat moss are not readily available everywhere, so a substitute may be needed. If you need to make up your own plug media, be aware of the physical properties each component brings to the final mix. Usually, good plug media will have at least two different components mixed together (mostly peat moss and vermiculite or perlite). However, some plug growers in Europe and the United States grow very well with only peat moss. Other growers use only rock wool with basically a hydroponic system. Whatever components or mix you use, make sure to have it tested for percentage WHC and AP. Only a few commercial laboratories conduct these types of physical tests, but you can do them yourself with the method outlined in appendix 2.

TABLE 7.3 GREENHOUSE GROWING MEDIA COMPONENTS

Component	pH	CEC	Weight	WHC	AP	Sterility
			Relative value of characteristic			
Calcined clay		+	+	+	+	+
Composted bark	Acid	+	+	+	+/−	+
Mineral soil		+	+	+	−	−
Perlite	Base		−	−	+	+
Polystyrene			−	−	+	+
Pumice			−	−	+	?
Rice hulls			−	−	+	−
Rock wool	Base		−	+	+/−	+
Sand			+	+/−	+/−	?
Sphagnum peat	Acid	+	−	+	+/−	+
Vermiculite	Base	+	−	+	+/−	+

CONTAINER SIZE AND SHAPE

To understand how container size and gravity affect water drainage from growing media, compare media to a sponge. Figure 7.1 shows very little water draining from the large bottom surface of a water-soaked sponge lifted horizontally (A). Tilting the sponge on its side increases drainage (B). Holding the sponge vertically, though—thereby creating the tallest (and heaviest) possible water column per square inch of bottom surface—causes water to drain the fastest (C). This same principle is true with containers. The taller the container, the better the media drains because of gravity's influence; there is more water bearing down per square inch. A shorter container not only drains slower, but it also contains less air space [2].

Container size determines how much air and water the media holds. In table 7.4, most of the commercial mixes have at least 20% air space when placed in a 6-inch pot [2]. However, when 273-plug trays are filled with these same commercial mixes, air content decreases to 2 to 4%. Notice that as air content decreases in smaller containers, water content increases. These two factors work opposite each other, making it more difficult to effectively water shallow plug trays.

FIGURE 7.1 How gravity affects water drainage from a sponge. Adapted from Fonteno, Know your media, *GrowerTalks.*

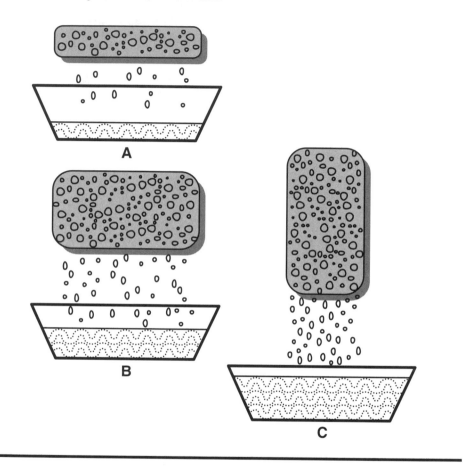

TABLE 7.4 CONTAINER SIZE AFFECTS AIR AND WATER CONTENT

Container		Metro 360	Fafard 4	Ball II	Jiffy Mix	ProGro 300
6-inch	Water content (%)	60	64	60	73	62
	Air (%)	23	17	24	20	22
4-inch	Water content (%)	67	70	67	79	68
	Air (%)	16	11	17	14	16
Bedding flat (48/tray)	Water content (%)	73	75	74	85	74
	Air (%)	9	6	10	9	10
273 plug tray	Water content (%)	80	80	81	90	80
	Air (%)	3	2	4	3	4

Source: From Fonteno, Know your media, *GrowerTalks.*

Many plug growers have experienced problems with plug trays being either too wet or too dry. Plugs can stay too wet because plug cells are too shallow to drain properly, capillary action being stronger than the force of gravity. They can be too dry because the cells contain such small media volumes, leading to quicker total evaporation. In the comparisons charted in table 7.5, note that the coarser the mix, the greater the drainage and air content. In the 273-cell plug tray examples, when cells are 2 inches deep, air content doubles or triples. With the smallest plug tray, the 648 waffle, the plug cells do not drain well, attaining only 1.8% air content with the coarsest plug mix [2].

TABLE 7.5   PLUG MIX AND CONTAINER COMBINATIONS

Container		Peat and vermiculite	Coarse plug mix	Medium plug mix	Fine plug mix
Bedding flat	Water content (%)	80	64	71	79
(48/tray)	Air content (%)	7	10	4	2
273 plug	Water content (%)	85	70	75	81
(1-inch tall)	Air content (%)	2	4	1	0.3
273 plug	Water content (%)	82	65	72	80
(2-inch tall)	Air content (%)	6	9	3	1
648 plug	Water content (%)	87	72	75	81
	Air content (%)	0.3	1.8	0.2	0.1

Source: From Fonteno, Know your media, *GrowerTalks.*

In table 7.6, four commercial plug mixes were evaluated in the 1-inch versus 2-inch-deep plug cell [3]. Normally, the 273-plug cells are 1 inch deep. Air content increased dramatically in the 2-inch plug, regardless of which mix was used. Up to 10% air content could be achieved with the deeper plugs. This difference in air content means that smaller plug cells have a greater chance of being improperly watered.

The shape of the plug cell or container affects the volume, or the root zone area. Square cells have greater volume (up to 33% more) than round cells when the number of cells per tray are the same [3]. This extra volume translates to more water being available to the plant and less chance of the cell's drying out. This extra volume does not necessarily increase air space percentage. However, the media surface area is increased, resulting in more area for roots to grow. Hexagonal, octagonal, and star-shaped plug cells ("star tray") have even greater surface areas, with root growth being improved and overwatering not being as much of a problem.

TABLE 7.6 AIR SPACE IN SHORT AND TALL PLUG CELLS

Commercial plug mix	Plug size	
	Short: 1 inch, 4.5 ml vol. (air space %)	Tall: 2 inches, 6.1 ml vol. (air space %)
Mix #1	2.7	10.0
Mix #2	1.3	5.1
Mix #3	1.2	4.8
Mix #4	2.4	7.4

Source: Adapted from Fonteno, How to get 273 plugs, *GrowerTalks.*

MEDIA HANDLING

The handling of a mix during tray filling and prior to seeding can greatly affect its air and water content. One factor is *compaction.* Plug trays should be lightly filled, the excess brushed away. This can be accomplished by hand or by machine flat fillers. *The media should not be packed down, and trays should not be stacked directly on one another.* Table 7.7, notes that the lighter the media is packed, the greater the air space. The coarser the plug mix, the more air space and the less unavailable water [2]. A fine plug mix heavily packed eliminates any chances of drainage and aeration.

The second consideration is mix moisture content prior to flat filling [3]. When water is added to dry peat moss particles treated with a wetting agent, they hydrate and swell, which helps create more aeration by reducing the tendency of the particles to nest within one another. This effect is not so dramatic with larger containers, but it can be the difference between 1 and 5% air space in a plug cell. Water should be added to the mix within a half hour before it is placed into the cells. Many growers use a nozzle or series of nozzles to apply water while the plug mix is in the flat-filler hopper or while it is going into the hopper if on a belt feeder.

The plug mix moisture content should be a minimum of 50% before tray filling. A moisture content between 50 to 70% is best for plugs [4]. Air space becomes more limited below 50% moisture content. Above 70%, the mix becomes more difficult to handle, and tray filling is cumbersome.

For plug production, it's important to determine mix water content and adjust it to a preferred level [4]. Percent moisture content is defined as:

([IW – DW] / IW) × 100

where IW = initial weight of a known volume of media, and DW = dry weight of that same volume of media.

TABLE 7.7 AIR SPACE AFTER FILLING AND STACKING PLUG TRAYS OR BEDDING PLANT FLATS

Container	Coarse plug mix	Medium plug mix	Fine plug mix
Bedding plant cell, 48/tray			
Filled and brushed			
Available water	45	48	47
Unavailable water	19	23	27
Air space	10	4	2
Filled, pressed, and refilled			
Available water	37	40	41
Unavailable water	27	29	32
Air space	3	0.3	0.2
273-cell plug tray, 1 inch deep			
Filled and brushed			
Available water	51	51	54
Unavailable water	19	23	27
Air space	4	1	0.3
Filled, pressed, and refilled			
Available water	40	41	41
Unavailable water	27	29	32
Air space	1	0	0
273-cell plug tray, 2 inches deep			
Filled and brushed			
Available water	46	49	53
Unavailable water	19	23	27
Air space	8	3	1.5
Filled, pressed, and refilled			
Available water	38	40	42
Unavailable water	27	29	32
Air space	3	0.1	0.1
648-cell plug tray (waffle)			
Filled and brushed			
Available water	53	52	55
Unavailable water	19	23	27
Air space	1.8	0.3	0.1
Filled, pressed, and refilled			
Available water	40	41	42
Unavailable water	27	29	32
Air space	0.3	0	0

Note: Numbers represent % volume of saturated media.

Source: From Fonteno, Know your media, *GrowerTalks.*

You can determine media moisture content with the following procedure [4]:

1. Fill three beakers half full of representative media samples.

2. Weigh the three samples and record as "initial weight."

3. Place them in a drying oven for 24 hours at 225F (107C).

4. Weigh them again and record as "dry weight."

5. Average the three initial weights and three dry weights separately. Calculate percent moisture content using the preceding equation.

Using table 7.8, you can determine how much water to add to your mix [4]. For example, if you are starting from dry-baled peat and vermiculite or perlite straight from the bag, add 20 gal/yd³ of mix to get 50% moisture. If your peat is wet, determine moisture content and adjust it accordingly. If you test your mix and it is at 33% moisture, add 10 more gal/yd³ to bring it to 50%.

TABLE 7.8   MOISTURE PERCENTAGE AND EQUIVALENT VOLUMES IN 1 CUBIC YARD OF PLUG MIX[a]

Moisture (%) [b]	Water volume (gal/yd³ mix)
10	2
20	5
33	10
50	20
60	30
67	40
72	50
75	60

[a] Peat-vermiculite or peat-perlite mix. Calculations based on dry bulk density of 0.1 g/cc (6.25 lb/ft³).
[b] Calculations based on mass wetness values of 0.1, 0.25, 0.5, 1.0, 1.5, 2.0, 2.5, and 3.0 g/g, respectively.
Source: Adapted from Fonteno, Bailey, & Nelson, "Squeeze" your plugs, *GrowerTalks.*

CHEMICAL PROPERTIES

Due to the small container size of a plug cell, the chemical properties can change rapidly, depending on how you water and fertilize, your water quality, and your growing environment. Whether you mix your own plug media or buy a commercial mix, you need to know (1) the starting pH and how it will change in the first two weeks, (2) the amount of soluble salts present,

(3) the nutrients available to the young seedling in the first two weeks, and (4) how to test the chemical properties of your plug media.

MEDIA PH

Growing media pH influences the availability and plant uptake of all essential nutrients. Most plug crops grow best in a slightly acid pH range of 6.2 to 6.8 in soil-based media and 5.8 to 6.2 in soilless media. Sphagnum peat moss, pine bark, and many composts are acid; peat moss can have a pH level of less than 4.0. Sand and perlite are neutral (pH 7.0). Vermiculite and some hardwood barks are alkaline (pH greater than 7.0). Field soil can range from acid (pH 3.5) to alkaline (pH 8.5). Rock wool can range from neutral to mildly alkaline [9]. If you make your own plug media, then it is important to check the pH level after formulation and adjust it to the proper level prior to planting. A commercial plug mix is usually adjusted to the proper pH level by the manufacturer. However, you should definitely test any commercial mix for pH before using, as variability can occur.

Nutrient availability is controlled by the root-media pH level (fig. 7.2). Low pH levels result in high proportions of soluble (available) Fe, Mn, and Al, all of which react with P to render it insoluble (unavailable). Also, at a low pH level, the available levels of Ca, Mg, S, and Mo decrease. On the other hand, high pH levels result in the tie-up of P, Fe, Mn, Zn, Cu, and B. Generally, if the pH in a peat-based media stays between 5.5 and 6.5, all nutrients will be available. In a soil-based media, the optimum range is 6.0 to 7.0. A lower pH range is allowed in organic (soilless) media for two reasons. First, in organic media there is less native Fe, Mn, and Al to convert to soluble forms and thus become toxic or cause a P tie-up. Second, higher quantities of Ca and/or Mg are required in organic media to attain a given pH level; thus, a sufficient level of Ca and Mg can be attained at a lower pH level than in soil [9].

To make up for the acidic nature of peat-based plug mixes, pulverized limestone is added to raise the pH level. Calcitic lime supplies only Ca, whereas dolomitic lime contains both Ca and Mg. Finely ground (pulverized) limestone will mostly pass through a 100-mesh sieve (0.01 inch, 0.25 mm). Know the mesh size of the limestone used in your plug media, as the smaller the size, the faster it will react in the media. Lime will not react in dry, stockpiled plug media; when the plug medium is moistened, however, finely ground lime will fully react within two weeks. How fast the pH goes up in the first two weeks depends on: (1) the buffering capacity (ability to resist change) of the growing media, (2) the mesh size and type of limestone; (3) how much moisture the plug media had during storage; and (4) watering

FIGURE 7.2 Nutrient availability changes with pH in peat-based media. Courtesy Ball Seed Co.

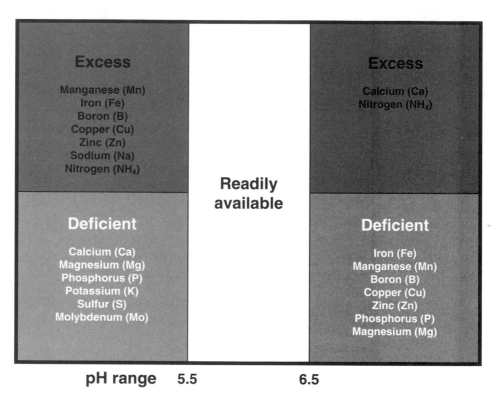

Excess

Manganese (Mn)
Iron (Fe)
Boron (B)
Copper (Cu)
Zinc (Zn)
Sodium (Na)
Nitrogen (NH₄)

Excess

Calcium (Ca)
Nitrogen (NH₄)

Readily available

Deficient

Calcium (Ca)
Magnesium (Mg)
Phosphorus (P)
Potassium (K)
Sulfur (S)
Molybdenum (Mo)

Deficient

Iron (Fe)
Manganese (Mn)
Boron (B)
Copper (Cu)
Zinc (Zn)
Phosphorus (P)
Magnesium (Mg)

pH range   5.5   6.5

frequency during germination (more water speeds up lime release). Water alkalinity also influences media pH.

To test how the lime in your plug media will react and change the media pH, fill some plug trays with your mix. Water them in with distilled or low-alkalinity (less than 80 ppm) water. Take a pH test after one hour. Continue to water these plug trays for the next two weeks as they need watering. Take further pH tests after one and two weeks. Compare the readings from Week 0 to Week 2 to determine how the media pH changed due to the lime. If the plug media pH is not within the proper range in the first week, you must either decide to not use this media and to switch to another source or adjust the media pH through amendments, fertilizers, or water alkalinity.

To raise the plug media pH, alkaline (basic) fertilizers containing calcium nitrate (15-0-15) can be used. Another possibility is high-alkalinity water, especially if acid injection is also being used to reduce the alkalinity. To get a quicker increase in media pH, use hydrated lime [calcium hydroxide, Ca(OH)₂] at 1 lb per 100 gal as a drench. Allow the mixture to settle, then apply the clear solution to the root media. Make sure to rinse off your plants after application. Some plants may be sensitive, so test a small area first [5]. Hydrated lime is more soluble than ground limestone, but not completely water-soluble. It reacts much faster than ground limestone yet has a shorter residual effect in the root media. A repeat application may be needed after one or two weeks. Do not use high-ammonium (more than 30% of total N) fertilizers either before or after using the hydrated lime treatment, as ammonia gas can be produced and damage plants.

To lower the plug media pH, acid fertilizers containing NH_4 or urea (21-7-7) can be applied. If acid injection is being used to control water alkalinity, then increased amounts of acid can be applied through the water on a temporary basis. Do not exceed 14 fl oz per 1,000 gal for phosphoric or sulfuric acid, or 32 fl oz per 1,000 gal for nitric acid. Use caution with acid treatments to avoid too much P, SO_4, and NO_3 in the media. To get a quicker decrease in plug media pH, use iron sulfate at 1 to 2 lbs per 100 gal as a drench. Make sure to rinse off your plants after application, as iron sulfate will burn the leaves. Iron sulfate will react in the media very quickly, but the residual effect lasts only a week; a repeat application may be needed. Caution: iron sulfate will raise soluble salt levels in the root media and may release toxic levels of minor elements from exchange sites or from compounds that are insoluble at a higher pH [5].

The ideal plug media starts at 5.8 pH and stays near there during the entire crop cycle. This pH is ideal for most crops. However, some crops, such as geranium, marigold, impatiens, and lisianthus, require the higher pH of 6.0 to 6.2 to grow properly. A plug grower does not need two different plug mixes to grow all crops adequately, though. For crops requiring higher soil pH, just use the pH-raising techniques described previously. Additionally, the pH can be raised by feeding these crops first with basic fertilizers, such as 15-0-15, 14-0-14, or 13-2-13-6-3.

If, however, the plug media pH is rising too fast in the first two weeks, you will need to find out why. Either there is too much limestone, it is too fine, or the water alkalinity is too high. Make the necessary adjustments or switch to another commercial source.

SOLUBLE SALTS

An excessive level (greater than 1.5 mmhos/cm, 2:1 dilution) of soluble salts in plug media can cause many problems. First, high soluble salts (greater than 1.0 mmhos/cm, 2:1 dilution) can reduce germination and burn off sensitive primary roots of emerging seedlings, particularly with vinca, snapdragons, impatiens, and begonia. Initial root growth will be slower. Wilting during bright times of the day, even though the root media is moist, may occur during Stages 3 and 4. Overall growth slows down. Roots die from the tips back, particularly in the drier zones of the root media. Such root rots as *Pythium, Phytophthora, Rhizoctonia,* and *Thielaviopsis* can then take over, causing greater loss of roots and seedlings. Leaves become necrotic due to high salts, in some cases along the margin, in others as circular spots scattered across the leaf blade. Ultimately, symptoms of deficiencies of many nutrients will occur as a result of radically impaired nutrient uptake by the injured root systems.

Soluble salts come from various sources. In the plug media, all soluble ions and nutrients such as NO_3, NH_4, K, Ca, Mg, Cl, Na, and SO_4 contribute to the soluble salt level. Many of these elements are added into the plug mix to give the emerging seedlings a starter growth fertilizer for the first 10 days after seeding. Some of these elements come with the individual components of the mix, such as in peat moss, vermiculite, and composted bark. High NH_4 (more than 10 ppm) may be found in organic matter that undergoes rapid decomposition in a plug mix, such as compost or peat humus. Some soluble salts must be present to ensure a proper level of fertilizer, but the level must not be too high.

Other soluble salts come from the water and from the fertilizers used during growing. Some of these salts are not desirable. For instance, excessive Na and Cl can be found in water sources around the world, particularly near coastlines. High Na in well water can also be found in alkaline areas in arid parts of the world. High calcium carbonates and bicarbonates can be found in well water in areas of limestone deposits. Run-off of nitrates, nitrites, and phosphates is a problem in shallow wells or ponds in agricultural areas.

Fertilizers vary in the manner in which they affect soluble salt levels (table 7.9). The nutritive value of these fertilizers should be taken into account, along with their salt indexes. As the fertilizer is utilized by the plants, the influence upon the soluble-salt level is reduced. Remember, fertilizers containing Na (in sodium nitrate or nitrate of soda) and Cl should be avoided for plug growing. Neither of these elements is needed by young seedlings and will just build up in the media, causing problems with root growth.

Seedlings are more sensitive to high soluble salt levels than are established plants, which vary in their resistance (table 7.10). A vinca seedling is highly sensitive to soluble salts when the primary root is just coming out. The exact level at which injury occurs depends to a large degree on watering practices. If the root medium is not permitted to dry, then a high salt content may be tolerated. When the medium dries, the salts become more

TABLE 7.9   RELATIVE SALT INDEX FOR SEVERAL FERTILIZERS

Fertilizer	Salt index
Potassium chloride (muriate of potash, 60% K_2O)	116
Ammonium nitrate	105
Sodium nitrate (nitrate of soda)	100 [a]
Urea	75
Potassium nitrate	74
Ammonium sulfate	69
Calcium nitrate	53
Potassium sulfate	46
Magnesium sulfate	44
Diammonium phosphate	34
Monoammonium phosphate	30
Concentrated superphosphate	10
48% superphosphate	10
20% superphosphate	8
Gypsum	8
Limestone	5

[a] Sodium nitrate was arbitrarily set at 100. The lower the index value, the smaller the contribution that the fertilizer makes to the soluble-salt level of the root media.

Source: Adapted from Rader, White, & Whittaker, A measure of the effect of fertilizers, *SoilSci.*

TABLE 7.10   RELATIVE SENSITIVITY OF BEDDING PLANTS TO SOIL SOLUBLE SALTS

Sensitive	Intermediate	Tolerant
Balsam	Cauliflower	Alyssum
Begonia	Celosia	Calendula
Geranium [a]	Onion	Petunia
Impatiens	Portulaca	
Marigold	Snapdragon	
Pansy		
Zinnia		

[a] Sensitive to ammonium concentration above 15 ppm in the soil.

concentrated (3 to 4 times more) right around the roots than indicated by a soil test, and injuries may ensue. Try to keep soluble salts at less than 0.75 mmhos/cm (2:1 dilution) during Stages 1 and 2.

Soluble salt buildup can be minimized by watering to cause some leaching. Watering the plug trays so a good amount of water drains out, then repeating this procedure one or two hours later, will reduce the soluble salt level sufficiently. Avoid using plug media with initially high soluble salt levels! Some plug media, especially grower-made, may be too low in soluble salts (less than 0.25 mmhos/cm, 2:1 dilution). These mixes will need early feedings of a balanced fertilizer in order for the seedlings to start their growth.

NUTRIENTS

If the soluble salts are greater than 1.0 mmhos initially and greater than 1.5 mmhos during growing in your plug media, then you need to know what salts are causing this problem. A soil test will measure not only pH and soluble salts but also the levels of nutrients that the plant needs. The main nutrients to test include NH_4, NO_3, total N, P, K, Ca, Mg, SO_4, and the minor elements of Fe, B, Mn, Cu, Zn, and Mo. In addition, it is important to know the levels of elements that are not plant nutrients but will affect plant growth, such as Na and Cl.

As mentioned, germinating seedlings need some nutrients available, but not at high levels. Once the cotyledons expand and new leaves start to come out, though, nutrient levels need to be increased, right up until transplanting. Table 7.11 shows the levels of nutrients in a high-quality plug mix before sowing. If your plug mix has considerably higher values than the ranges indicated here, you will need to leach considerably during germination, buy a new commercial mix lower in soluble salts, or reduce the fertilizer charge in the plug mix you make yourself.

When NH_4 is greater than 10 ppm initially in the plug mix, many growers have found reduced germination with crops such as begonia, snapdragon, vinca, verbena, and pansy. High levels of NH_4 also promote rapid seedling stretch (Color plate 47), even before the cotyledons have fully expanded. This problem shows up the most with snapdragon, tomato, impatiens, cosmos, flowering kale, and zinnia. High levels of total N or P also stimulate early stretch, depending on the crop. Commercial plug mixes used to have high starter charges, but now most of them have very low starter charges (less than 0.5 mmhos/cm, 2:1 dilution). Some manufacturers do not even put *any* fertilizer into their plug mixes. The net result is better control of early seedling growth and better germination percentages in many crops.

TABLE 7.11 ACCEPTABLE INITIAL PLUG MEDIA NUTRIENT LEVELS

pH	5.5–5.8 for most crops
	6.0–6.2 for low pH-sensitive crops
Soluble salts or EC (mmhos)	0.4–1.0, depending on crop
Nitrates (NO_3)	40–60 ppm[a]
Ammonium (NH_4)	<10 ppm
Phosphorus (P)	5–8 ppm
Potassium (K)	50–100 ppm
Calcium (Ca)	60–120 ppm
Magnesium (Mg)	30–60 ppm
Sulfur (S)	50–200 ppm
Sodium (Na)	<30 ppm
Chloride (Cl)	<40 ppm
Boron (B)	0.2–0.5 ppm
Iron (Fe)	0.06–6 ppm
Manganese (Mn)	0.03–3 ppm
Zinc (Zn)	0.001–0.6 ppm
Copper (Cu)	0.001–0.6 ppm
Molybdenum (Mo)	0.02–0.15 ppm

[a] ppm = mg/l

Note: Values based on the saturated media extract (SME) procedure.

The sodium level should be less than 30 ppm. The Ca, K, and Mg levels should be sufficient to counteract the competitive nature of Na. If you need to raise the Ca and Mg levels in the plug mix you make yourself, then use fine-mesh dolomitic limestone. If your media pH is already high enough but you still want to raise the Ca level, then use fine-mesh gypsum (calcium sulfate) in place of some of the limestone. If you are buying commercial mixes, then Ca, K, and Mg levels can be raised early with feedings of a low-NH_4 fertilizer, such as 14-0-14, 15-0-15, or 13-2-13-6-3.

The chloride level should be less than 40 ppm [6]. A high Cl level may come from your water or fertilizer, so make sure to test all such sources. Media chlorides can be removed by allowing the media to dry somewhat thoroughly between waterings, then leaching when watering again. Also, raise the soil temperature for two or three days while leaching. Chlorides will combine to form chlorine gas when the mix dries, then escape into the air, if the mix has good aeration.

MEDIA TESTING

The soilless media now in use by many growers have good moisture-holding and aeration properties but limited nutrient-holding capacities. As a result, fertility management in the greenhouse is more important than ever before. Prior to using any new lot of plug media, test for pH, soluble salt content, and available nutrient levels. Even though most companies maintain quality control programs, variations in growing media properties do occur. Knowing the initial chemical properties is essential to avoiding costly plant growth problems later. About 80% of all plug nutrient problems are caused by pH or soluble salts! You can set up a program to do your own pH and soluble salt tests, while sending in samples to a reputable testing laboratory to measure nutrients (appendix 4).

Determining the pH and soluble salt level in plug media can be complex and confusing to interpret. The three methods most commonly used by growers and commercial labs are 1:2 dilution, 1:5 dilution, and saturated-media extract (SME) using distilled water. For each of these methods, several factors—such as (1) when to sample, (2) time needed to extract samples, (3) whether to filter the solution or read in the slurry, and (4) gravity versus vacuum filtration—will influence your readings, as well as how your readings compare to those of the lab. Many growers have sent samples to five different labs and received back five very different interpretations.

SAMPLING

Reliable, consistent media analysis readings come from consistent procedures developed in sampling (grower stage) and analysis (laboratory stage). For plugs, a grower should sample several trays of a specific crop, harvesting several cells from each tray to collect media. You need to pool quite a few plugs together to get a large enough sample for most testing methods and laboratories. Some growers just place filled plug trays with no seed or plants in the growing area. They can then use these "blank" trays for media tests throughout the course of the crop. This method is good for the first two weeks, but not so good as the crop develops a good root system (Stages 3 and 4), which will quickly change pH, soluble salt, and nutrient levels.

Uniformly mix the collected samples to make up the pooled sample. Remove the tops of the plants, but keep the roots intact. For the 1:2 and 1:5 dilution methods, it is important to air-dry all samples to a standard moisture level. Since the 1:2 and 1:5 dilution methods are based on media-to-water dilution ratios, varying the media moisture content between samples or between sampling periods would significantly affect your results. For the SME method, the sample does not need to be dried.

Plugs should be sampled at least every week. Test every new batch of media before using. Then test sensitive crops every week during their crop cycles to see what the trends are in pH and soluble salts. If you change watering or fertilizer practices, you should test sensitive crops every week through a crop cycle. Otherwise, test when you see nutrition or growing problems. Again, monitor sensitive crops—such as petunia, vinca, snapdragon, impatiens, marigold, geranium, primula, and lisianthus—every week, but not necessarily every week of the crop cycle.

Plug crops should be sampled one to two hours after fertilizing [1]. You want to know what the soluble salt level is before the roots take most of the nutrients out of the media, as well as know the pH for nutrient availability. Remember to dry the samples if using a 1:2 or 1:5 dilution method. Above all, be consistent about when you sample.

TESTING METHODS

Basically, there are three different methods for testing media:

1. The saturated-paste or saturated-media extract (SME) test, in which the intent is to add only enough distilled water to saturate the media sample to a level typical of watering, when the media glistens but there is little or no freestanding water on top.

2. A 1:2 dilution test, in which 2 volume units of distilled water are added to 1 volume unit of dry media.

3. A 1:5 dilution test, in which 5 volume units of distilled water are added to 1 volume unit of dry media.

Let the sample equilibrate with the newly added distilled water for 30 minutes. There can be a slight change in pH and soluble salts within the first 30 minutes, but then readings tend to level off.

Whether you filter the solution or read directly in the slurry is largely determined by the types of pH and conductivity probes you use. If you are worried about damaging the probes, filter the solution. When using the SME method, you can either vacuum- or gravity-filter the solution, depending on how big the sample is and how long you want to wait. Be aware that pH values differ depending on which way you filter. Generally, expect about a 0.5-unit difference in pH, with the vacuum method being lower. When using the 1:2 or 1:5 dilution method, you can either read directly in the slurry or gravity-filter the solution. Slurry readings tend to give lower pH readings than filtered extract readings [8].

The electrical conductivity of the sample is measured with a Solubridge (conductivity meter) and expressed in millisiemens (mS) or millimhos/ centimeter (mmhos/cm). To convert this value to parts per million (ppm), multiply by 700. The EC value also varies depending on the testing method. Guidelines for interpreting soluble salt levels by each procedure are given in table 7.12. For plugs, the soluble salt levels for different growth stages should be lower than shown here, especially for germination and early seedling growth. During these beginning stages, try to keep the soluble salts at less than 0.75 mmhos/cm (1:2 dilution).

TABLE 7.12   MEDIA-TO-WATER RATIO EFFECT ON SOLUBLE SALTS

| | Solubridge (mS) | | |
Saturation extract	1 part media to 2 parts water	1 part media to 5 parts water	Comments
0–0.74	0–0.25	0–0.12	Very low salt levels; indicates very low nutrient status.
0.75–1.99	0.25–0.75	0.12–0.35	Suitable range for seedlings and salt-sensitive plants.
2.00–3.49	0.75–1.25	0.35–0.65	Desirable range for most established plants; upper range may reduce growth of some sensitive plants.
3.50–5.00	1.25–1.75	0.65–0.90	Slightly higher than desirable; loss of vigor in upper range; OK for high-nutrient-requiring plants.
5.00–6.00	1.75–2.25	0.90–1.10	Reduced growth and vigor; wilting, and marginal leaf burn.
6.00+	2.25+	1.10+	Severe salt injury symptoms, with crop failure likely.

Source: Adapted from Warncke & Krauskopf, *Greenhouse growth media.*

A fourth method of testing, the "squeeze" method, calls for sampling as already described [4]. Once you draw media plugs from the tray, however, place them in a piece of cheesecloth and squeeze or twist to force the solution out. Combine solutions from every tray before analysis. Be sure to wear clean plastic gloves or wash your hands before handling the media to avoid contamination. The solution you extract from the plugs can be analyzed the same way you would test extracts from 1:2 or saturated paste for pH, soluble salts, or specific nutrients.

The pH values for the squeeze method seem to be the same as those measured with the 1:2 and SME methods. Squeeze EC values are closer to those of SME than the 1:2 extraction system. Current guidelines show an EC range of 0.75 to 2.0 mmhos/cm for plugs [4].

Make sure to properly standardize and calibrate your equipment (fig. 7.3). Use fresh pH buffer solutions of 4.0 and 7.0. Calibrate conductivity meters in a solution of known conductivity. Also, make sure you adjust your equipment for the temperature of the solutions, unless you have automatic temperature compensation.

There is variability in sampling techniques, analysis methods, and procedures within each method. Be aware of how the testing lab you send samples to conducts its analysis. Ask your lab a lot of questions. For your own method, be consistent—do it the same way every time, no matter who does it. For the cost of a $400 pH and conductivity meter (appendix 4) and the time needed to sample, many plug crops have been saved!

Figure 7.3 Combination pH/EC meter. Courtesy Myron L Company.

Mixing your own versus buying commercial plug mixes

You must decide whether to mix your own media or buy a commercial, ready-to-use plug mix. This decision should not be based solely on economics. Before deciding, answer the following questions:

- Can I get the necessary components consistently to make up quality plug media?

- Do I have the necessary equipment and techniques to make a consistent media?

- Do I have the time?

If you answered no to any of these questions, consider buying a commercial, ready-to-use plug mix. (Appendix 4 lists some North American plug mix suppliers, some of whom ship internationally.) Commercial plug mixes are more expensive but are made to exacting standards and consistency.

If you answered yes to all three questions, take a look at what is needed to make up your own plug media. First, keep in mind the following attributes of quality plug media:

- Two or more components, for best balance between WHC and AP

- pH of 5.8 to 6.2, which stays there for first two weeks

- Starting EC of less than 0.75 mmhos/cm (2:1 dilution)

- Consistent every time regarding component particle sizes, pH and lime, soluble salts, and wetting agent

Second, the selection of components will generally depend upon their availability and cost. Dry peat moss, particularly when finely ground, can be exceedingly difficult to wet because it repels water. Therefore, *wetting agents* are incorporated into peat moss-based soilless media. Sphagnum peat has a waxy layer and repels water. The wetting agent breaks the surface tension and allows the water to move through the media. Use great caution in determining the correct wetting agent concentration, as damage may occur if it is too high. The best commercially available wetting agent is Aqua-Gro 2000 from Aquatrols Corp. (800/257-7797).

Third, other amendments will need to be added to your homemade plug mix, including dolomitic limestone, superphosphate, micronutrients, and N and K starter charge (table 7.13). Add dolomitic limestone to bring the pH level into the range of 5.5 to 6.0. If you find that you do not need to add much limestone to your media, then it is a good idea to add some gypsum ($CaSO_4$) to provide that needed Ca and S that you may not get with your fertilizer program. Phosphorus is added either as regular superphosphate (0-20-0) or as triple superphosphate (0-45-0). The regular superphosphate will provide some gypsum along with the P. Minor elements should be added to the media at half the recommended rate. Two common formulations are fritted trace elements (FTE 555) and granular chelates and salts (Micromax, Esmigram) [9]. If you want a starter charge in your plug mix to include N and K, you should add calcium nitrate and potassium nitrate at low rates.

You need to conduct your own trials and test your batches of media to determine exactly how much of these different amendments you need, based on the components you use (such as peat moss, vermiculite, perlite) and how you grow (wet versus dry). Never use slow-release fertilizers in a plug mix, as unequal distribution occurs, and you lose control over the feeding of your crop!

Finally, thorough mixing of media components is critical for uniform distribution. However, the mixing should not be so excessive as to cause breakdown of the components. Media may be blended by tumbling in a revolving bucket, blending on a traveling ribbon belt, mixing with an auger, and lifting with paddles. Several types of soil mixers are on the market from Bouldin & Lawson (800/443-6398) and Gleason (815/939-9746).

TABLE 7.13 NUTRIENT SOURCES COMMONLY ADDED INTO ROOT MEDIA DURING FORMULATION

Nutrient source	Rate per cubic yard (per m³)	
	Soil-based media	Soilless media [a]
To provide calcium and magnesium		
Dolomitic limestone	0 – 10 lb (0 – 6 kg)	10 lb (6 kg)
To provide phosphorus and sulfur [b]		
Superphosphate (0-20-0)	3.0 lb (1.8 kg)	4.5 lb (2.7 kg)
Superphosphate (0-45-0)	1.5 lb (0.9 kg)	2.25 lb (1.3 kg)
+ gypsum (calcium sulfate)[c]	1.5 lb (0.9 kg)	1.5 lb (0.9 kg)
To provide micronutrients: iron, manganese, zinc, copper, boron, molybdenum [b]		
F-555HF	3 oz (112 g)	3 oz (112 g)
F-111HF	1 lb (0.6 kg)	1 lb (0.6 kg)
Esmigram	5 lb (3 kg)	5 lb (3 kg)
Micromax	1 – 1.5 lb (0.6 - 0.9 kg)	1 – 1.5 lb (0.6—0.9 kg)
To provide nitrogen and potassium (optional)		
Calcium nitrate	1 lb (0.6 kg)	1 lb (0.6 kg)
Potassium nitrate	1 lb (0.6 kg)	1 lb (0.6 kg)

[a] For plug media, cut rates by half.
[b] Apply only one nutrient source per purpose.
[c] Apply superphosphate (0-45-0) + gypsum as a combined "single" source.
Source: From Nelson, *Greenhouse operation.* Reprinted by permission of Prentice Hall.

Components and amendments should be layered in the hopper to ensure more uniform distribution, with the most common component (peat moss) going in first. Moisture should be added so that the mix contains 50 to 70% moisture, allowing the mix to more readily absorb water added later. The moisture also reduces dust. Tumbling, grinding, and ribbon blending may break down softer particles, such as vermiculite. Mixing too long can also cause segregation of particle sizes and an increase in bulk density. Often, three to five minutes of mixing is sufficient, depending on the type of equipment. To determine the extent of particle degradation and segregation, a smaller batch (with equal properties) could be mixed by hand and compared with the machine batch. Prior to filling the plug trays, the mix may need to be screened to remove large particles. As large a mesh screen as possible will prevent reducing the quality of the media.

It is always best to mix only enough media as needed, to prevent drying or contamination. Throughout the mixing process, all components and amendments should remain clean, that is, the bags should stay unopened. Equipment should be cleaned regularly to remove any old media and prevent the establishment of disease. If the components are kept clean, then soil sterilization or pasteurization is not necessary, unless a known problem exists or if soil is being recycled. In fact, sterilization at excessive temperatures can kill off beneficial nitrifying bacteria, essential for converting NH_4 to NO_3, resulting in a buildup of NH_4. Steam sterilization does not increase the availability of the added nutrients.

Regardless of whether you buy commercial mix or make your own, make sure to test the media before using for pH, soluble salts, and available nutrients. Know the physical characteristics of your media (WHC versus AP). If a plug mix does not meet your specifications, change it or try a different mix. Commercial mixes are more expensive but will be more consistent than what you can make yourself. Many plug growers have switched mixes or decided to make their own to save a nickel, and lost a dollar instead, when their crops did not germinate or grow properly. A good, consistent plug mix is the most demanding to make but is the key to successfully growing a good plug crop!

KEY POINTS TO REMEMBER

- Good plug media must be able to hold water but still have enough air porosity. Plug media with air porosity less than 2% will hold too much water and not allow sufficient root and root hair development.

- Know the physical and chemical characteristics of each component in your mix. There are many choices of components to make up plug media. Peat moss is the most commonly used component, followed by vermiculite and perlite.

- The container size and plug media handling will affect the media water-holding capacity and air porosity. Gravity helps drainage with increasing plug cell depth. Water-holding capacity increases in smaller plugs, while AP decreases. Compression of media by stacking filled plug trays will result in lower AP. Adding some moisture to the peat-based mix before filling trays will improve the AP-to-WHC ratio.

- The pH of the media determines the nutrient availability to the seedlings. For best results, start with plug media of 5.5 to 5.8 pH for most crops. For geranium, impatiens, marigold, and lisianthus, increase starting pH to 6.0 to 6.2 within two weeks of seeding. When media pH is too high (greater than 6.5), micronutrients become deficient and Ca becomes excessive. When media pH is too low (less than 5.5 for most crops), micronutrients become excessive and macronutrients become deficient.

■ Know the amount and concentration of soluble salts in your plug media to start. Keep the beginning level less than 0.75 mmhos/cm (2:1 dilution). If soluble salts are higher than that, then make sure to have a laboratory test individual nutrients to see which make up the soluble salts. Germination will be increased and early seedling stretch more controllable if the starting soluble salt level is less than 0.75 mmhos/cm, with low N and P. If your plug medium has no starter charge, you need to start feeding early with 50 ppm N of a balanced fertilizer low in NH_4.

■ There is no substitute for a consistent, in-house media testing program. Buy yourself a good pH and conductivity meter, set up an area to do the tests, sample properly, decide on an extraction method, and do it the same way every time. Track your results over time to determine if adjustments are needed in pH and soluble salts. Work with a reputable testing laboratory and get to know how it does its tests. Always test every new batch of plug mix you bring in or make yourself.

■ Buy in a quality plug mix from a reputable manufacturer, rather than make up the plug mix yourself. The physical and chemical requirements of plug mixes are the most demanding in our industry (compared to other commercial mixes), and margins for error are too small. Your plug crop is dependent on having consistent, high-quality plug media to grow in, yet the cost of the media compared to the total cost of the plug is minimal (less than 10%).

REFERENCES

[1] Compton, A., and P.V. Nelson. 1996. Plug seedling soil sampling—timing is critical. *GrowerTalks* 59(13):60–66.

[2] Fonteno, W.C. 1988a. Know your media—the air, water and container connection. *GrowerTalks* 51(11):110-111.

[3] Fonteno, W.C. 1988b. How to get 273 plugs out of a 273-cell tray. *GrowerTalks* 52(8):68–76.

[4] Fonteno, W.C., D.A. Bailey, and P.V. Nelson. 1995. "Squeeze" your plugs for simple, accurate nutrient monitoring. *GrowerTalks* 59(9):22–27.

[5] Harbaugh, B.K. 1994. Root medium components and fertilizer effects on pH. *PPGA News* 25(11):2–4.

[6] Koranski, D.S. 1989. Production 101: Sorting out water quality. *GrowerTalks* 53(5):32–43.

[7] Kramer, P.J., and J.S. Boyer. 1995. *Water relations of plants and soils.* San Diego: Academic Press.

[8] Lang, H.J., and G.C. Elliott. 1993. Media analysis: What does it all mean? *FloraCulture International* 3(12):25–27.

[9] Nelson, P.V. 1991. *Greenhouse operation and management.* 4th Ed. Englewood Cliffs, N.J.: Prentice Hall.

[10] Rader, L.F., Jr., L.M. White, and C.W. Whittaker. 1943. A measure of the effect of fertilizers in the concentration of the soil solution. *Soil Sci* 55:201–208.

[11] Warncke, D.D., and D.M. Krauskopf. 1983. *Greenhouse growth media: testing and nutrition guidelines.* MSU Ag. Facts Ext. Bull. E-1736. East Lansing: Michigan State University.

CHAPTER 8

GERMINATION
FACILITIES

S uccessful seed germination is a direct result of a grower's ability to provide the proper microenvironment around the seed. The crucial factors for germination include soil temperature, moisture, light, and oxygen. The required measures of these factors vary with the crop. (Refer to plug charts included with this book for details.) This chapter will focus on how to set up facilities to control those factors and provide the best germination environment possible.

GERMINATION CONDITIONS

Seed germination takes place in two stages. Stage 1 is the time from seeding to when the root (radicle) emerges from the seed. Stage 2 is the time from radicle emergence to expansion of the cotyledon (seed leaves). Due to covering the seed, many crops may not exhibit visible signs of germination or emergence until they are into Stage 2, when the hypocotyl, or hook, appears above the covering.

Uniform soil temperature must be maintained throughout the germination facility. Different crop species and cultivars may require different temperatures for best germination, and this requirement may vary from year to year. For example, during Stage 1, petunias germinate best at 75 to 78F (24 to 25.5C), whereas geraniums need 72 to 75F (22 to 24C). High soil temperatures can result in poor germination in many species, possibly caused by thermodormancy in the seed. On the other hand, low soil temperatures greatly reduce the speed of germination and may not allow many seeds in a particular crop to germinate in time or at all. Mistakes in overwatering can also occur if the soil temperature is too low, due to the length of time required for germination. (Table 8.1 groups some crops by best germination soil temperature.)

TABLE 8.1   STAGE 1 PLUG SOIL TEMPERATURES

67F (19C)	72F (22C)	77F (25C)
Pansy	Aster	Ageratum
Perennials, some	Calendula	Alyssum
(also 60F)	Carnation	Begonia (both fibrous and
Phlox	Chrysanthemum	tuberous)
Poppy	Coreopsis	Browallia
Primula	Cosmos	Celosia
Ranunculus (60F)	Dahlberg daisy	Coleus
Viola	Dahlia	Gomphrena
	Dianthus	Hypoestes
	Dusty miller	Impatiens (<78F)
	F. kale/cabbage	Lobelia
	Gazania	Nicotiana
	Geranium	Pepper
	Lisianthus	Petunia (<78F)
	Marigold	Portulaca
	Pansy	Salvia
	Perennials, some	Verbena
	Poppy	Vinca
	Shasta daisy	
	Snapdragon	
	Stock	
	Tomato	
	Viola	
	Zinnia	

Seed germination in the plug tray is very dependent on the moisture applied to the seed. Too much moisture may bury the seed or not allow enough oxygen to reach it. Insufficient moisture inhibits the physiological processes of germination. In either case, erratic germination or death of the seed can result. A fine mist or fog system with a droplet size of 10 to 80 microns provides ample moisture and oxygen for optimum seed germination in Stage 1. The objective during Stage 1 is to provide 100% humidity around the seed and still provide air for the seed to breathe. Normal mist systems used for vegetative propagation have a droplet size of 300 to 500 microns, which is too large to allow sufficient oxygen for germination and may cause the seed to become buried in the media. Imbibition, or water uptake by the seed, starts with the initial watering immediately after seeding. The proper moisture levels need to start at that point and be watched throughout Stages 1 and 2 (see table 3.2).

To hold the moisture around the seed while still providing oxygen, apply a covering of coarse vermiculite, plug media, sand, or perlite over the plug tray; most plug growers use a good grade of coarse vermiculite. Certain crops benefit the most from this treatment (table 3.1). Large seeds need more moisture around them to germinate. Some crops need dark to germinate. Still other crops orientate their roots to go down into the media when they are covered.

Light is not required for germination of most crops. However, it may speed up germination, due to increasing the soil temperature, and light is needed for early seedling growth (Stage 2). Some crops actually germinate better in the dark, though, such as cyclamen, phlox, and vinca. Covering these crops with coarse vermiculite, sand, or plug media will give dark enough conditions for proper germination. Crops that may benefit from light levels of 10 to 100 footcandles (fc), 108 to 1,076 lux, during Stage 1 include

TABLE 8.2   IMPATIENS GERMINATION IN LIGHT AND DARK

	Germination percentage	
Cultivar	Light	Dark
Accent Pink	97	80
Accent Rose #1	94	64
Accent Rose #2	95	52
Accent Salmon	89	61
Impulse Rose	68	62
Rose Star	95	96
Super Elfin Coral	98	25
Super Elfin Lipstick	98	92
Super Elfin Orange	90	66
Super Elfin Orchid	85	71
Super Elfin Pink	96	26
Super Elfin Red	86	42

Source: Adapted from Koranski & Karlovich, Plugs: Problems, Concerns, *GrowerTalks.*

FIGURE 8.1 Average germination of 30 impatiens seed lots at different light intensities. Courtesy PanAmerican Seed Co.

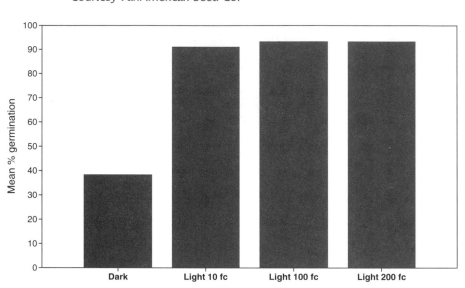

fibrous and tuberous begonias, gerbera, impatiens, lettuce, lisianthus, nicotiana, petunia, and primula. Some cultivars of impatiens are photodormant, whereas other varieties are not affected by absolute darkness (table 8.2) [3]. The minimum light level appears to be 10 fc (108 lux) for impatiens to overcome photodormancy (fig. 8.1) [1]. (Table 8.3 lists some crops that need light or darkness for improved germination.)

TABLE 8.3   CROPS THAT NEED LIGHT OR DARKNESS FOR IMPROVED GERMINATION

Light	Dark
Begonia	Cyclamen
Gerbera	Phlox
Impatiens	Vinca
Lisianthus	
Nicotiana	
Petunia	
Primula	
Snapdragon	

GERMINATION CHAMBERS

Germination chambers are environmentally controlled rooms in which seeded plug trays are placed to germinate. They are designed so that trays may be stacked vertically on movable carts or racks, then rolled or taken out of the room for observation or transportation to the growing-on area in the greenhouse. Temperature is closely controlled with heating and cooling systems. Moisture is initially provided by watering in plug trays directly after seeding. This moisture is maintained in the germination chamber by a fog system. Light may or may not be provided. The oxygen levels to the seed are improved by not oversaturating the seed with moisture or burying the seed in the plug media. Environmental control can be achieved through simple thermostats and timers or computers.

Generally, you can expect at least 10% greater germination in chambers than on the greenhouse bench. Advantages to germination chambers include higher germination percentage, faster germination, greater uniformity of germination, less space needed in the greenhouse, and less attention needed to provide proper moisture and temperature levels. The disadvantages include the cost of building them, having to handle trays in the product flow, and timing, which needs to be closely monitored to move trays from chamber to greenhouse to give best germination but no seedling stretching.

There is no one perfect design for a germination chamber. Most growers build them themselves out of exterior plywood and 2- x 4-inch lumber and improve them over time. Some growers buy prefabricated coolers and turn them into germination chambers. The type of chamber you build will depend on: (1) how much space you need to germinate plug trays, (2) how many different temperatures you need, (3) how long during the year you need the chamber, and (4) how much you want to spend. We have included three different plug chamber designs to give you an idea of what is possible (figs. 8.2, 8.3, and 8.4).

There are several key factors to consider in building a germination chamber. First, the capacity or size of the chamber must be calculated, depending on how many plug trays you need to germinate in a given time and how many chambers you need. The types of crops in the chamber will also affect the size. For example, begonias take about a week to germinate and take up chamber space longer than marigolds, which take about two days to germinate.

Make sure the chamber height is at least 8 feet (2.44 m) if no cooling system is needed, and at least 10 feet (3.05 m) if a cooling system will be hung from the ceiling. This height is needed for enough air space above the racks or carts to allow the fog to flow without condensing on the plug trays.

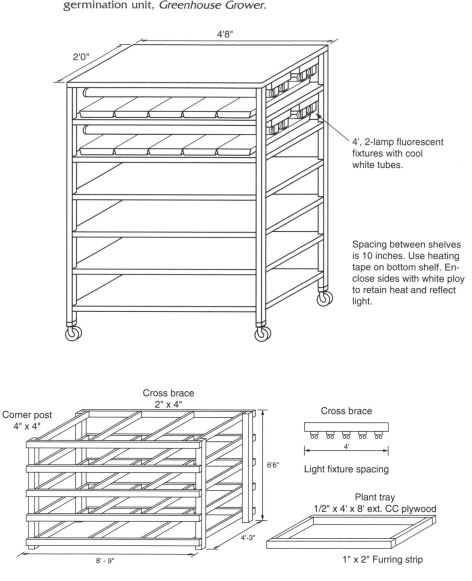

FIGURE 8.2 Small plug chamber design. From Bartok, Build your own germination unit, *Greenhouse Grower.*

Too often growers build the chambers too low, with the result that the plug trays on the top of the carts or racks get too wet from the fog.

The chamber ceiling should be sloped to prevent condensation from dripping onto the plug trays. Channel away condensation forming on the ceiling before it forms drops.

Insulate the germination chamber to an R-value of at least 20. This insulation will help maintain the temperature inside, regardless of where the

FIGURE 8.3 Germination chamber design.

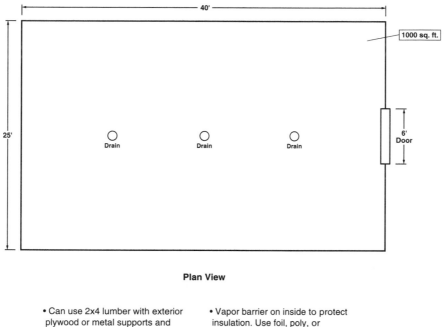

Plan View

• Can use 2x4 lumber with exterior plywood or metal supports and siding.
• Insulate to R-factor = 20 to 30, especially if any walls are exposed to outside conditions. Use 4" to 6" Styrofoam panels.

• Vapor barrier on inside to protect insulation. Use foil, poly, or fiberglass and seal properly.
• Cement floor should be 4" to 6" thick, sloped towards center where drains are located.

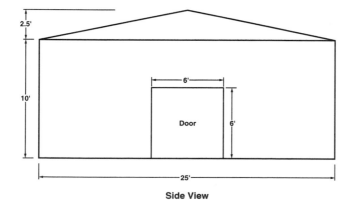

Side View

• Peaked roof to reduce drips.
• Make sure to insulate roof as well as walls (R = 20 to 30) and with vapor barrier.

• Sliding door (rollers) or insulated door/latch (like flower cooler door or meat locker).
• Wood doors and frame will warp and should not be used if using chamber > four months/year.
• Door should be as insulated as walls and ceiling.

FIGURE 8.3 continued

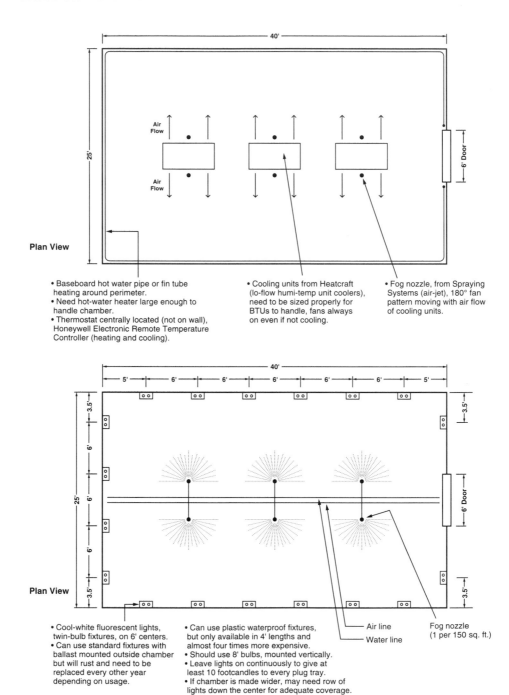

• Baseboard hot water pipe or fin tube heating around perimeter.
• Need hot-water heater large enough to handle chamber.
• Thermostat centrally located (not on wall), Honeywell Electronic Remote Temperature Controller (heating and cooling).

• Cooling units from Heatcraft (lo-flow humi-temp unit coolers), need to be sized properly for BTUs to handle, fans always on even if not cooling.

• Fog nozzle, from Spraying Systems (air-jet), 180° fan pattern moving with air flow of cooling units.

• Cool-white fluorescent lights, twin-bulb fixtures, on 6' centers.
• Can use standard fixtures with ballast mounted outside chamber but will rust and need to be replaced every other year depending on usage.

• Can use plastic waterproof fixtures, but only available in 4' lengths and almost four times more expensive.
• Should use 8' bulbs, mounted vertically.
• Leave lights on continuously to give at least 10 footcandles to every plug tray.
• If chamber is made wider, may need row of lights down the center for adequate coverage.

Air line
Water line

Fog nozzle (1 per 150 sq. ft.)

FIGURE 8.3 continued

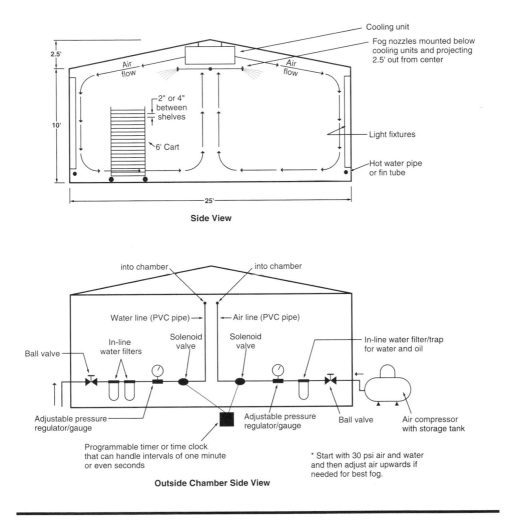

Side View

Outside Chamber Side View

* Start with 30 psi air and water and then adjust air upwards if needed for best fog.

chamber is located. Various materials can be used for insulation, with the R-value depending on the type and thickness of material (see table 8.4). Remember to take into account the floor when insulating your chamber.

Finally, provide a moisture barrier inside of the chamber. This material will protect the insulation from getting wet, which would reduce its R-value. Also, moisture will stay inside the chamber, where it belongs. Examples of moisture-resistant materials include polyethylene film, aluminum foil, and fiberglass.

Heating the chamber will be necessary during the winter and early spring months. If you are using fluorescent light fixtures, the heat will be

FIGURE 8.4 Advanced plug chamber design. Adapted from Polking et al., Germination chambers, *GrowerTalks*.

A. Dimensions

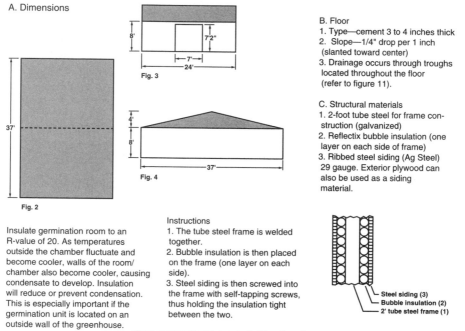

Fig. 3

Fig. 4

Fig. 2

B. Floor
1. Type—cement 3 to 4 inches thick
2. Slope—1/4" drop per 1 inch (slanted toward center)
3. Drainage occurs through troughs located throughout the floor (refer to figure 11).

C. Structural materials
1. 2-foot tube steel for frame construction (galvanized)
2. Reflectix bubble insulation (one layer on each side of frame)
3. Ribbed steel siding (Ag Steel) 29 gauge. Exterior plywood can also be used as a siding material.

Insulate germination room to an R-value of 20. As temperatures outside the chamber fluctuate and become cooler, walls of the room/ chamber also become cooler, causing condensate to develop. Insulation will reduce or prevent condensation. This is especially important if the germination unit is located on an outside wall of the greenhouse.

Instructions
1. The tube steel frame is welded together.
2. Bubble insulation is then placed on the frame (one layer on each side).
3. Steel siding is then screwed into the frame with self-tapping screws, thus holding the insulation tight between the two.

*These are frame dimensions, not actual door dimensions.

Steel siding (3)
Bubble insulation (2)
2' tube steel frame (1)

D. Framework of the chamber showing spacing and number of support beams (tube steel)

2. Diagrams

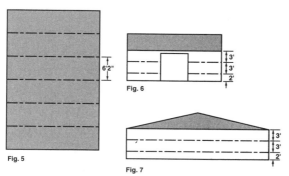

Fig. 6

Fig. 5

Fig. 7

E. Door Design (sliding door inside chamber)
1. Materials
–1/2-inch tube steel frame
–Ribbed steel siding (Ag Steel) 29 gauge on inside of door
–Flat steel (or similar flat material) on outside of door
–Reflectix bubble insulation (one layer on each side of frame) and frame

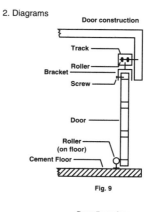

Door construction

Track
Roller
Bracket
Screw

Door

Roller (on floor)
Cement Floor

Fig. 9

Door dimensions

Fig. 8   7'3"   2'5"
2'5"
2'5"
7'2.5"

*Note—This drawing is not proportional to the other drawings.

FIGURE 8.4 continued

3. Diagrams
—Finn tube placement in the floor and in the area above the floor.

*Note—This heater is used to heat two of these growth chambers. A smaller unit may be enough if only one chamber is built.

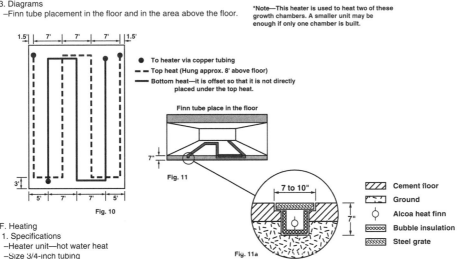

● To heater via copper tubing
- - Top heat (Hung approx. 8' above floor)
— Bottom heat—it is offset so that it is not directly placed under the top heat.

Finn tube place in the floor

Fig. 11

Fig. 10

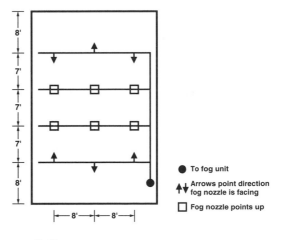

Fig. 11a

▨ Cement floor
▱ Ground
⚬ Alcoa heat finn
⬚ Bubble insulation
▨ Steel grate

*Note—The floor heat finn is placed in the ground between the slabs of cement in the trough made for both drainage and finn tube placement. This can be lined with bubble insulation for more heat reflection upward. Small holes should be cut in the insulation for drainage.

F. Heating
1. Specifications
—Heater unit—hot water heat
—Size 3/4-inch tubing
—Btu/hr. 250,000
—Booster pump—1/20 horsepower
2. Tubing
—Aluminum Alcoa Finn tube is used to radiate and distribute heat.
—Copper tube is used to connect the finn (inside the chamber) to the heater unit (outside the chamber).

G. Cooling—Fog system
1. Specifications
—1/2-inch copper tubing
—Number of nozzles—12
—Water particle size—5 to 10 microns

2. Placement of fog lines and nozzles

● To fog unit
▲▼ Arrows point direction fog nozzle is facing
☐ Fog nozzle points up

Fig. 12

TABLE 8.4   R-VALUES OR THERMAL RESISTANCE OF CERTAIN MATERIALS

Insulation (inches)				
Cork or mineral wool	Glass fiber or polystyrene	Urethane (sprayed)	Urethane (foamed in place)	R-value
	1			4
	2			8
4	3	2		12.6
5	4		2	16.4
6	5	3		19.6
8	6	4	3	25
10	8		4	33
	10	6		38.7
			6	50

supplied by the lights, which can be left on continuously. Remember, the ballast from fluorescent fixtures will contribute some of the heat, so locate the ballasts outside the chamber if you do not need that much heat.

The best method of accurately heating a germination chamber is to use a system of hot water piped around the baseboards from a separate hot water heater. Generally, the maximum temperature needed is 80F (26.5C). Provide secondary heating by heating, or tempering, the water going through the fog system into the chamber.

Cooling the chamber will be necessary if you use it during warm months, use lights for heating, or need to germinate crops that require cooler than normal temperatures (such as ranunculus or anemone). The desired temperature range should be from 60 to 80F (15.5 to 26.5C). Small chambers can be cooled by an air-conditioning unit mounted on top of the chamber, with the cool air entering the chamber through a perforated ceiling. Do not recirculate the humid air through the air conditioner, as ice will cause the unit to freeze up.

For larger chambers, look into cooling units designed for high humidity and low airflow (Heatcraft, Inc., 770/939-4450). These unit coolers can be mounted flush to the ceiling, pulling warm air up to the ceiling and discharging cool air through the coils on each side, thus providing even air distribution. Allow for about 1.5 feet (46 cm) for these units to hang from the ceiling. The chamber height should be increased if you use such units.

Remember, these cooling units will set up their own airflow patterns, so your fog system will need to be adjusted accordingly. Make sure to keep your set points 2F (1C) apart, so as not to have the heating and cooling systems running against each other all the time.

Moisture control is critical for chamber germination. Plug trays should not be hand-watered in the chamber, as seed could be washed out of the cells or buried. The proper amount of water should be added to the tray after seeding and before going into the chamber. A fog or very fine mist system (10 to 50 microns droplet size) will then maintain the high humidity inside the chamber to keep the original moisture level in the plug tray, neither adding nor subtracting moisture. The finer the droplet size, the better the distribution of the fog and the more uniform the temperature throughout the chamber. The greatest uniformity of moisture distribution will be attained with very little air movement. Too much air movement can cause uneven distribution, resulting in wet and dry spots in the chamber.

In a small chamber, a humidifier is sufficient. In a large chamber, a fog system—either using high pressure (up to 1,000 psi) or air-over-water nozzles—is needed. Use fog nozzles when the chamber is larger than 150 ft^2 (14 m^2). A high-pressure fog system (for example, from Mee Fog Systems, 800/732-5364, or Atomizing Systems Inc., 201/447-1222) requires a special air pump, special tubing, and special nozzles, which tend to clog up with less-than-perfect water quality. Make sure you size the system properly with the number of nozzles needed for the chamber size. Air-over-water fog nozzles (AirJet Fogger Nozzles, Spraying Systems Co., 630/665-5000) need an air compressor, operate at 30 psi air and water pressure, need no special tubing, and have larger nozzle orifices that keep them from clogging up (fig. 8.5). Output from these nozzles is much higher than from high-pressure nozzles, which means fewer nozzles per chamber. Generally, you need one air-over-water nozzle per 150 ft^2 (14 m^2) of chamber floor space.

With either fog system, you need to cycle the fog on and off, as running at

FIGURE 8.5 Air-over-water fog nozzle. Courtesy Spraying Systems Co.

capacity would oversaturate the chamber. Control can be achieved with electronic programmable timers (Cole-Parmer, 800/323-4340), simple time clocks or with humidity sensors that can operate accurately above 85% relative humidity. Environmental control computers can also regulate timing and maintain relative humidity.

Another measure used in controlling a chamber's fog system is the *vapor pressure deficit* (VPD). This is the difference between the amount of water held in the air immediately surrounding the media and seed, and the amount of water held in the ambient air. The higher the VPD (the more positive), the greater the rate at which water is lost from the media to the ambient air. If VPD is negative, the media is actually absorbing water from the ambient air. To determine VPD, you need to measure the soil and air temperature and the relative humidity of the air, then calculate the VPD using a table [4]. Fortunately, environmental control computers can do this in a flash.

Lights may or may not be used inside the germination chamber. With no lights, a chamber is commonly called a *sweat chamber*. Crops left in here for germination need to be monitored closely for root emergence, then pulled out and placed onto greenhouse benches for growing on. Remember, some crops need light to germinate sufficiently.

If you want to use lights to provide heat, to extend the time needed in the chamber for better germination, or to improve the germination of certain photodormant crops, then look into using cool-white fluorescent lights. You can install them horizontally over each shelf (fig. 8.3), or mount them vertically along the walls or between the carts (fig. 8.4). Mount two-tube fixtures about 3 to 4 feet (0.9 to 1.22 m) on center, thereby providing about 100 fc (1,076 lux) of light. High-output bulbs will give you the same fc desired with fewer fixtures but are more expensive. Lights should be placed no closer than 8 to 10 inches (20 to 25 cm) from the plug trays, as uneven drying and light distribution would otherwise result.

Metal fixtures will corrode within one or two years in the high humidity of germination chambers. You can extend the life of your lights by purchasing plastic, waterproof fixtures. However, such fixtures cost about three times as much as standard metal fixtures. If you are mounting lights vertically in a 10-foot-high (3.05 m) chamber, 8-foot (2.44 m) lights will provide uniform light. Otherwise, you will need some pattern of 4-foot (1.22 m) lights. Leave the lights on continuously unless you need to reduce the heat load in a small chamber.

Movable carts are required if the chamber is large, fixed racks if the chamber is small. Shelves should be spaced about 4 inches (10.2 cm) apart for good movement of fog and penetration of light, if used. Some large plug growers stack containerized benches on top of each other and roll them into the chamber on rails. It is essential that the fog can penetrate between these stacked benches and provide uniform soil temperature and moisture.

Timing of each crop in the chamber is critical. If left too long in the chamber, especially one with no lights, the seedlings will stretch rapidly, and the crop will be ruined. If taken out too quickly, before germination has really commenced, then total germination and uniformity will be reduced on the greenhouse bench. Use the information in this book's plug charts and in your own trials to determine how long any crop and variety should stay in the germination chamber.

Once you take the germinating plug trays out of the chamber, place them on a greenhouse bench to finish Stage 2. Make sure this area is protected from temperature extremes and high light levels, so that the fragile, tiny seedlings can acclimate to the different growing conditions. The light level should be lower than 1,500 fc (less than 16,140 lux). Maintain soil temperatures close to those in the germination chamber or slightly lower. Moisture levels should be closely monitored.

GERMINATION ON THE GREENHOUSE BENCH

A portion of a greenhouse can be devoted to plug germination if the proper conditions are maintained. Greenhouse germination allows easy access to, and close inspection of, the plug trays. Root-zone heating, with assistance from a perimeter or overhead heating system, should be set up to provide optimum soil temperatures. In warm weather a cooling system will reduce soil temperature to the proper range for germination. An overhead fog or fine mist system can supply the necessary moisture (fig. 8.6). Irrigation booms can be used if very fine nozzles (50 to 80 microns) are installed. Tempered water can also maintain soil temperatures, especially if cold well water is used during the winter season; heat the

FIGURE 8.6 Stationary mist system for bench germination.

water to 70F (21C). Moisture can be controlled with timers (fog or mist systems) or according to visual inspection (boom irrigators or hand-watering).

Some growers use capillary mats when germinating plugs on benches, especially if using root-zone heating without fog. The mats supply moisture and humidity to the plug trays and reduce the drying effects of the root-zone heating. The mats also help distribute heat evenly across the bench and help pull excess moisture through the plugs.

The disadvantages of capillary mats are: (1) roots may grow into them, (2) buildup of algae, fungus gnats, and shoreflies may occur; and (3) plug trays may actually stay too wet. Capillary mats are not as widely used in the United States as previously.

In northern areas during winter, HID lights are recommended to provide supplemental light energy (about 400 fc, or 4,300 lux, at plant level) for seedling development after germination. In the greenhouse, HID lights can provide both light and heat, raising the soil temperature 2 to 5F (1 to 3C). In sunny weather the greenhouse germination area should be shaded to provide less than 1,500 fc (less than 16,140 lux).

A microenvironment can be created for the seeds during Stages 1 and 2 by covering the plug trays (fig. 8.7). Coarse vermiculite, plug media, sand, and other materials have been used successfully by many growers. Other types of coverings can trap heat and humidity around the seeds, but they are then removed once germination is visible. These coverings include polyethylene film (clear and opaque), Vispore (plastic punched with holes), and frost covers (spun porous plastic, sometimes called Agricloth). Water can be applied to the plug trays through Vispore and frost covers, if someone watches carefully for water accumulation or dry spots. All these plastic products can be cleaned off and reused.

Using the greenhouse bench for germination requires careful grouping of crops by temperature and moisture requirements. Dividing this greenhouse area into temperature zones gives you more flexibility for placing crops in the best germination climates. How long a crop stays there depends on the temperature and moisture conditions, type of crop, variety, and seed quality. Once germination is visible, moisture and temperature may need to be lowered

FIGURE 8.7 Plugs trays covered with coarse vermiculite.

slightly to keep seedlings from stretching. If this is not possible in the germination area, trays will need to be moved to another part of the greenhouse for the rest of Stage 2 through Stage 4.

KEY POINTS TO REMEMBER

- Germination depends heavily on your ability to optimize and control soil temperature and moisture at the seed level for each specific crop. (Refer to plug charts included in this book for more information.) Germination chambers give you better control of temperature, moisture, and light, but they are more costly to build. Greenhouse benches make it easy to see germination, but a grower needs to pay more attention to controlling temperature and, especially, moisture.

- Space requirements can play a role in deciding what type of germination facility to use, especially during peak times of the year. Germination chambers will free up bench space for up to seven days, depending on the crop. Will you have enough quality bench space to germinate all your crops at the busiest time of the year?

- Chamber building costs should be determined through careful planning. Many growers build their own and improve them along the way.

- The type of germination facility you use will largely be determined by what types of crops you grow and at what time of year. Growers in the southern United States cannot germinate pansies very well on the greenhouse bench in July and August, when temperatures are above 90F (32C). Vinca will have difficulties germinating in the northern United States during January and February, when greenhouse temperatures are below 70F (21C).

- Finally, attention to detail is essential for high germination results, regardless of the type of germination facility. Be vigilant in removing trays from the germination chamber before stretching occurs. On the greenhouse bench, more attention must be paid to moisture levels, which may fluctuate rapidly, as well as soil temperature.

REFERENCES

[1] Armstrong, T., D. Cross, and R.C. Styer. 1995. Get the most germination from your impatiens seed. *GrowerTalks* 59(9):50, 52.

[2] Bartok, J., Jr. 1992. Build your own germination unit. *Greenhouse Grower* 10(11):21, 24.

[3] Koranski, D., and P. Karlovich. 1989. Plugs: Problems, concerns, and recommendations for the grower. *GrowerTalks* 53(8):28.

[4] Polking, G., D. Koranski, R. Kessler, and M. Khademi. 1990. Germination chambers guarantee success in the plug tray. *GrowerTalks* 54(8):62–69.

CHAPTER 9

ENVIRONMENT

The basics of plant growth are greatly influenced by the environment. Each of several key factors—temperature, light, carbon dioxide (CO_2), and humidity—has individual effects on processes from germination to photosynthesis to flowering. These factors also interact with each other and with nutrition to control plant growth and flowering, the effects varying with the crop and growth stage involved.

There are two main processes inside the plant that determine how it grows. In *photosynthesis* the plant takes CO_2, light energy, and water, to form carbohydrates (sugars), as expressed in the following equation:

$$CO_2 + H_2O + \text{light energy} \rightarrow \text{carbohydrate} + O_2$$

The light energy is trapped in the carbohydrate. Later, the carbohydrate can be translocated from the green stem and leaf cells, where photosynthesis occurs, to all other parts of the plant [25]. The carbohydrates can be converted into amino acids, proteins, fats, cellulose for cell walls, hormones, and DNA. The conversion into these other products results in plant growth, which can be detected as an increase in dry matter.

Nutrient uptake, protein formation, cell division, membrane maintenance, and other processes require energy inputs. This energy is obtained when compounds formed as a direct or indirect result of photosynthesis are broken down in the process of *respiration,* very much the reverse of photosynthesis:

$$\text{Carbohydrate} + O_2 \rightarrow CO_2 + H_2O + \text{Energy}$$

Respiration occurs in plants at all times. It is temperature-dependent, increasing with an increase in temperature [25]. Certain nutrients, such as

FIGURE 9.1 Factors influencing respiration in plug seedlings.

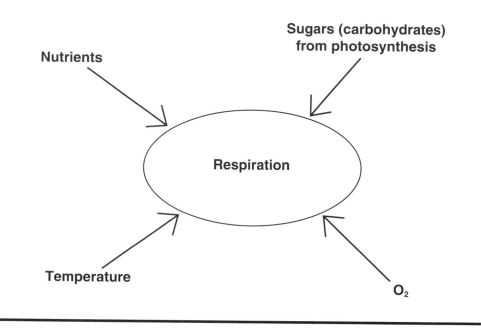

phosphorus, are also necessary for respiration to continue. (Figure 9.1 shows the various factors that influence respiration.)

Photosynthesis is dependent on such factors as temperature, light, CO_2, water, and nutrients (fig. 9.2). If one or more of these factors are not optimized, photosynthesis is limited. When photosynthesis is limited, for whatever reason, plant growth slows down. Photosynthesis occurs only during the daylight hours because of its dependence on light.

When photosynthesis exceeds respiration, net plant growth occurs (table 9.1). When they equal each other, net plant growth stops. If respiration exceeds photosynthesis, the plant declines in vigor and will eventually die. This decline in vigor may appear as leaf chlorosis, smaller leaf size, shoot stunting, root growth reduction, and other abnormalities [25].

TABLE 9.1   DEPENDENCY OF GROWTH ON PHOTOSYNTHESIS AND RESPIRATION

Photosynthesis	>	Respiration	→	Net growth
Photosynthesis	=	Respiration	→	Net growth stops
Photosynthesis	<	Respiration	→	Decline of vigor and death of plant

FIGURE 9.2 Factors influencing photosynthesis in plug seedlings.

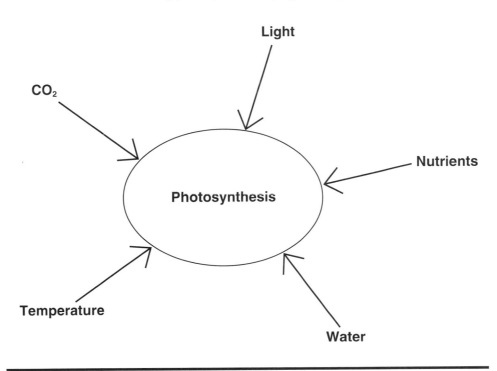

Controlling the environment is the reason we grow plants in greenhouses. Temperature can be raised in the winter season by adding heat inside the greenhouse. Light from the sun is optimized by a structure with nearly transparent coverings, allowing as much light to pass through as possible but still retaining the temperature needed for growing the plants. However, during warm times of the year, greenhouses become very difficult to cool enough to grow plants properly. A grower reduces the light levels through shading to reduce the heat load inside the greenhouse. This heat load is due to the fact that more than 80% of the sunlight energy is radiant heat, raising the temperature of the leaves, soil, and air. This radiant heat can easily raise the inside temperature 20 to 30F (11 to 17C) higher than the outside temperature. Cooling systems have to remove some of this radiant heat, as well as try to lower the inside temperature to a level below the outside temperature. Humidity levels can get quite high inside greenhouses, particularly at night, causing problems with plant disease and soft growth.

How much any plug grower can control the environment using available greenhouse facilities determines how much plug growth can be controlled. But how much control do you really have of temperature, light, CO_2, and humidity? Less than you think! During the winter season, most growers can provide enough heat to keep growth going, but light becomes limiting. In a tight greenhouse with vents closed during winter, CO_2 levels become limiting. Humidity levels can be reduced through dehumidification cycles in some greenhouses. During the summer season, most growers cannot cool their greenhouses enough to optimize plug growth. Light levels get too high, and shading must be applied. Humidity levels cannot be controlled at this time of year. So it appears that most plug growers can control temperature, light, CO_2, and humidity within only a certain range, but not with precision throughout the whole year.

Nevertheless, controlling the environment is a goal that every plug grower should keep striving to achieve. With the advent of better greenhouses, better shading, and computer control, more precision can be obtained, particularly during the winter season.

In this chapter we will cover the key environmental factors and how they influence growth from late Stage 2 through Stage 4 and beyond (the germination stages [Stage 1 and most of Stage 2] were covered in the previous chapter). Understand that these environmental factors rarely operate alone, but interact with each other simultaneously to control plant growth.

TEMPERATURE

The temperature of a plant at any given time is the result of a number of factors that have direct and indirect effects on heating or cooling the plant. For instance, a plant can be directly heated by the surrounding air through conduction or indirectly through convection. Conduction is the direct heating of the leaf particle by the air. Convection is a flow of air, brought about by unequal air temperature and density, resulting in more heat conduction to the leaf. Heat from chemical energy released during metabolism or by conversion of sunlight to heat can also increase plant temperature.

The primary mechanism through which a plant can control its temperature is transpiration. The evaporation of water requires energy, which results in a drop in the leaf temperature. When transpiring heavily, a leaf can actually dissipate as much as 50% of the energy it absorbs [9].

All plants respond to temperature similarly (fig. 9.3). No growth occurs below a certain temperature, referred to as the *base temperature*. Base temperatures vary from 32 to 50F (0 to 10C). Above the base temperature, growth increases linearly as temperature increases, until an *optimal temperature* is reached. At this point the growth rate of shoots and roots is maximized. Optimal temperatures for plant growth vary from 65 to 85F (18 to 29C) for most floricultural crops [9]. As temperature increases above the optimal temperature, plant growth decreases.

FIGURE 9.3 Typical temperature response curve. From Heins, Choosing the best temperature, *Greenhouse Grower.*

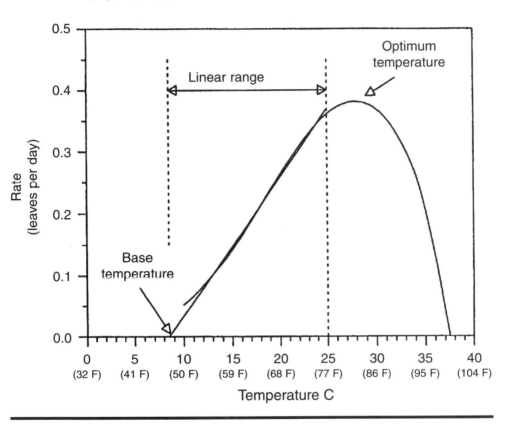

OPTIMAL TEMPERATURE

Optimal growth temperatures vary with plant species. Species that originate in warm climates tend to have higher optimal temperatures than species from cooler climates. For example, fuchsia, dianthus, and primula prefer cooler temperatures (60 to 70F, 15 to 21C), whereas zinnia, vinca, and New Guinea impatiens have higher optimal temperatures (70 to 80F, 21 to 26C) [9].

The optimal temperature varies at different stages of plant development. The optimal temperature for increase in plant mass tends to decrease as a plant ages [9]. Most bedding plants require a higher temperature for optimal germination than for the continued development. Recommended germination temperatures vary from 65 to 80F (18 to 26C) for most bedding plants. The recommended temperatures for the stem growth stage and cotyledon emergence vary from 62 to 75F (17 to 24C), for the growth and development of true leaves from 60 to 72F (15 to 22C), and for the final development prior to transplanting or shipping from 58 to 66F (14 to 19C) [20].

The time of day often also affects the optimal temperature. Higher day temperatures tend to promote higher rates of photosynthesis. Cooler night temperatures tend to decrease respiration or carbohydrate (sugar) depletion. Together, warmer days and cooler nights tend to promote high gains in plant mass or weight [9]. All biochemical reactions in the plant are controlled by enzymes, which are heat-sensitive. Above the optimal temperature, most enzymes will not function. Water and nutrient uptake are also influenced by the day or night temperature. Transpiration is reduced at low temperatures; therefore, the plant has little need for water uptake. Certain nutrients (P, Fe, and NH_4) are not taken up by the root system at low soil temperatures (less than 60F, 15C).

PLANT DEVELOPMENT AND TEMPERATURE

A crop's rate of vegetative development is often quantified by determining the *leaf-unfolding rate* [9]. A high leaf-unfolding rate demonstrates rapid development. In general, the leaf-unfolding rate has a temperature-response curve similar to that of plant growth (fig. 9.3).

The leaf-unfolding rate is proportional to the *average daily temperature* (ADT) when temperatures are maintained in the linear range [9]. The ADT is calculated by the following formula:

$$\frac{(Day\ temp)\ (Hrs\ of\ day) + (Night\ temp)\ (Hrs\ of\ night)}{24} = ADT$$

This concept means that to speed up plant growth or leaf-unfolding rate, a grower can increase the ADT within the linear range. To slow down the plant growth, reduce the ADT—but stay within the linear range, or growth will stop completely. Leaf-unfolding rate models are available or being developed for a number of crops [9]. Environmental-control computers applying these models can determine the ADT a plug grower needs to maintain to ensure that the crop is at the desired stage of development when it is to be used or marketed.

Plant height is determined by stem length, which is based on the number and length of internodes. The number of internodes is mainly dependent on the ADT, as just described. In contrast to leaf or node number, internode length for most crops is dependent on *how* temperature is delivered during a day-night cycle. Internode length increases as the *difference* between day and night temperature increases. This relationship, *DIF*, is simply formulated as the difference between the day temperature (DT) and the night temperature (NT): DIF = DT − NT [17].

In general, stem elongation can be reduced by one third by going from a higher DT than NT (+DIF) regime to a constant DT and NT (zero DIF)

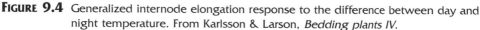

FIGURE 9.4 Generalized internode elongation response to the difference between day and night temperature. From Karlsson & Larson, *Bedding plants IV.*

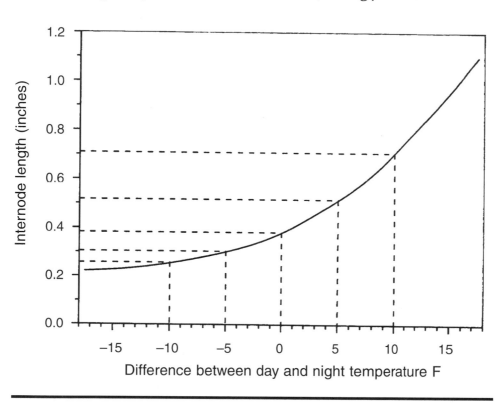

regime (fig. 9.4). Response to DIF is greater under short days than long days. Plant stem elongation is most sensitive to temperature during the first two to three hours of the morning, starting a half hour before sunrise. Do not let the temperature increase immediately in the morning when using a temperature drop at sunrise. Dropping the temperature for two to three hours does not greatly affect ADT, in most cases. The reduction in stem elongation due to a temperature drop is greatest when the drop is rapid, occurs at sunrise, and light intensity is high [9]. An alternate way to drop the temperature can simply be to water plants with cold (50F, 10C) water, which occurs commonly during the winter in the north [21].

In the linear range, most plants exposed to a positive, negative, or zero DIF grow at the same leaf-unfolding rate as long as the ADT is the same. For example, if plants were grown at a 12-hour day of 70F (21C) and 12-hour night of 60F (15C) (+DIF), or a 12-hour day of 60F (15C) and 12-hour night of 70F (21C) (−DIF), or at constant 65F (18C) for 24 hours (zero DIF), all the plants would develop at the same rate and would flower at the same time, because the ADT is the same (65F, 18C). However, the height of these plants

TABLE 9.2   PLUG GROWTH PROCESS RESPONSE TO ADT AND DIF

Process	ADT[a]		DIF	
	Increasing	Decreasing	Positive	Negative
Photosynthesis	↑	↓	↑	—
Respiration	↑	↓	—	↑
Leaf unfolding	↑	↓	—	—
Internode length	—	—	↑	↓
Leaf size	↑	—	↑	—
Stem thickness	—	↑	↑	—
Leaf color	—	—	↑	—

[a] Within linear range

would be very different due to their response to DIF. The plants grown at a negative DIF would be the shortest, while the plants grown at a positive DIF would be the tallest [16].

Stem caliber or mass, thickness, and/or dry weight are responsive to ADT and DIF. In general, stem caliber increases as ADT decreases and as DIF increases. As with stem caliber or mass, leaf size and dry weight partitioning are affected by ADT and DIF. Leaf color increases as DIF increases [9]. As mentioned previously, photosynthesis and dry weight accumulation are affected by ADT and DIF. During the day, a higher temperature may result in a faster photosynthetic rate, especially in high light conditions. Respiration increases in plants with increasing temperatures. During the night there is no photosynthesis, and a low temperature can be expected to result in slow respiration. High day temperature in combination with a low night temperature increases dry weight, but remember, it will also increase internode length, or stretch [20]. (Table 9.2 summarizes the plug growth processes that ADT and DIF affect.)

FLOWERING AND TEMPERATURE

Temperatures higher or lower than the optimal temperature can reduce flower number or inhibit flowering completely. Flower formation may be most sensitive to the temperature maintained only during the day, only during the night period, or during another particular period of the 24-hour daily cycle [9]. New Guinea impatiens flower number decreases dramatically when day or night temperature exceeds 76F (24C) or drops below 63F (17C), whereas zonal geranium flower number decreases as temperatures increase from 54F (12C). Fuchsia is a day-sensitive plant, and flower initiation will not occur if the day temperature exceeds 68F (20C). African marigold will not initiate flowers if the night temperature is higher than 74F (23C).

Some bedding plants can be induced to flower using temperature alone. The best example of this is primula, which can be induced to flower when the temperature is maintained below 63F (17C). Statice is another crop that can be *vernalized,* or induced to flower, with cool temperatures for a period of time in a plug. Many perennials also need or would benefit from vernalization in a large plug.

Both flower bud development and abortion are influenced by the ADT that the plants are grown under. The rate of flower bud development increases with temperature to about 75F (24C) in several bedding plant species, including geranium, New Guinea impatiens, and fuchsia. Higher temperatures than 75F (24C) will only result in slower flower development and increase the number of aborted flower buds. On species sensitive to temperature, the optimal temperatures for flower size tend to be lower than those for leaf unfolding or leaf expansion [9].

INTERACTIONS WITH OTHER FACTORS

Light. Temperature interacts with such other factors as light, CO_2, and nutrition. When temperature is optimal but the light level is low, photosynthesis will be limited, respiration will increase and deplete carbohydrates, and the plant will stretch (greater internode length). When temperature is optimal but light level high, photosynthesis will be maximized, and respiration will be high. The result is maximum plant growth, as long as such other factors as CO_2, nutrients, and water do not become limiting. High light levels can also raise leaf temperature above optimum, causing photosynthesis to shut down, resulting in temporary growth regulation.

When plants are grown at a low temperature (near base level), a low light level will combine with the low temperature to limit photosynthesis and respiration, resulting in a slow plant growth rate. If the light level is high but the temperature low, photosynthesis may still be limited, along with respiration, thereby limiting the plant growth rate. However, a high light level may again increase leaf temperature faster than air temperature and thereby increase photosynthesis above respiration. Growth in this situation would be increased.

Carbon dioxide. When the CO_2 level is increased above ambient levels, plant growth will increase. Combined with a daytime temperature increase of 5F (3C), CO_2 injection will promote more plant growth. The interactions

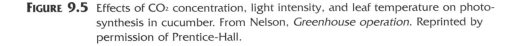

FIGURE 9.5 Effects of CO_2 concentration, light intensity, and leaf temperature on photosynthesis in cucumber. From Nelson, *Greenhouse operation*. Reprinted by permission of Prentice-Hall.

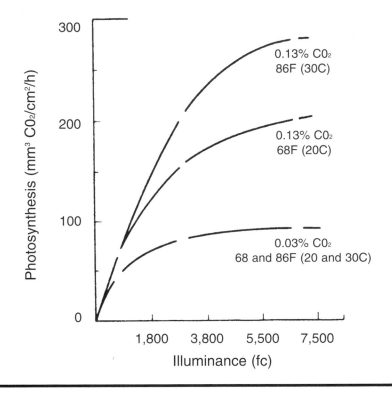

between this process and light levels are clearly illustrated in fig. 9.5. In the lowest curve, the rate of photosynthesis began to plateau at about 3,800 fc (40,000 lux) of light intensity, regardless of whether the temperature was at 68F or 86F; the 300 ppm level of CO_2 became a limiting factor at that point. When the temperature was held at 68F and the CO_2 level was increased to 1,300 ppm, the rate of photosynthesis increased. Then the 68F temperature became the limiting factor, because temperature increase to 86F at the same 1,300 ppm CO_2 level brought about another increase in photosynthesis [25].

Nutrition. Plant nutrients, particularly ammonium-nitrogen (NH_4), may also interact with temperature. At optimal temperatures and high NH_4, plants tend to increase internode length and the leaf-unfolding rate, resulting in soft, stretched plants. At low temperatures (less than 60F, 15C) and high NH_4, plants cannot use the NH_4, as it is not broken down by soil bacteria. Toxic levels of NH_4 can then easily occur, damaging the root system and causing foliar symptoms, as well.

Be careful when determining how high to raise the temperature because it affects processes in addition to photosynthesis. Generally, higher temperature results in faster growth, but with it a reduction in quality—longer stems, thinner stems and leaves, and smaller flowers—may occur.

LIGHT

The four most common types of light measurements are light quality, duration, intensity, and quantity (table 9.3 outlines several plant responses and the most valuable type of light measurement to use for each). Plant growth and yield (measured in terms of plant size, flower number, and other attributes) are primarily influenced by the total quantity of light a plant receives during the entire day. Plant morphology (height and shape) is primarily influenced by light quality, which refers to the wavelengths of light (such as blue, red, and far-red light). Flowering of photoperiodic species (short-day and long-day plants) is primarily influenced by light duration, or photoperiod, while light quantity is most important for flowering of day-neutral species. Photosynthesis is mainly affected by the light quantity and the light intensity [23].

TABLE 9.3   PLANT RESPONSE TO LIGHT MEASUREMENTS

Light measurement	Growth/yield	Morphology	Flowering	Photosynthesis
Light quality	+ [a]	++ [b]	+	
Light duration		+	++	
Light intensity	+			+
Light quantity	++		++	++

Source: Adapted from Moe, Physiological aspects, *Artificial Lighting in Horticulture.*

[a] Significant effect

[b] Greatest effect

LIGHT QUALITY

Light quality is defined by wavelength (nm), with visible light occurring between the wavelengths of 400 to 700 nm (fig. 9.6). Far-red light (700 to 750 nm) plays important roles in photoperiod and plant morphology. Ultraviolet light (UV) (300 to 400 nm) may help to keep plants shorter, but is screened out by most greenhouse coverings. Infrared light (750 to 800 nm) does not affect plant processes [25].

FIGURE 9.6 Radiant energy between 300 and 800 nm. From Nelson, *Greenhouse operation*. Reprinted by permission of Prentice-Hall.

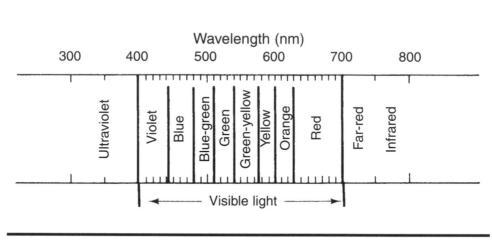

FIGURE 9.7 Photosynthetic activity under different qualities of light. From Nelson, *Greenhouse operation*. Reprinted by permission of Prentice-Hall.

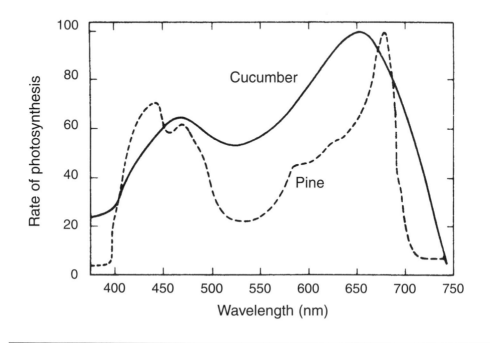

Photosynthetic activity occurs in the visible spectrum of light, with peak activity in the red and blue wavelengths (fig. 9.7). Radiant energy is captured in the leaves and stems of plants by pigments called *chlorophyll* and *carotenoids*. The radiant energy is then turned into chemical energy through carbohydrate synthesis. Photosynthesis requires high energy, about 150 to 500 micromoles for several hours [22]. (Footcandles, a measurement related to vision, mainly of yellow and green wavelengths, is inappropriate for photosynthesis; micromoles is the correct unit. Roughly, 1 micromole = 7 footcandles.)

Plant morphology is controlled primarily by pigments called *phytochrome*. The phytochrome system involves red and far-red wavelengths. The dominant one of these two wavelengths determines the plant form (table 9.4). When more red light is applied, plants have reduced stem elongation and more branching, and seed germination is improved in some species. When more far-red light is applied, plants have increased stem elongation, growth is soft, and seed germination in some species is inhibited [5].

TABLE 9.4   PLANT RESPONSES TO RED AND FAR-RED LIGHT

Plant characteristic	Red light	Far-red light
Stem elongation	Inhibits	Promotes
Branching	Promotes	Inhibits
Leaf color	Dark green	Light green
Leaf thickness	Thick	Thin
Leaf angle	Horizontal	Upright
Shoot: root ratio (dry weight)	Low	High

Source: Adapted from Erwin, *Build a better plug.*

The ratio of red to far-red light allows the plant to determine whether it is being shaded by surrounding plants. Green leaves preferentially absorb red light. Therefore, plants shaded by other plants are exposed to less red light than far-red light. A higher proportion of far-red light stimulates stem elongation and reduces branching, enabling a plant to grow through a canopy shading it, so it can compete better with adjacent plants [5]. Crowding of plants is common in a plug tray. Overlapping leaves filter out red light, resulting in greater stem elongation and less branching in lower internodes. Hanging baskets over the plug crop promote the same effect [8, 24].

The difference between the influence of light quality on plant photosynthesis and plant morphology (photomorphogenesis) is in the amount of energy required. Photosynthesis requires high energy, about 300 micromoles for several hours. *Photomorphogenesis,* on the other hand, is a low-energy process, requiring only about 2 to 5 micromoles for a few minutes [22]. This energy level could be supplied at the end of the day or in the middle of the night with supplemental or night-interruption lighting.

LIGHT DURATION (PHOTOPERIOD)

The mechanism in plants that tracks time is called *photoperiodism.* Photoperiodism, as the response of a plant to the day-night cycle, is very important for control of flowering. Plants are classified in regard to photoperiodism as long-day (short-night), short-day (long-night), and day-neutral plants. The time-tracking mechanism actually measures the dark period [25].

The pigment phytochrome serves as the light receptor in photoperiodic plants. When the plant is in daylight or artificial light, phytochrome exists in a form known as *Pfr,* which is sensitive to far-red light. If the plant is exposed to far-red light, Pfr phytochrome will quickly change to *Pr* phytochrome (Pfr→Pr), which is sensitive to red light. This same response will occur when the plant is placed in darkness, but it then occurs very slowly. The Pr form developed in darkness or under far-red light rapidly returns to the Pfr form when the plant is again exposed to daylight (Pr→Pfr). Remember, the Pfr form is rapidly produced in the light, whereas the Pr form is slowly produced in the dark.

The Pfr form is the active form that controls the photoperiodic response. It inhibits flowering in long-night plants and promotes flowering in short-night plants. Typical levels of Pfr for a long-night plant during summer and

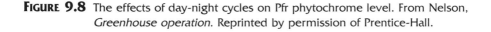

FIGURE 9.8 The effects of day-night cycles on Pfr phytochrome level. From Nelson, *Greenhouse operation.* Reprinted by permission of Prentice-Hall.

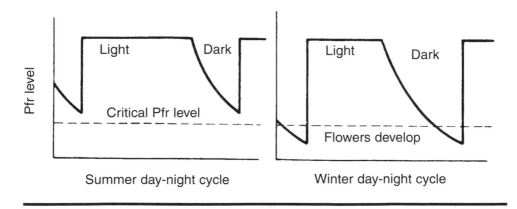

winter daily cycles are shown in fig. 9.8 [25]. Flowering develops in the long-night plant when the Pfr gets low enough.

Different bedding plant species cover all possibilities of photoperiodic combinations for flowering (table 9.5). Many are day-neutral and will flower in relatively the same period of time under any reasonable photoperiod, but they will respond preferentially to light quantity. Some species are short-night plants, while others are long-night plants. Salvia may be found in all three categories, varying by cultivar. The *S. farinacea* varieties are short-night responsive, needing 11 or fewer hours of dark. Red Pillar and Bonfire Elite are long-night in response, whereas Early Scarlet Pygmy is day-neutral [10]. Petunias respond to short nights in both time to flower and plant morphology between the temperatures of 55 to 70F (13 to 21C) [6]. Outside of this range, the plant responds to temperature instead of photoperiod. Induction of flowering in petunia can be accomplished in the plug stage with supplemental lighting to provide short nights (less than 11 hours). Tuberous begonias need to have short nights (less than 10 hours) to prevent tuber formation, which inhibits vegetative and reproductive growth. As soon as the begonia seed germinates, the plant is photoperiodic. The short-night requirement is *absolute,* meaning it cannot be reversed even after just one day of long nights [10].

TABLE 9.5   BEDDING PLANT RESPONSE TO PHOTOPERIOD

Short day (long night)	Long day (short night)	Day neutral
African marigold[a]	African marigold[a]	Alyssum
Basil	Ageratum	Balsam
Cleome	Centaurea	Begonia
Cosmos	Gaillardia	Carnation
Dahlia	Gypsophila	French marigold
Morning glory	Lobelia[a]	Gomphrena
Salvia[a]	Nicotiana	Impatiens
Zinnia	Petunia[b]	Lobelia[a]
	Phlox	Pansy
	Salvia[a]	Salvia[a]
	Scabiosa	Vinca
	Snapdragon	
	Verbena	
	Viola	

[a] Response varies by cultivar.

[b] Long day between 55 and 70F (13 and 21C). Affected by temperature out of this range.

Source: Adapted from Carlson, Kaczperski, & Rowley, Bedding plants, *Introduction to floriculture.*

Some African marigolds are long-night plants, whereas others may be short-night plants. Generally, you need to provide two weeks of long nights (15 or more hours) in Stage 3 to initiate the seedlings. Otherwise, the plants will take much longer to flower, and will do so erratically after transplanting, especially later in the spring-summer season. *Zinnia elegans* is also a long-night plant, needing 15 or more hours of dark for three weeks in the plug tray to speed up bud development [10]. Lisianthus responds to short nights (less than 10 hours), particularly when grown under cooler temperatures and low light levels [15]. Asters form a rosette-type of growth when nights are longer than a critical length, developing tall stems and initiating flower buds under shorter nights [25].

A plug grower can manipulate the photoperiod in the plug tray. If longer nights are required, an opaque screen (black cloth) will be necessary. Pull the screen closed at the end of the day (usually 5 to 6 P.M.) and open at 7 to 8 A.M. It will be difficult to keep temperatures from staying high, as this is the time of year when days are long and hot. If shorter nights are required, then incandescent, fluorescent, or HID lights will be needed. Usually, a two- to four-hour night break is all that is needed to provide short nights. Many plug growers who use HID lights for supplemental lighting turn them on at the end of the day and leave them on well into the night, providing 16 to 18 hours of light. For crops that need a night break, it would be better to use fluorescent or HID lights, as these two sources have less far-red light, which causes the seedlings to elongate rapidly, than incandescent lights. (Table 9.6

TABLE 9.6   INDUCTION OF FLOWERING BY PHOTOPERIOD OF SELECTED CROPS IN PLUG TRAYS

Crop	Short nights (<10 hrs)	Long nights (>12 hrs)
African marigold		✓
Ageratum	✓	
Dahlia	✓	
Lisianthus	✓	
Lobelia	✓	
Petunia	✓	
Salvia farinacea	✓	
Salvia splendens	✓	✓
Snapdragon	✓	
Tuberous begonia	✓	
Verbena	✓	
Zinnia		✓

summarizes the photoperiod requirements of some selected bedding plants whose flowering can be initiated in the plug tray.)

LIGHT INTENSITY

A light reading, an instantaneous measurement of light intensity, can be expressed as fc or lux (measuring light wavelengths visible to the human eye) or micromoles per square meter per second (measuring photosynthetically active radiation [PAR] in the 400- to 700-nm waveband). Light intensity is the amount of light energy available to the plant at a particular moment and affects photosynthesis the most (table 9.2). Light readings should be taken in a clear area of the greenhouse and level with the bench (fig. 9.9). Readings will increase if the sensor is turned toward the sun.

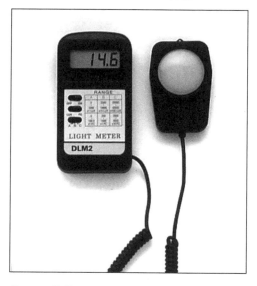

When all factors such as CO_2 level, temperature, and water are optimized for photosynthesis, optimum light intensity can be determined. If the light intensity is diminished, photosynthesis and growth slow down. If higher than optimal, growth again slows down because the intense light adversely affects photosynthesis.

Greenhouse crops are subjected to light intensities as high as 12,000 fc (129,000 lux) on clear summer days, but perhaps less than 300 fc (3,228 lux) on cloudy winter days. For most crops, neither condition is ideal. Many crops become light-saturated at 3,000 fc (32,280 lux) [25], meaning photosynthesis does not increase at higher light intensities. Of course, this is assuming that all leaves are exposed to an intensity of 3,000 fc (32,280 lux). This is rarely the case with larger plants, but it can be with small plug seedlings. Upper leaves of a larger plant cast shadows on lower leaves, thus reducing the light intensity at the lower leaves. Red light will also be absorbed by these upper leaves, while far-red light passes through to the lower leaves, resulting in a stretch signal to the plant. Fig. 9.10 shows how an individual leaf at the top of the plant may saturate at 3,000 fc (32,280 lux), while the plant as a whole may not reach light saturation until 10,000 fc (108,000 lux).

The excess radiant heat on an individual leaf after reaching light saturation (3,000 fc, 32,280 lux) will increase transpiration from the leaf until the

FIGURE 9.9 Light meter. Courtesy The Dickson Company.

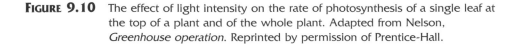

FIGURE 9.10 The effect of light intensity on the rate of photosynthesis of a single leaf at the top of a plant and of the whole plant. Adapted from Nelson, *Greenhouse operation.* Reprinted by permission of Prentice-Hall.

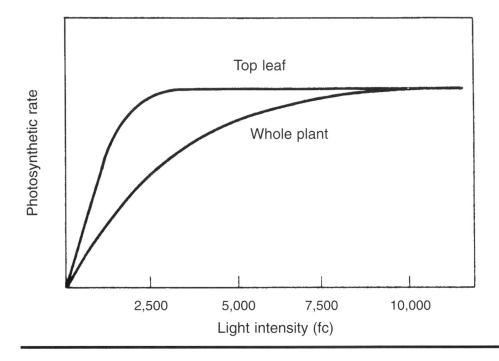

stomates close in self-protection. This stomate closing shuts down the photosynthetic process, as no CO_2 can get in, thereby stopping plant growth for the moment. On the other hand, when light intensity is low, transpiration is also low. This means that less water is being taken up through the roots and, therefore, less calcium is also taken up, since calcium is taken up by the roots only with water uptake. The net result of this process is a soft, stretched seedling with thin leaves, stems, and roots.

The shading response of the upper leaves on the lower leaves causes the plant to stretch. This shading response is eventually very strong in plug production due to the fact that seedlings are being grown at high densities, so the plant canopy becomes very crowded. You can improve light intensity with certain types of greenhouse coverings and by keeping them clean; with fewer structural supports; with proper greenhouse orientation, with no hanging baskets growing overhead (fig. 9.11); by coating metal supports with white reflective paint; and by growing in less dense plug trays, providing more space for seedlings. These techniques help all the leaves receive more of the red light.

Reducing light intensity is necessary to grow many crops through the summer season, such as pansy, primula, ranunculus, dianthus, and snapdragon. Too much radiant heat on the leaves would cause bleaching, burning, and stunting of plants, particularly young seedlings. Death may also occur if damage is severe and sud-

Figure 9.11 Hanging baskets over plug trays.

den. Therefore, many plug growers reduce light intensity either manually or automatically. The cheapest way is to spray a shading compound on the outside of the greenhouse covering. Difficulties with this method include the inability to calculate and control the amount of shading compound applied, the wearing away of the compound with rain, and not being able to daily manipulate the amount of light entering the greenhouse. This last point is particularly important when the weather is cloudy and rainy for several days, resulting in too low light levels and plugs that will stretch.

The most accurate method of reducing light intensity is automatic shading curtains, either hand- or computer-controlled. Each greenhouse zone can be set up with separate controls. Shading curtains are made for several different levels of light reduction, and some can double in winter as heat-retention curtains. The curtains could be closed for only the warmest and highest light periods of the day (such as 10 A.M. to 2 P.M.). Plants could then still receive plenty of light in the morning, late afternoon, and early evening, maximizing photosynthesis but controlling growth.

LIGHT QUANTITY

The total light a plant receives in a day is, simply, total light quantity. It is a measure of light intensity times duration, as expressed in moles per square meter per day. Light quantity affects photosynthesis, plant growth and yield, and flowering to some degree (table 9.3). Day-neutral plants flower better when the light quantity has reached a certain level. If light quantity is too high, some plug crops, such as celosia, French marigold, and larkspur, prematurely flower in the plug tray due to the stress imposed.

The growing point of seed-produced geraniums is the receptor of light energy, and that determines flower bud formation. Radiant energy is cumulative in nature, meaning seed geraniums are light accumulators. Supplemental lighting with them is most effective for initiating flower buds when started four to five weeks after sowing and continued for four weeks [19]. A growth regulator is very important to keep the leaf over the growing point small.

Light quantity ultimately affects plant growth and yield by its relationship to a plant's photosynthetic capacity. Light quantity also enters into play with the source-sink relationship [13, 14], which describes how the carbohydrate products of photosynthesis are allocated throughout the plant. The sources of the carbohydrates are the green parts of the plant, mostly the leaves. The sink is the high-priority part placing the greatest demand for the carbohydrates as building blocks and energy sources.

Under low light conditions, fewer carbohydrates are produced. To increase their amount, more photosynthesis is needed, so the shoots and immature leaves get first priority on the existing carbohydrates, with the roots getting second. Under high light conditions, more than enough carbohydrates are being produced to meet the demands of both top growth and the roots.

However, when the plant becomes reproductive, the flowers, and soon the developing seeds, take top priority, followed by shoots and, finally, roots. This source-sink distribution explains why it is so difficult to get seedlings that have flowered in the plug tray with a single stem and flower to turn vegetative again after transplanting. Most of the plant's food resources are devoted to the flowers, not the shoots or roots.

When light quantity is high, leaf temperature may get too high (greater than 90F, 32C) and shut down the photosynthetic process temporarily during the warmest times of the day. High light quantity also requires the seedling to use more nutrients. Plug growers must be aware to feed their crops more frequently when grown under high light quantity, as photosynthesis is being maximized, and provide enough water to keep the plants from wilting, as transpiration is greatly increased. More problems result, though, from growers overfeeding and overwatering plugs when light quantity is low, as in winter. The plug seedlings then become soft and stretch easily, with poorer root development.

SUPPLEMENTAL LIGHT

When light is limited during the winter season, the plants slow down all processes, particularly photosynthesis, and respond with slower growth, thinner stems, smaller leaves, and longer internodes. With supplemental lighting, plants respond with more breaks or branching, thicker stems, larger leaves, and better roots and are more compact. The end result of proper supplemental lighting is better plug quality and plants that grow faster [1].

All plants—including bedding, cut flower, and flowering pot crops—are more responsive to light when they are young. Light is usually effective once the first true leaves are visible, being the most beneficial for the first two to six weeks after the first or second true leaves are visible. Regardless of location, lighting seedlings will result in faster growth and better quality plants. Lighting for more than six weeks is of very little value to the plants and is not economical to the plug grower [1]. Crops that benefit the most from supplemental lighting for growth during the winter, tending to have one- to four-week faster crop times, include geranium, petunia, vinca, begonia, impatiens, lisianthus, and gerbera. Other crops will also benefit but may not show as great crop time reductions.

Crops receiving supplemental lighting are generally given a light period of 16 to 18 hours. This includes the time when lamps are on as well as the part of the day when it is bright enough to turn lamps off. Generally, lamps are turned off when the natural light exceeds about twice the level the lamps deliver [25]. Plants often do not grow appreciably more when lit for 24 hours compared to 16 to 18 hours [1]. A plug grower may turn on the lights at 4 P.M. and have them go off at midnight during a typical winter day.

The two best sources of supplemental greenhouse light are metal halide and HPS vapor lamps, both commonly called HID lights. Both are relatively efficient at converting electricity to visible light (20 to 25%), and both have proven effective over many years of trials. Metal halide lamps have the better light spectrum of the two, but HPS lamps are cheaper to purchase and operate. Most lamps being installed worldwide today are HPS lamps. Fluorescent lights are effective, but in order to achieve proper light intensities, so many fixtures are necessary that they block much of the natural light. Incandescent lights are useful only for low-intensity photoperiodic lighting.

The reflector is as important as the lamp because this part of the fixture is responsible for even distribution of light across the bench without hot spots and dark areas [1]. The average intensity being used today is about 400 to 500 fc (4,300 to 5,400 lux) at plant height. Lamp manufacturers and suppliers (see appendix 4) will determine for a grower the lamp height and spacing, according to the desired light intensity and configuration of the greenhouse. Expect the plant temperature to increase 2 to 5F (1 to 3C) when the lamps are on, benefiting crops such as vinca, which like it warmer to grow.

The economics of lighting depend on the location, light source, electricity cost, and crops grown. Lighting, combined with additional fertility and CO_2, will result in faster turnover and better plug quality. If the investment in lighting allows more trays to be sold from the same greenhouse space or a higher price per plug, it is worth considering. Plug growers in northern areas, in any case, need to light at least some of their plug crops through the winter.

CARBON DIOXIDE

Carbon dioxide, needed for photosynthesis (fig. 9.2), has been shown to be a limiting factor for proper plant growth and development in greenhouses during the fall, winter, and spring, when vents are normally closed to conserve heat for extended time periods. Without adequate ventilation, the CO_2 level drops below the normal (ambient) 300 ppm atmospheric level. With vents closed, the CO_2 is quickly used up during daylight hours. Plants with inadequate levels of CO_2 are put under stress from lower photosynthetic rates, resulting in poorer growth.

Research over many years has shown that elevating the CO_2 level to three to five times the ambient level will give increased yields, higher quality, and often shorter cropping times. Pansy plugs grown at elevated CO_2 concentrations could be transplanted earlier and required fewer days to flower than pansy seedlings grown at ambient CO_2 levels [3]. Similar results have been observed using CO_2 during geranium seedling development [18]. Begonia plugs that received four weeks of CO_2 under low light were ready for transplanting 10 days earlier than untreated plugs and reached flowering stage faster [2]. Impatiens plugs grown at 1,100 ppm CO_2 under 2,400 fc (25,800 lux) light were almost 50% larger (leaf area, dry weight) than the controls at ambient CO_2 [7].

As with other factors that influence photosynthesis, CO_2 levels interact with temperature, light, humidity, and nutrition. When using elevated levels of CO_2 in plug production, daytime temperature may need to be raised 5 to 10F (3 to 6C). As much light as possible should be provided. If supplemental lighting is used to extend the day, CO_2 injection can be continued until the lights go off. If light becomes limiting, not as much benefit may be gained from an elevated level of CO_2. At times when more light is available, more CO_2 will be needed. A high humidity level inside the greenhouse may reduce transpiration and influence leaf stomatal opening, which in turn regulates how much CO_2 is taken into the leaf. With higher levels of photosynthesis due to elevated CO_2, plants will require more nutrients and water. Roots and shoots develop more rapidly, along with greater leaf expansion. Plug growers will need to increase the frequency of fertilization, as much as doubling it, to keep up with the faster growth.

Since CO_2 is used during photosynthesis, which occurs only during daylight hours for most plants, additional CO_2 should be injected into the greenhouse from sunrise until one hour before sunset, or as long as the HID lights remain on. It should be injected only when the ventilation fans are off or, in the case of greenhouses cooled with vents, when the roof vents are open less than 2 inches (5 cm). Carbon dioxide cannot be injected during the warm seasons because cooling generally coincides with the daylight hours. Remember, the idea is not just to return CO_2 levels to ambient, but to maintain them at elevated levels during daylight hours. Rates most commonly used range from 600 to 1,500 ppm for plugs. Do not permit the CO_2 level to exceed 5,000 ppm, which would be dangerous to humans.

The main sources of CO_2 for greenhouse enrichment are liquid CO_2 (Liquid Carbonic, 800/299-7977) and the burning of fossil fuels, such as natural gas, kerosene, or propane. Liquid CO_2 is a clean source but usually more expensive than generating CO_2 by combustion. Larger greenhouse firms, however, find the cost of liquid CO_2 comparable to that of CO_2 generated from the combustion of fuel, but only because a large consumption volume is necessary in order to negotiate an economical, steady source of liquid CO_2 from the supplier. A rule of thumb for liquid CO_2 enrichment is that 1 lb liquid CO_2 per ft^2 per year is equivalent to 1,000 ppm.

Combustion units to generate CO_2 are either (1) an open-flame, non-vented, within-house "heater"; (2) a forced-draft, externally located, pre-cooled, CO_2-air mixture generator; or (3) highly developed systems with precombustion scrubbers to remove fuel contaminants and postcombustion absorption towers to remove products of incomplete combustion. The small, open-flame units are currently the most popular and the least expensive (Johnson Gas Appliance Co., 800/553-5422). When purchasing fuel for CO_2 generation, be sure your fuel supplier is aware that it will be used for CO_2. This will avoid delivery of batches with abnormally high sulfur content [12]. It is also important that sufficient oxygen supplies be provided to all fossil fuel burners so that noxious gases, such as ethylene and sulfur dioxide, are not produced, causing deleterious effects on plants.

Small greenhouses are generally enriched with a centrally located, small, open-flame burner (fig. 9.12). The warm CO_2 tends to diffuse readily throughout the greenhouse without circulation fans. However, fans will keep the CO_2 from rising to the roof and staying there. Larger greenhouses are enriched either by placing a number of small generating units around the greenhouse, or with a single large generating unit and a forced-air distribution system. Liquid CO_2 is stored outside the greenhouse and piped around the greenhouse through plastic tubing. Cool CO_2 from this liquid source will drop in the greenhouse and should be introduced near the tops of the plants.

Various CO_2 control systems can be used—everything from a simple time clock to a monitor-controller hooked into your environmental control computer. However, it is very important to know how much CO_2 is being injected. Simple CO_2 testers can be purchased for about $300. Levels should be sampled at the same time of day, preferably at 10 A.M. Avoid breathing close to the immediate sampling point, as human breath contains about 40,000 ppm CO_2. More sophisticated sensors are available for automatically monitoring the CO_2 level in the greenhouse and controlling the CO_2 generator. These sensors are priced in the range of $750 to $1,500. Information from these sensors can be received by an environmental control computer, which in turn controls CO_2 generation in each greenhouse.

FIGURE 9.10 Open-flame CO_2 generator. Courtesy Johnson Gas Appliance Co.

HUMIDITY

Another environmental factor that influences plant growth is humidity, which is important to the process of transpiration. Water moves out of the leaf via the stomates, evaporates, and cools the leaf surface. This movement of water out of the leaf—transpiration—forces the root system to bring more water into the plant; otherwise, wilting would occur.

Transpiration requires the stomates to be open. Stomates are open while photosynthesis is going on, as CO_2 is also taken in through the stomates. However, if the transpiration rate gets too high and water cannot easily be taken up through the roots to replace what was lost through the leaves, then the stomates will close down to protect the plant. This means that photosynthesis will stop, as no CO_2 is available in the leaves.

Factors that affect transpiration include temperature, evaporation in the greenhouse, humidity in the air, amount of watering within the greenhouse, amount of venting and air movement, and the type of greenhouse floor. At high temperatures, transpiration and evaporation increase. When plugs are grown cool, these processes slow down; therefore, the plants' water needs are lower. Warm air can hold more moisture than cool air, so humidity levels are usually higher in a greenhouse during the night than during the day. When light levels are sufficiently high for maximum photosynthesis, solid surfaces are heating up from the radiant sunlight energy and evaporation increases within the greenhouse. Evaporation occurs from the soil, leaves, containers, benches, and floors. This process will continue until the air inside the greenhouse cannot take up any more water vapor (reaching high humidity).

For plugs being grown in Florida, humidity levels are naturally high, especially during the rainy season. Plugs grown in California are subjected to much lower humidity levels, even though temperature and light levels may be similar. When plugs are watered, the humidity level soon goes up in the greenhouse. A greenhouse with a cement floor tends to be drier than one with a dirt floor. Adequate venting and air movement help remove the humidity from inside the greenhouse, providing that the humidity level outside the greenhouse is lower than inside.

The response of young seedlings to high humidity is to increase internode length (stretch), produce thin leaves and stems, have less branching, and produce fewer roots. Since transpiration is reduced at a high humidity level, water uptake is also reduced. Calcium, needed for cell wall thickness, can be taken up by the roots only through water uptake. Therefore, less calcium is taken up by the plant at a high humidity level. Plugs grown at low humidity level (such as in California) transpire more rapidly and continuously, thereby taking up more calcium and magnesium. These plugs will also close their stomates if water stress gets too great, and then plant growth is stopped. The result is shorter, more toned shoot growth and better root systems.

High humidity also affects plug growth when Stage 2 and 3 plugs are being grown in an area close to a Stage 1 fog zone or to a stationary mist system for bench germination. The higher humidity levels near these zones will cause plugs to stretch and grow faster. Benches located farther away grow slower and more toned. Be careful to keep these zones separate to control plug growth!

Syringing of plants (very light and frequent misting) is sometimes used to reduce leaf temperature during hot weather [11]. This technique will work, but has its drawbacks. First, frequent misting keeps moisture on the leaves longer, thereby promoting diseases. Second, frequent misting raises the humidity level directly around the plant, causing more stretch and soft growth. It is better to try to reduce temperature through better greenhouse cooling systems, air movement, and shade systems.

ENVIRONMENTAL CONTROLS

There are three basic levels of environmental controls: thermostat ($50 to $250); analog ($800 to $1,600); and computer ($3,000 to $50,000 or more). The main differences between these levels are the amount of control and versatility, the complexity of operation, and the expense. On-off thermostats simply switch (heat or vent) with a change in temperature. Proportioning thermostats provide a continuously variable resistance that changes with temperature [4]. It is important to place the thermostat near the center of the greenhouse and near the crop height. A sensor of this type also needs to be protected from the direct rays of the sun, which would result in inaccurate readings.

Both analog and computer controls use proportioning thermostats or electric sensors (thermistors) to gather temperature information. Analog controls use amplifiers and electronic logic (decision-making) circuitry, whereas computer controls use a microprocessor. The computer can combine inputs from a variety of sensors to make complex judgments for controlling the greenhouse environment [4].

To summarize the levels of environmental controls, thermostats regulate one piece of equipment and are available from local heating contractors. An analog temperature controller only regulates one environment and is available from companies such as Wadsworth (STEP) or Acme (Grotron). A computer typically regulates several environments using multiple sensors in each environment. They are available in North America from companies such as Wadsworth, Q-Com, Priva, and Argus (see appendix 4).

Plug growers need to make their own decisions about how much environmental control they need. If you have a small plug range, all you may need are thermostats and time clocks. However, if you have two acres or more of plug greenhouses with multiple growing zones, you need to look into environmental control computer systems. Basically, the bigger your plug range and the more complex but flexible you want the control, the more you need computers. Growers in Florida need these control systems just as much as growers in the north.

Knowing what you want to control, and how, are the keys to working with an environmental control computer system. You must understand how the system works and how to make adjustments! Some systems allow you to make more program adjustments than others. Computers can record weather data on a continuous basis, provide a permanent record of greenhouse conditions in every zone and graph them out, provide much more precise and faster control than other systems, and do it when no one is around. Environmental control computers can easily handle DIF, dehumidification cycles, CO_2 injection, shade and black cloth curtains, venting, heating to within 1F, and multiple zones at the same time. Shop around and ask a lot of questions before buying a system. Growers who already have a particular system are good references for how the system really works.

KEY POINTS TO REMEMBER

■ Temperature affects photosynthesis, respiration, enzyme activity, and uptake of water and nutrients. Shoot and root growth increases proportionally with temperature increase from 50 to 85F (10 to 29C). There is an optimal temperature for each species for maximum growth, which may not be the same for flowering. The leaf-unfolding rate is proportional to the ADT the plants are grown under when temperatures are maintained in the linear range. DIF is used to control internode length (stretch). Temperature interacts with light, CO_2, and nutrition to control plant growth.

■ Light quality affects plant morphology and is determined by the ratio of red to far-red light. Light duration, or photoperiod, controls flowering, either through short or long nights. Light intensity determines plant growth and yield through photosynthesis. The light saturation point is about 3,000 fc (32,280 lux) on the leaf for photosynthesis. Shading response (due to far-red light) causes plant stretch. Light quantity (intensity times duration) affects photosynthesis, growth and yield, and flowering of day-neutral plants. The source-sink relationship for carbohydrates from photosynthesis favors flowers and seeds first, shoots second, and roots third. HID lights, mainly using HPS lamps, are the main supplemental lighting in areas with low natural light and short days.

■ Plugs respond to higher levels of CO_2 than ambient levels (300 ppm). The suggested range for CO_2 injection is 600 to 1,200 ppm after the first true leaves appear. Increased CO_2 levels interact with temperature, light, humidity, and nutrition.

■ Humidity controls the rates of evaporation and transpiration in plants. High humidity causes plugs to stretch and be soft due to lack of calcium uptake.

■ Environmental controls for small plug greenhouses involve thermostats/time clocks or analog systems. For more than 2 acres, use environmental control computers. Know what you want to control, and how, and ask other growers how they like their systems.

REFERENCES

[1] Armitage, A.M. 1989. Let there be light. *Greenhouse Grower* 7(11):50, 52.

[2] ———. 1990. Why you should use CO_2 on plugs. *Greenhouse Grower* 8(1):60, 63.

[3] ———. 1993. CO_2 decreases plug and bench time. *Greenhouse Grower* 11(11):36, 38–39.

[4] Ball, V. 1991. Controlling the greenhouse atmosphere, from *Ball redbook*, 15th ed., Ball Publishing, Batavia, Ill.

[5] Ballare, C.L., A.L. Scopel, and R.A. Sanchez. 1995. Plant photomorphogensis in canopies, crop growth, and yield. *HortScience* 30(6):1172–1181.

[6] Carlson, W.H., M.P. Kaczperski, and E.M. Rowley. 1992. Bedding plants. In *Introduction to floriculture*. 2nd ed. San Diego: Academic Press.

[7] Dreesen, D.R., and R.W. Langhans. 1989. Maximize plug growth. *Greenhouse Grower* 7(13):74–78.

[8] Erwin, J. 1992. *Build a better plug*. Presentation given at International Plug Conference, Orlando, Fla.

[9] Erwin, J.E., and R.D. Heins. 1993. Temperature effects on bedding-plant growth. *Minnesota Commercial Flower Growers Association Bulletin* 42(3):1–10.

[10] Ewart, L.C. 1994. *Flowering out of season*. Presentation given at Ohio Floral International Short Course, July 11, Cincinnati, Ohio.

[11] Faust, J.E., S. Verlinden, and R.D. Heins. 1994. Pulsing temps at sunrise. *Greenhouse Grower* 12(1):82–85.

[12] Freeman, R. 1991. The importance of carbon dioxide. Chapter 23 in *Ball redbook*. 15th ed. ed. Vic Ball. Batavia, Ill.: Ball Publishing.

[13] Graper, D.F., and W. Healy. 1991. High pressure sodium irradiation and infrared radiation accelerate petunia seedling growth. *J. Amer. Soc. Hort. Sci.* 116(3):435–438.

[14] ———. 1992. Modification of petunia seedling carbohydrate partitioning by irradiance. *J. Amer. Soc. Hort. Sci.* 117(3):477–480.

[15] Harbaugh, B.K. 1995. Flowering of *Eustoma grandiflorum* (Raf.) Shinn. cultivars influenced by photoperiod and temperature. *HortScience* 30(7):1375–1377.

[16] Heins, R.D. 1990. Choosing the best temperature for growth and flowering—How temperatures affect plant response. *Greenhouse Grower* 8(4):57–59.

[17] Heins, R., and J. Erwin. 1990. Understanding and applying DIF. *Greenhouse Grower* 8(2):73–78.

[18] Kaczperski, M.P., and A.M. Armitage. 1993. Accelerating growth of geraniums in plugs with light and carbon dioxide. *HortScience* 28(5):520.

[19] Kaczperski, M.P., and R.D. Heins. 1995. The effect of timing and duration of supplemental irradiance on flower initiation of plug-grown seedlings. *HortScience* 30(4):760.

[20] Karlsson, M., and R. Larson. 1994. Light, temperature, and carbon dioxide. In *Bedding plants IV*. ed. E.J. Holcomb, 185–196. Batavia, Ill.: Ball Publishing.

[21] Koranski, D., and R. Kessler. 1990. News from the cutting edge of plug research. *GrowerTalks* 54(8):20–24.

[22] McMahon, P. 1995. *Controlling plant growth and flowering with light*. Presentation given at the Ohio Floral International Short Course, July 10, Cincinnati, Ohio.

[23] Moe, R. 1994. Physiological aspects of high irradiance lighting in horticulture. Third International Symposium, *Artificial Lighting in Horticulture*, January 23–27, Nordwijkerhout, the Netherlands.

[24] Moore, S.R. 1995. Filtered light has potential as growth regulator. *GrowerTalks* 59(10):62, 64.

[25] Nelson, P.V. 1991. *Greenhouse operation and management*. 4th ed. Englewood Cliffs, N.J.: Prentice Hall.

CHAPTER 10

MOISTURE MANAGEMENT

M oisture management, or watering, accounts for the greatest loss in plug production for many operations. Watering looks so easy and simple when done properly by an experienced plug grower. In many operations, however, it is also boring. Unfortunately, this job is often assigned to an inexperienced employee with little or no training. Watering at the wrong time or in the wrong way adversely affects plug crops, and the job is made harder by the number of crops that need varying amounts of water.

Water is essential in plants for many processes. Cell division and elongation depend on proper amounts of water. Imbibition and seed germination require adequate amounts to be immediately and continuously available around the seeds. Photosynthesis depends on water as a key factor in the production of carbohydrates. Nutrient uptake is regulated by water uptake. Calcium, in particular, is directly taken up by water flow into the roots. The maintenance of turgor pressure within the plant is proportional to the amount and availability of water taken up.

Plugs must never be allowed to dry completely. Saturated media, however, contains almost no oxygen (0 to 2%); therefore, cells must dry out somewhat to allow increased oxygen for optimum germination and growth. The smaller the cell size, the more vulnerable the plug is to fluctuations in moisture. Deeper plug cells provide more drainage from the media and better aeration.

The sign of a good plug grower is the ability to deliver the right amount of moisture at the right time to all plugs. In doing this job correctly every day, the plug grower can get the best germination possible from the seed lot, control growth (both roots and shoots), and reduce disease. However, watering is the hardest job to learn and teach, whether watering by hand or by boom irrigator. The discussion in this chapter will mainly focus on Stages 2 through 4, the active plug growth stages.

PLUG MEDIA AND WATER MOVEMENT

The characteristics of plug media most important for good root growth, such as WHC and AP, depend largely on soil structure and texture. Soil structure and amount of pore space depend on particle size and diversity of particle sizes. The relative amounts of capillary and noncapillary pore space (fig. 10.1) strongly affect soil drainage and aeration [3]. *Capillary pore space* consists of small pores (30 to 60 microns or less) that retain water against gravity. This determines the *field capacity* (*container capacity*), the amount of water retained in plug media after watering thoroughly. *Noncapillary pore space* is the fraction of soil volume from which water drains by gravity, providing the air space so important for good root aeration.

Water applied to the plug cell enters the pores at the top and adheres to the particle surfaces surrounding the pores. Additional water is too much for these particles to hold onto, and gravity pulls this water down to the next particles below. These particles in turn hold onto some of the water, but

FIGURE 10.1 Plug cell pore spaces and water movement.

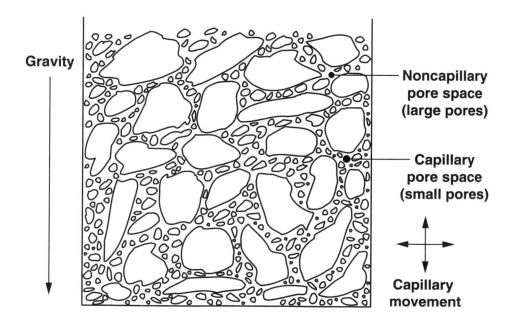

additional water then moves down to the next layer of particles. This process repeats itself until water reaches the bottom of the plug cell and flows out the drainage hole.

This downward movement of water, largely caused by gravity, depends on the rate at which water is supplied to the wetting front. Water moves rapidly through the moist soil behind the wetting front because of gravity, but very slowly into the dry soil in front of it. This sharp boundary between wet and dry soil after a partial watering of dry soil in a container can easily be seen or felt. It also explains why all the soil cannot be rewetted to a partial percentage of container capacity by the addition of a limited amount of water, because part of the soil is wetted to 100% container capacity, and part is not wetted at all [3].

This concept applies to watering dry soil in a container. When there is already some moisture throughout the whole plug cell, movement of added water is much quicker, as all particles are already covered by a water layer of some thickness. An individual particle does not need to be rewetted, but just needs its existing water layer added to. This principle is very important in watering larger plug cells (288 deep and larger) where the bottom of the cell is not totally dry and the grower does not want to saturate the plug media. Watering halfway down the container will allow the moisture to get to the bottom of the container within an hour of watering.

Water moves in this manner by *capillary action*. The small pore spaces between small particles allow water to move up and down and also across the container. This movement is much slower than gravity and not as visible. Capillary movement of water is a response to osmotic potentials, which means that water moves with a gradient from a wetter to a drier area. Upward movement of water (*capillary rise*) toward the soil surface is caused chiefly by evaporation from the surface and removal of water by roots of transpiring plants. Upward flow to an evaporating surface is about twice as rapid in a fine-textured as in a coarse-textured soil [3]. Soil water in the vicinity of the roots of rapidly transpiring plants sometimes tends to become depleted during the day because water absorption exceeds the rate of movement of water through the soil toward the roots, resulting in a water-depleted zone around them. Fortunately, the soil in this zone is usually rewetted overnight, but the rate at which this occurs depends on the hydraulic conductance of the soil. This decreases rapidly as the soil dries because the larger pores are emptied first, decreasing the cross-sectional area available for capillary water movement.

Several key factors influence water availability and movement within a plug cell (fig. 10.2). Water is removed from media by evaporation and root uptake, or absorption, which is controlled mainly by transpiration.

FIGURE 10.2   Factors influencing availability and movement of water within a plug cell.

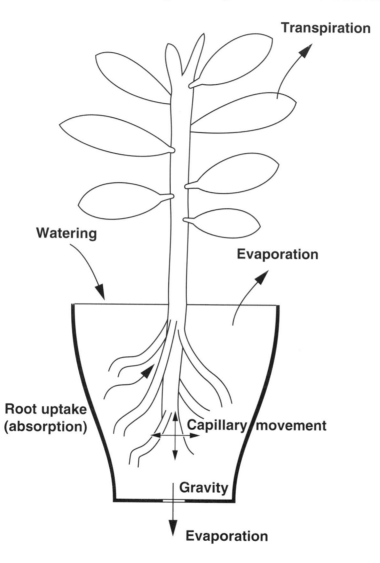

Sometimes the factors of evaporation and transpiration, as they relate to plants, are lumped together into the term *evapotranspiration.* Evaporation, the loss of water from the soil surface to the atmosphere, is controlled by environmental conditions inside the greenhouse. With increasing temperature in the soil, and particularly at the soil surface, evaporation increases. A high light level hitting the soil surface will heat it up and speed up evaporation. Root-zone heating systems also heat up the soil. Evaporation is reduced when the plant canopy forms over, and cools, the surface of the plug tray. Reduced humidity draws water out of the plug media and into the air.

Active or *osmotic absorption* occurs in slowly transpiring plants. *Passive absorption* occurs in rapidly transpiring plants, where water is pulled in through the roots, which act merely as absorbing surfaces. During transpiration, water evaporates from leaf cells, which decreases their water potential, causing water to move into them from the xylem of leaf veins. This movement continues on down to the roots, which then are required to take up more water from the soil. Passive absorption often lags quantitatively behind transpiration during the day (fig. 10.3). An absorption lag on a hot summer day can result in wilting of the plug seedling, even with moist plug media. In cool, cloudy weather, the same plant may show little stress in relatively dry soil [3].

Absorption of water also depends on the type of crop grown (cool-season, warm-season crops) and the temperature the crop is grown at (fig. 10.4). Cool soil reduces water absorption. At low temperatures, roots increasingly resist water movement through them. The reduced water absorption through cooled roots is usually accompanied by a reduction in stomatal conductance and photosynthesis, a decrease in leaf water potential, and an inhibition of leaf expansion [3].

The final piece of the water availability and movement puzzle is the plug medium itself. The WHC and air porosity of a plug mix are somewhat opposite each other. If the plug mix is too fine, it will have a high WHC but a low AP, holding more water longer but providing less air for root growth. Plug mixes containing at least three different component sizes will have enough

FIGURE 10.3 Absorption lagging behind transpiration. Sunflower supplied with water by an autoirrigator system on a hot summer day. Note the midday decrease in transpiration, probably caused by a temporary water deficit and partial closure of stomata. Adapted from Kramer & Boyer, *Water relations.*

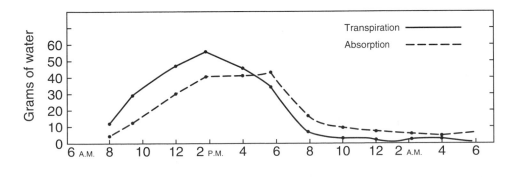

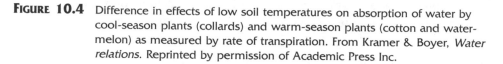

FIGURE 10.4 Difference in effects of low soil temperatures on absorption of water by cool-season plants (collards) and warm-season plants (cotton and watermelon) as measured by rate of transpiration. From Kramer & Boyer, *Water relations*. Reprinted by permission of Academic Press Inc.

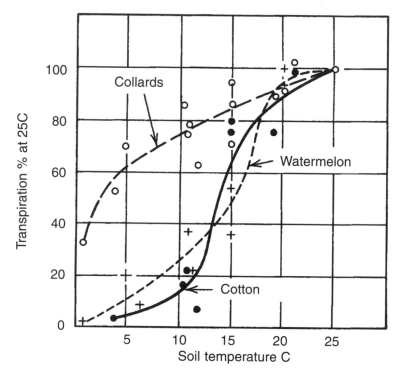

AP to grow good roots, due to a better balance between WHC and AP, or between capillary and noncapillary pore spaces. Media compaction during the tray-filling process (Stage 0) or through heavy initial watering will reduce the AP.

Due to the small container size of individual plug cells, gravity does not have much of an effect on water movement. However, with a deeper plug cell, gravity becomes more important. The taller the container, the better the media will drain (refer to fig. 7.1).

ADDING WATER TO THE PLUG MEDIA

Knowing how much water to add to plug media, when to water, and how to apply this water require considering: (1) the wide range of crops grown in plugs, (2) different environments, (3) different sizes of plug trays, and (4) different stages of growth. Complicating this picture is many plug growers' need to water by hand, which requires careful training. Automatic watering systems, either mist nozzles, sprinklers, or boom irrigators, can allow a grower to water more crops faster than by hand, but one must make sure plug quality is not sacrificed in the pursuit of labor savings.

Generally, in Stage 1 most crops require uniformly high moisture levels for best germination (fig. 10.5). Once radicle emergence occurs, the moisture level should be reduced for many crops (Stage 2). This means that a slight color change from surface drying can become visible before you apply more moisture. By allowing the soil surface to dry out slightly, the roots will tend to go down into the media. Early hypocotyl stretch can be minimized by reducing moisture levels during this stage for crops such as snapdragon, tomato, cabbage, pansy, and impatiens.

Once crops enter Stage 3, germination is finished, and leaves and roots are actively growing. Moisture levels are lower, on the average, with wider swings between wet and dry conditions (fig. 10.5). To tone the plug crop or hold it past transplant date (Stage 4), seedlings are allowed to dry out further—to the point of wilting, in some cases—before watering. Notice how the alternating wet/dry pattern increases in depth with advancing growth stages. This pattern will produce the best root growth with the greatest control of shoot growth for most all crops.

FIGURE 10.5   Variations in moisture levels by plug stage.

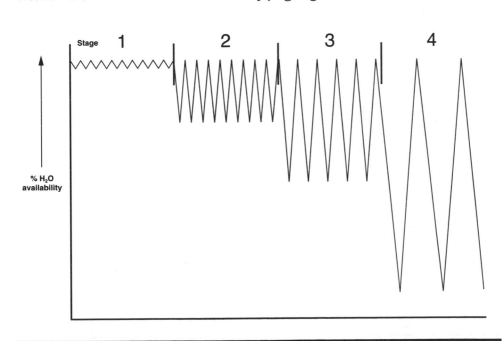

Some crops, however, are exceptions to this pattern. A begonia seedling in Stage 2 and early Stage 3 has a very shallow and fibrous root system (fig. 10.6). The plug grower must manage the moisture level at the soil surface with close attentiveness. If surface drying occurs, the seedlings will stall out, resulting in uneven seedling growth one or two weeks later. With too much moisture, algae growth will increase, and nutrients will leach in that top layer, also resulting in stalled and uneven growth. On the other hand, a lisianthus seedling at the same stage of development sends its roots down deep quickly (fig. 10.6). Therefore, the plug grower needs to manage not the surface layer of the plug media, but the whole plug cell. More surface drying can occur for lisianthus, which will control algae development. Too many plug growers treat these two crops the same way during critical plug stages, with poor results for one or both.

Other crops cannot be dried down as much in Stages 3 and 4 (table 10.1). Sensitive crops wilt easily upon nearing the permanent wilting point (PWP), where there is no more available water for the roots to take up. Once these crops wilt, they will not recover with additional watering; other crops, such as impatiens and many vegetables, will recover sufficiently with a thorough watering. Celosia is not only sensitive to wilting but will prematurely flower in the plug tray with moisture stress. Geraniums will produce reddish lower leaves, have uneven growth, and lose some roots when dried to PWP (Color plate #60). This result is common near the edges of geranium plug trays. Salvia (splendens type) cotyledons will yellow and drop off quickly under moisture stress. All the crops in table 10.1 should be monitored more closely for moisture stress than other plug crops.

Many plug growers water some or all their plugs by hand. Due to the plant density, the high cost of hand-watering is spread out over many seedlings. Hand-watering can be done at any plug stage, but different watering nozzles

FIGURE 10.6   Differences in root system in Stage 2 and early Stage 3 between begonia and lisianthus.

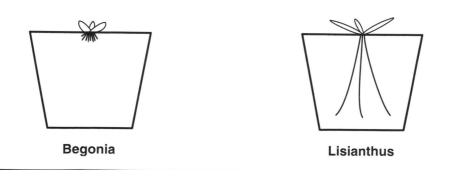

Begonia   **Lisianthus**

TABLE 10.1 CROPS SENSITIVE TO WILTING IN STAGES 3 AND 4

Ageratum	Pansy
Browallia	Phlox
Celosia [a]	Primula
Geranium [b]	Salvia [c]
Lettuce	Viola

[a] Also causes premature flowering in plug tray
[b] Causes reddish lower leaves, stunting, loss of roots, and fewer flowers
[c] Causes cotyledons to become yellow and drop off

and techniques are needed. For watering small-seeded crops in Stages 1 and 2, such as begonia, a grower should use a fine-mist nozzle, such as a Fogg-It nozzle (see appendix 4 for suppliers). This nozzle puts out a fine mist particle in the range of 50 to 100 microns, which keeps from flooding the small seeds or blowing them away. Some plug growers combine two or three Fogg-It nozzles onto a mini-boom made of PVC pipe to cover more territory quicker (fig. 10.7). Larger-seeded crops and covered crops can be watered with a coarser stream, but not so high of a volume that the plug trays wash out, flood over,

FIGURE 10.7 Mini-boom of Fogg-It nozzles for germination area.

or get too much water (fig. 10.8). Coarser-drop nozzles include Gardena, Wonder Wand, and Dramm. For watering larger plug trays and larger seedlings in Stages 3 and 4, a plug grower can use higher capacity nozzles— commonly called breaker, soaker, or shower-head nozzles (fig. 10.9)— which are the most common nozzles available for hand-watering in the greenhouse business.

No matter what nozzle is used for hand-watering, successful technique depends entirely on how well the plug grower is trained in the art of watering. Proper coverage of all trays, especially at the edges, is necessary no matter the benching system. The plug grower must know how much water to give different crops at different stages of growth, even if all these crops are growing in the same greenhouse at the same time. Also, daily adjustments must be made for changes in the weather and other conditions! When germi-

FIGURE 10.8 Gardena nozzle.

nating on the bench, adjustments must be made several times a day if the weather is warm and sunny. It is not uncommon to use a Fogg-It nozzle on germinating impatiens and begonia plug trays three times or more a day, just to be able to keep the surface layer at the optimum moisture level.

Adjustments also need to be made for different plug cell sizes. Many operations grow more than one plug size at the same time, especially if the plugs are sold. The proper moisture level for a 512 tray is different than that for a 128 tray. Generally, the bigger the plug cell size, the less attention the cell needs for watering, especially during Stages 3 and 4. Many growers provide proper moisture to small-celled trays (800 trays) but then overwater large-celled trays (128 trays), or vice versa. The large-celled trays may take two to four times as long to dry out as the small-celled trays. This drying out includes surface drying, as

FIGURE 10.9 Dramm soaker nozzle. Courtesy Dramm Corp.

more water is available through capillary action to replace moisture lost due to evaporation in the large-celled trays.

Some plug operations utilize *stationary mist systems* for moisture management, mainly during Stages 1 and 2 on the greenhouse bench. Such mist systems are usually mounted on risers coming up from the bench, with proper overlap between mist nozzles (fig. 10.10); Dramm mist nozzles are frequently used. Stationary mist systems can also be installed overhead and used for Stages 3 and 4 as needed—generally, on weekends, when

FIGURE 10.10 Stationary mist system for bench germination.

less help is available, and when the weather is warm and dry and the grower cannot keep up with the watering. A mist system can be controlled with an automatic timer or manual switch. Mist particles range from 50 to 400 microns in size, depending on the type of nozzle used.

Boom irrigation systems have been developed based on outdoor growing technology. On the most basic level, a boom is a pipe with several nozzles that is held above the bench or floor to water the crop. Differences between boom systems include motor size, type of hose reel, the way the boom is moved from bay to bay, and the different commands the boom can follow (see appendix 4 for list of suppliers).

The greatest thing boom irrigation has to offer is uniformity. The consistent watering and fertilizing helps to produce a high-quality product. This is particularly critical if you are growing plugs. The range of nozzles available lets you control the amount of mist and irrigation during germination and later growth stages (fig. 10.11).

With this consistency in watering and fertilizing comes long-term cost savings. Manufacturers estimate that booms use 40% less water than hand-watering and 25% less than upright

FIGURE 10.11 Watering boom.

sprinklers [2]. Growing space is gained by eliminating the wide aisles previously needed for hand-watering. Labor savings are perhaps the greatest advantage of automated watering booms. Booms are also faster than hand-watering. Booms can apply insecticides, fungicides, and growth regulators and are adaptable to a wide range of greenhouse sizes. The more area you have one boom cover, the faster the return on your investment.

While boom irrigators are becoming more popular and, in many cases, more necessary for large-scale plug production, they cannot handle all watering duties for most operations. Spot-watering in late Stage 2 and Stages 3 and 4 still needs to be done by hand, with a grower pulling a hose along the bench and touching up small areas and edges of trays that are drier than the rest. When many different crops are grown in the same greenhouse and bench area, boom irrigators are less effective. The constant adjustments for different crops, stages of development, and tray sizes may be made easier by a plug grower well trained in hand-watering than by a boom irrigator. Of course, computerized boom irrigators can now handle many of these tasks, but it still takes an expert plug grower to walk the crop and program the boom irrigator as to what to water, when, and how much.

CONTROLLING MOISTURE

A grower should look at several factors in determining which plug trays need water and which are moist enough. For trays that are not covered, a slight change in surface color from darker to lighter indicates that the surface is drying out. This sign is especially important in the germination stages (1 and 2). When trays are covered with coarse vermiculite, a slightly lighter color will again indicate a need for more moisture. Touching the surface and pushing your finger into the media will also tell you how much moisture there is in the plug cell. With a deeper plug cell, you may need to dig down to find out if the bottom half of the cell has moisture in it before watering. Picking up a tray with one hand is a good way of determining moisture level by weight. Know the weight differences between the different plug sizes and moisture levels (wet, medium, dry). The timing of the last irrigation can also be used as an indicator of when to water. Look at the bottom of the trays to see if the medium is dry.

The plants themselves are good indicators of how much moisture is available because they integrate the atmospheric and soil factors that affect plant water status. Early indicators of plant water deficit are changes in leaf color (begonia), wilting or flagging of leaves (impatiens, tomato), leaf angle (pepper, lettuce), and leaf rolling (ageratum, hypoestes). As mentioned previously, some crops should not be allowed to show symptoms of wilt before watering, as permanent damage can occur (table 10.1). Plants will also show symptoms of overwatering. Tall, soft shoots with thin, big leaves and poor root systems are good indicators of too frequent watering. So is the widespread presence of diseases, such as root rot and *Botrytis.*

Controlling moisture levels for plug growing also takes a thorough understanding of the interactions of moisture with temperature, light, humidity, and nutrition:

- Higher temperature and light levels cause faster evaporation and transpiration, thereby resulting in plug cells drying out faster.

- When greenhouse humidity is high due to cool, cloudy weather or poor ventilation, plug trays dry out slowly. Photosynthesis will still be active, and the plug seedlings will probably stretch if too much moisture is available.

- Adjust fertilizer levels according to how much leaching is occurring with each watering, whether clear water is being applied and how often between feedings, and what type of fertilizer is being used.

- When the plug seedlings have well-developed root systems (Stage 4), more water will be taken up quicker; therefore, the plug trays will dry out faster than expected. Put this situation together with warm, sunny weather, and these plugs will wilt almost every day.

Probably the greatest problem in growing plugs is to decide which of your growers are "wet" growers and which are "dry" growers, then to change their practices to make all plug growers in an operation water the same way. Wet growers typically water too frequently without allowing some drying to take place. Many of them are scared of those tiny plugs wilting to death! Recognizing wet growers is not so much looking at how much water they apply at one time, but at how frequently they apply it. Plugs tend to be soft and stretched, with poor root systems and a lack of root hairs. Often, more fungicides are needed to control damping-off, root rots, *Botrytis,* and leaf spots.

Dry growers typically wait until the last minute to water plug seedlings. Many of them are scared of overwatering plugs. They may or may not water plug cells all the way through with clear water. Edges of plug trays may suffer from permanent wilting. Germination may be reduced in some cases due to lack of moisture. Plug seedlings tend to be short and toned, with less disease and better root systems and root hairs.

If your plug-growing operation has several growers, some who are wet and some who are dry, what should you do to get everyone watering the same way? Generally, it is better to be more dry, depending on the crop needs. However, remember that dry growers can go too far and lose germination and plants by not watering soon enough. Most inexperienced plug growers start out as wet growers and, after better training and experience, may become dry growers. But how can you get wet growers to change their habits? Try to get them to dry out and wilt plants in the center of plug trays, not the edges. They may lose a few plants or trays, but don't yell at them for this result. Once they recognize how far they can control moisture before the plant dies, they know how much water will be needed. Anyone can kill plants around the edges of a plug tray! Controlling the moisture in the center of the tray is the hard part, whether watering by hand or with a boom.

In Stages 1 and 2, the bottom half of the plug cell is never allowed to dry out. Moisture management is done on the top half of the cell, where the seed will germinate and the developing seedling emerges. In Stages 3 and 4, moisture management is done throughout the whole plug cell, with emphasis on how much moisture is available in the bottom half of the cell. As shown in Figure 10.5, cycles of alternate wet/dry periods are needed in these latter two stages for best root development. Plug growers can achieve this moisture cycle by watering through the cell to achieve about 10% leaching. When fertilizing or drenching with fungicides, thorough watering is a necessity. When watering with clear water, most times the watering is through the cell.

However, there may be times when watering halfway down the cell is appropriate: (1) weather change from sunny to cool and cloudy, (2) very high greenhouse humidity level, (3) some capillary moisture still available in the bottom half of the plug cell, or (4) setting up the plug seedlings to be fertilized the next morning. Growers in warm climates very effectively use this halfway-watering technique to control seedling stretch. However, it requires more attention by the grower and proper knowledge of just how much water is enough.

EFFECTS OF WATERING ON PLANTS

When water is not applied frequently enough, plants wilt, thus retarding photosynthesis and growth. The elongation of young, developing cells is reduced, resulting in smaller leaves, shorter stem internodes, and a hardened appearance to the plants. In more extreme cases, marginal leaf burning may appear and spread inward, affecting whole leaves [4]. Root tips may also be burned off in geranium, pansy, and impatiens. The soluble salts around the roots increases three to four times under severe moisture stress. Sometimes, plants will drop their cotyledons or lower leaves (salvia, pepper). In some crops (begonia, impatiens), plant stands are reduced due to low moisture levels during Stages 1 and 2. Overall, plants are shorter and more toned with better root systems when moisture stress is used effectively.

When water is applied a little too frequently, new growth may become large but soft as a result of high water content. Plants tend to stretch and be taller. These plants will also wilt easily under bright light or dry conditions, and they do not ship or hold well. If water is supplied even more frequently, plug media air porosity is reduced, resulting in root damage. A damaged root system cannot readily take up water or nutrients. In addition, root rot and damping-off diseases become more prevalent. *Botrytis* and various leaf spots will cause problems with certain crops, resulting in more fungicide usage. Reduced plant stands in such crops as verbena, vinca, dahlia, and portulaca will occur due to too much moisture during Stages 1 and 2. To control plant height, more growth regulators will be needed. Overall, plants will be taller, softer, have poorer root systems, and more diseases when too much moisture is applied over time.

As Allen Hammer [1] states, "Watering is one of the most important tasks in the greenhouse, and it should not be assigned to the least experienced person in your operation. A great deal of knowledge and experience are required to manage watering. The grower must recognize the interaction between plant, root medium, and environment, and be able to manipulate each factor to produce the desired results. As a grower, you are managing a plant growing system, not just a root medium. If we take this approach, we will have fewer watering problems." Have growers who are in charge of watering visit other operations to get the fine points on how one should water plugs. The fine art of watering cannot be totally communicated by spoken or written word, but through example you can learn the correct process.

KEY POINTS TO REMEMBER

- Water moves in plug media through pore spaces by gravity and capillary action. Gravity has little effect on small plugs. Capillary action is a slower process than gravity.

- Water moves out of plug media through evaporation and root absorption. Transpiration ultimately controls the uptake by roots.

- Temperature, light levels, humidity, and the physical characteristics of the plug media all interact with movement of water in and out of the plug cell.

- Plugs can be watered by hand, by mist systems, by boom irrigators, or by any combination of these methods. Moisture should be added based on type of crop, growth stage, tray size, and environment.

- Being a dry grower is usually better for controlling plug growth than being a wet grower.

- Moisture management is the key to growing plugs successfully!

References

[1] Hammer, P.A. 1994. Watering. *GrowerTalks* 58(7):78.

[2] Kelley, M.K. 1995. Boom irrigation basics and buyer's guide. *GrowerTalks* 58(11):48, 50.

[3] Kramer, P.J., and J.S. Boyer. 1995. *Water relations of plants and soils.* San Diego: Academic Press.

[4] Nelson, P.V. 1991. *Greenhouse operation and management.* 4th ed. Englewood Cliffs, N.J.: Prentice Hall.

CHAPTER 11

FERTILIZERS AND NUTRITION

We discussed the importance of certain nutrients for plug growth in previous chapters, as well as the role of substrate pH on the availability of these nutrients. In this chapter we will discuss the third part of the nutrition triangle, the role of water-soluble fertilizers applied postplanting.

Fertilization is difficult for crops grown in plugs. The very small containers (the cells in the trays) leach very quickly, media pH changes rapidly, and salts can build up and damage the root systems of tender seedlings. No single fertilizer scheme covers all species of plug crops grown. Even within a single crop, fertilizer rate and formulation must be altered according to growth stage, desired growth rate, and shifts in substrate pH. When only one crop, such as tomato, is being grown in a greenhouse, fertilizing is less of a problem. When a grower has 200 or more varieties of bedding plants in different plug sizes and at different stages of growth, the fertilizer program becomes complicated.

So, why not just feed with one type of fertilizer and be done with it? After all, that's how seedling flats were grown for years. The problems with applying this philosophy relate to three factors: nutrient availability, the nutrient balance, and controlling plant growth with nutrients on a daily basis. Nutrient availability is determined by media pH. For soilless mixes, all nutrients are generally available between pH 5.5 and 6.5. However, in a small plug cell, media pH is not constant, influenced by the water alkalinity, limestone in the media, the type of fertilizer, and the plant itself. These small plug cells have little buffering ability, partly due to the small cell size, small particle size, and the use of peat moss, which has less buffering

193

ability than soil. If just one fertilizer is used, some nutrients may become excessive, and some may become deficient.

In the past, seedling mixes had a high starter charge, with enough limestone and phosphorus (P) added to feed the plants until transplanting, which was done earlier than with plugs. Now commercial plug mixes have low starter charges, less limestone to keep pH around 5.5, and less P, meaning plugs need to be fertilized starting 10 days or so after seeding until being transplanted. Controlling plug growth can be achieved by carefully examining what type of fertilizer to use, when, and how much.

INTERACTION OF NUTRITION WITH WATER AND MEDIA QUALITY

The fertilization program initially depends on your water and media quality. Water quality is important for three main reasons: *alkalinity, soluble salts* or *EC,* and *nutrients in the water.* Alkalinity, a measure of the water's buffering capacity, is more important than the water pH. The more alkaline the irrigation water, the more bicarbonates there are to consume hydrogen ions in the substrate and, consequently, the higher the pH level will become in the substrate. Adding alkaline water to a plug crop is equivalent to applying limestone. Acid can be used to help neutralize a high alkalinity level in irrigation water. The soluble salt content of the water should not be greater than 0.75 mmhos. Soluble salts, cumulative between water, media, and fertilizer, will hinder root development and promote root rot. The amounts of nutrients in the water should also be considered (table 6.3).

Media quality also contributes to pH control, soluble salts, and nutrient levels. In peat-based soilless mixes, the pH is initially low (4.0 to 4.5) and needs to be raised by adding limestone. The particle size and amount of limestone will determine how fast the media pH moves up and stabilizes. Some plug mixes have no lime added, whereas other mixes have large amounts. Test your plug media over the first two weeks of watering to determine what the lime will do to your media. The soluble salt level should be less than 0.75 mmhos (2:1 dilution). The amount of starter fertilizer (charge) added for initial seedling development will, to a large extent, determine the soluble salt level of the plug mix. Have a reputable lab test to learn the soluble salt level and what nutrients make up the soluble salts.

The higher the CEC, the more the media holds onto nutrients, making them available for the seedling's use. Finally, the plug mix porosity will affect watering frequency and nutrient leaching. With greater air porosity, the plug mix dries out faster and therefore needs to be watered more frequently. How the plug grower applies this water will dictate the amount of leaching. A wet grower tends to water more frequently and leach more than a dry grower.

Media pH is controlled by water alkalinity and the limestone in the media. The acidic or basic reaction of the dissolved fertilizer added to the growing medium postplanting will also control media pH. The pH of peat-based soilless media needs to be between 5.5 and 6.5 for nutrients to be readily available (fig. 7.2). In soil-based mixes, the pH range should be 6.0 to 7.0. If the media pH gets out of this range, some nutrients will become unavailable to the plant, while other nutrients may become too available and be toxic to the plant.

All fertilizers are made up of soluble salts and will add to the soluble salt level of the water and media to which the young seedling roots are exposed. If the total soluble salt level is too low (less than 0.5 mmhos, 2:1 dilution), there is not enough feed to make the seedling grow. If the total soluble salt level is high (greater than 1.5 mmhos, 2:1 dilution), the seedling may grow too much. With even higher soluble salt levels, root growth is inhibited, and total plant growth becomes affected. It is important to know how much fertilizer is being delivered to the plug each time and what the total soluble salt level is in the media. The most important reason for using fertilizers is to add nutrients that the seedling needs and at the right times. The water and media may already be providing some of them. The feeding program needs to provide the rest.

POSTPLANTING FERTILIZATION

INDIVIDUAL NUTRIENTS

Nitrogen. Nitrogen (N) is used by the plant for amino acids, proteins, enzymes, and chlorophyll. There are three forms of N in fertilizers: nitrate nitrogen (NO_3^-), ammonium or ammoniacal nitrogen (NH_4^+); and urea (NH_2-CO-NH_2). Urea is considered to be the same as NH_4, since urea needs to be converted to NH_4 to be assimilated by plants. The NO_3 form is readily taken up by roots, is very mobile within the plant, and can be stored within the plant at high levels with no toxicity. However, for NO_3 to be used inside the plant, it must be reduced (through nitrate reduction) to ammonia (NH_3). Some NH_4 can be taken up directly by roots, but most of it needs to be changed to NO_3 by bacteria in the soil before root uptake can occur. This bacterial conversion of NH_4 to NO_3 is dependent on soil temperature and soil pH. Cool temperatures (less than 60F, 15C) and low soil pH (less than 5.5) significantly reduce the conversion, and NH_4 toxicity can occur. Most of the

NH_4 taken up directly by roots has to be incorporated into organic compounds in the roots. Plants can store NH_4 only at low levels without suffering from toxicity [6].

For a given species, the proportion of NO_3 reduced in the roots increases with temperature and plant age. The uptake rate of the accompanying cation also affects this proportion. With K as the accompanying cation, translocation of both K and NO_3 to the shoots is rapid; correspondingly, NO_3 reduction in the roots is relatively low. In contrast, when Ca is the accompanying cation, NO_3 reduction in the roots is considerably higher [6]. This means that when Ca accompanies NO_3, the roots get more of it to use themselves, resulting in greater root dry weight. When K accompanies NO_3, the shoots get more to use than the roots, resulting in greater shoot dry weight.

When total N content increases, storage carbohydrates decrease, but the content of lignin (a component of cell walls) increases. High N levels compete with K (2N:1K), which is important in sucrose loading in the phloem of plants. High NH_4 levels (greater than 10 ppm) will inhibit uptake of Ca and copper (Cu) (table 11.1). The plant will correspondingly have faster shoot growth than root growth, thinner leaves and stems, and dark green color when NH_4 inhibits Ca uptake.

TABLE 11.1   NUTRIENT INCOMPATIBILITY

Excessive	Inhibited
N	K
NH_4	Ca, Cu
K	N, Ca, Mg
P	Cu, Fe, Zn, B
Ca	Mg, B
Mg	Ca
Na	Ca, K, Mg
Mn	Fe, Mo
Fe	Mn
Zn	Mn, Fe
Cu	Mn, Fe, Mo

Nitrogen deficiency is not difficult to detect. The green chlorophyll pigmentation fades to a lighter green and eventually to a yellow color (chlorosis). The telltale sign is the development of chlorosis in the older leaves (Color plate 36) because N is a mobile element. Some bedding plants that normally develop red or bronze pigmentation, such as amaranthus, celosia, coleus, and begonia, develop a light red color, even pink, rather than their normal deep red or bronze color when N is deficient. Marigolds may develop an abnormal red color or red spots across the lower leaves, and the overall plant is stunted [8].

The symptoms of NH_4 toxicity for petunias consist of chlorosis along the margins of the older leaves as well as the rolling up of the margins of these leaves (Color plate 37). Geraniums exhibit interveinal chlorosis of older leaves, with a red discoloration developing within the chlorotic area. For crops in general, the sequence of NH_4 toxicity symptoms starts with a wilted appearance of older leaves, even though these leaves remain turgid (not wilted). Affected leaves become thickened and leathery. Chlorosis develops in older leaves. In some species, it can be interveinal, but in many it is very irregular and does not fit a pattern. Necrosis soon follows chlorosis on the older leaves. All symptoms progress up the plant from older to younger leaves. Root tips also are killed from high levels of NH_4. Often, reddish brown color goes along with the death of root tips [8]. Coleus, cosmos, geranium, petunia, salvia, and zinnia are bedding plants that are particularly susceptible to NH_4 toxicity.

To correct problems with N deficiency, fertilize with a N fertilizer on a regular basis, depending on the crop and growth stage. Constant feed (with each watering) or an increase in concentration (ppm) may be needed to get plants going again. Keep media soluble salts between 0.5 and 1.2 mmhos (2:1 dilution). High light (more than 3,000 fc, 32,280 lux) and high temperatures (more than 75F, 24C) will decrease available N levels quickly. Make sure the roots are growing and healthy looking for N to be taken up into the plant.

To correct problems with NH_4 toxicity, keep soil temperatures greater than 65F (18C) when using fertilizers with NH_4 or urea in them. Keep soil pH levels above 5.5 for NH_4 conversion to NO_3 to occur [7]. Reduce the amount of NH_4 in the fertilizer program by substituting the NO_3 form, reducing concentration and frequency, and leaching. Ammonium toxicity is a greater problem in the winter than in the summer, and more so in northern regions than in southern.

Potassium. The most versatile and necessary plant nutrient is potassium (K). It is important in cell elongation, protein synthesis, enzyme activation, and photosynthesis. Potassium functions as a carrier across cell membranes for other nutrients and carbohydrates. As a carrier, it is responsible for sucrose loading in the phloem of plants, whereby photosynthates are transported from leaves to flowers, seeds, fruits, and roots. Potassium plays a major role in contributing to osmotic potential of cells and tissues (turgor).

It functions in the opening and closing of leaf stomates due to changes in turgor pressure (accompanying photosynthesis). Plants withstand drought stress with less decrease in photosynthesis at high K levels [6].

Uptake of K is highly selective and closely coupled to the plant's metabolic activity. Potassium is highly mobile in plants at all levels. Potassium is needed in plants at the same level as N and Ca. Potassium-deficient plants are more susceptible to frost damage and fungal attacks [6].

The first sign of K deficiency is the development of chlorosis along the margins of older leaves. For some species, such as tomato, it may start as large yellow (chlorotic) spots across older leaves. This chlorosis quickly gives way to necrosis. This transition occurs so rapidly that chlorosis is often unnoticed. For most species, the necrosis occurs along the leaf margin, particularly at the leaf points (Color plate 38). For species that form chlorotic spots across the leaf, necrosis will show up in these same spots. These symptoms progress from leaf to leaf up the plant [8].

One problem with some bedding plants that form red pigmentation, such as coleus, begonia, and celosia, is that both N and K deficiencies cause an abnormal, pale red discoloration or pink color on these lower leaves. Marigolds and salvia exhibit yellow-orange spots on the lower leaves along the edge. Marigolds can also develop very short leaf petioles, and the lower leaves may curl down. A very bushy-looking marigold plant results from K deficiency. These distortions almost resemble a 2,4-D injury; however, the symptoms start at the base of the plant for K deficiency, rather than at the top [8].

To correct K deficiency, make sure K levels are approximately the same as N and Ca by providing a balanced fertilizer program. Potassium is very leachable and must continually be replaced with the feed program. High levels of N (2N:1K) and Na will inhibit K uptake (table 11.1). Check your water quality for Na levels (keep under 40 ppm). If K becomes excessive, it will inhibit uptake of N, Ca, and Mg. Under conditions of cool, cloudy weather, K will be taken up more than Ca, and an imbalance can result.

Phosphorus. An adequate phosphorus (P) supply is important for root system development, rapid shoot growth, and flower quality. Phosphorus is easily taken up by the roots and can be stored in the plant. The biggest role P plays is in the energy compounds, such as ATP, that the plant needs for synthesis and degradation [6].

Generally, in greenhouse crops, growers tend to overfertilize with P (Color plate 39). Phosphorus is only needed at one fifth to one tenth the quantity of N and K. On the other hand, P can be very leachable in soilless mixes. Marconi and Nelson [5] showed that P does not leach in soil-based mixes, but will leach almost 40% more in peat-based soilless mixes. Much of the P can be supplied preplant by means of superphosphate (0-20-0), which contains 50% gypsum (calcium sulfate), or treble superphosphate (0-44-0), which does not contain gypsum. Generally, regular superphosphate is available as a powder, while treble superphosphate is a coarse prill. The former is more desirable for plug mixes and trays because there is a better chance that a uniform amount will be distributed into each tiny plug cell [7].

With the frequent waterings that plug trays receive, coupled with the low CEC of the plug mixes, P will need to be supplemented with the feed program at low rates. A grower using phosphoric acid to neutralize water alkalinity will not need to add any more P, as 10 fl oz of 85% phosphoric acid per 1,000 gal of water supplies 36 ppm P. This amount of phosphoric acid will neutralize about 90 ppm or 1.5 meq/l alkalinity.

Uptake of P by the root system is greatly reduced under cool soil temperatures (less than 55F, 13C) or high media pH (greater than 6.5). Raising the soil temperature 5F (3C) or lowering the media pH to less than 6.5 will enable the plants to grow out of this condition more easily than will the addition of more P. An excessive P level may reduce the ability of a plant to take up and utilize several of the micronutrients (table 11.1).

The symptoms of P deficiency begin with darker green foliage color than normal and stunting of top growth, which eventually becomes very severe. These symptoms make P deficiency difficult to detect unless there are normal plants nearby to compare with. The next symptom in many species, such as tomato, is purple pigmentation of older leaves, particularly on the undersides. A few species do not form this color. Chlorosis on older leaves occurs next, followed after some time by necrosis of older leaves. These symptoms progress up the plant. Bedding plants that have red pigmentation tend to form more of a purple burn on older leaves. Marigolds develop red pigmentation on the margins of the older leaves [8].

To correct P deficiency, supplement the feed program with 20-10-20 or similar fertilizers that contain some P. Staying on a feed program with 13-2-13 or 14-0-14 will not provide enough P to some crops in certain environments (high temperature or high light). Determine how much P is in your plug mix in the beginning with a lab soil test. Keep media pH 5.5 to 6.5 for best availability. Make sure soil temperatures are warm enough for the roots to take up P. Consider using phosphoric acid if you need to neutralize a high alkalinity level in your water and need a source of P.

Calcium. Calcium (Ca) is very much involved in cell walls, membrane stability (plasma membrane), cell division, and cell extension (elongation). Calcium improves the plant's resistance to fungal and bacterial infections through its involvement in the cell wall and the plasma membrane. It also serves as a messenger in signal conduction between environmental factors and plant responses for growth and development [6].

Calcium uptake is very much dependent on water flow into the roots and through the plant. Since Ca moves almost exclusively through the xylem, its uptake is affected by low root temperature and by restricted water movement through the plant, due to dryness or salinity in the media or to excessive atmospheric humidity [14]. When plants are transpiring, more water is taken up, and thus more Ca is taken up. When the weather is cool and cloudy, transpiration is greatly reduced, as are water flow and Ca uptake.

Availability of Ca for plant uptake is also dependent on the growing media pH and levels of other cations present, especially K, Na, Mg, P, and NH_4 (table 11.1). Calcium becomes less available when the media pH is less than 5.5 in a peat-based soilless mix. For some crops, such as geranium, marigold, impatiens, and lisianthus, the pH needs to be at 6.0 for Ca to be taken up and for micronutrients not to be excessively taken up. At high media pH (greater than 6.5), Ca becomes too available and inhibits other nutrients, such as Mg and B.

Generally, enough Ca is available from the water and the media. High-alkalinity water usually contains $CaCO_3$. Limestone or dolomitic limestone (containing Ca and Mg) is added to peat-based soilless mixes to bring the media pH up to 5.5. This limestone will release Ca over a period of time (two to four weeks) for the seedling to use. The rate of limestone use varies with the quality of the peat moss and differs from one company to another. Some plug mixes have no limestone added! For growers making their own plug media, incorporation of dolomitic limestone is a must. Gypsum can also be added to supply Ca and SO_4 without affecting the media pH; it also helps compete against Na.

Calcium is not mobile within the plant; therefore, Ca deficiency will first show up at the top of the plant (Color plate 40). Margins of young leaves fail to form, sometimes yielding strap leaves. The growing point ceases to develop, leaving a blunt end. Light green color or uneven chlorosis of young tissue develops. Root growth is reduced in that roots are short, thickened, and without root hairs [8]. Calcium deficiency shows up readily on poinsettia cuttings, petunia, pansy, begonia, and marigold.

To correct Ca deficiency, incorporate $Ca(NO_3)_2$ into your fertilizer program. Check to make sure media pH is 5.5 or higher. High levels of competing cations will inhibit Ca uptake; maintain a balance of 1N:1K:1Ca:1/2Mg. Sodium levels should be lower than 40 ppm. Check the soil temperature to make sure the roots can take up Ca. High relative humidity inside the greenhouse will keep plants from taking up Ca but not

K. Improve air movement and dehumidify the greenhouse periodically to improve transpiration of plug seedlings.

Magnesium. The main function of magnesium (Mg) in plants is as the central mineral in the chlorophyll molecule, necessary for photosynthesis.

Low pH levels (lower than 5.5 in peat-based soilless mixes) tie up Mg. The rate of uptake of Mg by the roots is strongly depressed by other cations, such as K, Ca, Mn, Na, and NH_4 (table 11.1). Some soilless mixes are low in available Mg unless the pH has been adjusted with dolomitic lime, which contains Ca and Mg. Growth media containing vermiculite usually have adequate Mg levels, since vermiculite naturally contains Mg [13]. Geraniums will need more Mg than the vermiculite can supply. A high level of Mg will inhibit uptake of Ca (table 11.1); keep the Mg levels to half of the Ca level.

Magnesium deficiency symptoms begin at the base of the plant and progress upward. Yellowing and interveinal chlorosis of recently mature or older leaves is the main symptom [8] (Color plate 41). Plants may generally look pale in color, and some plants will show chlorosis up to immature leaves. To correct Mg deficiency, test your water and media to determine how much Mg is available from these two sources. If making up your own plug mix, incorporate dolomitic limestone as your lime source. Use Mg-containing fertilizers (1.0% or higher), such as 14-0-14 or 13-2-13-6-3, in your feed program. Using 15-0-15 will not help, as it contains no Mg. Magnesium sulfate (Epsom salts) can be drenched at 1 lb per 100 gal of water every four weeks (table 11.2). When injecting magnesium sulfate into the watering system, do not mix it with any other material unless you are sure it does not contain Ca or P, as a precipitate would form and clog up the injector.

Sulfur. Plants require significant amounts of sulfur (S), as much as P, for optimum growth [10]. There is a balance between N and S. Without enough S, a plant cannot efficiently use N and other nutrients to reach its full yield and quality potential. For optimum growth, plants require about 1 part S for every 10 parts N. A level of 20 ppm S or more is sufficient [10, 11].

Plants take up S as sulfate (SO_4^-). Sulfate is readily soluble and subject to loss by leaching [10]. Irrigation water can be a good S source, but natural S levels in water vary greatly by location. If water smells like rotten eggs, it may have dissolved sulfide. Sulfides, produced under waterlogged conditions, such as found in drainage ponds, are toxic to plants! Sulfide oxidizes to sulfate upon exposure to air [11].

Soilless media can have added S by incorporating $CaSO_4$ or superphosphate (which contains gypsum) when mixing. Triple superphosphate does not contain S. Most common water-soluble fertilizers are not formulated

TABLE 11.2   FERTILIZER CORRECTION OF NUTRIENT DEFICIENCIES

Deficient nutrient	Fertilizer source	Rate of application[a] oz/100 gal	g/l
P	Switch to a complete fertilizer containing N-P-K for the continual program		
Ca	Switch part or all of the N source to calcium nitrate for a few weeks		
Mg	Magnesium sulfate (Epsom salts) Switch part of the N source to magnesium nitrate	16	1.2
S	Magnesium sulfate	16	1.2
Fe	Iron chelate (Sequestrene 330) or Ferrous sulfate	4 16–32	0.300 1.2–2.4
Mn	Manganese sulfate	2	0.150
Zn	Zinc sulfate	2	0.150
Cu	Copper sulfate	2	0.150
B	Borax or Solubor	0.5 0.25	0.038 0.019
Mo	For soil-based media, drench once with sodium or ammonium molybdate. For soilless media, drench once with sodium or ammonium molybdate.	0.027[b] 2.67	0.002 0.200

[a] These corrective procedures are to be applied once. Subsequent applications should be made only after soil and foliar analysis tests indicate the need. All fertilizers are to be applied to the root media.

[b] Dissolve 1 ounce sodium or ammonium molybdate in 40 fluid ounces of water. Use 1 fluid ounce of this stock solution in each 100 gallons of final-strength fertilizer solution.

Source: From Nelson, Greenhouse operation and management. Reprinted by permission of Prentice-Hall.

with S. Micronutrients added after planting, such as STEM, are sulfate forms and can provide additional S. If Mg is also needed, drenching with $MgSO_4$ at 1 lb per 100 gal water every four weeks will provide adequate S. Maintain media S levels between 20 to 40 ppm for best availability [11].

Sulfur deficiency is not easily diagnosed. Deficiency symptoms usually appear as light green or yellow immature leaves, reduced leaf size, rolled-down leaf margins, red or purple coloration, shortened internodes, and stunted growth—similar to N deficiency symptoms. Sulfur symptoms usually begin in younger leaves, while N symptoms begin in older leaves [10]. Geraniums, poinsettias, and impatiens may be prone to S deficiency.

Iron. Iron (Fe) is probably the most important of the plant micronutrients. It has special importance in biological systems, such as photosynthesis.

Iron uptake is best at low media pH (5.5 to 6.0). In peat-based soilless mixes, Fe starts being tied up once media pH goes above 6.5. Iron competes very closely with Mn. When the substrate is cool (less than 60F, 15C) and wet, roots cannot take up Fe very effectively. Warming the media up 5F (3C) and drying it out will correct this type of Fe deficiency. At low media pH (less than 6.0 for some crops, less than 5.5 for most crops), Fe, along with other micronutrients, will become readily available and be taken up by the roots to toxic levels.

Iron deficiency is characterized by interveinal chlorosis of young leaves (Color plate 42). As the interveinal chlorosis moves down the plant, the youngest leaves become totally yellow and later necrotic. Root elongation is also inhibited [8]. Iron toxicity invariably leads to Mn deficiency, unless the media pH is lower than 5.5.

Iron can be supplied for most plants by adding a micronutrient package while mixing media. Many commercial fertilizers have micronutrients added (such as Peat-Lite Plus). Iron, along with other micronutrients, can be added post-planting with a soluble micronutrient formula, such as STEM, once or twice during the crop cycle. If severe Fe deficiency occurs, use iron chelate (Sequestrene 330) or iron sulfate at recommended rates, preferably as a drench (table 11.2). Make sure to rinse off the plants immediately after using iron sulfate, as it will burn the tender foliage. Check your media pH to make sure it is lower than 6.5. If it is not, lower it with an application of iron sulfate, ammonium sulfate, diluted acid, or acid fertilizer (21-7-7). To provide Fe quickly to the plant, it may be better to use iron chelate if the pH is greater than 7.0. Iron sulfate rapidly releases Fe into the soil solution, where it precipitates at very high pH, thereby requiring additional applications. Iron chelate will still be available to the plant at this high pH [7].

Iron toxicity can be corrected by monitoring media pH and manganese levels. If pH is too low (less than 5.5), raise it with high-alkalinity water, calcium nitrate fertilizers, or hydrated lime (1 lb per 100 gal). Maintain the Fe:Mn ratio at 2:1 (3:1 for geraniums). Some micronutrient packages may contain more Mn than Fe.

Manganese. Like Fe, manganese (Mn) plays an important role in biological systems such as photosynthesis. A large number of enzymes are activated by Mn as a cofactor. Manganese is also involved in root cell elongation and in resistance to root-infecting pathogens [6].

Manganese availability is controlled by substrate pH. At pH levels greater than 6.5, Mn is tied up. It is most available at pH levels lower than 5.5, at which it can become toxic to plants. Manganese competes with other divalent cations, such as Zn, Cu, Mg, Ca, and most of all Fe (table 11.1). Keep the Mn:Fe ratio at 1:2 for best results.

Deficiency symptoms start with interveinal chlorosis on young leaves. On heavily chlorotic leaves, small, light tan, sunken spots develop randomly between the veins (Color plate 43), which sets Mn deficiency apart from Fe deficiency. Root growth may also be inhibited. Manganese toxicity symptoms start with necrosis developing at the tips and margins of older leaves, or as spots across older leaves. A high Mn level also causes Fe deficiency symptoms [8].

Manganese can be supplied in proper quantities through micronutrient packages either preplant or postplant. Check the media pH to make sure it is neither too high nor too low. Have the media tested for levels of Fe, along with those of other competing divalent cations. Use manganese sulfate at the recommended level as a drench one time only (table 11.2).

Boron. Boron (B) is essential in plants for good pollination, fruit set, and seed development. It plays key roles in sugar transport, carbohydrate synthesis, cell wall synthesis and structure [6].

Roots take up B with water when plants are actively transpiring. Boron uptake is inhibited by high media pH (greater than 6.5), high Ca and low Mg levels, and high P levels. It is also very leachable in soilless mixes. A sufficient K level helps with B uptake. Boron becomes readily available at pH lower than 6.0 and especially at pH from 4.5 to 5.5. Excessive B can come from irrigation water or as a contaminant in raw fertilizers [3, 4].

Boron deficiency symptoms start with the new growth. At first the foliage is dark green. Young leaves develop thicker than normal, with a leathery feel (Color plates 44 and 45). Leaves may curl downward from end to end, giving a wilted appearance; however, they are turgid. Young leaves become chlorotic; rusty brown to orange necrotic spots appear across them. These leaves then become crinkled or develop puckered surfaces. Stem internodes become shortened. The terminal shoot aborts, and later the lateral shoots abort. This often leads to a cluster of stems, known as a witch's broom. Brown necrotic notches of missing cells may occur in leaf petioles, stems, and flower stems [8]. The most sensitive crops include petunia and pansy, especially in warm weather, when more watering is done along with less feeding.

Toxicity symptoms appear as chlorosis and burn on margins of older leaves (Color plate 46), and stunted shoot and root growth. Sensitive crops include begonia, gerbera, impatiens, marigold, lantana, pansy, and zinnia [4]. Satisfactory B levels, according to Scotts lab tests, are: water, less than 0.5 ppm; soil, 0.25 to 0.6 ppm; and tissue, 60 to 80 ppm.

Use care when applying B, as the difference between deficiency and toxicity is very small. Boron is usually provided in sufficient quantity through micronutrient packages either preplant or postplant, except during warm weather conditions. Check your water source to determine how much B it provides. Acid injection and reverse osmosis systems will *not* remove excessive B from the water [9]. Check your raw fertilizer sources for B contamination. High-grade commercial fertilizers do not have problems with B as a contaminant. If high B could be a problem, then use a fertilizer with no B in its micronutrient package. A high Ca level (greater than 150 ppm) will also help control excessive B. Adding $CaSO_4$ to the media will help.

For a low B level, supplement with Borax or Solubor at the recommended rates (table 11.2) as a one-time application only. Uniform application is very important and is best done as a liquid solution (drench). Keep the Ca level in line and at a 2:1 ratio with Mg. Keep media pH at less than 6.5 for best B availability.

Zinc. Zinc (Zn) plays a large role in certain enzymes and enzyme reactions, and helps protect cell membranes [6]. The Zn uptake is greatly influenced by substrate pH and P levels. Keep media pH less than 6.5 for best availability. When media pH gets lower than 5.5 (lower than 6.0 for some crops), Zn becomes very available and can build to toxic levels in the seedling. Cool, wet media also reduce root activity for taking up Zn. High P levels compete with Zn (table 11.1). High levels of Zn compete with Mn and Fe.

Zinc deficiency shows up as a chlorosis of young leaves, somewhat in an interveinal pattern. Internodes are very short (rosetting). Leaves are greatly reduced in size (little leaf). Shoot tip abortion occurs in severe situations. Zinc deficiency is not very common, but sensitive crops include carnation and kalanchoe [7, 8]. Normally, a micronutrient package applied either preplant or postplant in the media provides sufficient Zn, along with micronutrients included in commercial fertilizers. Check the media pH to make sure it is less than 6.5. Check P levels to keep from inhibiting Zn uptake. If needed, apply a one-time drench of zinc sulfate at the recommended level (table 11.2).

Copper. Copper (Cu) is important in plant respiration and photosynthesis. Copper availability is greatly reduced at substrate pH levels greater than 6.5, whereas it is readily available at low pH (less than 5.5) and can build up to a toxic level in the plant. High levels of N, particularly NH_4, and high levels of P interact with Cu, affecting its availability and mobility. High levels of Cu will interfere with uptake of Mn, Fe, and Mo (table 11.1). When spraying plug seedlings with copper fungicides, do not apply them more than once or twice during the crop cycle, as copper toxicity could occur.

Deficiency symptoms appear on youngest leaves as interveinal chlorosis. Unlike with Fe deficiency, the leaf tips remain green. More severe deficiencies result in leaf blade tissue collapse as the leaf expands. This results in very small leaves, which appear to have been burned back due to desiccation. The burning symptom will affect a few leaves and then stop. After a few nearly normal leaves appear, the burn can occur again [8]. Copper deficiency is not very common. Normally, a micronutrient package applied either preplant or postplant in the media provides sufficient Cu, along with micronutrients included in commercial fertilizers. Check the media pH to make sure it is lower than 6.5. Check NH_4 and P levels to keep from being excessive. If needed, apply a one-time drench of copper sulfate at the recommended level (table 11.2).

Molybdenum. Molybdenum (Mo) is essential in protein synthesis and nitrogen metabolism. Molybdenum is opposite of the rest of the micronutrients discussed, in that it is less available at low media pH, and deficiency symptoms show up on the oldest leaves first. This micronutrient is needed in such a small quantity that it is very rare to find a problem with deficiency in plug crops.

FERTILIZER FORMULATIONS

Whether you are mixing your own fertilizers or buying commercially available ones, three key factors help you understand what any fertilizer will do for your plugs. On a commercial fertilizer, these three key factors are on the label: (1) percentage of total N as NH_4 and urea, (2) how acidic or basic the fertilizer is, and (3) the availability of Ca and Mg.

Nitrogen form. There are three forms of nitrogen that have different effects on plug growth: nitrate nitrogen (NO_3), ammoniacal nitrogen (NH_4), and urea nitrogen. Nitrate nitrogen is the form most readily available to the plant and can be provided with K, Ca, Na, Mg, or ammonium nitrate. Ammoniacal nitrogen, coming from ammonium fertilizers, must be broken down by soil bacteria to become available to the plant in the form of NO_3. This bacterial conversion slows down greatly below 60F (15C), resulting in NH_4 toxicity. Urea nitrogen must be converted to NH_4 first, then converted to NO_3 to be used by the plant.

Ammoniacal nitrogen fertilizers promote larger and softer amounts of shoot growth, longer internodes and larger, greener leaves. Root growth is not promoted. Vegetative growth is promoted more than reproductive growth (flowering). Vegetative growth occurs when the N proportion in the NH_4 form is 25% or higher and the remaining N is NO_3. Do not apply more than 50% of total N in the NH_4 form, as such a high rate can cause plant injury [7]. Ammonium sensitivity increases with cooler substrate temperatures in winter and in northern latitudes. Lower substrate pH levels increase crop sensitivity to NH_4. Under cool temperatures and low substrate pH conditions, NH_4 is not converted as rapidly to NO_3 by soil bacteria.

Nitrate nitrogen fertilizers keep plants compact. Nitrate nitrogen favors root growth over shoot growth, resulting in shorter internodes, smaller and lighter green leaves, but thicker leaves and stems. This occurs when the NO_3 proportion of total N is greater than 75% (NH_4 is less than 25%). Reproductive growth is promoted more than vegetative growth with potassium nitrate.

Research has shown that many plants grow better with a combination of NH_4 and NO_3 as opposed to either source alone. You can manipulate the type of growth that you put on your plugs using N nutrition. High-urea and NH_4 fertilizers (greater than 30% NH_4) will promote softer, lusher growth, while high-NO_3 fertilizers (greater than 70% NO_3) will bring about more of a harder and toned appearance. A grower should be aware of this while either pushing or toning plug crops.

We have listed some common commercial fertilizers used by plug growers in table 11.3. Note how much they vary in the percentage of total N in the NH_4 + urea forms. You can calculate this percentage from the information on the label. For instance, Peters 20-10-20 fertilizer has 20% total N. However, this N is made up of 12% NO_3 and 8% NH_4, giving the 20% total N. To calculate the percentage of total N as NH_4, take the 8% NH_4 and divide by the 20% total to get 40% of the total N as NH_4. In table 11.4 we have listed some single-element fertilizers that growers can use to make their own complete fertilizers. Note that urea provides 100% of N as NH_4, while ammonium nitrate provides 50%. Keep these percentages in mind when selecting a fertilizer for plug growth. Do you want to push the plugs (speed up growth, usually shoot growth), or do you want to slow the crop down and tone it up (favor root growth and thicker leaves and stems)?

Reaction or pH control. Although the substrate pH level may be correct at the start of a plug crop, it may change over time. High-alkalinity water will raise it. Heavy watering at the start may activate the limestone in the media quicker and raise the pH. Application of water-soluble fertilizers may also raise or lower the pH level. You can lower, hold constant, or raise postplant substrate pH level by selecting the proper fertilizer.

High NH_4 and urea-containing fertilizers will cause an acidic reaction in the soil solution and will bring the pH of the media down over time. Ammonium nitrate, ammonium sulfate, and the ammonium phosphates are acidic. Urea is only slightly acidic, not as much as ammonium nitrate. High NO_3 fertilizers will cause a moderate alkaline reaction in the soil solution and will slowly raise media pH over time. Calcium nitrate and sodium

TABLE 11.3   COMMERCIAL PLUG FERTILIZERS [a]

Fertilizer	NH₄ [b] (%)	Potential acidity [c]	Potential basicity [d]	Ca [e] (%)	Mg [e] (%)
21-7-7	100	1560		—	—
9-45-15	100	940		—	—
20-20-20	69	583		—	—
20-10-20	40	422		—	—
21-5-20 (Excel)	40	418		—	—
15-15-15 [f]	52	261		—	—
15-16-17 [f]	30	165		—	—
20-0-20	25	40		5	—
17-5-17	24	0	0	3	1
17-0-17	20		75	4	2
15-5-15 (Excel)	28		135	5	2
13-2-13	11		200	6	3
14-0-14	8		220	6	3
15-0-15	13		420	11	—

[a] List of some commercially available fertilizers used for plugs. Not all formulations are the same from every company. Check the labels!

[b] NH₄ (%) is the total nitrogen percentage that is in the ammonium plus urea forms; the remaining nitrogen is nitrate.

[c] Pounds of calcium carbonate limestone required to neutralize the acidity caused by using 1 ton of the specified fertilizer.

[d] Application of 1 ton of the specified fertilizer is equivalent to applying this many pounds of calcium carbonate limestone.

[e] Only where % Ca or % Mg were 1% or greater.

[f] Contains sodium nitrate (nitrate of soda), which adds unwanted sodium to plugs.

Source: From Nelson, Fertilization, *Bedding plants IV.*

nitrate will raise media pH, with magnesium nitrate and potassium nitrate neutral (there is some disagreement on this point!) (table 11.4). To check the potential acidity or basicity of a commercial fertilizer, look on the label (table 11.3). For example, 20-10-20 has 40% of the total N as NH₄ and a potential acidity of 422. This means that it would require 422 pounds of limestone to neutralize the acidity produced in the substrate by the addition of 1 ton of this fertilizer. Compare this to 20-0-20, which has 25% of total N as NH₄ and a potential acidity of only 40. This means that 20-0-20 will change the media pH less than 20-10-20. On the other end, 15-0-15 has 13% of the total N as NH₄, with a potential basicity of 420. This means that applying a ton of 15-0-15 is like applying 420 pounds of limestone to the media.

TABLE 11.4 SINGLE-ELEMENT FERTILIZERS FOR MACRONUTRIENTS

Name	Fertilizer Analysis	% of N as NH$_4$	pH Reaction in soil
Ammonium nitrate	33-0-0	50	Acid
Potassium nitrate	13-0-44	0	Neutral
Calcium nitrate	15.5-0-0	6	Basic
Sodium nitrate	16-0-0	0	Basic
Magnesium nitrate	11-0-0	0	Neutral
Ammonium sulfate	21-0-0	100	Acid
Urea	45-0-0	100	Slightly acid
Monoammonium phosphate	12-62-0	100	Acid
Diammonium phosphate	21-53-0	100	Slightly acid
Potassium sulfate	0-0-53	—	Neutral
Potassium chloride	0-0-60	—	Neutral
Monopotassium phosphate	0-53-34	—	Basic
Dipotassium phosphate	0-41-54	—	Basic
Magnesium sulfate	—	—	Neutral

Note: These analysis values were obtained from commercially available products. The analysis of compounds may vary slightly from listed values as a result of processing differences among various chemical companies.

Two fertilizers labeled "Excel" in table 11.3 are available from Scotts and use proprietary technology concerning urea phosphate. Urea phosphate produces the equivalent of one-third ounce of 75% phosphoric acid in 100 gal at 100 ppm N, which may be sufficient to reduce moderate levels (120 to 200 ppm) of water alkalinity when used on a constant basis. However, urea phosphate does not influence the long-term potential acidity or basicity of the fertilizer solution in the media. The 15-5-15 fertilizer will still raise the media pH over time, regardless of the urea phosphate in it.

Calcium and magnesium. Whether a particular fertilizer supplies any Ca or Mg is of primary importance to a plug grower. As seen in table 11.3, most fertilizers do not contain any appreciable amounts. If the fertilizer is acidic, more than likely it will contain neither Ca nor Mg. Calcium plays an important role in cell walls and root growth, helping leaves and stems become thicker and more toned, while promoting root growth. Magnesium is important in chlorophyll synthesis, the overall green color of the leaves and good photosynthetic activity. Until the past five to 10 years, Mg was not available in most fertilizers. Now magnesium nitrate is being used more often, providing a steady supply of Mg. However, fertilizers containing both Ca and Mg tend to be basic, causing the media pH to increase over time if used continuously.

Most acidic fertilizers cannot have Ca and Mg in them because of their interaction with SO_4 and phosphates (PO_4). Calcium combines with SO_4 and PO_4 to produce insoluble precipitates of calcium sulfate and calcium phosphate. Magnesium combines with PO_4 to produce an insoluble precipitate of magnesium phosphate. Acidic fertilizers tend to have substantial amounts of P, whereas basic fertilizers have very low levels. Sulfates come from ammonium sulfate (acid), potassium sulfate (neutral), or magnesium sulfate (neutral). The latter two compounds are rarely used in commercial fertilizers.

Growers have been able to get around this problem of Ca and Mg precipitating out with PO_4 or SO_4 by setting up two separate concentrated stock tanks and a dual-head injector to add 20-10-20 and 14-0-14 at the same time (fig. 11.1). Other growers alternate feeding between the two opposite fertilizers. There are additional options for supplying Ca and Mg while still providing some P. The Excel line of fertilizers has urea phosphate (5% P) to keep from precipitating with Ca and Mg, allowing the grower to use concentrated forms of Ca and Mg from different Excel fertilizers in the same stock tank. Greencare

FIGURE 11.1 Multihead fertilizer injector with two stock tanks.

and Masterblend both make a fertilizer that provides 2% P along with 6% Ca and 3% Mg without precipitating (13-2-13-6-3). These P levels are sufficient for most crops most of the time. (Appendix 4 lists some suppliers of commercial water-soluble fertilizers.)

Most media Ca and Mg can be supplied by dolomitic limestone. Additional amounts may come from the water source. However, dolomitic limestone activates within the first two weeks in a plug crop and may run out for longer-term plug crops. Also, plug media manufacturers have been adding less limestone in order to have the media start and stay at a lower pH (5.5 to 5.8). Therefore, it is important for a plug grower to use some fertilizers containing Ca and Mg in the feed program to supplement the other sources and help control plug growth. Remember that Ca and Mg are antagonistic toward each other. Try to maintain a 2:1 ratio of Ca:Mg at all times. A higher level of either will inhibit uptake of the other nutrient.

Micronutrients. Generally, sufficient quantities of micronutrients are provided in commercial plug mixes and fertilizers. However, not all fertilizers have added micronutrients. Check the fertilizer label to be sure. If you are mixing your own plug media or your own fertilizers, then you need to add a micronutrient package. (Table 11.5 lists some commercially available micronutrient formulations in addition to the micronutrient packages [Esmigram, Micromax]). Follow the label for recommended rates. Some of these packages are for media, and some are for fertilizers. You may need a package with dye to determine if fertilizer is coming out of your water line.

Micronutrients come in three forms: chelates, sulfates, and fritted. Chelates are large organic chemical structures that encircle and tightly hold the micronutrients Fe, Mn, Cu, and Zn [7]. Plant roots can absorb the micronutrient-chelate combination. The micronutrient is then released inside the plant as needed. Alternatively, a plant can absorb micronutrients alone as they are slowly released into the soil solution by chelates. Chelated micronutrients are protected from precipitation at high media pH, depending on the chelation.

There is usually an advantage to using chelated iron when the pH level is adversely high for the crop (over 7.0), but if the pH level is normal, the cheaper iron sulfate form is sufficient. The sulfate forms of Mn, Zn, and Cu are much cheaper than the chelates and are recommended for correcting nutrient deficiencies. Fritted micronutrients are contained in a solid, finely ground, glass powder. The glass slowly dissolves in root media, releasing nutrients over an extended time.

As long as the media pH stays between 5.5 and 6.5, the micronutrients should remain available. Some crops, such as geranium and marigold, need to be grown at the higher pH of 6.0 to 6.2 in order to avoid micronutrient toxicity. During very warm weather, B may be leached out more than it is being replaced; STEM, Solubor, or Borax can provide supplemental B at these times. If the plug media stays cool and wet, micronutrient deficiencies may show up. Simply warm up the media to 65F (18C), dry it out, and the problem should go away.

Buying versus blending your own. Developing a fertilizer program presents the plug grower with an array of alternatives. Most growers choose commercial water-soluble fertilizers for their crops. Some growers prefer to mix their own fertilizers. High-quality crops can be produced either way; there are advantages and disadvantages for both.

TABLE 11.5   COMMON COMMERCIAL MICRONUTRIENT FORMULATIONS

Company	Product name	Nutrients in formulation (%)									Form
		Zn	Fe	Mn	Cu	B	Mo	Mg	Ca	S	
Frit Industries, Inc.	Frit Micro-Control	4	20	4	2	0.05	0.07	2.5	5	—	Fritted
	F-101 HF	1.5	3	1.5	1.5	0.05	0.015	—	—	—	Fritted
	F-111 HF	1	3	1	0.3	0.05	0.015	—	—	—	Fritted
	F-176 HF	2.5	25	3	2.5	1	0.025	—	—	—	Fritted
	F-2682 HF	1.5	3.5	1.5	0.6	0.03	0.005	—	—	—	Fritted
	F-503	7	18	7.5	3	1.5	0.02	—	—	—	Fritted
	F-504 HF	7	14	7	7	3.8	0.07	—	—	—	Fritted
	F-504 LB	7	14	7	7	2.8	0.07	—	—	—	Fritted
	F-555	5	14	5	1.5	0.8	0.07	—	—	—	Fritted
Greencare Fertilizers	Liquid Multi-purpose Micronutrients	0.9	1.8	0.9	0.9	0.36	0.01	—	—	3.5	Chelated
	Water Soluble Micronutrient Blend	5.29	8.26	4.05	3.55	0.69	0.07	—	—	21.3	Sulfates
Plant Marvel Labs	Chemec	0.64	1.26	0.64	0.625	0.25	0.01	—	—	—	Chelated
	Sol-Trace	4.5	7.5	8.15	3.2	1.45	0.046	—	—	14.75	Sulfates
The Scotts Co.	Peters STEM	4.5	7.5	8	3.2	1.35	0.04	—	—	14	Sulfates
	Peters Compound III	0.075	1.5	0.74	0.1136	0.232	0.0242	0.74	—	—	Chelated
J.R. Simplot Co.	APEX	1	13	1.5	0.5	0.1	0.005	1.2	2.4	13	Sulfates
Vaughan's Seed Co. Fertilizer Division	Masterblend Water Soluble Micronutrient Blend	4.5	7.5	8	3	1.5	0.05	—	—	15	Sulfates
	Masterblend Formula 222 Micro Additive	0.15	3	0.24	0.237	4.65	0.215	—	—	—	Chelated

Commercial fertilizers are often chosen for their high solubility. Most are manufactured from chemicals of higher grade than many other agricultural fertilizers, making them easier to dissolve, even at the high concentrations needed for injector stock solutions. In addition to N-P-K, newer commercial plug fertilizers can supply Ca and Mg, along with micronutrients, at levels to satisfy the demands of plug growing. Additional advantages are the labor savings from not making up your own fertilizer solutions and the technical backup you can get from the horticultural fertilizer companies. The main disadvantage of commercial fertilizers is their cost [1].

Mixing your own fertilizer has advantages, too. Many growers report significant savings in fertilizer cost by mixing their own. They also like the flexibility of customizing the fertilizer to their needs. Consider the additional labor involved in mixing, as well as additional equipment for more stock tanks and multihead injectors, if you use this type of fertilizer system. Some fertilizers for farm crops have coatings or other materials that can settle out, clogging injectors and fertilizer lines [1]. Agricultural-grade chemicals may also have contaminants—such as Na, Cl, B, and other chemicals—that you do not want or need. When you mix your own fertilizers, buy horticultural-grade chemicals, keeping in mind the NH_4 percentage, how acid or basic your fertilizer will be, and incorporating P, Ca, and Mg, as well as micronutrients (table 11.6).

FERTILIZING BASED ON CROPS AND GROWTH STAGES

Fertilizer levels by growth stage. The beginning of this book defined four different plug growth stages based on environmental and nutritional requirements. These stages are Stage 1, from sowing to radicle emergence; Stage 2, from radicle emergence to full expansion of cotyledons; Stage 3, from cotyledon expansion to full growth of true leaves; and Stage 4, from full growth of true leaves to transplanting or shipping. In Stage 1, if there is a starter charge (fertilizer) in the media, no further fertilization is needed. The starter charges in most commercial mixes will last about seven to 10 days, depending on how much you water the media during germination. For a grower germinating on the bench, the starter charge will generally not last as long, due to more watering being done. For a grower germinating in a chamber, the starter charge should last up to 10 days. Remember, some plug media have very low or no starter charge in them. If this is the case, you may need to start feeding plugs as soon as germination is visible. Feed 25 to 50 ppm N from a low NH_4 fertilizer until Stage 2. Potassium nitrate can also be beneficial for helping to break seed dormancy.

TABLE 11.6 FERTILIZER SOLUTIONS TO YIELD N AND K₂0 CONCENTRATIONS

Fertilizer	NH₄ + urea (%)	N and K₂O concentration (ppm)						
		50	100	200	300	400	500	600
20-20-20	70	3.3	6.7	13.3	20.0	26.7	33.4	40.0
15-15-15	52	4.5	8.9	17.6	26.7	35.6	44.5	53.4
15-0-15	13	4.5	8.9	17.8	26.7	35.6	44.5	53.4
13-2-13 (-6 Ca-3 Mg)	11	5.1	10.3	20.5	30.8	41.0	51.3	61.5
14-0-14 (-6 Ca-3 Mg)	8	4.8	9.5	19.0	28.6	38.1	47.6	57.1
17-0-17 (-4 Ca-2 Mg)	20	3.9	7.8	15.7	23.5	31.4	39.2	47.0
20-10-20	40	3.3	6.7	13.3	20.0	26.7	33.4	40.0
Ammonium nitrate	36	1.4	2.9	5.7	8.6	11.4	14.3	17.1
+ Potassium nitrate (23-0-23)		1.5	3.0	6.1	9.1	12.1	15.2	18.2
Calcium nitrate	0	3.0	6.0	12.0	18.0	24.0	30.0	36.0
+ Potassium nitrate (15-0-15)		1.5	3.0	6.0	9.0	12.0	15.0	18.0
Ammonium nitrate	40	1.2	2.5	4.9	7.4	9.9	12.3	14.8
+ Potassium nitrate		1.5	3.0	6.0	9.0	12.0	15.0	18.0
+ Monoammonium phosphate (20-10-20)		0.5	1.1	2.2	3.2	4.3	5.4	6.5
Potassium nitrate	0	1.5	3.0	6.1	9.1	12.1	15.2	18.2
+ Calcium nitrate		1.8	3.5	7.0	10.5	14.1	17.6	21.1
+ Magnesium nitrate (13-0-13-6.6 Ca-3.3 Mg)		1.8	3.5	7.0	10.5	14.1	17.6	21.1

Note: Numbers are oz of fertilizer or fertilizer salts per 100 gal water to make solution with given N and K₂0 concentrations. oz/100 gal = 0.075 g/l.

Source: From Nelson, Fertilization, *Bedding plants IV.*

In Stage 2, the young seedling is starting to photosynthesize and make sugars for itself. Fertilization should be done one or two times per week (more often if watering more) with 50 to 75 ppm N, generally alternating between 20-10-20 and a low NH₄ fertilizer, such as 14-0-14. In this stage some crops start to rapidly stretch, due partly to maintaining high moisture levels to finish germination and partly to availability of fertilizer, particularly NH₄. (Table 11.7 indicates which crops should be grown with lower EC in Stages 2 and 3.) The lower starter charges in commercial plug mixes have also addressed this early stretch.

The active growth of leaves and roots in Stage 3 requires more nutrients to be available to the young seedling. Increase the concentration to 100 to 150 ppm N one or two times a week, depending on how often you water. Again, alternate between 20-10-20 and 14-0-14 or similar fertilizers to avoid

TABLE 11.7 FERTILIZER LEVELS BY CROP AND PLUG GROWTH STAGE

Plug stage and feeding program	Low	Medium	High
Stage 2	**<0.5** [a]	**0.5–0.75** [a]	**>0.75** [a]
50–75 ppm N			
1–2x/week	Cabbage	Ageratum	Begonia
	Celosia	Browallia	Geranium
	Eggplant	Cyclamen	Gerbera
	F. kale/cabbage	Dianthus	Hypoestes
	Lettuce	Dusty miller	Nicotiana
	Pansy (fall)	Impatiens	Petunia
	Pepper	Lisianthus	
	Snapdragon	Marigold	
	Tomato	Pansy (spring)	
		Primula	
		Salvia	
		Verbena	
		Vinca	
Stage 3	**0.5–0.75**	**0.75–1.0**	**1.0–1.5**
100–150 ppm N			
1–2x/week	Cabbage	Ageratum	Begonia
	Eggplant	Cyclamen	Browallia
	F. kale/cabbage	Dianthus	Coleus [b]
	Lettuce	Dusty miller	Geranium
	Pepper	Impatiens	Gerbera
	Snapdragon	Marigold	Lisianthus
	Tomato	Pansy	Nicotiana
		Primula	Petunia
		Salvia	
		Verbena	
		Vinca	
Stage 4		**Most crops 0.5–0.75**	
100–150 ppm N			
1–2x/week, only when needed; use mainly nitrate fertilizer			

[a] Soil EC expressed as mmhos/cm from a 2:1 extraction.

[b] Only certain slow varieties.

providing too much NH_4. For most plugs, maintain pH at 5.8 and soluble salts around 1.0 mmhos. Some crops need more fertilizer (table 11.7). These crops are not necessarily more tolerant of high salts but need more nutrients to maintain their desired growth rates. Begonia reacts very well to NH_4 fertilizers such as 20-10-20 during Stage 3, but still needs some Ca and Mg from 14-0-14. The fertilizer program for this crop would shift more to 20-10-20 (table 11.8). Impatiens will stretch too much if given more 20-10-20 like begonia. To control growth of impatiens, the fertilizer program would use more 14-0-14 than 20-10-20. Fertilizers such as 13-2-13-6-3 are excellent for growing crops such as impatiens, snapdragons, and vegetables, where low NH_4 and higher Ca levels are needed. However, these fertilizers may not have enough NH_4 to satisfy crops such as begonia (Color plate 48) and petunia. A new fertilizer (17-5-17-3-1), with 25% of total N as NH_4 and containing Ca and Mg, is now available from Greencare. This fertilizer may be used in place of alternating between 20-10-20 and 14-0-14 in northern areas during the spring season.

TABLE 11.8   PLUG CROP EXCEPTIONS TO ALTERNATING 20-10-20 AND 14-0-14 FERTILIZER PROGRAM

Crops needing more 20-10-20	Crops needing more 14-0-14
Begonia	Cyclamen
Coleus (slow varieties)	Flowering kale/cabbage
Gerbera	Impatiens
Nicotiana	Most vegetables
Petunia	Snapdragon

Note: Other crops can be alternated between 20-10-20 and 14-0-14. Adjust such crops based on weather conditions and speed of growth.

Once the desired number of leaves, height, and root growth have been achieved, it may be necessary to tone the plug or slow down the growth before transplanting or shipping (Stage 4). Some growers who immediately transplant their own plugs never go through this stage. In Stage 4 it is necessary to provide cooler temperatures (lower than 65F, 18C) to slow down the growth. The fertilizer program should include 100 to 150 ppm N from high NO_3 fertilizers only when needed. At these cool temperatures, NH_4 is not converted by soil bacteria fast enough to be used by the plant and will build up in the media and become toxic. The high NO_3, high Ca fertilizers promote thicker leaves and stems, resulting in a harder, more toned plug. Root growth will also be improved.

Maintain media pH at less than 6.5 to avoid micronutrient deficiencies, and keep the media EC less than 1.0 mmhos. Many plug growers will not feed at all during this stage, even though they may hold plugs for one or two weeks. This technique is dangerous in that the plug may lose its root hairs if too dry, lose its chlorophyll, and not grow out well after transplanting. Vegetable plug growers can keep nutrient levels from 0.5 to 0.75 mmhos until three days prior to transplanting, at which time the fertilizer concentration can be increased to 150 to 300 ppm N (commonly called pumping or spiking).

It is very important that all nutrients be present and available at all times. It is necessary to maintain the balance of nutrients with each other, not just strictly an absolute amount (ppm) for one or more. For optimum plug growth, try to maintain ratios of 1N:1K:1Ca:1/2Mg:1/5–1/10P. The ratio of Fe to Mn should be 2:1. Keep B levels between 0.25 and 0.5 ppm. The Na level should be lower than 40 ppm. If not, increase Ca, Mg, and K, and water thoroughly to leach out Na.

To increase vegetative growth, use fertilizers with more ammonium nitrate. To increase reproductive growth (flowering), use more potassium nitrate and calcium nitrate and no ammonium nitrate.

For soft, fast growth, use ammonium nitrate and P. For hard, slow growth, use calcium nitrate and potassium nitrate. Make sure the media pH stays within the desired range when using any of these fertilizers.

To promote shoot growth, use fertilizers containing ammonium nitrate, potassium nitrate, P, and Mg. To promote root growth, use fertilizers containing calcium nitrate, potassium nitrate, Mg, and P. Notice that no one fertilizer can do all these things. Monitor the type of growth occurring, then use the fertilizer and concentration needed to achieve the final product.

FERTILIZING BASED ON ENVIRONMENT AND MOISTURE

Temperature. The desired growth of plug seedlings will vary according to the growing temperature. Both shoot growth and root growth are affected. Crops grown at 65F (18C) ADT will grow slower than the same crops grown at 70F (21C) ADT. Plug seedlings are most sensitive to root zone temperature; therefore, you need to measure soil temperature, not just air temperature (fig. 11.2). In a normal greenhouse bench with above-bench heating, the air temperature can be as much as 5 to 10F (3 to 6C) different from the soil temperature. With a root-zone heating system, the air temperature becomes less important and may actually be kept below the soil temperature.

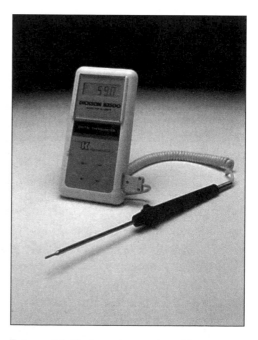

FIGURE 11.2 Digital thermometer for measuring soil temperature. Courtesy The Dickson Company.

When soil temperature is lowered to slow down plug growth, the feeding program also needs to be changed. Below 60F (15C), NH_4 is converted to NO_3 much more slowly by soil bacteria. Since the plant is growing more slowly and the NH_4 is accumulating in the media, NH_4 toxicity can occur. This could show as high-salts damage, NH_4 toxicity symptoms, or N deficiency symptoms. Plug crops being grown at lower temperatures should be fed with low-NH_4 fertilizers, such as 13-2-13-6-3 or 14-0-14. Generally, less fertilizer is needed at lower temperatures to maintain color.

When soil temperature is increased due to warmer weather or if you are pushing the crop, the feeding program needs to be monitored for the amount of NH_4 fertilizers used and the increase in internodal length (stretching). The NH_4 will be used very quickly by plug seedlings as soil temperatures rise above 65F (18C). If too much NH_4 has been provided, the seedlings will grow rapidly, resulting in stretched and soft shoot growth, with root growth trailing behind. However, under high light and warm temperature conditions, the plug seedling needs more NH_4 in order to continue to grow and maintain dark green color. High NO_3 fertilizers may not be able to keep up with the plant's photosynthetic needs under such conditions, resulting in small, pale leaves and restricted shoot growth.

Plug growers who use DIF to control plug height should be aware of the ADT, as well as the plug's nutritional needs. When using a negative DIF throughout the day, it is likely that the ADT may be getting close to the 60F (15C) level, where NH_4 fertilizers should not be used. Make sure to use high-NO_3 fertilizers (such as 13-2-13-6-3, 14-0-14) if using negative DIF, to avoid NH_4 toxicity. Also, negative DIF may cause chlorosis in certain crops, such as salvia (Color plate 51) and gerbera, resembling a nutrient disorder. This chlorosis is *not* due to nutrient deficiency and can be quickly alleviated in most crops by restoring the plug seedlings to a normal growing temperature. Be careful about trying to correct plug seedling chlorosis with fertilizers when growing at negative DIF!

Light. Under low light conditions (less than 1,500 fc, 16,140 lux), as is very common during the winter, most plug seedlings in Stages 3 and 4 stretch. Leaf growth will be large and soft. Root growth will be less than shoot growth. The fertilizer program needs to be adjusted when light is reduced for even just a few days. Frequency and rates (ppm) of feeding should be reduced. Use fertilizers with low NH_4 but high NO_3, particularly with Ca.

When light levels are high (greater than 2,500 fc, 26,900 lux), plug seedlings are photosynthesizing at maximum rates and therefore need more food. Higher NH_4 fertilizers (such as 20-10-20) may be needed to support this maximum growth. High light may also act as a growth regulator, if leaf temperature gets too high. The plant will shut down photosynthesis in order to protect itself; when the leaf temperature gets lower, photosynthesis resumes. Regardless, the plug seedlings will be utilizing nutrients faster and may need higher rates or more frequent applications of fertilizer to sustain their growth.

Longer photoperiods result in more light in a 24-hour period getting to the plug seedling. This means that the plug seedling will be photosynthesizing more on a spring day than on a winter day. When photosynthesis increases, the plant needs more nutrients. Adjust the frequency and rates accordingly. You may need to incorporate more NH_4 fertilizer as well.

Humidity. In the greenhouse, humidity levels can get quite high, especially at night (more than 90% RH). When the weather gets very humid, the daytime humidity level inside the greenhouse also goes up. This results in lower transpiration rates for the plug seedlings. Reduced transpiration means not as much water is going up through the plants from the roots through the leaves.

When transpiration is reduced, Ca uptake is also reduced. Potassium uptake will continue, though, resulting in a possible imbalance between Ca and K. The plug seedlings will also tend to stretch, with leaf growth being more rapid and thin. Try to dehumidify the greenhouse, especially at night. Keep air moving to promote leaf dryness and transpiration. Change the fertilizer to higher Ca, lower K, and lower NH_4.

Plugs grown under low humidity levels, especially during the day, will transpire at high rates. Water uptake by the roots may or may not be able to keep up with the transpiration loss through the leaves, depending on the water availability in the media. Calcium uptake is maximized and kept in balance with K. Shoot growth will be shorter, and root growth will be more in balance with the shoots. However, these plugs will also need more NH_4 fertilizer in order to put on the desired leaf expansion and color.

Carbon dioxide. During the winter season, many greenhouses stay closed tight while plug growth is occurring. It is not uncommon at all for CO_2 levels to be as low as 150 ppm, which is detrimental to plant growth. Some plug growers are now injecting CO_2 into their greenhouses to raise the levels as high as 1,000 ppm (levels higher than 1,000 ppm are not economical and may inhibit plug growth). Increasing CO_2 levels to between 400 to 1,000 ppm will improve photosynthesis if other factors, such as temperature, light, water, and nutrients, are not limiting. When injecting CO_2, photosynthesis is increased, along with root and shoot growth; therefore, frequency and rates of fertilizer will also need to be increased. You may need to use more NH_4 fertilizers, as well. Failure to change the fertilizer program when injecting CO_2 may result in nutrient deficiencies, particularly of N.

Moisture. Plug growers can typically be divided into "wet" or "dry" growers by how they water their plug trays. Suffice it to say that wet growers like to water more often, and dry growers like to hold off watering. When you water more frequently and water comes out the bottom of your plug trays, you need to feed more frequently, as you are leaching out nutrients. Wet growers tend not to be able to control plug growth very well, with more problems of stretching, soft growth, and disease. This is because at high moisture levels, nutrients are taken up very well by the roots, higher humidity causes soft shoots and thin leaves, and root rot and *Botrytis* are more prevalent on this soft growth. Make sure you use low NH_4 fertilizers with more Ca.

Dry growers tend to hold off watering until plants wilt, which may be a problem with crops such as primula, ageratum, and pansy, as these crops do not recover from wilting. By growing on the dry side, these growers can control shoot growth much better and promote root growth with more oxygen in the media. Dry growers need to fertilize less frequently, but they must watch the media soluble salt levels, which will build up around the roots two to four times higher under dry conditions.

Leaching percentage is a more important factor than most people realize (fig. 11.3). A grower maintaining a low leaching percentage, such as 10 to 15%, will be successful using a low concentration of fertilizer (50 to 100 ppm N). A grower using a 50% leaching fraction may need to double the fertilizer concentration (100 to 200 ppm N). When developing a fertilization program, be sure to select a leaching level and adhere to it. A major problem with uniformity comes when two or more people are assigned to watering or fertilizing a plug crop, and one is a wet grower and the other is dry.

Interactions. In growing plugs, none of the preceding factors occurs by itself. A plug grower must consider temperature, light, humidity, CO_2, and moisture all at the same time in deciding when to fertilize, with what, and how much. Too often the plug grower is reacting to changes in the weather, from warm and sunny to cool and cloudy—but for how long will the weather stay one way? One day? A week? What happens if you fertilize your plugs now, and then the weather turns cool and cloudy? The nutrients you apply now will show up in a leaf analysis within three days. Some crops (tomato, impatiens, celosia) seem to stretch within one day after you feed them—and then the weather changes.

A plug grower needs not just to react to weather changes but to anticipate them. Watching the weather forecast for the next two or three days is the first step. If a storm moving in will cause cool, cloudy weather for the next three days, you should fertilize with a low NH_4 fertilizer (such as 13-2-13-6-3 or 14-0-14), maybe at a lower concentration. If the weather is going

FIGURE 11.3 Recommended nitrogen (N) fertilization rates based on plug stage of development, frequency of fertilizer application, and degree of leaching during irrigation. Courtesy of Paul Nelson, North Carolina State University.

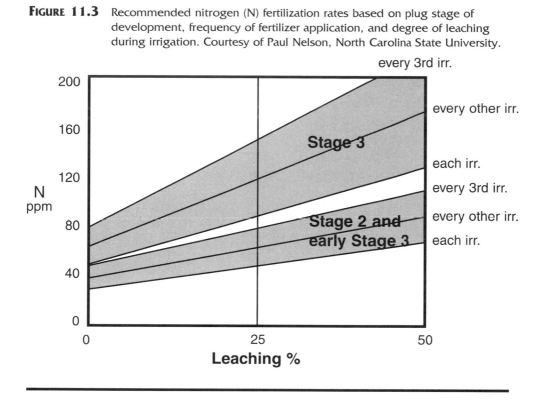

to turn warm and sunny, you can feed with a higher-NH_4 fertilizer (such as 20-10-20) and at a higher concentration. Most plug growers have the greatest problems with cool, cloudy, wet periods of weather. They generally lose control of shoot growth, cannot get enough roots, and have more problems with disease. Remember to control moisture very carefully during such periods, provide good air movement, and fertilize at lower rates with a high-NO_3 fertilizer containing more Ca. And then pray for sun!

PROBLEM SOLVING

To solve plug nutritional problems, you need several key pieces of information. First, what are the plant symptoms? Table 11.9 is a key to the classical symptoms of various nutrient deficiencies. Second, do you know the quality of your irrigation water? The optimum range of soluble salts and nutrients in the water appear in table 6.3. Test your water at least every six months for growing plugs, more often if using acid injection for correcting high alkalinity. Third, do you know the pH, soluble salt, and nutrient level of your plug media? Finally, you can get a tissue test for symptomatic and non-symptomatic plants to determine nutrient levels (table 11.10). However, the

TABLE 11.9   KEY TO THE CLASSICAL SYMPTOMS OF VARIOUS NUTRIENT DEFICIENCIES

Deficiency symptom	Deficient nutrient
a. The dominant symptom is chlorotic foliage.	
b. Entire leaf blades are chlorotic.	
c. Only the lower leaves are chlorotic, followed by necrosis and leaf drop.	Nitrogen
cc. Leaves on all parts of plant are affected and sometimes have a beige cast.	Sulfur
bb. Yellowing of leaves takes form of interveinal chlorosis.	
c. Only recently mature or older leaves exhibit interveinal chlorosis.	Magnesium
cc. Only younger leaves exhibit interveinal chlorosis. This is the only symptom.	Iron
d. In addition to interveinal chlorosis on young leaves, gray or tan necrotic spots develop in chlorotic areas.	Manganese
dd. While younger leaves have interveinal chlorosis, the tips and lobes of leaves remain green, followed by veinal chlorosis and rapid, extensive necrosis of leaf blade.	Copper
ddd. Young leaves are very small, sometimes missing leaf blades altogether, and internodes are short, giving a rosette appearance.	Zinc
aa. Leaf chlorosis is not the dominant symptom.	
b. Symptoms appear at base of plant.	
c. At first, all leaves are dark green, and then growth is stunted. Purple pigment often develops in leaves, particularly older leaves.	Phosphorus
cc. Margins of older leaves become chlorotic and then burn, or small chlorotic spots progressing to necrosis appear scattered on old leaf blades.	Potassium
bb. Symptoms appear at top of plant.	
c. Terminal buds die, giving rise to a witch's broom. Young leaves become very thick, leathery, and chlorotic. Rust-colored cracks and corking occur on young stems, petioles, and flower stalks. Young leaves are crinkled.	Boron
cc. Margins of young leaves fail to form, sometimes yielding strap leaves. Growing point ceases to develop, leaving a blunt end. Light green color or uneven chlorosis of young tissue develops. Root growth is poor, in that roots are short and thickened.	Calcium

Source: From Nelson, *Greenhouse operation and management.* Reprinted by permission of Prentice-Hall.

TABLE 11.10 TISSUE ANALYSIS PARAMETERS FOR BEDDING PLANTS

Nutrient	Minimum	Maximum
N	3.50%	4.60%
P	0.40%	0.67%
K	2.00%	8.80%
Ca	1.00%	2.60%
Mg	0.40%	1.90%
B	50 ppm	175 ppm
Fe	90 ppm	250 ppm
Mn	75 ppm	300 ppm
Cu	5 ppm	28 ppm
Zn	25 ppm	100 ppm
Mo	0.20 ppm	5 ppm
Al	NA [a]	NA
Na	NA	NA

[a] NA = Not available

Source: From Scotts Testing Laboratory, Allentown, Penn.

plants are usually so small as to make tissue sampling very tedious and difficult. For larger plugs, tissue testing may be more appropriate. Always test the media and tissue from the same plug trays.

Media testing is best as a preventative measure, rather than a corrective measure. Sample once a week for certain key crops, and follow some of these crops through their crop cycle. Table 11.11 lists some key indicator crops for low- and high-pH problems, crops that will probably show symptoms first. For more information on nutrient levels and to double-check your own pH and soluble salt readings, send out media samples occasionally to a professional testing lab.

The importance of testing your media as you are growing your plug crops cannot be overstated. Consider growing plugs like driving your car. What are the two most important dashboard gauges you monitor, without whose proper functioning, you would not be able to drive? Your speedometer and gas gauge! You need the speedometer to tell you the range of speed you need to stay within. You look at your speedometer to tell how fast you are going so you do not get a ticket, but also to make sure you do not go too slow and take too long to get wherever you are going. The media pH tells you the same thing. You need to stay within the range of 5.5 to 6.5 for most crops; otherwise, problems show up. If you do not know if you are in the

TABLE 11.11   INDICATOR CROPS

High pH (low Fe)	Low pH	High EC
Pansy	Geranium	Pansy
Petunia	Impatiens	Snapdragon
Primula	Lisianthus	Vinca
Snapdragon	Marigold	
Vinca		

High NH₄	Low B
Salvia	Pansy
Snapdragon	Petunia
Vinca	

range, are you relying on the young seedlings to tell you? By that time, it may be too late!

The gas gauge on your car tells you how much gas you have. The media EC is somewhat similar. If you have high EC readings (greater than 1.5 mmhos on a 2:1 extraction), the plants have either too much feed (in danger of high-salt damage) or they do not need any more. However, if you have low EC readings (less than 0.5 mmhos on a 2:1 extraction), your plants will run out of gas soon!

Most plug nutritional problems are related to media pH (Color plates 34 and 35). If your pH is greater than 6.5, then you need to lower into the acceptable range by one of the following methods:

- Use fertilizers that are more acid and that contain NH_4. However, be aware that seedling growth will increase quickly, maybe more than you want. Under cool, cloudy conditions, you do not want to use high NH_4 fertilizers.

- Use dilute acid (preferably sulfuric acid) to lower the media pH. If you are already using sulfuric acid to control water alkalinity, increase the amount of acid to bring down the media pH. Once it is down to an acceptable level, go back to your normal level of acid injection.

- Use iron sulfate at 1 to 2 lb per 100 gal as a drench. Make sure to rinse off the plants immediately after with clear water, as iron sulfate will burn the foliage. Iron sulfate will form sulfuric acid in the soil and combine with carbonates to lower pH [2].

If your media pH is less than 5.5 (less than 6.0 for certain crops), you need to raise it into the acceptable range. You can use one of the following methods:

- Use high-alkalinity water with no acid injection, if you have it. Alkalinity, limestone in the water, will raise the media pH.

- Use high NO_3 fertilizers, particularly those containing Ca. Remember that this type of fertilizer will keep plants shorter, with more toned growth. It will not rapidly expand leaves or promote fast growth, so if you are behind on your plug schedule, a high calcium nitrate fertilizer will not help you make up time.

- Use hydrated lime (calcium hydroxide, $Ca[OH]_2$) at 1 lb per 100 gal as a drench. Hydrated lime will not all dissolve, so you should use the solution and not the undissolved portion. Leave overnight to get the most into solution before using. You may need to rinse off the plants immediately after drenching, depending on the stress on the plants at the time.

These solutions are short-term fixes. They may need to be repeated if the media pH is still not in the acceptable range after treatment. You should also determine why the media pH is out of line and develop a longer-term fix.

For high soluble salt problems, leaching is the most effective solution. Water the plugs first with clear water, then water them again with clear water about one hour later, making sure to have water coming out of the bottom of the trays before moving on. Reduce the fertilizer concentration and frequency, and monitor regularly. For high NH_4 problems, you should leach thoroughly, switch fertilizers to a high NO_3 type, and warm up the soil temperature. For low B, check the media pH and Ca levels first. Then if you need to, add more B in the form of Solubor (1/4 oz per 100 gal) or Borax (1/2 oz per 100 gal) as a one-time-only drench.

Once you know what your water, media, and tissue results are, you can begin to solve any plug nutritional problem. Keep in mind that the environment and culture will interact with nutrition to exaggerate problems. For further practice at solving nutritional problems, we have included four common plug problems in appendix 3 for you to work on. Use the water and media quality guidelines, along with tissue guidelines, included in appendix 3 to diagnose and correct the nutritional problems. Remember, there could be more than one solution to solving a problem.

KEY POINTS TO REMEMBER

- The fertilizer helps control media pH, along with water alkalinity and limestone in the media. Fertilizers can be acidic or basic. Fertilizers containing high amounts of NH_4 (more than 25%) tend to be acidic in the soil solution, whereas fertilizers containing high amounts of NO_3 (more than 75%), particularly calcium nitrate, tend to be basic. Media pH determines nutrient availability to the plant. Nutrients are most readily available at pH between of 5.5 and 6.5.

- Maintain a nutrient balance of 1N:1K:1Ca:1/2Mg:1/5–1/10P for best growth. Keep the Fe to Mn ratio at 2:1. Keep the B level between 0.25 and 0.5 ppm. Keep the Na level at less than 40 ppm.

- Three factors are key to understanding what any fertilizer will do for your plugs: percentage of total N as NH_4/urea, potential acidity or basicity, and amounts of Ca and Mg in the fertilizer. Ammonium will promote shoot growth over root growth and encourage big, green leaves. It also will favor vegetative growth over flowering. The potential acidity or basicity tells you how much influence the fertilizer will have on the media pH. Calcium and Mg are necessary for root growth, thicker stems and leaves, and photosynthesis. Many fertilizers have little or no Ca and Mg.

- To control plug growth, monitor the balance between NH_4 and NO_3, depending on the environment, moisture, crop, and growth stage. Plugs need both compounds, but not the same amount of each. Make sure to supply some Ca and Mg. Regulate with frequency and concentration of feeding as well as type of fertilizer. One fertilizer will not work for all crops at all times!

- Media pH and EC are responsible for more than 80% of all plug nutritional disorders. Learn how to test pH and EC yourself on indicator crops. Know the basic symptoms of nutrient deficiencies and how to correct them. Better yet, know how to *prevent* them!

REFERENCES

[1] Cox, D. 1989. To buy or to blend? *Greenhouse Grower.* 7(5):34, 36–37.

[2] Finck, A. 1982. *Fertilizers and fertilization.* Weinheim, Germany: Verlag-Chemie GmbH.

[3] Knauss, J.F. 1986. The role of boron in plant nutrition. *GrowerTalks* 50(9):106–112.

[4] Laffe, S.R., and R.C. Styer. 1989. Too B or not too B—Learn to recognize boron deficiency. *GrowerTalks* 53(8):66.

[5] Marconi, D.J., and P.V. Nelson. 1984. Leaching of applied phosphorus in container media. *Scientia Horticulturae* 22:275–285.

[6] Marschner, H. 1995. *Mineral nutrition of higher plants.* 2nd ed. San Diego: Academic Press.

[7] Nelson, P.V. 1991. *Greenhouse operation and management.* 4th ed. Englewood Cliffs, N.J.: Prentice Hall.

[8] ———. 1994. Fertilization. In *Bedding plants IV,* ed. E.J. Holcomb, 151–75. Batavia, Ill.: Ball Publishing.

[9] Osmonics Engineering Memo #13. 1993. Minnetonka, Minn.: Osmonics, Inc.

[10] Reddy, S.K., and P.A. King. 1992. Sulfur—an emerging star. *GrowerTalks* 55(12):79, 81.

[11] Reddy, S.K., and M.A. Madore. 1995. Is there enough sulfur in your water? *GrowerTalks* 58(9):92.

[12] Scotts Testing Laboratory. Allentown, Penn.

[13] Warncke, D.D., and D.M. Krauskopf. 1983. *Greenhouse growth media: Testing and nutrition guidelines.* MSU Ag. Facts Ext. Bull. E-1736. East Lansing: Michigan State University.

[14] Winsor, G., and P. Adams. 1987. *Diagnosis of mineral disorders in plants.* Vol. 3, *Glasshouse crops.* London: Her Majesty's Stationery Office.

CHAPTER 12

CONTROLLING SHOOT AND ROOT GROWTH

P revious chapters have detailed how water and media quality, environment, nutrition, and moisture management affect plug growth. Some factors affect shoots more than roots and vice versa. The key to growing a quality plug is to incorporate the many factors previously covered into controlling the shoot:root ratio. But first, we need to define the characteristics of a quality plug:

- Proper height, with short internodes and lateral branching, if possible

- Solid green leaf color when appropriate

- Sufficient leaf expansion, with proper number of leaves for plug size

- No buds or flowers evident for most crops

- Active, healthy root system with root hairs when visible, resulting in readily pullable plug when moist

- No disease or insects

- Timely flowering after transplanting

- Every plug is uniform, depending on crop and plug cell size

- Tone or hardness to leaves and shoots when being shipped

To obtain the proper shoot:root ratio in any plug, we first need to review and tie together the effects of water quality, media quality, environment, nutrition, and moisture management on shoots and roots. Sometimes a plug crop will be growing too fast, and you need to slow it down. At other times, you need to push the crop to get it ready to transplant. When shoot growth is ahead of root growth, how do you get the roots to catch up? When the plug height is small but the roots are great, how do you get the shoots to expand?

EVALUATING SHOOT AND ROOT GROWTH

To control plug shoot and root growth, a grower must first evaluate the growth and determine if it is ahead or behind schedule. A clear picture of desired quality in each crop and in each plug size is needed, whether you are transplanting your own plugs or shipping them to other growers.

SHOOT GROWTH

Height. Most growers evaluate shoot growth by how tall the plug is above the soil line. Height can be judged by internode length, petiole length, or leaf length. For single-stem crops, such as celosia, snapdragon, and tomato, internode length is the main determinant of plug height. Tall plugs have elongated internodes but may still have the proper number of true leaves. Crops that grow from a crown or rosette, such as pansy, cyclamen, anemone, delphinium, and ranunculus, will be judged on petiole length, not internode length. Petiole length is controlled by the same factors as internode length. Leaf length is important for height in crops such as begonia and petunia, where there is a crown-type of growth but no long petioles. As the petunia plug gets older, however, a central stem will begin to elongate and greatly determine the height of the plug.

Leaf color. A second shoot growth criterion is the color of the leaves, which, for most crops, should be solid green. This includes the lower leaves, where yellow color may indicate that the plugs are underfed, stressed in some way, or have root rot such as *Pythium* or *Thielaviopsis.* The lowest leaves may just be shaded too much, turn yellow, and drop off (as with geranium and salvia). Dark green leaves, on the other hand, may indicate too much ammonium (NH_4) fertilizer. Pale green leaves may indicate a lack of nitrogen (N), NH_4 toxicity, or a lack of magnesium (Mg).

Some crops do not produce uniformly green leaves, or at least it is not desirable that they do, being known for their colored leaves, which are generally dependent on anthocyanin pigmentation. Dark-leaf begonias should have dark, not pale-colored leaves. Coleus and hypoestes have variegated or spotted pigmentation of different colors in addition to green. Dusty miller should have silvery dust on the youngest leaves when plugs are produced in 406 or larger plug cells. Lack of colored pigmentation in such crops may indicate too much NH_4 fertilizer or a lack of stress during growing (which should come from moisture, light, or temperature).

Leaf size or expansion. Another key way to evaluate shoot growth is by leaf size or expansion. Leaves should be properly expanded for the particular crop. For many crops, the leaves should completely cover the plug tray before transplanting or shipping. Small leaf size will cause the plug tray to look sparse. Customers who receive such plug trays may think there are too few usable plugs or the plugs are too small. Plug customers will definitely complain if begonia plugs have small leaves, but they will rarely complain if they have large leaves, unless using an automatic transplanter. Small leaf size may be caused by not enough NH_4 fertilizer, too much chemical growth regulator, or too intense light.

On the other hand, large leaves that are thin cause the plug tray to look overgrown and too tall. These soft leaves are particularly prone to diseases such as *Botrytis* and leaf spots. Large, soft leaves also make the plug more susceptible to damage during shipping and transplanting and may adversely affect growth after transplanting, especially in vegetable plugs transplanted into the field.

Number of true leaves. An indication of the plug's physiological age, the number of true leaves, is a direct result of the leaf-unfolding rate. Crops grown too cool will have fewer true leaves than they should. Too many true leaves, though, may indicate the plug is too old, has been grown too warm, or has been grown with too much NH_4 fertilizer, resulting in a tall plug. The number of true leaves will also depend on the plug cell size. For example, to be considered of sufficient age and size to be shipped and transplanted, pansies may have three true leaves when grown in an 800 tray, four true leaves in a 406 tray, five true leaves in a 288 tray, and six true leaves in a 128 tray.

Buds or blooms. The appearance of buds or blooms on the shoots is generally not desirable in a plug tray. Budding or blooming is usually a sign that the plugs are too old or have been stressed too much. For single-stem, single-flower crops, such as petunia, celosia, French marigold, salvia, and zinnia, the appearance of buds and blooms in a plug tray will mean delayed vegetative growth after transplanting, thus resulting in delays in finished production or an undesirable finished product. The plant will put all its energy into that main flower, and only later will it put energy into more vegetative growth (branching). For crops that are multiple-branched or multiple plants per cell, such as alyssum, portulaca, and impatiens, plug tray budding or blooming does not present problems after transplanting, as the plants will continue to grow vegetatively and flower at the same time. In fact, many plug customers want their impatiens plugs to be branched and budded when they transplant, as the crop will finish faster and with more blooms (fig. 12.1).

ROOT GROWTH

Pullability. To evaluate root growth, a grower must first pull up, or try to pull up, plugs to look at the roots. This is usually more difficult than looking at the tops of the plug trays to determine shoot growth. In evaluating root growth, a grower should look for plug pullability, root amount and location, root hairs and root thickness, and root rot. For a plug to be usable for transplanting, it needs to be pullable from the tray when moist. This means that the root system is developed enough to allow the plug media in the cell to be pulled intact and transplanted together with the roots. Otherwise, a grower will be transplanting a bare-rooted seedling. Generally, all plugs should be pullable about one week before transplanting or shipping. If not, the root growth is behind schedule.

FIGURE 12.1 Branched and budded impatiens plug.

Root amount and location. The amount and location of the roots gives a plug grower an idea of the effectiveness of the moisture management, nutrition, and environmental control programs. Roots located mainly in the top half of the plug cell can be a result of frequent, light waterings, with the bottom half staying too dry. On the other hand, the bottom half may be staying too wet, and only the top half dries out enough to support roots. Either way, the plug will not be pullable on time.

Roots will mainly be located on the outside of the media and at the bottom of the cell, less so through the center of the cell. This is due to the fact that more air is available at the interfaces between the plastic sides of the cell and the plug media and at the bottom of the cell where the hole allows drainage and evaporation. Some crops, such as ranunculus, send down a thickened taproot, which winds around at the bottom of the cell; only later will roots come up into the rest of the plug cell.

Root hairs and root thickness. Located mainly on the outside and bottom of the cell, long, thin roots, often called *hydroponic* or *water roots,* indicate overwatering or a plug media with little air porosity. Generally, these roots also lack root hairs, the fuzziness on the roots. Root hairs are necessary for expanding the root surface area, which improves uptake of the water and nutrients needed for plant growth. The plug system greatly enhances the seedling's ability to produce roots with root hairs. Bare-rooted seedlings from seedling flats do not produce any root hairs at all. Root hair development on such crops as pansy, petunia, and impatiens indicates good moisture management (fig. 12.2). There is enough water available for growth, but also enough air moving into the plug media pore spaces for roots to thrive.

Once root hairs are produced, they can be lost due to high salts or overdrying, however. Root hair loss will stunt growth, delay takeoff of root growth after transplanting, and may open up the root system to root rots, such as *Pythium* or *Thielaviopsis.*

FIGURE 12.2   Root hairs on pansy plug.

HOW TO ADJUST THE SHOOT:ROOT RATIO

Since growing a young seedling in a plug system is a very dynamic process, it is very difficult to keep the desired ratio between shoots and roots throughout the plug crop every time. Thus, a plug grower will always be making adjustments for every crop to promote the shoots or roots, or to speed up or slow down plug growth, based on the production schedule.

TOO MUCH SHOOT GROWTH

The main problem with plug quality that most plug growers have is a high shoot:root ratio, or too much shoot growth. Symptoms include tall, stretched plugs; large, soft leaves; and poor root growth. Petunia and impatiens frequently exhibit this problem. Many a plug grower has achieved luxuriant top growth but poor rooting, regardless of the plug tray size. Looking at the shoot growth, the plugs seem like they should be ready to transplant; they are not pullable, though, due to less-than-desirable root growth.

Corrective measures for a high shoot:root ratio include: (1) reducing temperature or using negative DIF, (2) reducing moisture levels, (3) changing fertilizer to one with more NO_3 and Ca, (4) increasing light levels, and (5) using chemical growth regulators. Growth of shoots and roots increases linearly with increasing temperature until an optimal temperature is reached (table 12.1). Average daily temperature determines the leaf-unfolding rate when temperatures are maintained in the linear range for growth. To slow down shoot growth, reduce the ADT—but stay within the linear range (usually 50 to 80F, 10 to 26C), or growth will stop completely. However, root growth will also slow down with a lower ADT. Internode length in most crops mainly depends on how temperature is delivered during a day-night cycle or on the difference between day and night temperatures. A negative DIF (day cooler than night) will keep internodes short, while allowing roots to grow.

TABLE 12.1 ENVIRONMENTAL AND CULTURAL FACTORS PROMOTING SHOOT AND ROOT GROWTH

| Factor | Level promoting growth | |
	Shoots	Roots
Temperature	Increasing (between 50 to 80F) +DIF	Increasing (50 to 80F) −DIF
Light intensity	Low (less than 1,500 fc)	High (more than 1,500 fc)
Moisture	High	Low
Nutrition	High NH_4 and P	High NO_3 and Ca
CO_2	High (1,000 ppm)	High (1,000 ppm)
Humidity	High	Low

A good alternating wet-dry moisture cycle (creating moisture stress) will promote roots, while keeping shoot growth from being too rapid. If your plug medium is not drying out within two days during the winter, or every day during the spring, then evaluate its water-holding capacity and air porosity. It may be that the plug medium contains too many fine particles with not enough air space for good root growth and good drainage. Media compaction, through handling and stacking filled plug trays on top of each other, will also squeeze the air spaces right out of the plug media. Using watering nozzles that deliver heavy streams of moisture may compact the media when plug seedlings are very young. Overwatering of plugs is the most common problem plug growers encounter, particularly with smaller plug sizes. Provide air movement and dehumidification cycles to promote evaporation and transpiration.

Changing to a high NO_3—low NH_4 fertilizer with at least 6% Ca (still not enough if there is low Ca in water) will favor root growth, while toning the shoot growth. Calcium is needed for cell wall thickness and root cell division and elongation. High NO_3 will keep the plant from stretching but still supply enough N for maintaining growth (fig. 12.3). It may also be necessary to reduce the total N to keep shoots from stretching. This NO_3 fertilizer can also be used when growing the plugs at soil temperatures lower than 60 to 62F (15 to 17C). Examples of high NO_3/ high Ca fertilizers include 15-0-15, 14-0-14, and 13-2-13-6-3. Remember that some of these fertilizers are basic and will raise the media pH over time.

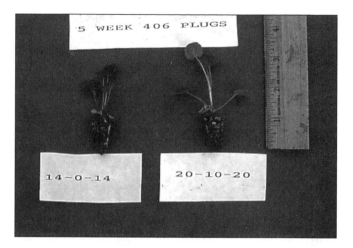

FIGURE 12.3 Difference in shoot growth of pansy plugs due to type of fertilizer only.

Increasing light levels or intensity will increase photosynthesis, thereby providing more sugars (carbohydrates) to the roots. At low light levels (less than 1,500 fc, 16,140 lux), leaves have first priority on the carbohydrates. At higher light levels (1,500 to 3,000 fc, 16,140 to 32,280 lux), roots get their fair share of the sugars needed for growth. Light intensity greater than 3,000 fc (32,280 lux) on the leaf will cause its temperature to go above the threshold (above 90F, 32C) for photosynthesis to continue safely. The stomates in the leaves then close to protect the plant, resulting in a temporary growth regulation. Once leaf temperature is back in the safe range, the stomates open and photosynthesis continues. Also, higher light levels tend to dry out the plug media more quickly through evaporation. Transpiration is also increased, resulting in more plant uptake of Ca.

Light quality affects plant appearance (table 9.4). The ratio of red to far-red light allows the plant to determine whether it is being shaded by surrounding plants. Green leaves preferentially absorb red light compared to far-red light, but leaves shaded by other leaves are exposed to less red light than far-red light. A high level of far-red light stimulates stem elongation and reduced branching, enabling a plant to grow through a canopy shading it to compete effectively with adjacent plants. Plant crowding is common in a plug tray. The overlapping leaves filter out red light, resulting in greater stem elongation and less branching in lower internodes. Hanging baskets over the plug crop promote the same effect [1, 2].

Chemical growth regulators are traditionally used when shoot growth is ahead of root growth. These chemicals block the synthesis or activation of GA, which would promote internode elongation. Some chemicals, such as

Bonzi and Sumagic, also stimulate root growth while keeping shoot growth from expanding, particularly in impatiens [3].

Slowing down shoot growth while simultaneously speeding up root growth is not an overnight process. It may take up to a week or longer, depending on the conditions available for manipulation and the crop being grown, to get enough roots. This process is different from just applying a chemical growth regulator and stopping the shoot growth within a day. Controlling growth through moisture and feed consists of decisions that should be made wisely each day for each crop.

TOO MUCH ROOT GROWTH

In some cases, plugs may have very good root systems, but the shoot growth is too small for the age of the plug. This results in a low shoot:root ratio. Symptoms of root growth being ahead of shoot growth include small and light-colored leaves, small tops with very short internodes, and lots of roots, making the plug very pullable. Commonly, growers in warm areas with low humidity and high light levels (such as California and Israel) may experience this problem.

Corrective measures for promoting more shoot growth (table 12.1) include: (1) increasing temperature or using positive DIF, (2) increasing moisture levels, (3) increasing use of fertilizers containing more NH_4 and P and less NO_3 and Ca, (4) reducing light levels, 5) increasing humidity levels around the plugs, and (6) minimizing use of chemical growth regulators. Shoot and root growth increases linearly with increasing temperature until an optimal temperature is reached, above which plant growth decreases. Average daily temperature determines the leaf-unfolding rate when temperatures are maintained in the linear range for growth (usually 50 to 80F, 10 to 26C). To speed up shoot growth, a grower can increase the ADT within the linear range until optimal temperature is reached. A positive DIF (day warmer than night) will increase internode length, or stretch, and increase plant dry weight.

To keep the plug cells from drying out too far, water more frequently and more thoroughly. You do not want to lose the good roots you have gained so far by keeping the media moist all of the time, though. Too much moisture for too long will promote foliar diseases *(Botrytis,* leaf spots) and root rots *(Pythium, Rhizoctonia).* In climates that tend to be very dry with high light levels, plug growers should evaluate plug media with higher water-holding capacity and less air porosity.

Fertilizers higher in NH_4/urea and P and lower in NO_3 and Ca will promote rapid shoot growth (fig. 12.3). Plants growing in conditions with warm temperatures, high light levels, and dry air are working very hard, with maximum photosynthesis and respiration, and need more energy. More NH_4/urea and P are needed to expand the leaves and internodes and keep the green color. Less Ca is needed, with the plant actively taking up available Ca through rapid water uptake. Higher rates of total N (ppm) may also be required.

To expand shoot growth, light levels should be reduced with shading to less than 2,500 fc (26,900 lux). A high light level can act as a growth retardant by heating up leaf temperature and shutting down photosynthesis. A lower light level will keep the stomates from closing by keeping the leaf temperature below the danger level (less than 90F, 32C). Evaporation and transpiration will also be slowed down under lower light levels. Providing more far-red than red light will also promote rapid shoot growth (table 9.4).

Increasing the humidity levels around the plugs can be accomplished by maintaining higher moisture levels or by introducing fog intermittently through the greenhouse. Fog systems can also cool the greenhouse or aid in the germination process on the bench. Pad and fan cooling also add humidity to dry greenhouses. High humidity levels reduce transpiration, or water loss from the plants, as well as reduce evaporation of media water.

When plants are grown in warm, dry areas with high light levels, chemical growth regulator use should be reduced to only what is really necessary. For many crops, such environmental conditions will be enough to keep shoot growth from rapidly expanding and keep internodes short. All chemical growth retardants should be closely trialed so as not to overdose a whole crop of seedlings. However, when the weather turns cloudy or rainy for several days, the plug grower may need to use such chemicals to keep the plugs from rapidly stretching.

Generally, if root growth is sufficient but shoot growth lags behind, it is easier to speed up the shoot growth by using positive DIF, feeding with more NH_4, cutting down the light levels, and keeping more moisture in and around the plugs. Within three days, shoot growth increases should be evident. Many plug growers hold back on the feed levels, particularly with vegetables, until about three days before shipping and planting. Then the growers pump the seedlings up with 300 to 400 ppm N from fertilizers such as 20-10-20 to green them up and get them growing again. This technique works well when the environmental conditions cooperate with the desired shoot growth. However, under conditions of warm temperature, high light, and dry air, it may take longer than three days for the shoot growth to expand sufficiently from fertilizer alone.

BEHIND SCHEDULE

When a plug crop is behind schedule and overall seedling (root and shoot) growth needs to be speeded up, a grower can: (1) increase the ADT by 5F (3C), (2) use positive DIF, (3) practice a good alternating wet-dry watering cycle, (4) increase feed levels to 150 to 250 ppm N, using more NH_4/urea fertilizer (such as 20-10-20) and feeding more frequently, and (5) provide light levels of 1,500 to 2,500 fc (16,140 to 26,900 lux). Keep a close eye on media EC and pH levels so as not to run into any major problems with root growth or nutrient uptake.

AHEAD OF SCHEDULE

When a plug crop is ahead of schedule and overall growth of roots and shoots needs to be slowed down, a grower can: (1) decrease ADT by 5F (3C) or more, (2) use negative DIF of 5 to 10F (3 to 6C), (3) run the plugs drier before watering, (4) decrease feed levels to under 100 ppm N using more NO_3 and Ca fertilizers (such as 14-0-14 or 13-2-13-6-3), (5) increase light levels to greater than 2,500 fc (26,900 lux) but less than 4,000 fc (43,040 lux), and (6) use chemical growth regulators judiciously. Late applications of Bonzi or Sumagic may cause delays in plugs growing out after transplanting. Again, monitor media pH and EC levels, particularly when using the basic fertilizers just mentioned and drying out the plugs more thoroughly. Soluble salt levels around the roots will increase three to four times under dry conditions.

KEY POINTS TO REMEMBER

- Plug quality is determined by the shoot:root ratio, along with leaf color and other attributes.

- Learn to recognize what makes a good shoot or good root system for each type of plug crop you grow.

- Factor levels (such as light, moisture, and fertilizer) promoting shoot growth may be the opposite of those promoting root growth.

- To speed up shoot growth, increase temperature up to the optimal level or use positive DIF, increase moisture levels, increase feeding with NH_4 and P, and decrease light levels.

- To speed up root growth, use negative DIF, increase light levels, increase feeding with NO_3 and Ca, and decrease moisture levels.

REFERENCES

[1] Erwin, J. 1992. Build a better plug. Presentation given at International Plug Conference, Orlando, Fla.

[2] Moore, S.R. 1995. Filtered light has potential as growth regulator. *GrowerTalks* 59(10):62, 64.

[3] Styer, R.C. 1989. Control impatiens height in the plug stage with Sumagic or Bonzi. *GrowerTalks* 52(10):52.

CHAPTER 13

HEIGHT CONTROL

*P**lug quality* is popular phraseology today. Growers who grow for themselves or who buy or sell plugs strive to achieve quality plugs. What is *quality*? Each grower has special requirements and definitions, but most would agree that *quality* refers to a well-formed root system, good branching, controlled height, good color, timely flowering, and absence of pests and disease.

Of these attributes, the one most growers see first or put the most emphasis on is height control. Plugs that are too tall will not transplant easily, are generally soft and easily bruised, may not flower early, may have poor root systems, will neither ship nor hold well, and are more susceptible to insects and disease. Plugs that are too small are generally hard to transplant, have poor root systems, show poor counts in the plug trays, and may require the customer to grow on in the plug trays before transplanting. Growers who grow plugs for themselves are not as critical about height control as those who buy plugs from others. The advent of automatic transplanters for both field and greenhouse transplanting increases the need for consistent, predictable plug height—regardless of the crop or time of year.

This chapter discusses nonchemical and chemical growth regulators for height control. Every effort should be made to control the crop's environment and culture to minimize the need for chemical growth regulators. The banning of B-Nine on vegetable transplants puts renewed focus on the height-control effects of temperature, moisture, nutrition, light, and mechanical means. Growers of flowers and ornamentals should pay attention to these factors and cultivar selection. Chemical growth regulators not only cost money, they also are difficult to consistently apply, and cause problems with worker reentry into treated greenhouse areas.

The information presented in this chapter does not constitute a recommendation or an endorsement of particular chemicals or techniques. Rules for chemical usage vary between different countries and sometimes between different states in the United States. Each grower has different growing conditions and techniques; therefore, any control measure, chemical or natural, should be tested on a limited scale before being applied to the full crop. Always read and follow label directions, and use proper precautions in applying chemicals.

NONCHEMICAL GROWTH CONTROL

Growers have long manipulated temperature, moisture, nutrition, and light to modify plant growth—and now to produce plugs. How well they do it determines the amount of chemical growth regulators needed, as well as final quality.

To understand this point, imagine that growing a plug is like driving your car. You have a gas pedal and a brake pedal. When you want to go forward in your car, you put your foot on the gas pedal. When a grower wants a plug to grow, "gas" is provided by higher temperature, higher moisture or relative humidity levels, more ammonium nitrogen (NH_4) fertilizers or higher fertilizer levels, or lower light levels. When you want to stop your car, you put your foot on the brake pedal. A grower can slow down plug growth by lowering temperature, lowering moisture or relative humidity levels, replacing NH_4 fertilizers with calcium/potassium nitrate fertilizers or lowering fertilizer levels, increasing light levels, or using chemical growth regulators. Too often, a grower applies chemical growth regulators to slow down plants, yet keeps providing optimum environmental and cultural conditions for plug growth. This is like trying to drive a car with your feet on the gas and brake pedals at the same time. The key is to take your foot off the gas pedal before applying the brake!

TEMPERATURE

The cooler the temperature, the slower and shorter a plant will grow, until a temperature is reached where no growth will occur. For most plants, this level is between 41 and 50F (5 to 10C). Low-temperature control applied before flower initiation, or for an excessive period of time after flower initiation, may cause stunting and flower delay. Tomatoes do not tolerate cold and will not respond to such treatment. Neither will begonias, impatiens, or vinca [7]. Petunias grown too cool before flower initiation will take much longer to bloom, even though more branching occurs [9].

Both root and shoot growth increase linearly with temperature between the general range of 50 to 85F (10 to 30C) (fig. 9.3). This means that to speed up plant growth, a grower can increase the ADT. To slow down plant growth, reduce the ADT—but stay within the general range, or growth will stop completely.

Regulating day and night temperatures affects plant height and development and is described by a relationship called DIF, discussed in chapter 9. Internode elongation and final plant height can be reduced either by keeping day and night temperatures the same (zero DIF) or by reducing day temperature below that of night (negative DIF). Internode elongation can be increased by keeping day temperatures greater than night temperatures (positive DIF), the normal situation in a greenhouse.

The first two or three hours of morning light are the most critical time for using DIF effectively. Cooling the first two or three hours in the morning can produce as much height control as maintaining cooling all day long [8]. The air temperature must be at the low point before sunrise. The set-point adjustment timing is dependent on the heating system. A system with a slow response time, such as a hot water system, may require its set-points to be lowered 45 to 60 minutes before sunrise. A system with a fast response time, such as a unit heater, should have its set-points lowered about 15 minutes before sunrise.

Not all plants respond the same way to DIF (table 13.1). Photoperiod also influences the effectiveness of DIF. The longer the night period (short days), the more effective DIF is [7]. This may be due to more red light being available during long days, and to the shorter nights not allowing more build-up of the stretch-promoting phytochrome.

On seedlings, start DIF treatments for most crops once germination is finished and a full set of mature leaves is evident. Remember, you must also calculate the ADT in order not to delay the overall growth rate of your plug crop. Too often growers use DIF but forget about ADT, and have the crop take longer than expected to reach transplantable size. If using the two- to three-hour dip method in the morning, then ADT is minimally affected. ADT is changed when using zero or negative DIF through the whole day.

Negative DIF often causes chlorosis of young leaves, particularly in salvia (Color plate 51) and gerbera. This chlorosis is not due to a nutrient deficiency and is readily reversible when the plants are placed in a positive DIF environment. Try to avoid negative DIF beyond 15 to 20F (8 to 11C). It is best to achieve zero DIF.

TABLE 13.1 SPECIES RESPONSE TO DIF

Large response		Small or no response
Asiatic lilies	Petunia	Aster
Celosia	Poinsettia	French marigold
Chrysanthemum	Portulaca	Hyacinth
Dianthus	Rose	Narcissus
Easter lily	Salvia	Platycodon
Fuchsia	Snap bean	Squash
Geranium	Snapdragon	Tulip
Gerbera	Sweet corn	
Hypoestes	Tomato	
Impatiens	Watermelon	
Oriental lilies		

Source: From Heins & Erwin, Understanding and applying DIF, *Greenhouse Grower.*

Internode elongation can be promoted or reduced on a daily basis. Internode elongation can be slowed immediately by reducing DIF. This method works very well on most vegetable transplants, for which no chemical growth regulators are labeled for use in the United States.

MOISTURE

Low moisture levels produce slow plant growth and a more compact habit. Leaves and stems may be thicker and root growth improved. However, low moisture levels may also cause stunting and flower delay. The key is to know just when to water and how much. Certain crops, such as celosia and French marigold, may prematurely flower in the plug tray due to low-moisture stress. Premature flowering will not allow the plant to grow out sufficiently after transplanting. On the other hand, moisture stress can keep impatiens compact and force budding and branching, giving the grower a much better transplant that will finish faster after transplanting.

Relative humidity levels within the greenhouse can also influence plant height. High relative humidity caused by cool wet weather and poor air circulation will cause many crops to stretch in the plug tray due to reduced evapotranspiration. Reduce relative humidity at night by increasing heating and venting before sundown for short periods of time (dehumidification cycles) and by increasing air movement through venting or HAF fans. Keep Stage 3 plants away from fog zones used for Stages 1 and 2.

NUTRITION

High levels of starter fertilizer in a plug media (greater than 0.75 mmhos, 2:1 dilution) will promote rapid seedling growth even before the first true leaves emerge. Crops such as tomato, snapdragon, godetia, lettuce, celosia, and cosmos will quickly get too tall even before Stage 3 starts, thereby making it more difficult to control plant height. Test your plug media soluble salts before using. The EC level should be lower than 0.75 mmhos/cm (2:1 dilution).

Reduce the amounts of fertilizer given to crops that stretch quickly, particularly in cloudy weather. Monitor the EC levels in your plug trays, and give less ppm N, if needed. Ammonium nitrogen (NH_4) fertilizers (including urea) promote soft growth. Potassium and Ca sources of NO_3 promote more toned growth. Shift to low NH_4 fertilizers (13-2-13-6-3 or 14-0-14) during winter months, and cloudy periods to control plant height. Low light levels (less than 1500 fc, 16,140 lux) during such periods, along with higher humidity, will promote soft, stretched shoot growth.

Phosphorus is another nutrient most growers, particularly vegetable plug growers, limit [7]. A mild P deficiency keeps plants short and purplish. However, with increasing P deficiency, symptoms may become too severe, and plants may not grow out properly after transplanting. Phosphorus should be added to the feed program in small amounts. Normally, a plug grower only needs one fifth to one tenth the amount of P as N, K, and Ca.

LIGHT

In Stage 3, light levels should be close to 2,500 fc (26,900 lux) for best growth of most crops. When light levels drop well below this level for several days, plants will elongate (stretch) and become soft. For many plug growers in northern areas during the winter months, natural short days and greenhouse light levels of 150 fc (1,614 lux) do not provide enough light to grow high-quality plugs. HID lights can provide an extra 450 to 600 fc (4,842 to 6,456 lux) of light and extend the winter day length to 16 to 18 hours. This extra light will speed up plant growth but help keep the plant shorter with better branching and better leaf development.

Plants grown in glass greenhouses are shorter than those grown in double-polyethylene greenhouses, due to more light transmission. Greenhouses with retractable roofs (the whole roof opening up) allow more UV light to the plant, resulting in more compact growth (fig. 13.1).

High light levels (greater than 2,500 fc, 26,900 lux) during Stage 3 will also help keep plant height shorter. Photosynthesis in the leaf becomes light-saturated at about 3,000 fc (32,280 lux). Any more light above this level is received as heat. The subsequent reduction in plant growth is primarily caused by sunlight increasing the leaf temperature above 90F (32C), causing the leaf stomates to close. Essentially, photosynthesis stops for the period that the leaves are too hot. Therefore, high light acts as a growth regulator. Be careful about too much high light, as the leaves may bleach out or burn, particularly with begonia. Fertilizer levels will probably need to be increased when plugs are grown under higher light levels.

High light can also cause stress on plants, making them flower faster. With crops like celosia and French marigold, high light levels promote premature flowering, as does moisture stress. Keep these crops under moderate light levels to avoid premature flowering.

FIGURE 13.1 Retractable-roof greenhouse. Courtesy Cravo Equipment Ltd.

MECHANICAL METHODS

Various ways of mechanically disturbing the plant have shown positive results in controlling plant height. These methods include brushing, shaking, and increasing air movement. The plant bending that occurs, however brief, stimulates ethylene production within the plant. Ethylene is a plant growth hormone that tends to promote lateral branching and inhibit apical growth.

Brushing different vegetable transplants several times a day has yielded significant height reductions, with best results on tomato [1, 10]. Care must be taken to avoid scraping the leaves and causing quality to decrease. Pepper transplants have suffered more damage than benefit from brushing [11].

Several growers brush by extending plastic sheets from their boom irrigators and running them over their plug crops on a timer anywhere from one to four times a day during Stage 3. Brushing for height control may also be advantageous in an integrated pest-management program to control aphids and thrips [12]. Increasing air movement inside the greenhouse with HAF fans, or by rolling the plug trays outside, also helps to keep plants short.

CHEMICAL GROWTH REGULATORS

Synthetic growth-regulating chemicals prevent a plant's natural production of gibberellins, although at different parts of the pathway. Their primary use is to achieve a shorter plant through reduction of internodal elongation below the growing meristem, not through fewer leaves or nodes. In many cases, the leaves become greener, branching is increased, and root growth may be increased. However, flowering may be slowed down (except for Cycocel acting on geranium). Not all chemical growth regulators have the same effects on the same crops, nor do they work on all crops.

COMMERCIAL PRODUCTS

B-Nine is the trade name for daminozide, manufactured by Uniroyal Chemical Company. It is applied only as a spray, not as a drench, and is generally applied to runoff. It is taken up easily through leaves, is very mobile within the plant, and moves to all parts after application. Concentrations for plugs range from 1,250 to 5,000 ppm (table 13.2), with repeat applications needed. Many crops grown in warm temperatures are not responsive to B-Nine, primarily due to the rapid plant growth in warm temperatures, not because B-Nine breaks down. Also, B-Nine may evaporate from the leaves

TABLE 13.2   B-NINE SPRAY DILUTIONS

| Desired level | | B-Nine needed | | | Water needed | |
%	ppm	tsp/gal	oz/gal	g/l	gal/1 lb B-Nine	gal/1 cup B-Nine [a]
0.08	800	1.3	0.13	0.9	127	37.5
0.1	1,000	1.6	0.16	1.2	101	30.0
0.15	1,500	2.4	0.24	1.8	68	20.0
0.2	2,000	3.2	0.31	2.4	50	15.0
0.25	2,500	4.0	0.39	2.9	41	12.0
0.3	3,000	4.8	0.47	3.5	33	10.0
0.35	3,500	5.6	0.55	4.1	29	8.6
0.375	3,750	6.0	0.59	4.4	27	8.0
0.4	4,000	6.4	0.63	4.7	25	7.5
0.5	5,000	8.0	0.79	5.9	20	6.0
0.75	7,500	12	1.18	8.8	14	4.0
1.0	10,000	16	1.57	11.8	10	3.0

[a] The values are only approximate; use weight measurements whenever possible.
Source: From Barrett & Nell, Altering retardant spray rates, *PPGA News.*

TABLE 13.3 EFFECTIVE PLUG GROWTH REGULATORS

Crop	B-Nine	A-Rest	Bonzi	Sumagic	Cycocel + B-Nine
Ageratum	♦	♦	♦	♦	♦
Alyssum	♦	♦			
Begonia [a]		♦			♦ [b]
Celosia			♦	♦	♦
Coleus		♦	♦	♦	♦
Dahlia	♦	♦	♦	♦	♦
Dianthus		♦	♦	♦	♦ [b]
Dusty miller	♦	♦	♦		
F. kale/cabbage	♦		♦	♦	
Geranium		♦	♦	♦	♦ [b]
Hypoestes		♦	♦	♦	♦ [b]
Impatiens		♦	♦	♦	
Lobelia	♦				
Marigold		♦	♦	♦	♦
Nicotiana	♦		♦	♦	♦
Pansy	♦	♦	♦	♦	♦
Petunia	♦	♦	♦	♦	♦
Portulaca	♦	♦			
Salvia	♦	♦	♦	♦	♦
Snaps (not cuts)	♦	♦	♦	♦	♦
Torenia			♦		
Verbena	♦		♦	♦	♦
Vinca	♦	♦		♦	♦
Viola	♦	♦			
Zinnia	♦	♦	♦	♦	♦

[a] On begonias, especially tuberous, you can use Bayleton (Strike) at quarter to half rate or Zyban at half to full rate (also good for mildew control).

[b] You can also use Cycocel alone.

Note: Important—these chemicals are not necessarily labeled for such use!

quicker at warm temperatures, thus restricting the amount of active ingredient getting into the plant. For these reasons, plug growers in northern areas get more response from B-Nine than southern growers. Impatiens, marigolds, snapdragon, and geranium may show little or no response to B-Nine (table 13.3).

Cycocel is the trade name for chlormequat chloride, manufactured by BASF and sold in the United States only by Olympic Chemical. It can be applied as a spray or a drench. The primary ornamental use is on poinsettia, azalea, geranium, and hibiscus, although many plug growers are using it on tuberous begonia, hypoestes, and dianthus (table 13.3). The Cycocel U.S. label is being expanded to include all bedding plant crops. Spray concentrations on plugs range from 750 to 3,000 ppm (table 13.4). Sprays of Cycocel can cause phytotoxicity as chlorotic spotting or a halo effect on newly expanded leaves (Color plate 52). These symptoms, appearing in three to five days, are due to damage to the chloroplast.

TABLE 13.4   CYCOCEL SPRAY DILUTIONS

Dilution ratio [a]	Desired ppm [a]	fl oz/gal	ml/l	ml/gal
1:118	1,000	1.1	8.5	32.1
1:80	1,500	1.6	12.7	48.1
1:70	1,685	1.8	14.3	54.1
1:60	2,000	2.2	16.9	64.2
1:50	2,500	2.7	21.2	80.2
1:40	3,000	3.3	25.4	96.2
1:34	3,500	3.8	29.7	112.3
1:30	4,000	4.3	33.9	128.8
1:25	4,500	4.9	38.1	144.4
1:23	5,000	5.4	42.4	160.4
1:21	5,500	6.0	46.6	176.5
1:20	6,000	6.5	50.8	192.5

[a] Approximate

Source: From Barrett & Nell, Altering retardant spray rates, *PPGA News.*

In some cases, most notably with poinsettia and pansy, a tank mix of B-Nine (2,500 ppm) and Cycocel (1,500 ppm) is used. Combining the two chemicals provides a synergistic effect, greater than the sum of the two chemicals alone, but is dependent on the cultivar selection. This synergistic effect occurs because the different chemicals affect slightly different steps in GA production. This tank mix is not labeled for pansy, but growers of summer/fall pansies are using it effectively without having as many problems with the leaf halo effect. With the recent expansion of the Cycocel label in the United States, however, the tank mix will be legal to use on plugs. The tank mix is very effective and will be more widely used by plug growers as it is publicized. Choose a Cycocel rate that will not cause phytotoxicity and then raise or lower the B-Nine rate to adjust the activity [4].

A-Rest is the trade name for ancymidol, manufactured and sold by SePro. This chemical is more active than Cycocel or B-Nine and can be used on most all major crops (table 13.3). Applied as a spray or a drench, it readily moves around the plant. Plug spray concentrations are between 5 and 25 ppm (table 13.5). The high cost of A-Rest has prevented many growers from using this very effective chemical. However, A-Rest works well on pansy and vinca at about 10 ppm, which many plug producers find cost-effective because of its ease of use and fewer problems with overstunting.

TABLE 13.5   A-REST SPRAY DILUTIONS

Desired ppm	fl oz/gal	ml/l	ml/gal
10	4.8	38	143
25	12	95	359
33	16	125	473
50	24	189	717
66	32	250	947
75	36	284	1,076
100	49	379	1,435

Source: From Barrett & Nell, Altering retardant spray rates, *PPGA News.*

Bonzi, trade name for paclobutrazol from Uniroyal Chemical Company, and *Sumagic,* trade name for uniconazole from Valent U.S.A., are two of the newer chemicals classified as triazoles, which are very active and affect almost all plant species. These two chemicals are very similar and affect the same part of the GA pathway; therefore, they will be discussed together. They do not readily move within the plant. They are very active when applied as a drench, because they are absorbed by the roots and translocated to the growing shoot tips, where they are active. These chemicals are not taken up through the leaves but through the stems and roots.

The optimum concentrations for different plug crops vary more with Bonzi and Sumagic than with other chemical growth regulators. They are so much more active that the potential for excessive growth control is great. Bonzi is generally used at concentrations ranging from 2 to 90 ppm (table 13.6), whereas Sumagic is generally used at half the concentrations of Bonzi (table 13.7). Pansy (Color plate 54), geranium, and vinca are very sensitive, while snapdragon is the least sensitive (table 13.8). Begonias are so sensitive that the labels for both chemicals do not include them. Bonzi causes black spots on vinca leaves (Color plate 53), whereas Sumagic does not. High rates of Bonzi and Sumagic may delay impatiens flowering.

TABLE 13.6 BONZI SPRAY DILUTIONS

Desired ppm [a]	fl oz/gal	ml/l	ml/gal
1	0.032	0.25	0.95
6	0.2	1.6	6.0
8	0.25	2.0	7.5
10	0.32	2.5	9.5
16	0.5	3.9	15.0
25	0.8	6.3	24.0
31	1.0	7.8	30.0
47	1.5	11.7	44.0
50	1.6	12.5	47.0
63	2.0	15.5	59.0
75	2.4	18.8	71.0
94	3.0	23.4	89.0
100	3.2	25.0	95.0
109	3.5	27.3	105.0
125	4.0	31.2	120.0
200	6.4	50.0	190.0
300	9.6	75.0	285.0

[a] Approximate

Source: From Barrett & Nell, Altering retardant spray rates, *PPGA News.*

Some fungicides have plant growth regulator activity and may be used on certain crops. Remember, though, these fungicides are *not* labeled as growth regulators! Bayleton (Strike) is a triazole fungicide that controls mildews. Zyban, a combination fungicide containing mancozeb and thiophanate-methyl, will also control mildews and other leaf spots. Some plug growers use either of these fungicides on begonias (both fibrous and tuberous) at less than the labeled rate to control plant height and powdery mildew (table 13.3).

APPLICATION PROBLEMS

Chemical growth regulator effectiveness is often determined by the absorption mechanism. The active ingredient must move through the waxy layer of leaves and stems into the plant and be translocated to the growing points. Water-soluble growth retardants (B-Nine and Cycocel) move slowly into the wax layer, whereas growth retardants that are poorly soluble in water (A-Rest, Bonzi, and Sumagic) move rapidly through it. For Cycocel and B-Nine,

TABLE 13.7   SUMAGIC SPRAY DILUTIONS

Desired ppm	fl oz/gal	ml/l	ml/gal
1.0	0.25	2	7.5
2.0	0.5	4	15.0
2.5	0.625	5	18.75
3.0	0.75	6	22.5
4.0	1.0	8	30.0
5.0	1.25	10	37.5
6.0	1.5	12	45.0
8.0	2.0	16	60.0
10.0	2.5	20	75.0
12.0	3.0	24	90.0
15.0	3.75	30	112.5
16.0	4.0	32	120.0
20.0	5.0	40	150.0
24.0	6.0	48	180.0
30.0	7.5	60	225.0
40.0	10.0	80	300.0

Source: From Barrett & Nell, Altering retardant spray rates, *PPGA News.*

movement into the wax layer occurs only while the leaf is still wet; once the leaf dries off, no further movement occurs. Therefore, it is necessary to apply B-Nine and Cycocel at the end of the day, or during conditions of high humidity, so that the leaves stay wet for 12 to 18 hours. If the plants are watered overhead before this time period is up, the chemicals are washed away. Many growers do not leave these chemicals on long enough and thus do not get as much control with them.

A-Rest, Bonzi, and Sumagic move into the plant rapidly, complete absorption occurring within minutes. Therefore, these chemicals can be applied at any time of day. The best is during the morning, as the grower can then irrigate later in the day without worrying about washing off these chemicals.

Application volume (measured not in ppm, but as to amount of active ingredient applied per plant) is more important with A-Rest, Bonzi, and Sumagic than with B-Nine and Cycocel. B-Nine can be sprayed to run off. B-Nine and Cycocel are absorbed through the leaves, putting the spraying emphasis on uniform leaf coverage. However, Bonzi and Sumagic are absorbed through the stems and roots. A-Rest is active when applied to leaves, but it is more active through the roots.

TABLE 13.8   OPTIMUM BONZI AND SUMAGIC RATE RANGES FOR BEDDING PLANTS

| Relative level | Optimum rate range (ppm) [a] | | Crops |
	Bonzi	Sumagic	
High	30–60	15–30	Afr. marigold [b]
			Ageratum
			Petunia
			Snapdragon [b]
Medium	15–30	5–15	Celosia
			Coleus
			Dahlia
			Fr. marigold [b]
			Salvia [b]
			Verbena
			Most other crops
Low	5–15	1–3	Geranium
			Impatiens
			Pansy
			Vinca

[a] Use low end of rate for starting point for plug applications. Growers in northern areas may need to use half the low end of rate.

[b] Sumagic better than Bonzi.

Note: Begonia—Warning! Do not even use!

Source: From Barrett, Bedding plant height control, Grower Expo.

Bonzi and Sumagic are rate- and volume-sensitive chemicals, meaning that a plug grower must not only use the correct rate (ppm) but apply the chemical the same way every time. The suggested volume is 2 qts per 100 ft^2. Nonuniform spray techniques and different spray personnel can cause variation between plants within a bench or from week to week.

Application costs of chemical growth regulators differs dramatically (table 13.9). B-Nine used to be the cheapest chemical to apply, but its price has steadily increased in recent years. Bonzi and Sumagic are cheap to use, since the amount of chemical per application is very low. A-Rest is the most expensive, but for high-value crops such as plugs, it may be very economical. A-Rest will give control similar to Bonzi and Sumagic but is more forgiving. A-Rest works better on more crops than B-Nine or Cycocel.

TABLE 13.9   COSTS OF GROWTH RETARDANT SPRAY APPLICATIONS

Chemical	Container price[a]	Application rate		Cost ($)[b] per 100 ft²
		ppm	Amount/gal	
A-Rest	$55/qt	5	2.4 fl oz	2.06
		15	7.3 fl oz	6.18
B-Nine	$65/lb	1,250	0.2 oz	0.41
		5,000	0.79 oz	1.64
Bonzi	$95/qt	5	0.16 fl oz	0.24
		20	0.64 fl oz	0.96
Cycocel	$65/qt	800	0.9 fl oz	0.90
		1,500	1.6 fl oz	1.62
Sumagic	$98/qt	1	0.25 fl oz	0.38
		4	1.0 fl oz	1.53

[a] Average of three sources; based on smallest available unit, therefore higher cost than for most growers.

[b] Based on spray volume of 2 qt/100 ft². Does not include labor. Actual costs for grower will vary depending on container costs, application rate, and application volume.

Source: Courtesy Jim Barrett, University of Florida.

INTERACTION WITH CULTURAL AND ENVIRONMENTAL FACTORS

Crops produced in cooler climates or during cooler months require smaller amounts of growth retardants than ones in warmer conditions. Many plug growers report B-Nine does not work on crops grown in warm temperatures but will work in cooler temperatures. This response is most likely due to the crops outgrowing the growth retardant at the warmer temperatures and not due to reduced chemical activity at high temperatures. Growth retardant rates need to be increased as the weather warms up, particularly in spring and summer.

For Bonzi and Sumagic, the temperature after application is just as important as how fast the plant is growing. If the temperature gets cooler for the two to 10 days after a Bonzi or Sumagic application, the growth retardant will have a stronger effect than anticipated. A plug grower using DIF, or during rapidly changing weather, should pay special attention to the chemical rate. Only 1 ppm may become as strong as 10 ppm due to temperature changes.

FIGURE 13.2   Plant size of White Flash petunias in 4-inch pots was affected by fertilizer level, drought stress, and Bonzi. Stressed plants were not irrigated until wilted, and nonstressed plants were not allowed to wilt. The dotted section on each bar shows the effect of Bonzi on plants with that fertilizer and stress treatment. The striped section shows size of plants without Bonzi, and the dotted section shows size of plants sprayed with Bonzi at 45 ppm. *Source:* From Barrett and Nell, *ActaHort.*

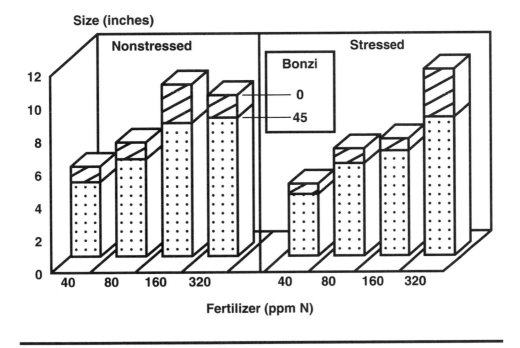

Moisture stress and type and amount of fertilizer affect growth rates and alter retardant effects. Figure 13.2 shows the effect Bonzi had on petunias grown with and without moisture stress and with different levels of fertilizer [6]. Bonzi's greatest effect occurred on the most vigorous plants. However, if growth was reduced due to moisture stress or a low fertilizer level, there was less height reduction from Bonzi. This figure illustrates again the concept of taking your foot off the gas pedal before applying the brake!

Make sure plugs are properly turgid before applying growth retardants. If not, leaf margin burn, stunting of plants, and spotting of leaves may occur. Plugs grown under a low fertilizer program may not be able to outgrow the growth retardant applied. Switching to a low-NH$_4$ fertilizer that also contains Ca will prevent the plant from rapidly stretching.

As you know by now, there are no universal recommendations for how much growth retardant to use and when. Plug growers need to do their own trials to determine what works for them. Jim Barrett at the University of

Florida [2] summarizes this need by offering these 10 suggestions for more successful trials.

1. Do not schedule trials during peak production periods.

2. Do trials in a manner similar to your production.

3. Do not use the poorest greenhouse space for your trials.

4. Clearly mark trials in the greenhouse.

5. Test one factor at a time.

6. Maintain accurate records.

7. Include control plants.

8. Randomize and replicate your treatments.

9. Do the work before the information is needed.

10. Conduct trials.

Plug growers should not become overly reliant on chemical growth retardants. Control environmental and cultural factors that influence plug growth first, then use growth retardants. When needed, chemical growth regulators should be used based on a complete understanding of rate, volume, stage of plant development, environment, and crop. Remember, no chemical growth regulators are labeled for use on vegetable transplants in the United States.

KEY POINTS TO REMEMBER

- Take your foot off the gas pedal before applying the brakes! Use all nonchemical methods—such as low temperature, low moisture, high light, low fertilizer or fertilizers low in P and NH_4—first before applying chemical growth retardants.

- The difference between day and night temperature (DIF) is very effective in controlling stem elongation in plugs. Use a zero DIF or a negative DIF of 5 to 10F (3 to 6C) (day temps cooler than night). Apply the cooler day temperature for the first two to three hours around sunrise.

- B-Nine and Cycocel move slowly into leaves, as long as the leaves are moist. Apply these chemicals at the end of the day for best uptake.

- A-Rest, Bonzi, and Sumagic move quickly into the plant, within 30 minutes.

- B-Nine is effective on a wide range of crops but not at warm temperatures. The Cycocel label in the United States will be expanded to include using a tank mix of B-Nine and Cycocel on bedding plants.

■ A-Rest works on a wide range of plug crops, but it is the most expensive chemical. Consider using A-Rest on plug crops that have difficulty with other chemicals, such as pansy and vinca.

■ Bonzi and Sumagic are taken up quickly by the stems and roots, not the leaves. They are very strong chemicals and effective on a wide range of plug crops. They are also rate- and volume-sensitive, meaning you need to pay attention not only to rate (ppm) used but also to coverage of plants with the spray volume.

■ Do your own trials to determine which chemicals work best for you and under what environmental and cultural conditions.

REFERENCES

[1] Baden, S.A., and J.G. Latimer. 1992. An effective system for brushing vegetable transplants for height control. *HortTechnology* 2(3):412–414.

[2] Barrett, J. 1993. Ten suggestions for more successful research trials at your greenhouse. *Greenhouse Manager* 11(11):127.

[3] ———. 1994. Bedding plant height control; growth retardants. Presentation given at Grower Expo, Chicago, Ill.

[4] ———. 1995. Enhancing the activity of B-Nine and Cycocel. *Greenhouse Management & Production* 14(8):72.

[5] Barrett, J.E., and T.A. Nell. 1989. Altering retardant spray rates helps growers adapt to varying conditions. *PPGA News* 20(2):8–9.

[6] ———. 1990. Factors affecting efficacy of paclobutrazol and uniconazole on petunia and chrysanthemum. *ActaHort.* 272:229–234.

[7] Carlson, W. 1990. Height control in vegetable transplants. *Greenhouse Grower* 8(2):16–17.

[8] Heins, R., and J. Erwin. 1990. Understanding and applying DIF. *Greenhouse Grower* 8(2):73–78.

[9] Koranski, D.S. 1987. Growing plugs—from A to Z. *GrowerTalks* 50(9):64–79.

[10] Latimer, J.G. 1991. Mechanical conditioning for control of growth and quality of vegetable transplants. *HortScience* 26:1456–1461.

[11] ———. 1994. Pepper transplants are excessively damaged by brushing. *HortScience* 29(9):1002–1003.

[12] Latimer, J.G., and R.D. Oetting. 1994. Brushing reduces thrips and aphid populations on some greenhouse-grown vegetable transplants. *HortScience* 29(11):1279–1281.

CHAPTER **14**

DISEASES AND INSECTS

M ost plug seedlings are produced in relatively short time. They are
smaller and nonflowering compared to posttransplanted crops, thus
making plugs not as likely to have many problems with diseases and insects.
However, with their intensive, high-density culture and the many crops that
may be grown at the same time, certain diseases and insects can become
major problems even during the short plug cycle. With longer-term plug
crops, such as lisianthus, gerbera, cyclamen, and begonia, diseases and
insects have a better chance to adversely affect quality.

In this chapter we will cover the major diseases and insects you will
likely encounter in plug production, their symptoms, hosts, and controls.
Tables are included for registered, effective plug fungicides and insecticides
in the United States.

DISEASES

DAMPING-OFF

Damping-off and crown and root rots are the most common plug diseases.
Damping-off results when a fungus attacks the germinating seed or seedling
at or just below the surface of the growing media. The fungus invades and
weakens the stem, causing the seedlings to fall over, even though the roots
are healthy. Under damp conditions, fungi are visible as weblike growths
over seedlings. In some cases, the roots may also become infected, resulting
in yellow leaves, stunted growth, and dieback. Damping-off can easily be
spotted due to the circular pattern of dying seedlings within the plug tray.

Several fungi can cause damping-off, and it may be difficult to tell which one is responsible. *Pythium, Phytophthora, Rhizoctonia, Fusarium,* and *Botrytis* can either separately or in combination be responsible. The most likely crops to be affected include those that are multiple-seeded, such as alyssum (Color plate 1), lobelia, and portulaca, and those that require dry conditions but are grown too wet, such as vinca, celosia, tomato, and pepper. Be careful not to confuse damping-off with soluble-salt damage or excessive drying of the growing media. Excessive drying between waterings commonly causes soluble-salt damage, which may weaken plants and may indeed lead to damping-off infection.

The first step in reducing losses, which are promoted by too much moisture or humidity, is cultural control:

■ Well-drained media

■ Proper watering techniques

■ Proper covering with vermiculite or media

■ Control of drips and wet spots

■ Reasonable fertilization

■ Reduced seedling density

■ Increased air movement

These good greenhouse sanitation practices also reduce the risk of damping-off:

■ Controlling weeds

■ Removing plant debris

■ Disinfecting equipment and greenhouse surfaces from time to time

■ Disinfecting plug trays, if reusing

■ Not reusing plug media

■ Keeping hose ends off the floor

■ Removing standing water

Disinfectants are quite reactive and break down quickly on contact with air and organic matter. Therefore, cleaning surfaces of organic matter or soilless media first greatly increases the effectiveness of disinfectants. For safe disinfecting, use quaternary ammonium salt compounds, such as Physan 20, Prevent, or Greenshield. Objects or surfaces should be soaked for 15 to 20 minutes for best results. Treated surfaces should not be rinsed after sanitation.

Fungicides for plug tray damping-off control (table 14.1) are best drenched into media, or sprayed heavily onto the plants and the surface of the

TABLE 14.1   FUNGICIDES USED ON ORNAMENTAL CROPS IN THE U.S. TO CONTROL MAJOR DISEASES [a]

Disease	Fungicide Common name	Trade names (U.S.)
Bacterial diseases	Cupric hydroxide	Kocide 101
	Copper sulfate pentahydrate	Phyton 27
Botrytis blights, spots, and stem rots	Chlorothalonil	Exotherm Termil, Daconil 2787
	Cupric hydroxide	Kocide 101
	Copper sulfate pentahydrate	Phyton 27
	Dicloran	Botran
	Iprodione	Chipco 26019
	Mancozeb	FORE, Dithane M-45, Dithane F-45, Dithane DF, Manzate 200 DF, Protect T/O
	Thiophanate-methyl	Cleary's 3336, Fungo Flo
	Thiophanate-methyl + mancozeb	Zyban, Duosan
	Vinclozolin	Ornalin
Botrytis damping-off and cutting rot	Iprodione	Chipco 26019
	Mancozeb	FORE, Dithane M-45, Dithane F-45, Dithane DF, Manzate 200 DF, Protect T/O
	Thiophanate-methyl	Cleary's 3336, Fungo Flo
Fusarium crown and root rot	Copper sulfate pentahydrate	Phyton 27
	Etridiazole + thiophanate-methyl	Banrot
	Thiophanate-methyl	Cleary's 3336, Fungo Flo
Leaf spots and blights	Chlorothalonil	Exotherm Termil, Daconil 2787
	Cupric hydroxide	Kocide 101
	Copper sulfate pentahydrate	Phyton 27
	Folpet	Phaltan
	Iprodione	Chipco 26019
	Mancozeb	FORE, Dithane M-45, Dithane F-45, Dithane DF, Manzate 200 DF, Protect T/O
	Thiophanate-methyl	Cleary's 3336, Fungo Flo
	Thiophanate-methyl + mancozeb	Zyban, Duosan
	Triadimefon	Bayleton TOF, Strike
	Vinclozolin	Ornalin
Downy mildews	Mancozeb	FORE, Dithane M-45, Dithane F-45, Dithane DF, Manzate 200 DF, Protect T/O
	Metalaxyl	Subdue

TABLE 14.1 CONTINUED

Disease	Fungicide	
	Common name	Trade names (U.S.)
Powdery mildews	Dinocap	Karathane
	Fenarimol	Rubigan EC
	Copper sulfate pentahydrate	Phyton 27
	Piperalin	Pipron
	Thiophanate-methyl	Cleary's 3336, Fungo Flo
	Thiophanate-methyl + mancozeb	Zyban, Duosan
	Triadimefon	Bayleton TOF, Strike
	Triforine	Triforine
Rhizoctonia damping-off, root and crown rot	Etridiazole + thiophanate-methyl	Banrot
	Iprodione	Chipco 26019
	Quintozene	Terraclor, PCNB, Defend
	Thiophanate-methyl	Cleary's 3336, Fungo Flo
	Triflumizole	Terraguard
Thielaviopsis root rot	Etridiazole + thiophanate-methyl	Banrot
	Thiophanate-methyl	Cleary's 3336, Fungo Flo
	Triflumizole	Terraguard
Water mold damping-off, root and crown rot (*Pythium* and *Phytophthora*)	Fosetyl-Al	Aliette
	Etridiazole	Truban, Terrazole
	Etridiazole + thiophanate-methyl	Banrot
	Metalaxyl	Subdue
	Propamocarb	Banol

[a] Benlate no longer has a label for use on ornamentals in the United States. It can still be used on vegetables. Not all fungicides listed here are labeled for all ornamental crops. Test-spray a few plug trays and look for phytotoxicity symptoms after a few days, before applying the fungicide to the whole crop.

Source: Adapted from Powell and Lindquist, *Ball pest & disease manual.*

planting media. Check the label before using to determine if a fungicide is registered for the crops to be treated. Use recommended protective equipment during application and know the reentry periods for each fungicide used.

Banrot is a combination of Cleary's 3336 (thiophanate-methyl) + Truban (etridiazole) to control *Pythium* and *Phytophthora* as well as *Rhizoctonia* and *Fusarium*. Banol (propamocarb), Truban or Terrazole (etridiazole), Subdue (metalaxyl), and Aliette (fosetyl-al) control only *Pythium* and *Phytophthora*. Benlate (not on ornamentals in the United States), Cleary's 3336 or Domain (thiophanate-methyl), Terraclor (quintozene), Terraguard (triflumizole), and Chipco 26019 (iprodione) control *Rhizoctonia.* For *Fusarium* control, only Benlate (for vegetables only), Cleary's 3336, and Domain are labeled. Check the labels for rates, how often to treat, and compatibility with other chemicals. To avoid toxicity to tiny seedlings, treat with drenches or heavy sprays when the growing media is moderately moist and plants are not moisture-stressed.

CROWN AND ROOT ROTS

Crown and root rots, such as *Pythium, Rhizoctonia,* and *Thielaviopsis,* may be as important and damaging as damping-off but harder to diagnose. *Pythium* and *Thielaviopsis* may not show obvious symptoms right away, whereas *Rhizoctonia* can easily be confused with *Botrytis.* Symptoms of *Pythium* root rot (Color plate 3) include: (1) yellow lower or upper leaves, (2) stunted growth, (3) roots that slough off when pulled, (4) root tip ends that are stubbed or brown, (5) loss of roots, and (6) death of the plant.

Thielaviopsis symptoms are similar to those of *Pythium* (Color plate 4). However, *Thielaviopsis* differs from *Pythium* in that there will be darkened or black areas of the root system (Color plate 5), in which dark chlamydospores can be seen with a hand lens. For proper diagnosis of *Thielaviopsis,* wash the root system carefully to find the blackened areas and chlamydospores. Make sure the plant disease diagnostic laboratory you send your samples to uses this quick diagnostic technique for *Thielaviopsis,* as this fungus does not grow well in culture.

Rhizoctonia symptoms show mainly at the soil surface and top of the plant, rarely on the roots themselves. These symptoms include a blackened stem area at the soil line, constriction of the stem, with the seedling falling over (wire-stem), and a circular pattern of dying seedlings in a plug tray (Color plate 2). *Rhizoctonia* moves up the stem and collapses the plant from the crown upward. The difference between *Botrytis* and *Rhizoctonia* is that the brownish, weblike mycelium of the *Rhizoctonia* fungus often can be seen growing on the leaf and lower stem tissue as tissue is rotting [2]. The *Botrytis* fungus readily colonizes weak plant tissue and fresh plant debris, such as old, yellowing plug leaves (Color plate 8). This organism quickly spreads under ideal conditions, and produces a toxin that kills adjoining live plant tissue. You can detect *Botrytis* in your crop by the masses of fuzzy-looking, brown or gray spores it produces.

There are now available root rot pathogen detection kits (Sigma, 800/325-3010, or Neogen Corp., 800/234-5333). The kits enable a plug grower to take a small sample of rotted root, grind it up, place it on the three test surfaces, and find out if *Pythium, Phytophthora,* or *Rhizoctonia* is present and active. This on-site testing can speed up disease diagnosis and treatment.

Environmental and cultural conditions that promote the development and spread of these crown and root rot diseases are similar to those with damping-off:

- Too wet

- Too cool or too hot (depending on the crop)

- High levels of salts

- Reused media

- Trays not properly disinfected

- Drips in the greenhouse

- High media pH (greater than 6.5)

- Overfeeding with fertilizers high in NH_4

- Too much covering with media or coarse vermiculite

Provide good cultural conditions and use sound greenhouse sanitation procedures, as indicated previously for damping-off. The diseases and the crops most affected by them are:

- *Pythium*—seedling geraniums, vinca

- *Rhizoctonia*—celosia, vinca

- *Thielaviopsis*—pansy, petunia, vinca

- *Botrytis*—seedling geraniums, salvia, lisianthus

Chemical controls are the same as indicated for damping-off (table 14.1). Make sure the chemical is labeled for the crop, use the labeled rates, and be aware of the reentry times. Best chemicals for controlling these diseases in plug production are Subdue or Banol (*Pythium* and *Phytophthora*); Cleary's 3336, Domain, or Terraguard (*Rhizoctonia* and *Thielaviopsis*); and Daconil or Chipco 26019 (*Botrytis*).

LEAF SPOTS

Leaf spot can show up in plug production and may be caused by fungi or bacteria. Generally, if spots appear water-soaked or have yellow halos, they are probably caused by bacteria. The most common bacterial leaf spots are due to *Pseudomonas* and *Xanthomonas* species. Major crops affected include tomato, pepper (Color plate 21), and impatiens (Color plate 22). Fungal leaf spots may be tan, purple, black, or gray in color, and mycelia and spores may be evident. Generally, symptoms show up on the lowest leaves first, but they may quickly spread to the whole plant under the proper conditions. The most common fungal leaf spots include anthracnose, *Alternaria,*

DIAGNOSING PLUG PROBLEMS

COLOR PLATE SECTION

1
Damping-off on alyssum.
←

2
Rhizoctonia on vinca.
Courtesy A.R. Chase, Chase
Research Gardens, Inc.
→

C1

3
Pythium root rot aggravated by fungus gnats on geranium. Courtesy Margery Daughtrey, Cornell University.

←

4
Lower yellow leaves and dieback on pansy caused by *Thielaviopsis*.

→

5
Black root rot (*Thielaviopsis*) on pansy plugs. Healthy roots at left, diseased roots, right. Courtesy Margery Daughtrey, Cornell University.

←

6
Fusarium root and crown rot on cyclamen. Courtesy Margery Daughtrey, Cornell University.

→

7
Fusarium root and crown rot on tomato. Courtesy Robert J. McGovern, University of Florida.

←

8
Botrytis on lower leaves of geranium.

→

9
Aerial *Phytophthora* on vinca. Note dieback of tips. Courtesy A.R. Chase, Chase Research Gardens, Inc.

←

10
Alternaria leaf spot on zinnia.
Courtesy Margery Daughtrey,
Cornell University.

←

11
Alternaria leaf spot on vinca.
Courtesy A.R. Chase, Chase
Research Gardens, Inc.

→

12
Alternaria leaf spot on impatiens.
Courtesy Margery Daughtrey,
Cornell University.

←

13
Alternaria leaf spot on pansy.
Courtesy A.R. Chase, Chase
Research Gardens, Inc.

→

14
Alternaria leaf spot on
African marigold.

←

15
Early blight on tomato caused by
Alternaria solani. Courtesy Robert J.
McGovern, University of Florida.

→

16
Alternaria leaf spot on
dusty miller. Courtesy A.R.
Chase, Chase Research
Gardens, Inc.

→

17
Botrytis leaf spot on pansy.
Courtesy A.R. Chase, Chase
Research Gardens, Inc.

←

18
Cercospora leaf spot on pansy.
Courtesy A.R. Chase, Chase
Research Gardens, Inc.

→

19
Cercospora leaf spot on tomato.
Courtesy Robert J. McGovern,
University of Florida.

←

20
Bacterial leaf spot on zinnia
caused by *Xanthomonas*.
Courtesy Margery Daughtrey,
Cornell University.

→

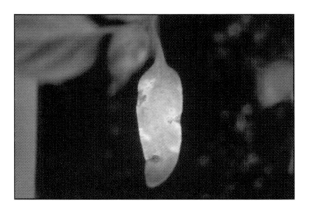

21
Bacterial spot on pepper caused by *Xanthomonas.* Courtesy Robert J. McGovern, University of Florida.
←

22
Pseudomonas leaf spot on impatiens. Courtesy Margery Daughtrey, Cornell University.
→

23
Downy mildew on snapdragons. Note grayish cast to leaves. Courtesy Margery Daughtrey, Cornell University.
←

24
Downy mildew on alyssum. Courtesy Margery Daughtrey, Cornell University.
→

25
Powdery mildew on zinnia.
Courtesy Margery Daughtrey,
Cornell University.

←

26
Impatiens necrotic spot virus
(INSV) on exacum. Courtesy
Margery Daughtrey, Cornell
University.

→

27
INSV on begonia. Courtesy
Margery Daughtrey, Cornell
University.

←

28
INSV on impatiens. Courtesy
A.R. Chase, Chase Research
Gardens, Inc.

→

29
Leafminer tunnels in leaves.
Courtesy Richard K. Lindquist,
Ohio State University.

←

30
Cabbage looper, a common
worm on vegetables and fall-
grown crops. Courtesy Richard
K. Lindquist, Ohio State
University.

→

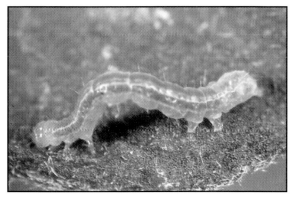

31
Beet armyworm, a common
worm on vegetables and fall-
grown crops. Courtesy Richard
K. Lindquist, Ohio State
University.

←

32
Western flower thrips adult.
Courtesy Richard K. Lindquist,
Ohio State University.

→

33
Slime trail and leaf injury caused by slugs. Courtesy Richard K. Lindquist, Ohio State University.
←

34
Marigolds, at left, show bronzing of lower leaves caused by low media pH and micronutrient toxicities. Courtesy Margery Daughtrey, Cornell University.
→

35
Upper yellow leaves on petunia caused by high media pH and iron deficiency.
←

36
Nitrogen deficiency on petunia. Note lower yellow leaves. Courtesy J.S. Huang and Paul V. Nelson, North Carolina State University.
→

37
Ammonium (NH_4) toxicity on petunia. Note curled leaves. Courtesy Ken Goldsberry.

←

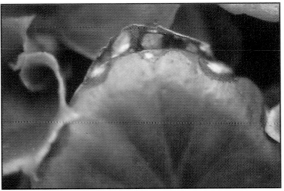

38
Potassium deficiency on lower leaves of begonia. Courtesy J.S. Huang and Paul V. Nelson, North Carolina State University.

→

39
Stretching of marigold plugs with additional phosphorus in the fertilizer. Courtesy Paul V. Nelson, North Carolina State University.

←

40
Calcium deficiency on newest leaves of poinsettia. Note incomplete leaf formation and marginal chlorosis. Courtesy Paul V. Nelson, North Carolina State University.

→

41
Magnesium deficiency on tobacco. Note interveinal chlorosis. Courtesy Paul V. Nelson, North Carolina State University.

←

42
Iron deficiency on ixora. Courtesy Paul V. Nelson, North Carolina State University.
→

43
Manganese deficiency on petunia. Note tan spots on young leaves with terminal chlorosis. Courtesy Paul V. Nelson, North Carolina State University.

←

44
First signs of boron deficiency on petunia. Note twisted, strapped new leaves.
→

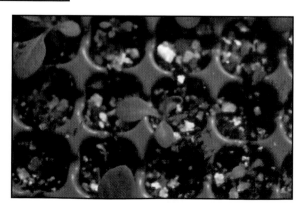

45
Boron deficiency on pansy. Note cupped, crinkled new leaves on plant at left.

←

46
Middle stages of boron toxicity on Rieger begonia. Courtesy Paul V. Nelson, North Carolina State University.

→

47
Seedling stretch due to high ammonium-nitrogen (NH_4) starter charge in the plug media.

←

48
Cupped down leaves and stunted growth of fibrous begonia due to high calcium, low ammonium fertilizer.

→

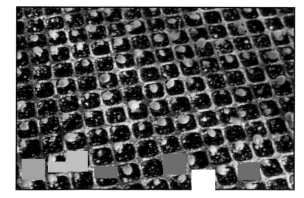

49
Tip abortion on impatiens can be caused by many factors.

←

50
Upper yellow leaves on impatiens caused by cold temperatures.

→

51
Chlorosis on upper leaves of salvia caused by too much negative DIF.

←

52
Halo effect from Cycocel on begonia. Courtesy Jim Barrett, University of Florida.

→

53
Black spotting on vinca leaves from Bonzi. Courtesy Jim Barrett, University of Florida.

←

54
Overdose of Bonzi on pansy.

→

55
Residual effects of Sumagic applied in the plug stage on vinca plugs after transplanting. Plants at left had no Sumagic, middle plants had 0.5 ppm Sumagic applied once, and plants at right had 2.0 ppm Sumagic applied three times in the plug stage. Courtesy Jim Barrett, University of Florida.

←

56
Chemical burn of snapdragons.

→

57
Fertilizer or chemical burn on vinca.

←

58
Ethylene damage on impatiens. Look for twisted, yellow leaves with stretched petioles.

→

59
Stunting in gerbera can be caused by many factors.

←

60
Reddish lower leaves on geranium caused by allowing plugs to get too dry.

→

and *Botrytis* (Color plate 17). Anthracnose is a major problem on pansy and cruciferous vegetables. *Alternaria* causes leaf spot on zinnia (Color plate 10), African marigold (Color plate 14), dusty miller (Color plate 16), and pansy (Color plate 13), and can be seed-transmitted.

Leaf-spotting bacteria and fungi require water on leaf surfaces for infection to occur, then splashing water for spread of spores from leaf to leaf. Stressful environmental conditions, such as cool, wet weather, also promote the development of leaf spots. Pansies have more problems with leaf spots under hot, humid conditions in the summer and early fall. Leaf spots may be controlled through venting and heating at sundown to dry the greenhouse air (dehumidification cycle). Do not crowd plants, avoid splashing water, and water early in the day so plants dry rapidly. Good air movement also helps control leaf moisture.

Fungicides and bactericides may also help control leaf spots (table 14.1) but will be effective only for the time they stay on the leaves. Frequent watering will wash off the chemicals and therefore reduce the effectiveness of chemical control. The most commonly used chemicals for leaf spots include chlorothalonil (Daconil), thiophanate-methyl + mancozeb (Zyban), iprodione (Chipco 26019), mancozeb (Dithane M-45, Manzate 200, Protect T/O), vinclozolin (Ornalin), thiophanate-methyl (Cleary's 3336, Domain), and copper (Kocide, Phyton 27). The thiophanate-methyl compounds are not effective against *Alternaria*. Consult the label for registered crops, concentrations, application methods, and reentry times. Do not use mancozeb on marigolds, as severe burning will result. Test on a small scale first to determine any phytotoxicity problems. Leaf spots mainly become a problem in the last one or two weeks before shipping and when holding the plugs. Chemicals should thus be applied during this time and rotated for best control.

MILDEWS

Mildews are not common in plug production, but may show up on certain crops and under certain environmental conditions. Powdery mildew, appearing as a white growth on leaves and stems, will occur in spots in the greenhouse under conditions of cool, night dampness and dry, sunny days [2]. Major crops affected include begonia, zinnia (Color plate 25), verbena, and snapdragon. Move the plants into a warmer place with good air movement, then apply the proper fungicide two or three times (table 14.1). Effective fungicides include thiophanate-methyl (Cleary's 3336, Domain), thiophanate methyl + mancozeb (Zyban), fenarimol (Rubigan), triforine, and triadimefon (Bayleton TOF, Strike). Be careful about fungicide resistance (to thiophanate-methyl), as well as plant stunting from overuse of triadimefon fungicides.

Downy mildew can cause major problems on snapdragon plugs (Color plate 23). It may go unnoticed in the plug stage, but it soon causes great trouble if contaminated plugs are transplanted. Downy mildew on alyssum (Color plate 24) and pansy causes lower leaves to yellow, mimicking nitrogen deficiency. Environmental control is the best method and is the same as for *Botrytis*. Mancozeb (Dithane, Manzate, Protect T/O) is the only approved fungicide in the United States, but metalaxyl (Subdue) sprays have also proven effective in grower experience (not labeled!).

VIRUSES

Viruses are systemic-disease-causing agents that live and multiply only within living host cells. They are usually spread by workers handling plants or by such insects as aphids, thrips, and leafhoppers. Some viruses may be seed-transmitted. Generally, vein banding, mosaic (a mixture of irregularly shaped dark and light green areas on the leaf), flecking, or spotting will show up on leaves, depending on the virus. Sometimes growth abnormalities similar to weed-killer damage may appear (abnormal leaf growth, twisting and etiolation of leaves). Viruses may also cause stunting of plants.

The three most common viruses that may show up in plug production or shortly after transplant are tomato spotted wilt virus (TSWV), impatiens necrotic spot virus (INSV), and tobacco mosaic virus (TMV). TSWV/INSV are spread by thrips and have a wide host range. Symptoms vary greatly, depending on the crop. Most commonly infected crops include all types of impatiens (Color plate 28) and begonia (Color plate 27), gloxinia, cyclamen, tomato, pepper, and fuchsia. TSWV/INSV are more of a problem with cutting-produced plugs, but they will quickly spread to seed-produced plugs via thrips. Once the disease shows up, there is not much to do except discard the entire production run, including apparently healthy plants. Furthermore, TSWV/INSV will infect many crops, including perennials, but not cause symptoms (asymptomatic) until the plants are under stress or at a certain age. Use a reputable testing service (such as Agdia, 800/622-4342) or test kits from Agdia or Sigma for on-site diagnosis. Use indicator petunias (Calypso, Supermagic Blue, Summer Madness) to detect the presence of thrips carrying the viruses before the crops show symptoms [4].

Tobacco mosaic virus is spread by mechanical means (workers handling plants or brushing against plants). Crops most affected include tomato, pepper, petunia, and nicotiana. Do not allow smoking in the plug greenhouse! All workers need to wash their hands with a disinfectant (Physan 20, Greenshield) before handling plants. Discard all plants showing symptoms.

INSECTS

FUNGUS GNATS AND SHORE FLIES

The main problem insects in plug production are fungus gnats and shore flies. Large numbers of adults create a nuisance and leave fly specks on leaves. More seriously, adults and larvae have been shown to transmit some fungal root rots, such as *Pythium*. Fungus gnat larvae also feed on roots, thereby exposing them to root rot. Controlling these two insects is a must, as they will quickly spread throughout the greenhouse. Control measures are basically the same, except for certain differences based on whether you have shoreflies, fungus gnats, or both.

Telling them apart is the first job in controlling them. Fungus gnat adults have long antennae and long, thin bodies; and are lazy fliers, like mosquitoes (fig. 14.1). Shore fly adults have short antennae and short, stout bodies; and are active fliers, like flies. Yellow sticky cards placed close to the plug trays will allow you to see which pest you have. The fungus gnat larva has a black head, whereas the shore fly larva doesn't.

The life cycles of these two insects are similar. Eggs are laid in the soil and hatch into larvae. The larvae, found within the top inch of soil, feed on algae and fungal materials. Fungus gnat larvae feed on roots, if necessary. The larvae will pupate and can persist through drought and temperature extremes in the soil. Adults emerge when environmental conditions are suitable. The

FIGURE 14.1 Greenhouse pest life cycles. Left, fungus gnat; right, shore fly. It is important to be able to distinguish between the two species in order to control them. Adapted from Robb, Cultural practices, *Greenhouse Manager*, 121.

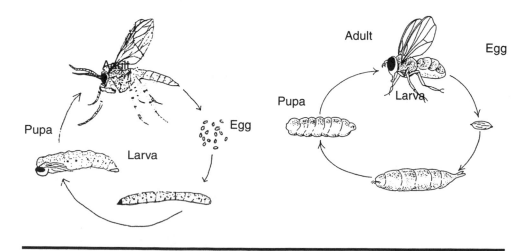

life cycle is temperature-dependent and ranges from two to four weeks. Development time decreases as the temperature increases (for example, 20 days at 75F, 24C; 50 days at 55F, 13C).

Both shore flies and fungus gnats need high moisture levels to develop, so conditions that favor algae and fungal growth enhance these insect problems. To control these insects, you can:

- reduce excess water use and runoff

- prevent water from collecting under benches or on floors

- control algal development with less moisture, reduced fertilizers, and quaternary ammonium salts (Physan 20, Greenshield) or Agribrom

- keep floors and benches clear of plant debris and soil

- keep the greenhouse weed-free

The areas under benches can be kept weed-free and inhospitable to fungus gnats and shore flies by using hydrated lime, copper sulfate, or Agribrom. Hydrated lime is mixed as a slurry at 1.5 lb per gal water and sprayed under benches. Copper sulfate is used at 1 lb per gal water and should be effective for three months [5]. Both of these materials are highly phytotoxic and should never contact the crop. Avoid overuse of these chemicals, as problems can develop with potential runoff.

Most pesticide applications are directed at the larvae (table 14.2). Make applications as drenches or coarse sprays to the growing media surface, getting the chemical at least into the top half inch of soil. Materials reported to provide good control against larvae include Gnatrol (*Bacillus thuringiensis*, for fungus gnats only), microencapsulated diazinon (Knox-Out) or dursban (DuraGuard), oxamyl (Vydate), kinoprene (Enstar II), neem (Azatin), cyramozine (Citation), microencapsulated pyrethrin (X-clude), and parasitic nematodes (X-Gnat, for fungus gnats only). Follow label directions for repeating treatments. With insect growth regulators—such as kinoprene, neem, and cyramozine—or with parasitic nematodes, do not expect immediate kill, but repeat the applications weekly. For best control, use one chemical for two or three weeks and then rotate to another.

When populations of adults get too high, aerosols may be needed (table 14.2). Materials reported to provide good control of adults include cyfluthrin (Decathlon), pyrethrin (X-clude), and resmithrin (PT 1200). Repeat applications for adults weekly until the population is reduced, and be sure to combine with applications for larvae. Adult control is best obtained with a fog or aerosol. Adults will move from one part of the greenhouse to another if a spray is used.

TABLE 14.2 **INSECTICIDES USED ON ORNAMENTAL CROPS IN THE U.S. TO CONTROL MAJOR PESTS** [a]

Pest	Pesticide Common name	Trade names (U.S.)
Aphids	Acephate	Orthene, PT 1300
	Bifenthrin	Talstar
	Bendiocarb	Dycarb, Turcam
	Chlorpyrifos	DuraGuard (Dursban)
	Cyfluthrin	Decathlon, Tempo
	Diazinon	Knox-Out
	Dichlorvos	Vapona, DDVP
	Endosulfan	Thiodan
	Fenpropathrin	Tame
	Fluvalinate	Mavrik
	Horticultural oil	Sunspray
	Insecticidal soap	M-Pede
	Lambda-cyhalothrin	Topcide
	Neem	Neemazad, Azatin
	Nicotine sulfate	Nicotine
	Permethrin	Ambush, Pounce, Astro
	Pyrethrum	PT 1100, X-clude
	Resmethrin	PT1200, Resmethrin
	Sulfotepp	Dithio, Plantfume 103
Caterpillars (worms)	Acephate	Orthene, PT 1300
	Bacillus thuringiensis	Dipel
	Bendiocarb	Dycarb
	Bifenthrin	Talstar
	Chlorpyrifos	DuraGuard (Dursban)
	Cyfluthrin	Decathlon, Tempo
	Diflubenzuron	Adept
	Fenpropathrin	Tame
	Fluvalinate	Mavrik
	Lambda-cyhalothrin	Topcide
	Neem	Azatin, Neemazad
	Permethrin	Ambush, Pounce, Pramex
	Pyrethrum	PT 1100, X-clude
	Resmethrin	PT1200, Resmethrin
Fungus gnats, shore flies	*Bacillus thuringiensis* H-14	Gnatrol
	Bendiocarb	Dycarb
	Chlorpyrifos	DuraGuard (Dursban)
	Cyfluthrin	Decathlon, Tempo
	Cyromazine	Citation
	Diazinon	Knox-Out
	Diflubenzuron	Adept
	Fenoxycarb	Precision, Preclude
	Kinoprene	Enstar II
	Neem	Azatin
	Nematodes	X-Gnat, Larvanem, Scanmask

TABLE 14.2   CONTINUED

Pest	Pesticide Common name	Trade names (U.S.)
	Pyrethrum	PT 1100, X-clude
	Resmethrin	PT 1200, Resmethrin
Leafminers	Abamectin	Avid
	Chlorpyrifos	DuraGuard (Dursban)
	Cyromazine	Citation
	Diazinon	Knox-Out
	Dichlorvos	Vapona, DDVP
	Lambda-cyhalothrin	Topcide
	Neem	Azatin, Neemazad
	Permethrin	Ambush, Pounce, Pramex
Slugs	Metaldehyde	Bug-Geta, Deadline, Slugit, Snarol
	Methiocarb	Grandslam, Mesurol, PT 1700
Thrips	Abamectin	Avid
	Acephate	Orthene, PT 1300
	Beauveria bassiana	Naturalis-O
	Bendiocarb	Dycarb, Turcam
	Bifenthrin	Talstar
	Chlorpyrifos	DuraGuard (Dursban)
	Cyfluthrin	Decathlon, Tempo
	Diazinon	Knox-Out
	Dichlorvos	Vapona, DDVP
	Fenoxycarb	Preclude, Precision
	Fenpropathrin	Tame
	Fluvalinate	Mavrik
	Lambda-cyhalothrin	Topcide
	Naled	Dibrom
	Nicotine sulfate	Nicotine
	Neem	Azatin, Neemazad
	Resmethrin	PT 1200, Resmethrin
	Sulfotepp	Dithio, Plantfume 103
Whiteflies	Acephate	Orthene, PT 1300
	Beauveria bassiana	Naturalis-O
	Bifenthrin	Talstar
	Cyfluthrin	Decathlon, Tempo
	Dichlorvos	Vapona, DDVP
	Endosulfan	Thiodan
	Fenoxycarb	Preclude, Precision
	Fenpropathrin	Tame
	Fluvalinate	Mavrik
	Horticultural oil	Sunspray
	Insecticidal soap	M-Pede
	Kinoprene	Enstar II
	Lambda-cyhalothrin	Topcide
	Naled	Dibrom

TABLE 14.2 CONTINUED

Pest	Pesticide Common name	Trade names (U.S.)
Whiteflies	Neem	Azatin, Neemazad
	Permethrin	Ambush, Pounce, Astro
	Pyrethrum	PT 1100, X-clude
	Resmethrin	PT 1200, Resmethrin
	Sulfotepp	Dithio, Plantfume 103

[a] Not all insecticides listed here are labeled for all ornamental crops. Test-spray a few plug trays and look for phytotoxicity symptoms after a few days, before applying the insecticide to the whole crop.
Source: Adapted from Powell & Lindquist, *Ball pest & disease manual.*

LEAFMINERS

Leafminers can cause problems on plugs of salvia, verbena, gerbera, and others, particularly those grown in warm areas of the world. Leafminers are larvae of small, black and yellow flies. The larvae cause most injury by feeding between the upper and lower leaf surfaces, leaving narrow, winding trails, or "mines" (Color plate 29). Adults can also cause noticeable injury, making small feeding and oviposition punctures in the leaf surface that soon turn white, giving leaves a speckled appearance. Monitor your crops with yellow sticky cards placed close to the plug trays of susceptible crops.

Chemical controls must be applied thoroughly to all leaf surfaces if applied as high-volume sprays. They must have even distribution throughout the greenhouse if applied as ultra-low-volume sprays or aerosols. The best chemicals include abamectin (Avid), cyromazine (Citation), neem (Azatin), and permethrin (Ambush, Pounce).

APHIDS

Aphids are another insect problem that will show up infrequently on plugs, but they will present problems when they do. Crops most susceptible to aphids include vegetables and cuttings. Aphids are soft-bodied, sluggish insects that multiply rapidly.

Early aphid detection is very important in managing them in plug production. Certain changes in seasons or weather may bring large numbers into your greenhouses from outside. Keep the inside of the greenhouse weed-free, and establish a weed-free perimeter outside all greenhouses.

Aphids have been known to become resistant to some chemicals. For best chemical control (table 14.2), use acephate (Orthene, PT 1300), pyrethrum (X-clude), or oxamyl (Vydate). Rotate between chemicals after two or three applications. Spot applications may be all that's needed at times of low populations.

WORMS

Caterpillars, or worms, are the larvae of *Lepidoptera* species, most commonly known as butterflies and moths (Color plates 30 and 31). Certain vegetable crops, such as cabbage, broccoli, and ornamental kale and cabbage, are very prone to worm attack. Damage may start in certain areas of the greenhouse or plug tray and progress outward as the worms move. Moths are night-fliers and are attracted to lights within the greenhouse. At certain times of the year, there may be outbreaks of many moths or butterflies, thereby increasing potential of worm damage. Screening the vents is an easy and economical method of worm control. Scouting the crops daily is the best method of detection. For chemical controls (table 14.2), use *Bacillus thuringiensis* (Dipel), acephate (Orthene, PT 1300), neem (Neemazad), permethrin (Ambush, Pounce), or pyrethrum (X-clude).

THRIPS

Thrips are small, slender insects less than an eighth of an inch long that feed on flowers, foliage, and pollen (Color plate 32). These insects can become problems on certain crops, such as all types of impatiens and begonias, gloxinia, cyclamen, fuchsia, and many others. The main problem with thrips is their ability to transmit TSWV/INSV. Thrips are difficult to control because they infest flowers and hide very well in weeds. When producing plugs, keep them in greenhouses separate from flowering crops. Maintain a weed-free greenhouse interior, and set up a weed-free perimeter outside of the greenhouses. Place yellow sticky cards close to the crops to monitor populations. Insect screening can be used over vents, but you will need to increase the fan and vent areas to account for a 40 to 50% reduction in airflow with screening small enough to exclude thrips.

For chemical control (table 14.2), use different methods of application—such as high- and low-volume sprays, aerosols, and fogs—to attack thrips where they are hiding, and apply at least weekly. The best chemicals include acephate (Orthene, PT 1300), bifenthrin (Talstar), endosulfan (Thiodan), bendiocarb (Dycarb), abamectin (Avid), fluvalinate (Mavrik), and neem (Azatin, Neemazad). Rotate chemicals after two or three applications.

SLUGS

In greenhouses with wet dirt floors, slugs can pose problems for many plug crops. Generally active at night, they are found beneath flats and foliage. Cool, wet conditions are best for slug survival and development. Characteristic plant injury consists of irregular holes eaten in foliage. Sometimes entire plants are stripped of leaves. Usually, a shiny, slimy trail of mucouslike substance is present (Color plate 33).

Eliminate slug habitats through sanitation, raising flats off the floor, and eliminating excessive moisture. Chemical control is achieved with baits containing pesticide, such as metaldehyde or methiocarb (Grandslam, Mesurol).

WHITEFLIES

Whiteflies are generally not a problem on plug crops, but they may show up on gerbera, poinsettia cuttings, and some vegetables, especially in certain parts of the world. Whiteflies have piercing, sucking mouthparts and can spread some viral diseases. All developmental stages usually occur on leaf undersides.

Chemical control must be thoroughly applied as high- or low-volume sprays, aerosols, or fogs and repeated weekly or as needed. The best chemicals to use (table 14.2) include bifenthrin (Talstar), cyfluthrin (Decathlon, Tempo), fluvalinate (Mavrik), kinoprene (Enstar II), neem (Neemazed), oxamyl (Vydate), permethrin (Ambush, Pounce), and pyrethrum (X-clude). Use Talstar + Azatin or Mavrik + Enstar II for best controls. Rotate chemicals after two or three applications to prevent pesticide resistance from developing. By all means, do not use Marathon 1%G on plugs!

KEY POINTS TO REMEMBER

- Most disease problems are caused by overwatering, poor air movement, humid greenhouses, poor sanitation, and poor weed control. Most insect problems are caused by poor monitoring procedures, improper pesticide applications, no insect screening, and poor weed control.

- The biggest disease problems in plugs are root and crown rots, along with damping-off (*Pythium, Rhizoctonia, Thielaviopsis*). Know how to recognize and control them.

- The biggest insect problems in plugs are fungus gnats and shore flies. Know how to tell them apart and how to control them.

- When using a fungicide or insecticide for the first time, make sure you follow label instructions, and test-spray a few plug trays first before applying it to the whole crop. Any phytoxicity should show up within two or three days after application.

- Your water pH should be from 5.5 to 6.5 for best efficacy of pesticides. Lower the pH of the water in the spray tank with acid if needed. Sulfuric acid is the most commonly used acid for this purpose.

- Make sure you are using proper application methods for the pesticide being applied and the crop being treated. High-volume sprays need to cover all parts of the plant. Drenches need to get all the way through the soil volume to be effective. Low-volume sprays need some fan movement for best coverage. Aerosols should be used at proper spacing and with closed greenhouses to get the best coverage.

- When applying any insecticide or fungicide, do not apply to moisture-stressed plants. Leaves should be dry when applying pesticides. Avoid applying during high temperatures.

- Minimize applications of emulsifiable concentrate and oil and soap formulations. *Never* tank-mix two liquid emulsifiable concentrates or flowable chemicals together, especially in hot weather or when soluble salt levels are high. This rule also applies when mixing two liquid fungicides, a liquid fungicide and a liquid insecticide, or a liquid pesticide of any sort with a fertilizer [1].

REFERENCES

[1] Lindquist, R., and C.C. Powell. 1995. Integrate your pest management for top-quality plugs. *GrowerTalks* 59(9):40–44.

[2] Powell, C.C. 1995. Managing diseases of bedding plants. *OFA Bulletin* 793:9–11.

[3] Powell, C.C., and R.K. Lindquist. 1997. *Ball pest & disease manual,* 2nd edition. Batavia, Ill.: Ball Publishing.

[4] Pundt, L., J. Sanderson, and M. Daughtrey. 1992. Petunias are your tip-off for TSWV. *GrowerTalks* 56(7):69–72.

[5] Robb, K. 1991. Cultural practices, chemicals help solve fungus gnat, shore fly problems. *Greenhouse Manager* 10(6):121–122.

CHAPTER 15

HOLDING PLUGS

U nder ideal conditions, seeds are germinated, and plugs are transplanted when they reach the correct size. Unfortunately, plugs are often ready for transplanting before a grower can transplant them. When this occurs, the grower must delay the growth of the seedlings until they can be transplanted. This process starts in Stage 4, the conditioning or toning stage up to the time of transplanting or shipping.

During this time (generally up to a week long), special cultural procedures need to be followed to tone or harden the plugs. The greenhouse temperature may be lowered to 55 to 60F (13 to 15C) for up to two weeks for most crops, providing flower initiation has occurred (as with petunias). The temperature should not be lower than 50F (10C), nor plugs held more than two weeks, to avoid flower delay and reduction in size and number of flowers after transplanting (except for cool-season crops, such as pansy). Apply moisture only as needed to maintain leaf turgor, with morning watering to allow foliage to dry quickly. Monitor soil pH and conductivity levels closely. Calcium and potassium nitrate fertilizers can supplement nutrition and still promote toned plant growth. Soluble trace elements can be added, if needed. Ammonium-containing fertilizers should *always* be avoided at low temperatures. High light levels (greater than 2,500 fc, 26,900 lux) can keep plants shorter, but care must be taken not to bleach or burn the leaves.

To successfully tone plugs for transplanting, shipping, or holding, a separate greenhouse zone is needed. If the temperature is lowered to recommended levels and Stage 3 plugs (in an active growth stage) are also in the same zone, then these younger plugs' growth will be seriously slowed.

At certain times of the year, more than half the plugs produced in the United States are grown on speculation. Because of poor planning, inclement weather, and a lack of sales, a grower cannot always transplant at the proper stage. What happens when transplanting backs up due to weather, customers cancel or delay shipments of their plugs or finished flats, and your plugs are now getting old? That small area for Stage 4 cannot hold all the plugs it needs to. Many growers who produce plugs for their own use are reluctant to throw away old plugs (two weeks or longer past transplant stage). Even when the plugs are twice as tall as they should be, these growers will find a way to use them (fig. 15.1). Unfortunately, hanging onto these old plugs also seriously affects the plug crops coming ready to transplant each of the next several weeks, and using old plugs adversely affects finished crops in several ways.

FIGURE 15.1 Overgrown petunia plug.

NEGATIVE EFFECTS OF HOLDING PLUGS

The most notable problem in holding plugs past transplant stage is stretching. Due to their high density, competition for space and light is intense. The young seedlings continue to grow taller due to the leaf-shading effect, the phytochrome response to far-red light. Internode stretch becomes greater once the canopy fills in, so it is much tougher to keep 800 plugs short than 128 plugs. Trays that have no airholes between the cells create a more humid climate in the middle of the tray. This results in a mounding effect, as the plugs in the center get taller, while the plugs around the edges stay smaller due to drying out faster and having more space (fig. 15.2). For many crops, it is difficult to produce a quality finished plant when the plug is too tall. Some crops can be planted deeper (tomato, pepper, marigold, salvia, snapdragon) with no detrimental effect. However, many crops cannot be planted deeper, due to a crown (cyclamen, petunia, begonia) or stem (vinca, celosia, pansy) that is very susceptible to rot from *Rhizoctonia* and other fungi.

Another problem of holding plugs is flowering in the plug tray. In most cases, early flowering creates difficulties after transplanting. Some crops prematurely flower or form flower buds in the plug tray and, therefore, do not grow enough vegetatively after transplanting. This problem is very noticeable in cut flowers, where the resultant flower stem is too short and not of good quality. The crops most affected include cut lisianthus and larkspur.

Other crops having problems with premature flowering are single-stem/single-flower types, where the first flower is produced in the plug tray (fig. 15.3). Once transplanted, this plant will continue to put energy into this flower and not into further vegetative growth. The result is a poor-quality finished container or a delay in shipping while waiting for more vegetative growth. Crops most affected by this problem include celosia, marigold, petunia, pansy, viola, and salvia. Early plug tray flowering is not as much of a problem in multiple-seedling, multiple-branched, and multiple-flowering crops, including impatiens, lobelia, alyssum, and portulaca. *Botrytis* on the flowers during shipping is the main problem to guard against with these crops.

FIGURE 15.2 Mounding of overgrown petunia plug trays.

The best advantage a good-quality plug can have is an active root system, with lots of root hairs, which promotes rapid rooting out after

FIGURE 15.3 French marigold plug trays in flower.

transplanting. However, when a plug is held too long, this root system becomes very rootbound. In many cases, you cannot even see any media when the plug is pulled out of the tray! Root binding promotes long roots that are not very active, tend to be thicker, and have less root hairs.

Sometimes plugs will have developed excellent root systems with a lot of root hairs, only to lose these root hairs during holding.

The loss of root hairs can expose plugs to root rots, such as *Pythium, Rhizoctonia, Thielaviopsis,* and *Phytophthora.* Diseases become more of a problem with older plugs that have lost root activity or have become so crowded that the lower foliage does not dry off. *Botrytis* under the canopy is a major problem on geranium, salvia, and vinca. Once the lower leaves yellow and die off, *Botrytis* moves in very quickly and may be difficult to see, due to the canopy density. Fungal leaf spots may also cause problems on certain crops because of moisture staying on the leaves. *Alternaria* can be a problem on dusty miller, zinnia, and vinca. Pansies during the fall season are more susceptible to a variety of leaf spots. Mildews can cause problems on old plugs of cabbage, cauliflower, broccoli, and snapdragon.

If the root system is adversely affected during holding, it is more than likely that flowering after transplanting will be delayed or at least be nonuniform [1, 4]. Starved plugs will also not grow quickly after transplanting [5]. This delay results in a longer crop schedule than planned. Therefore, the problem of holding onto plugs too long when there are younger plugs waiting to be transplanted can be solved easily: better to throw out the oldest plugs and transplant the rest more on time, so as not to delay your production schedule, which is based on flowering time. In addition, it costs money to hold plugs past their transplant date, with even more money lost due to delays in growing out and flowering.

Finally, the worst effect of holding plugs is plant death. Overly mature plugs dry out faster due to their greater root mass. Holding areas are usually the last areas to get attention, so watering may be delayed. Often, whole trays of plugs wilt to the point of no return before someone gets there to water. A dead plug cannot be transplanted! Sometimes the plug dies shortly after transplanting, due to the stress imposed in holding.

HOLDING PLUGS IN THE GREENHOUSE

Now that you are aware of the negative effects of holding plugs, let's discuss how you can successfully hold plugs in the greenhouse for up to two weeks. Since greenhouse holding conditions are likely to be variable, it is difficult to completely stop plant growth. More than likely the root system will continue to grow and become rootbound. Plugs should not be held in a greenhouse zone any longer than two weeks. Some crops, such as zinnia, celosia, and larkspur, should not be held at all.

The first factor to pay attention to is temperature. Plugs can be held on the greenhouse bench if the temperature is lowered to 50 to 60F (10 to 16C) and maintained in that range for the time needed. Make sure you have enough space in the greenhouse to create this temperature zone and not affect other plugs that are actively growing. Unfortunately, in the summer and early fall, such cool temperatures just cannot be provided.

To slow plant growth, provide higher light levels (greater than 2,500 fc or 26,900 lux). High light acts as a growth regulator, in that it heats up the leaf temperature and shuts photosynthesis down. However, you need to be careful about burning or bleaching the leaves.

Moisture control is another successful technique to control growth. Let the plugs dry down thoroughly before watering. This cycle of alternate wetting and drying will check the growth. Older plugs have a greater root ball and will dry down faster than younger plugs. Most crops can be dried down to the wilting point and rewatered with no negative effects, providing that the soil EC level is low (less than 0.75 mmhos/cm, 2:1 dilution). However, some crops do not like to be dried out to wilting (primula, pansy, and geranium). Moisture should be applied thoroughly and evenly to all plugs. Due to the cool temperatures being maintained, watering should be done first thing in the morning, so that the foliage can dry off before evening. This will help control disease on the dense foliage.

Changing to a calcium and potassium nitrate fertilizer program will also help tone plugs and slow down growth, yet still help maintain color. Ammonium-based fertilizers should never be applied to plugs being held at cool temperatures! The ammonium is not broken down by soil bacteria at low temperatures, and it will just build up and become toxic to the plug seedlings. Calcium and potassium nitrate fertilizers, such as 14-0-14, 15-0-15, or 13-2-13-6-3, will provide nitrogen in the form the plug seedlings can use at low temperatures to maintain color and desired growth. However, these fertilizers also tend to raise the media pH. Fertilize only when necessary with 100 to 150 ppm N. Monitor media pH and soluble salts during the holding stage. Keep the media pH below 6.5 for most crops and above 6.0 for impatiens, lisianthus, marigolds, geranium, and cyclamen. Soluble salts should stay at less than 0.75 mmhos/cm (2:1 dilution).

Reducing moisture, increasing light levels, and changing the fertilizer program will all help control plug growth during holding. However, these techniques may also promote premature plug flowering. Most affected are celosia, marigold, larkspur, lisianthus, aster, and zinnia. Be careful how much you rely on these growth control techniques if you are holding these sensitive crops.

Chemical growth regulators can also control the height of held plugs. These chemicals include B-Nine, Cycocel, A-Rest, Bonzi, and Sumagic. The main questions to ask before using chemical growth regulators to hold plugs are: (1) When do I apply them, and how much? (2) Are they effective at this late stage, and on what crops? (3) Will the plugs grow out of the treatment? Generally, it is best not to use chemical growth regulators in the holding zone, as the cool temperature will exaggerate their effects. Also, it is more difficult to get thorough coverage of each plug due to the high tray densities. Bonzi and Sumagic are very dependent on growing point coverage and moving into the media to be taken up by roots. If you want to treat with chemical growth regulators, do so one or two days before moving plants into your cool holding zone.

Disease can become a problem in holding mature plugs at high densities in a cool greenhouse. Root rots, such as *Pythium, Phytophthora, Rhizoctonia,* and *Thielaviopsis*, can become established if root systems are damaged due to cultural practices. Try not to place the plug trays on the floor during holding. Monitor media pH and soluble salts and keep them within acceptable ranges. Be careful about drying out plugs too much and losing root hairs. Use preventative fungicides as needed.

Botrytis can be the biggest problem, especially on geranium, salvia, and vinca. This disease will grow underneath the plant canopy on the oldest leaves. Look through the foliage to check trays for *Botrytis*. Spray thoroughly, almost as a drench, with Daconil (chlorothalonil) or Chipco 26019 (iprodione) every week once the plant canopy fills in. Provide good air movement to allow foliage to dry off before the end of the day. Fungal leaf spots (such as *Alternaria*) and mildew (both powdery and downy) can also spread quickly on susceptible crops in the holding environment. Look for *Alternaria* on dusty miller, zinnia, African marigold, and vinca. Examine snapdragon, flowering kale/cabbage, broccoli, and verbena plugs closely for mildews. Pansies in the summer-fall season are particularly susceptible to a number of fungal leaf spots. Use preventative sprays as needed, but make sure to keep leaves dry as much as possible.

STORING PLUGS IN A COOLER

One alternative to using stress to hold plugs is using low temperature, which can be applied in the plug production area as long as you have a definite greenhouse zone for holding. Otherwise, growth of younger plugs will be slowed down. Storing plugs in a cooler or refrigerated truck trailer (reefer) makes scheduling easier because they can be held for several days or even weeks before transplanting. However, the plug grower must understand how holding plugs under variable light and temperature conditions will affect seedling growth after transplanting.

Much research on holding plugs has been done [1, 3, 4]. The most comprehensive and definitive research was conducted by Dr. Royal Heins and his group at Michigan State University [2]. This research determined how plugs should be handled before they are cooled, and how long they could be stored under various light and temperature combinations without adversely affecting growth and flowering time after transplanting (table 15.1). In general, plants should not be stored at temperatures lower than those shown in table 15.1 unless storage duration is equal to or less than that listed for the species and temperature in table 15.2 (dark storage) and table 15.3 (light storage).

TABLE 15.1   OPTIMAL PLUG STORAGE TEMPERATURE AND MAXIMUM DURATIONS

Species	Optimal storage temperature F	Maximum storage in dark (wks)	Maximum storage in light (wks) [a]
Alyssum	36	5	6
Cyclamen	36	6	6
Geranium	36	4	4
Pansy	36	6	6
Petunia	36	6	6
Begonia, fibrous	41	6	6
Begonia, tuberous	41	3	6
Dahlia	41	2	5
Lobelia	41	6	6
Marigold, French	41	3	6
Salvia	41	6	6
Ageratum	45	6	6
Impatiens	45	6	6
Portulaca	45	5	5
Tomato	45	3	3
Verbena	45	1	1
Celosia	50	2	3
Vinca	50	5	6
New Guinea impatiens	55	2	3

[a] Minimum of 5 fc

Source: From Heins, et al., *Plug storage.*

TABLE 15.2   TEMPERATURE AND MAXIMUM PLUG STORAGE DURATION IN DARK

Species	32F (0C)	36F (2.5C)	41F (5C)	45F (7.5C)	50F (10C)	55F (12.5C)
			Weeks			
Ageratum	1	1	5	6	3	3
Alyssum	5	4	4	2	1	1
Begonia, fibrous	0	4	6	5	5	0
Begonia, tuberous	3	3	3	4	3	3
Celosia	0	1	1	1	2	2
Cyclamen	6	6	6	5	5	4
Dahlia	1	2	2	2	2	2
Geranium	4	4	4	4	4	2
Impatiens	0	2	3	6	5	4
Lobelia	0	5	6	5	4	0
Marigold, French	0	1	3	3	2	2
New Guinea impatiens	0	0	0	0	0	2
Pansy	6	6	6	6	6	6
Petunia	6	6	6	5	5	4
Portulaca	1	3	5	5	6	6
Salvia	0	0	6	6	4	4
Tomato	0	1	2	3	1	1
Verbena	1	2	1	1	1	1
Vinca	0	2	3	4	5	5

Source: From Heins, et al., *Plug storage.*

A grower may want to store crops with different storage requirements in the same cooling facility, so a compromise will have to be made. The best temperature to use for one cooler is 45F (7.5C), with the addition of at least 5 fc (54 lux) from cool-white fluorescent bulbs on a continuous basis (table 15.4). Note that New Guinea impatiens from cuttings will not store at all at this temperature. There may be other crops that react the same way, so conduct your own trials on additional crops.

Moisture control is more difficult when storing plugs in a cooler. Plug trays should be watered thoroughly, but the foliage should be dry before the trays are moved into the cooler. The humidity level inside the cooler will affect how quickly plug trays dry out. Fans should be running continuously for best air and temperature circulation. With lower humidity, plug trays dry out faster, but *Botrytis* is better controlled. With higher humidity, plug trays

---

TABLE 15.3 TEMPERATURE AND MAXIMUM PLUG STORAGE DURATION AT 5FC LIGHT

Species	32F (0C)	36F (2.5C)	41F (5C)	45F (7.5C)	50F (10C)	55F (12.5C)
			Weeks			
Ageratum	1	2	6	6	6	6
Alyssum	6	6	6	6	3	3
Begonia, fibrous	0	6	6	6	6	4
Begonia, tuberous	3	4	6	6	4	4
Celosia	0	1	1	1	3	3
Cyclamen	6	6	6	6	6	6
Dahlia	1	4	5	6	6	5
Geranium	4	4	4	4	4	4
Impatiens	0	2	3	6	6	6
Lobelia	0	5	6	5	4	4
Marigold, French	0	3	6	6	5	3
New Guinea impatiens	0	0	0	0	0	3
Pansy	6	6	6	6	6	6
Petunia	6	6	6	6	6	6
Portulaca	1	3	5	5	6	4
Salvia	0	0	6	6	6	6
Tomato	0	1	2	3	1	1
Verbena	3	2	1	1	4	4
Vinca	0	2	3	6	6	6

Source: From Heins, et al., *Plug storage.*

---

may go 10 to 12 days without needing to be watered, but *Botrytis* becomes a problem. Plug trays should be stored on carts or racks with space in between for air movement and light penetration. When trays dry out, move the carts outside the cooler and either water thoroughly from overhead or subirrigate the trays. If watering overhead, allow the foliage to dry off before moving the trays back into the cooler. It is not necessary to fertilize plugs in cold storage.

To minimize *Botrytis,* make sure the plugs are not grown too lush (soft). A well-toned plug will withstand the storage conditions and *Botrytis* much better than a big, soft plug. On the other hand, do not starve your plugs before putting them into the cooler, or they will not have enough energy to withstand those conditions. The last watering the plug trays receive before going into the cooler should also include a drench or thorough spray

TABLE 15.4 MAXIMUM STORAGE DURATIONS, IN WEEKS, FOR 19 SPECIES STORED AT 45F AND 5FC OF LIGHT

Species	45F with light (7.5C with light)
Ageratum	6
Alyssum	6
Begonia, fibrous	6
Begonia, tuberous	6
Celosia	1
Cyclamen	6
Dahlia	6
Geranium	4
Impatiens	6
Lobelia	5
Marigold, French	6
New Guinea impatiens	0
Pansy	6
Petunia	6
Portulaca	5
Salvia	6
Tomato	3
Verbena	1
Vinca	6

Source: Adapted from Table 15.3.

(enough to get down under the canopy) of Daconil (chlorothalonil). We have found this fungicide to be the best for *Botrytis* control with no known resistance. No phytotoxicity has been observed when Daconil is applied at half the labeled rate on plug trays. Additional control may be gained by combining half-rate Daconil with half-rate Chipco (iprodione). Rates higher than these may cause phytotoxicity in some crops. Make sure the foliage is dry before moving the trays into the cooler.

As with any technique, there are limits to storing plugs in a cooler. The young seedling's respiration is greatly slowed down, and photosynthesis and other food-making processes are not going on at this low temperature. Therefore, the key limitation is how many weeks you can keep the plug trays in storage before losing quality (refer to table 15.4 for guidelines).

KEY POINTS TO REMEMBER

- Criteria for holding plugs in the greenhouse:
  - Keep temperature between 50 and 60F (10 and 15C).
  - Maintain high light levels (greater than 2,500 fc, 26,900 lux), without raising temperature, if possible.
  - Water plugs only when needed, and then thoroughly. Keep foliage dry at night.
  - Fertilize only when needed with 100 to 150 ppm N from calcium and potassium nitrate fertilizers.
  - Maintain a low media EC of less than 0.75 mmhos/cm (2:1 dilution) and pH between 6.0 and 6.5.
  - Be *very* careful when using any chemical growth regulators during this stage.
  - Treat plugs with a recommended fungicide for root rot, *Botrytis,* leaf spots, or mildews when needed.
  - When transplanting, add up to five days to the normal production schedule for some delayed flowering.
  - The key is maintaining the root hairs and a healthy root system, yet keeping the plant from growing.
- Criteria for holding plugs in a cooler:
  - Start with well-toned, healthy plugs.
  - Make sure roots are moist but foliage dry before trays enter the cooler.
  - Treat all trays with recommended fungicide for *Botrytis.*
  - Keep trays in a cooler set for 45F (7.5C), continuous air circulation, and continuous light levels of at least 5 footcandles (54 lux).
  - For highest quality, keep track of how long plug trays are in the cooler.
  - Acclimate plug trays before transplanting.
- Criteria for shipping plugs:
  - Start with well-toned, healthy plugs.
  - Precool plug trays, especially during hot times of year, before shipping.

- Set the temperature in the reefer for 45F (7.5C) with *continuous* operation.

- Ship plugs with moist roots but dry leaves.

- Treat sensitive crops with recommended fungicide for *Botrytis*.

- Try *not* to use any chemical growth regulators within five days of shipping.

REFERENCES

[1] Al-Hemaid, A., and D. Koranski. 1990. Keep the transplanting line on schedule for top-quality plants. *GrowerTalks* 54(8):76–80.

[2] Heins, R., N. Lange, T.F. Wallace, Jr., and W. Carlson. 1994. *Plug storage.* Reprint from *Greenhouse Grower*, Willoughby, Ohio: Meister Publishing Co.

[3] Kaczperski, M.P., and A.M. Armitage. 1992. Short-term storage of plug-grown bedding plant seedlings. *HortScience.* 27:798–800.

[4] Koranski, D., P. Karlovich, and A. Al-Hemaid. 1989. The latest research on holding and shipping plugs. *GrowerTalks* 53(8):72–79.

[5] Melton, R.R., and R.J. Dufault. 1991. Tomato seedling growth, earliness, yield, and quality following pretransplant nutritional conditioning and low temperatures. *J. Amer. Soc. Hort. Sci.* 116:421–425.

CHAPTER 16

SCHEDULING PLUGS AND FINISHED BEDDING PLANTS

M ost plug users, in countries where plugs have been available for some time, base their plug-size purchasing decisions on cost comparisons between producing their own (they may not always know the exact cost) and purchasing plugs and using them. As customers get more demanding and competition more fierce, cost becomes the principal criterion. Plugs become viewed as commodities, where only availability and price are important. However, plug size is also significant, and its selection should also be based on the following criteria besides cost: (1) finishing time required, (2) ease of handling (holding, transplanting), (3) availability of plugs in various sizes, (4) space requirements, (5) growing skill, and (6) the quality of plant that will result from the plug.

In the past many growers would simply build more greenhouses to meet the expanding market. Presently, more growers, interested in expanding production capability without expanding greenhouse facilities, are looking into concentrating on how fast they can turn a crop. The more crop turns you can get from your greenhouse and sell, the more profitable you will be. This concept makes the greenhouse operation more efficient, rather than larger.

This chapter covers production schedules for plugs of all types and sizes, as well as finished bedding plants. You can use this information whether you grow your own plugs or buy them in. We will also show how you can optimize greenhouse time and space and become more profitable by calculating square foot weeks.

PLUG AND FINISHED BEDDING PLANT SCHEDULING

One of the major components for success in the plug production industry is proper planning and scheduling. The information in this chapter was obtained from growers who produce plugs in various sizes in different parts of the United States. Table 16.1 provides plug crop times for many bedding plants in different plug sizes. Table 16.2 lists some plug crop times (in northern California conditions) for common cut flower crops from seed. Table 16.3 shows plug crop times for some flowering pot crops, whereas table 16.4 contains plug crop timing for many perennials (in Midwest conditions). Finally, table 16.5 lists vegetable plug times for field usage. Generally, all these guidelines are for crop times during the *main* plug production season for each crop in the United States. Keep in mind that all these plug schedules are to be used as approximate guidelines only. Your actual crop time will differ, depending on plug size, environmental and cultural growing conditions, time of year, and type of market served.

The main factors affecting plug crop timing include temperature, light quantity, watering practices, type of fertilizer, time of year, location or latitude, and chemical growth regulators. The role that each has on plug growth has been discussed thoroughly in previous chapters. To review, soil temperature greatly affects the plant growth through photosynthesis, respiration, and uptake of water and nutrients. Plug growth (of both roots and shoots) increases as temperature increases between 55 and 85F (13 and 30C). Beyond these end points, growth drops off dramatically or stops. Light quantity (intensity × duration) also affects photosynthesis. Low light levels during the winter season slow down crop time while causing problems with shoot elongation and poor rooting. HID lights have greatly improved plug growth and reduced crop timing for some crops.

Watering practices affect the shoot:root ratio. A "wet" grower may have shorter plug crop timing but poorer root systems. A "dry" grower may need to add plug crop time to get more shoots but will have very good roots. Fertilizers high in NH_4 promote more shoot growth than root growth. Fertilizers high in NO_3 and Ca promote root growth and a toned plug. Growing plugs in the short days of winter takes longer than in the long days of summer. Growers in northern latitudes (or very southern latitudes in the southern hemisphere) need to provide HID lighting and maybe CO_2 enrichment, as well as better root-zone heating, to promote plug growth. Finally, chemical growth regulators, such as Bonzi, Sumagic, and A-Rest, can slow down crop growth, resulting in maybe an extra week at certain times of the year. In some crops and growing conditions, however, such chemicals may actually decrease crop timing by improving root growth.

TABLE 16.1   BEDDING PLANT PLUG CROP TIMES, BY TRAY SIZE

| Crop | Weeks from sowing to transplant | | | |
	800-tray	406-tray	288-tray	128-tray
Ageratum	4–5	5–6	6–7	7–8
Alyssum	4–5	5–6	6–7	7–8
Asparagus springeri	—	10–12	—	12–14
Aster	3–4	4–5	5–6	—
Begonia, fibrous	7–8	8–9	9–10	10–11
Begonia, tuberous	8–9	9–10	10–11	11–12
Browallia	6–7	7–8	8–9	9
Cabbage	—	4–5	5	—
Calendula	3	4	5	—
Carnation	4–5	5–6	—	7–8
Celosia	4–5	5–6	6	6
Coleus	5–6	6–7	7	7–8
Dahlia	—	4–5	5–6	6–7
Dianthus	4–5	5–6	6–7	7–8
Dracaena spike	—	12–16	—	18–20
Dusty miller	5–6	6–7	7–8	8
Eggplant	—	5–6	6–7	7
Flowering kale/cabbage	—	3–4	4–5	—
Gazania	5	5–6	6–7	7–8
Geranium	—	5	6	7
Impatiens	4–5	5–6	6–7	7–8
Lisianthus	9–10	10–11	11–12	12–13
Lobelia	5	6	7	7
Marigold	3–4	4–5	5–6	5–6
Nicotiana	4–5	5–6	6–7	7–8
Pansy	4–5	5–6	6–7	7–8
Pepper	—	5–6	6–7	7–8
Petunia	4–5	5–6	6–7	7–8
Portulaca	5–6	6–7	7–8	7–8
Primula acaulis	—	8–10	10–12	12–14
P. malacoides	—	9–11	11–12	12–14
P. obconica	—	8–10	10–12	12–14
P. polyantha	—	8–10	10–12	12–14
Ranunculus	—	9–11	11–12	12–14
Salvia farinacea	5–6	6–7	7–8	8
S. splendens	4–5	5–6	6–7	7
Snapdragon	4–5	5–6	6–7	7
Tomato	—	4–5	5–6	6–7
Torenia	4–5	5–6	6–7	7–8
Verbena	4–5	5–6	6–7	7–8
Vinca	4–5	5–6	6–7	7–8
Viola	4–5	5–6	6–7	7–8
Zinnia	—	3	4	—

TABLE 16.2   CUT FLOWER PLUG CROP TIMES, BY TRAY SIZE

Crop	390-tray	288-tray	200-tray	128-tray	73-tray [a]
		Weeks from sowing to transplanting			
Achillea		5	6–7		
Ageratum			5–6		
Ammi majus			6–7		
Anemone	6–7	8–9			12–13
Aquilegia			8–9		
Asclepias			6–7		
Aster		4–5	5–6		
Campanula			8–10		
Celosia			5		
Centaurea			6–7		
Cirsium			7		
Craspedia			7–9		
Delphinium			8–9		
Dianthus			7–8		
Didiscus			5–6		
Godetia			4–5		
Gomphrena			6–7		
Gypsophila			6–7	7–8	
Helianthus			3		
Helichrysum			5–6		
Larkspur			5–6		
Lisianthus	8–10	10–11			
Matricaria			6–7		
Platycodon			9–10		
Ranunculus			11–12		
Scabiosa			6–7	7–8	
Snapdragon	5–6	6	7		
Statice caspia			9–10		
S. latifolia			8–9		
S. perezii			6–7		
S. sinuata			5–6		
S. suworowii			5–6		
S. tartarica			9–10		
Stock	4–5		5–6		
Trachelium		9	10–11		
Veronica			8–9		
Zinnia			3		

[a] Transplanted from smaller tray; total crop time.

TABLE 16.3   POT CROP PLUG CROP TIMES, BY TRAY SIZE

	Weeks from sowing to transplanting		
Crop	**406-tray**	**128-tray** [a]	**55-tray** [a]
Calceolaria	7–8	8–9	
Cineraria	5–6	7–8	
Cyclamen	9	14	17
Exacum	6	9	
Gerbera	6	8–9	10–11
Gloxinia		10	
Schizanthus	4	6	
Streptocarpus		15–16	

[a] Transplanted from smaller trays; total crop time.

Calculating space needs for your plug production will depend on your season, greenhouse capacity, type of crops, plug ccll size, and how much you can zone the greenhouse to provide proper conditions for the various stages of plug growth. Remember the four stages of plug growth:

Stage 1— seeding to radicle emergence

Stage 2— radicle emergence to cotyledon expansion

Stage 3— cotyledon expansion to growth of all true leaves and roots

Stage 4— toning or holding phase

The germination process occurs during Stages 1 and 2. Whether you germinate most crops in a germination chamber or on the greenhouse bench will determine how much space you need for this critical stage. Long-term crops, such as begonia, lisianthus, ranunculus, primula, and cyclamen, have long germination periods. You may want to optimize your bench space by starting these crops in a chamber (Stage 1). Stage 3 for most crops requires the most growing space and time. About 50% of the crop time is spent in this stage. Stage 4 requires from a few days to two weeks, depending on how long you want to hold the plugs. The growing requirements are not as precise in this final stage as in the previous three stages, which means you can use a lower-cost greenhouse for Stage 4.

As can be seen in tables 16.1 through 16.5, the larger the plug size, the longer the crop time. Some crops naturally take longer than other crops to grow. Growing during the summer takes less time than during the winter. If growing plugs for your own needs, as compared to shipping plugs to other customers, you may not need to be as precise on timing or quality. However,

TABLE 16.4   PERENNIAL PLUG CROP TIMES, BY TRAY SIZE

| Crop | Weeks from sowing to transplanting [a] | |
	350-tray	120-tray [a]
Achillea	5–7	7–9
Agrostemma	5	7
Althaea	4	5
Alyssum	5–7	7–9
Anaphalis	6	8
Anchusa	5	7
Anthemis	6	8
Aquilegia	7–9	9–10
Arabis	6	8
Arenaria	6	8
Armeria	8	10
Asclepias	6	8
Aster	5–6	7–8
Astilbe	8–9	10–11
Aubrietia	6	8
Bellis	4–5	7–8
Bergenia	9	10–11
Campanula carpatica, persificola, and *rotundifolia*	8–9	11–12
C. glomerata	7–8	9–10
C. poscharskyana	12	14
Catananche	6	8
Centaurea	5–6	8
Centranthus	6	8
Cerastium	6	8
Cheiranthus	5	7
Chrysanthemum coccineum	6–8	8–10
C. maximum, leucanthemum, and *parthenium*	5–7	7–9
Coreopsis	6–7	8–10
Coronilla	5	7
Cortaderia	6	8
Delphinium	6–8	8–10
Deschampsia	7	9
Dianthus	5–7	7–9
Digitalis	6–7	8–9
Doronicum	6	8
Echinacea	5–7	7–9
Echinops	6	8
Euphorbia	6	8
Festuca	6–7	7–9
Gaillardia	5–7	7–9
Geum	6–8	9–11
Gypsophila	5–6	8–9
Helenium	8	10

TABLE 16.4 **CONTINUED**

| Crop | Weeks from sowing to transplanting [a] | |
	350-tray	120-tray [a]
Heliopsis	6–7	8
Heuchera	7–8	10–11
Hibiscus	3–5	5–6
Iberis	6–8	8–10
Kniphofia	8	10
Lathryus	7	9
Lavendula	8–9	11–12
Leontopodium	8	10
Liatris	8	10
Linum	6	8
Lobelia	7–8	9–10
Lunaria	7	9
Lupinus	4	5
Lychnis	6	8
Lythrum	5	7
Monarda	6–7	7–8
Myosotis	5–7	7–9
Nepeta	5	6
Oenothera	7–8	9–10
Papavar (poppies)		
P. nudicale	7–9	9–11
P. orientale	7–8	8–10
Penstemon	5	7
Physalis	5	7
Physostegia	7	9
Platycodon	6	8
Polemonium	7	9
Potentilla	6	8
Primula veris	8–10	12–14
Rudbeckia	6–7	8–9
Salvia superba	6	8
Santolina	8	10
Saxifraga	9–10	11–12
Scabiosa	4–5	6–7
Sedum	7–8	9–10
Sempervivum	10–11	13–14
Stachys	5–6	6–7
Statice	7–8	9–11
Teucrium	8	10
Thymus	7	9
Veronica	5	7
Viola	5–7	6–8

[a] 50/55-trays are also available (not shown), and are all transplanted from smaller plug sizes and vernalized for at least four weeks.

TABLE 16.5   VEGETABLE PLUG CROP TIMES FROM SOW TO TRANSPLANT

Crop	Tray size (inches) [a]	Crop time (weeks)
Broccoli	$^3/_4$	5–6
Cabbage	$^3/_4$–1	5–6
Cauliflower	$^3/_4$–1	5–6
Celery	$^3/_4$–1	8–9
Cucumber	1 $^5/_{16}$	3–4
Eggplant	1	6–7
Lettuce	1	4–5
Muskmelon	1 $^5/_{16}$	4–5
Onion	$^3/_4$	8–9
Pepper	1	7–8
Squash	1 $^5/_{16}$	3
Tomato	1	6–7
Watermelon	1 $^5/_{16}$	5–6

[a] Tray size is square-celled Styrofoam tray.

for most robotic transplanters to work properly, there are greater demands on home-grown plug quality, as the root systems need to be just right, and the plugs cannot be too tall.

The following tables give finishing times for selected bedding plant crops produced from plugs of different sizes and grown at 60F (15C) minimum night temperature. Table 16.6 gives crop timing for 72-cell packs, table 16.7 for 48-cell packs, table 16.8 for 36-cell packs, and table 16.9 for 4-inch pots. These tables are to be used as guidelines only. Actual crop times will depend on grower practices. Use the previously discussed methods to modify crop times to meet your production programs. For the deep 606 flat (36 plants/flat), add about one week to the crop times given in table 16.8, as it takes longer to get a deeper root system than it does to put on enough top growth and flowering. For hanging baskets, add three to four weeks to the 128-plug/4-inch pot crop time in table 16.9, depending on the number of plugs used and the size of the hanging basket; add more plugs per hanging basket to decrease crop time.

TABLE 16.6   CROP FINISHING TIMES OF PLUGS TRANSPLANTED INTO 72-CELL PACKS

| Crop | Weeks to finish [a] | |
	800 plug	406 plug
Ageratum	7	5
Alyssum	6	4
Begonia, fibrous	6	5
Browallia	6	5
Celosia	5	4
Coleus	5	4
Dianthus	6	5
Dusty miller	6	5
Impatiens	5	4
Lobelia	6	5
Marigold, African	5	4
Marigold, French	4	3
Nicotiana	—	5
Pansy	7	5
Petunia	6	5
Portulaca	6	5
Salvia	5	4
Snapdragon	5	4
Verbena	—	5
Vinca	7	5
Viola	7	5
Zinnia	—	4

[a] 60F (16C) minimum night temperature

HOW TO OPTIMIZE TIME AND SPACE

When planning a finished bedding plant production program, a grower has two variables to manage: crop time and production space. By adjusting the amount of time a crop spends in the plug compared to the finished container stage, the grower can significantly increase the number of turns per season. Knowing how to calculate square foot weeks (sq ft wk) lets the grower integrate time and space to maximize production without building more greenhouses.

For each type of crop, you need to know how long it will take to produce a certain size of plug and finish it in a certain size of container. Figure 16.1

TABLE 16.7   CROP FINISHING TIMES OF PLUGS TRANSPLANTED INTO 48-CELL PACKS

Crop	800 plug	Weeks to finish [a] 406 plug	288 plug
Ageratum	8	6	—
Alyssum	7	5	—
Begonia, fibrous	7	6	5
Browallia	7	6	—
Celosia	6	5	3
Coleus	6	5	3
Dianthus	7	6	5
Dusty miller	7	6	4
Geranium	—	10	8
Impatiens	6	5	3
Lobelia	7	6	—
Marigold, African	6	5	4
Marigold, French	5	4	3
Nicotiana	—	5	—
Pansy	8	6	5
Petunia	7	5	4
Portulaca	7	5	—
Salvia	6	5	4
Snapdragon	6	5	—
Verbena	—	6	5
Vinca	8	6	5
Viola	8	6	—
Zinnia	—	4	3

[a] 60F (16C) minimum night temperature

shows that impatiens grown for six weeks in a 390 plug require five weeks to finish in a 36-cell pack, for a total crop time of 11 weeks. Compared to an 800 plug, the time spent in the plug stage is increased 50%, while time in the final pack is decreased almost 28%. Now compare a 288 to an 800 impatiens plug. Plug time increases 75%, and the pack crop time decreases 43% [1].

To summarize fig. 16.1, as the plug size increases, the posttransplant time decreases. This reduction in finish time is very important when trying to schedule a crop into a specific production period, such as the normally short spring season. A grower may start out the season with small plugs (512 or 800) since there is adequate time to finish them. Later in the season, the grower may use larger plugs (288), matching the shorter crop times with the available production windows.

TABLE 16.8   CROP FINISHING TIMES OF PLUGS TRANSPLANTED INTO 36-CELL PACKS

Crop	800 plug	Weeks to finish [a] 406 plug	288 plug
Ageratum	8	7	—
Alyssum	8	7	—
Begonia, fibrous	8	7	6
Browallia	8	7	—
Celosia	7	6	4
Coleus	6	5	4
Dianthus	8	7	6
Dusty miller	8	6	5
Geranium	—	10	9
Impatiens	7	5	4
Lobelia	8	7	—
Marigold, African	7	6	5
Marigold, French	6	5	4
Nicotiana	—	6	
Pansy	8	7	5
Petunia	8	6	5
Portulaca	7	6	—
Salvia	8	6	4
Snapdragon	7	6	—
Verbena	—	7	6
Vinca	9	7	6
Viola	9	7	—
Zinnia	—	5	4

[a] 60F (16C) minimum night temperature

Using only crop times provides only half of the picture for production planning. Space calculations must also be made along with times, or the grower will run out of room very quickly. Here is a simple formula for calculating square foot weeks (sq ft wk), a valuable time and space use concept:

flats or trays needed for each crop and turn × 1.7 sq ft/flat × # weeks to finish (depends on plug size) = sq ft wk

A standard U.S. bedding plant flat occupies 1.7 sq ft. If the finished crop requires five weeks to produce, then it takes 8.5 sq ft wk to finish a flat. In a 5,000 sq ft production area (25,000 sq ft wk), 2,941 flats can be finished in five weeks.

TABLE 16.9   CROP FINISHING TIMES OF PLUGS TRANSPLANTED INTO 4-INCH POTS

| Crop | Weeks to finish [a] | | |
	406 plug	288 plug	128 plug
Ageratum	8	7	5
Alyssum	8	—	—
Begonia, fibrous	8	7	6
Browallia	8	—	5
Celosia	7	6	5
Coleus	6	6	5
Dianthus	8	7	7
Dusty miller	7	6	6
Geranium	11	9	8
Gomphrena	8	—	5
Impatiens	6	5	4
Impatiens, New Guinea	—	8	7
Lobelia	8	—	—
Marigold, African	7	5	4
Marigold, French	6	4	3
Nicotiana	7	—	5
Pansy	8	7	6
Petunia	7	6	5
Portulaca	7	—	6
Salvia	7	5	4
Snapdragon	7	—	5
Verbena	8	7	6
Vinca	8	7	6
Viola	8	—	6
Zinnia	6	5	4

[a] 60F (16C) minimum night temperature.

The sq ft wk measure allows the grower to quickly determine what plug sizes will finish in a specific number of sq ft wk. Table 16.10 shows the impact of using different plug sizes on the sq ft wk needed to produce an impatiens crop. A 288 plug uses 43% fewer sq ft wk than an 800 plug, allowing more turns during the season [1].

Now let's apply this information to a spring-season planning schedule. Table 16.11 illustrates some of the common timing problems growers observe. Because of the perceived cost savings, some growers use 800 plugs for the first turn (example A) assuming they can finish later crops without any problem. Unfortunately, if the grower uses 390 plugs for the second

FIGURE 16.1   Impatiens crop times finished in 36-cell pack, by plug size. Adapted from Healy & Szmurlo, Figuring time and space, *GrowerTalks.*

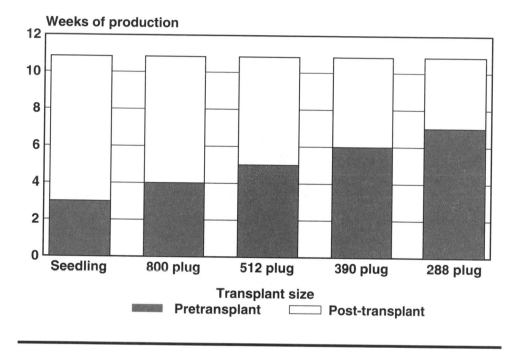

TABLE 16.10   CROP TIME TO FINISH 36-CELL PACKS, IN WEEKS AND SQUARE FOOT WEEKS

Plug size	Impatiens	Petunia Crop time (wks)	Begonia
800	7	8	8
512	6	7	7
390	5	6	6
288	4	5	5
		Sq ft wk [a]	
800	11,900	13,600	13,600
512	10,200	11,900	11,900
390	8,500	10,200	10,200
288	6,800	8,500	8,500

[a] 1,000 flats

Source: Adapted from Healy & Szmurlo, Figuring time and space, *GrowerTalks.*

TABLE 16.11   PRODUCTION PLANNING FOR IMPATIENS

Planting	Plug size	Sq ft wk used	Sq ft wk available after turn	Production period
Example A		25,500 at start		
Turn 1	800	11,900	13,600	Wk 9–15
Turn 2	390	8,500	5,100	Wk 16–20
Turn 3	390	8,500	0	Wk 21–25
Example B		25,500 at start		
Turn 1	800	11,900	13,600	Wk 9–15
Turn 2	288	6,800	6,800	Wk 16–19
Turn 3	288	6,800	0	Wk 20–23

Source: Adapted from Healy & Szmurlo, Figuring time and space, *GrowerTalks*.

turn, there is inadequate time to finish a third turn because the first turn requires too many sq ft wk, which leaves the third turn about two weeks short of finishing. Depending on when Easter is, the second crop will not finish until after Mother's Day. By using 288 instead of 390 plugs for the second and third turns, crops are salable the week before Mother's Day and by the week after Memorial Day (example B). The larger plugs require fewer sq ft wk to finish and therefore allow for more turns [1].

Calculating sq ft wks is an easy technique for accurately planning crop timing and space use. You can use it when growing plug trays, as well as finished containers. You can also use it whether growing plugs for your own use or buying in plugs. The key is to determine what size of plug to use, for what size of container, and for what part of the season. By optimizing these decisions, a grower can make the greenhouse facility more efficient, producing more product in a certain period of time without building more greenhouses.

CHANGING TRENDS

As with most things in this world, nothing stays the same very long in the plug and greenhouse business. One of the most noticeable changes in the United States lately is the trend toward larger finished containers, particularly for mass markets. It used to be that the standard finished bedding flat contained 72 plants. Now the trend is moving more toward 36 plants, with more 48- and 54-cell packs being grown now than ever before too. In fact, few parts of the country still grow 72-cell packs. In addition to having fewer plants per flat, the container has been made deeper to provide a better root zone, allowing the plants to hold up longer in chain stores. The deep 606 flat (36 plants/flat) provides a better plant to the chain store and to the consumer.

This larger container trend is also promoting the usage of a greater number of larger plugs, especially the 288 plug, for faster turns. Even though planting an 800 or 512 plug into a deep 606 is cheaper, the finishing time is much longer and ultimately costs the grower more (table 16.12). Another factor promoting 288 plugs is the ever-increasing presence of robotic transplanters, which need to handle well-rooted plugs that are not overgrown.

TABLE 16.12 ECONOMIC COMPARATIVE ANALYSIS OF PLUG SIZES

Crop—Impatiens	Crop A (512 plug)	Crop B (288 plug)
Flat size	1204	1204
Plugs/flat	48	48
Tags/flat	8	8
Finish time (wks)	5	3
Number flats to be produced/turn	10,000	10,000
Number of turns [a]	2	3.33
Cost/sq ft/week	$0.180	$0.180
Cost/plug	$0.043	$0.070
Cost/flat & insert	$0.500	$0.500
Cost/flat for soil	$0.350	$0.350
Cost/1,000 tags	$8.000	$8.000
Average flat selling price	$8.00	$8.00
Loss factor (% dump)	2.0	2.0
Total cost of production/flat	$4.422	$5.140
Total cost of production	$88,435	$171,170
Total production at selling price	$160,000	$266,400
Net sales	$156,800	$261,072
Profit/flat	**$3.42**	**$2.70**
Net profit/turn	**$34,183**	**$26,998**
Profit all turns	**$68,365**	**$89,902**
Profit/sq ft/week	**$0.43**	**$0.56**
Increased profits		**$21,537**

[a] Assumes 10-week selling window.

Source: Economic analysis provided by the Ball Seed Co., West Chicago, Illinois.

One of the main types, the MetroPlanter from MetroPlanter USA Inc., could initially transplant only 288 plugs, nothing smaller. It worked so well that many growers started paying attention to using 288 plugs. Now transplanters can handle many different plug sizes, but the 288 plug is still the plug of choice for a faster turn in bedding flats ranging from 36 to 54 plants per flat. Try figuring out your own costs and production schedule, and see if you find room for a larger plug in your operation.

The customer's knowledge of using plugs will determine the plug size needed. In a country where a plug market is new, a larger size of plug is generally needed first. This is mainly due to new customers, whether farmers or greenhouse operators, not being familiar with what a plug is and what it can do. They may be used to handling much larger plants, especially ones to put into the field. Later on, with more customer knowledge and more competition, a smaller plug may be needed to meet the demands for a cheaper priced plug. Again, the educational process continues, with plug growers needing to educate customers about how to handle small plugs. Finally, different usages may develop for the same crop. Growers may want to transplant plugs into larger containers, such as hanging baskets. This requires a larger size of plug, such as a 128 plug. Be aware of such specialty demands for different plug sizes! As the old saying might go, "One size does not fit all!"

KEY POINTS TO REMEMBER

- Use the scheduling tables as guidelines only. Your crop times may vary, depending on how, where, and when you grow.

- There is no one best size of plug for any container or purpose. Explore the different plug sizes and determine which combinations of sizes you can use.

- Cost should not be the only criterion for plug size. Also, consider finishing time, ease of handling, availability, growing space, growing skill, and quality of finished plant needed in determining what plug sizes to grow or buy.

- Optimize time and space usage by calculating square foot weeks. Use this measure to expand your production without expanding your greenhouse facilities, turning more crops in a given amount of space. The net result is more profit!

- Be aware of changing trends in plug and container sizes. What worked for you five or 10 years ago may not work tomorrow!

REFERENCES

[1] Healy, W., and G. Szmurlo. 1995. Figuring time and space to maximize your bedding turns. *GrowerTalks* 58(10):57–60.

CHAPTER 17

TRANSPLANTING PLUGS

Whether you are growing your own plugs or buying them in, getting them transplanted on time and with great results is not as easy as it might sound. No matter how good your plug production schedule is, there will always be times during the busy season when transplanting gets backed up due to poor weather. Plugs may have to be held one or two weeks before transplanting can resume. If the plugs had not been toned properly or held under the right conditions, they would quickly stretch, lose their roots and root hairs, get diseased, or generally not be of good quality for transplanting.

Many times a grower will buy in high-quality plugs but not succeed with them. Good plugs can be ruined during holding, transplanting, or the critical first week after transplanting. Poor-quality plugs, on the other hand, rarely make a high-quality transplant, no matter what the grower does.

To successfully transplant plugs, a grower needs to pay attention to many of the same factors as for growing them, including water quality, media quality, environment, nutrition, moisture management, height control, and insects and disease. Simple things—such as how deep to plant the plug, pulling or dislodging plugs from the trays, feeding them immediately after transplanting, and what temperature to grow them at—can make the difference between rapid, uniform take-off after transplanting and unevenness in growth and flowering.

This chapter will cover the basics of handling plugs, transplanting them manually or with robotic transplanters, and getting through the critical first week after transplanting. We will also discuss common problems that growers have with plugs both before and after transplanting. Growing a quality plug or buying one in is only part of the process. Getting that plug to take off and produce the quality finished plant you want is the other part.

HANDLING PLUGS

When growing your own plugs to be transplanted on time, there is generally no need to tone or harden them, unless they will be transplanted directly out in the field or grown under less than ideal greenhouse conditions after transplanting. Most plugs, however, are not transplanted on time, so toning is necessary. Toning the plug is done during Stage 4, when temperature can be reduced to 55 to 60F (13 to 15C); moisture is reduced, the plugs drying out thoroughly between thorough waterings; the fertilizer is changed to one with more NO_3, and feeding is less frequent; and light levels are higher (greater than 2,500 fc, 27,000 lux). Stage 4 usually lasts from three to seven days, depending on the crop, plug size, and time of year. Toning plugs is absolutely necessary for field vegetable transplants, many of which go out into harsh field conditions.

Shipping and handling can cause stress on perishable material such as plugs. To reduce stress and maintain plug quality, suppliers precondition, or harden off, plugs prior to shipping. Specially designed cardboard containers protect the product from damage while in transit. Where possible, air freight, Federal Express, or temperature-controlled truck trailers are used to transport the plugs efficiently (fig. 17.1). Delivery is normally made in two days, though one-day delivery may be possible in certain situations.

Upon plug arrival, you should open the boxes and inspect the contents immediately. Check the packing list to compare the varieties and quantities with what was ordered.

Next examine the condition of the plant material. Yellow or drooping leaves may be evidence of shipping stress. The plugs might have been in the box too long, the shipping temperature might not have been controlled, or the media might have been too wet or dry. Mold and decay may indicate that the media was too wet when shipped, the plugs were frozen in transit, or the shipment was delayed. Material could also have been damaged if the shipping container was upset, dropped, or crushed.

Report any discrepancies or damages to your plug supplier or broker immediately after receipt (definitely within 72 hours), so that replacements or credit can be arranged as quickly as possible. Take photographs of damaged product. If disease or insects are apparent on the plug trays, report this situation immediately to your supplier or broker, and do not plant these plugs without further treatment. Diseased samples may be sent for diagnosis to your lab of choice.

To acclimate plugs, place the trays in a predetermined area of the greenhouse for one or two days. Partial shade (30 to 50%) should be provided when light levels are high. Good air circulation is needed to remove excess moisture and any accumulated gases produced by seedlings during shipping, such as ethylene. Plugs should be clear-watered thoroughly with high-quality water (alkalinity lower than 120 ppm, EC lower than 1.0, Na less than 40 ppm). Maintain soil temperature between 62 and 65F (17 and 18C) until transplanting. No fertilizer, fungicides, or chemical growth regulators should be applied, unless the plugs will be held for more than three days.

Not all plugs are shipped in their trays in cardboard boxes or on racks in trucks. Some plugs, particularly vegetables for field transplanting and 10-week geraniums, are pulled from trays and packed in cardboard boxes for shipping longer distances, thereby saving money on freight (fig. 17.2). The large-celled trays they are grown in, along with the large size of the plants, would make shipping in the tray very expensive. These *pull-and-pack plugs* must be unboxed immediately and transplanted within one day of receipt. The conditions discussed for acclimating plugs do not apply to pull-and-pack plugs. Field vegetable growers, particularly, have problems with this shipping method when the weather keeps them from getting into their fields to transplant. The boxes may be held in a cooler set at 45F (7C), but only for a limited time. The close plant density and moisture inside the box allow diseases like *Botrytis* to develop rapidly.

FIGURE 17.1 Plug trays shipped in boxes (above) and racks on trucks (below).

Many large-celled perennial plugs are vernalized, and, when shipped to customers, look like they are dead. Many of these plants are dormant or semi-dormant and appear brown, have minimal or no top growth, or have discolored foliage. They are neither dead nor even diseased. These plugs usually have well-developed, healthy root

FIGURE 17.2 Pull-and-pack tomato seedlings. Courtesy Speedling Inc.

systems, which will push up new top growth once transplanted and warmed up. Do not fertilize until new root and shoot growth is visible. Grow on at cool temperatures (50 to 60F, 10 to 15C), depending on the timing of the finished crop.

TRANSPLANTING

Transplanting preparations should be made in advance of the scheduled date. Use a high-quality growing media. New containers should be filled and ready, although many growers now use mechanical flat fillers tied directly into their transplanting lines. The plugs should be watered at least two to three hours prior to transplanting to make extraction from the trays easier. The flats should be watered in thoroughly with high-quality water immediately after transplanting.

Bedding plants grow well in both soilless media and media with soil (but less than 20%). The growing media must have moderate water-holding capacity (65 to 70%), with 15 to 20% air porosity to allow drainage and air exchange. The grower should sterilize field soil before using it as part of growing media, growing a few plants of the main crops to test for contaminants in the soil media. The mix quality should be repeatable. The pH of the soilless mix should be 5.5 to 5.8, except for geranium, lisianthus, marigold, and impatiens, which need a pH of 6.0 to 6.2. For mixes with soil, pH can be 0.5 units higher. Soluble salts of the growing mix should be at less than 1.5 mmhos (2:1 extraction). A complete media analysis should be made prior to planting, and growing media pH and soluble salts should be monitored regularly during the crop cycle.

Transplanting can be done manually or mechanically. Use a dibble to create uniform holes in the container soil to reduce the potential of plug root damage. Dibble somewhat moist media to retain the shape of the hole. Dibbling devices can be purchased or are included with many types of mechanical flat fillers, or you can make your own dibble-board (fig. 17.3).

Make sure to adjust the dibble for the plug size you are transplanting, no deeper.

FIGURE 17.3 Dibbler on flat filler. Courtesy Gleason Equipment.

Use a plug dislodger or popper to prevent breakage or tearing the plug by pulling. The correct plug dislodger template needs to be used for each plug tray size. (Appendix 4 lists plug dislodger, or popper, suppliers.) Place the plug in the soil only *slightly* deeper than the top of the root ball, then firm the soil around the plug. Cyclamen plugs need to be planted evenly with the top of the root ball, so that the corm sits on the surface. If the dibble hole was made correctly for the plug size, you may not need to firm the soil around the plug.

The first watering-in will settle the media around the plug roots. Separating multiple seedlings will cause damage to seedling roots (making bare-root seedlings) and is not recommended. Water the flats thoroughly with clear water (alkalinity less than 120 ppm, EC lower than 1.0, Na less than 40 ppm) immediately after transplanting. No fertilizer or fungicide should be applied until after the roots have started to root out, in approximately three days at 65 to 70F (18 to 21C). If rooting-out is not observed in three days, the grower should check and adjust environmental and cultural practices, particularly temperature, moisture, and soluble salts.

Many bedding plant growers use a transplanting line to manually transplant the plugs into the finished containers (fig. 17.4). This work, generally done in the headhouse area, involves a transplanting crew working in assembly-line style. The typical transplanting line has a conveyor belt on which the containers are transported at a certain speed after being filled by a mechanical flat filler and dibbled. The crew people sit or stand on either side of the conveyor, with plug trays in front of and above them. The plugs have been dislodged from the trays, making it easy to grab a handful of plugs and place them into the dibbled containers' holes. Tags are then placed into the containers, which are then run through a watering tunnel and taken to the greenhouse to be grown on.

Some growers transplant bedding plants into containers in the greenhouse areas where the containers will be grown. The difficulty with this method is that it does not allow for efficient product movement and quality control. More labor has to be used, as this transplanting may be taking place in a number of greenhouses at the same time.

Transplanting into soil beds in a greenhouse, as in cut flower operations, requires the beds to be prepared ahead of time with the cor-

FIGURE 17.4 Manual transplanting line.

rect fertilizer, EC, pH, and soil texture. Steam or methyl bromide (where legal) fumigation may be done once a year. Some soil moisture is needed before transplanting can be done. Plugs are normally transplanted into the ground in furrows or holes made by fingers, with the soil firmed around the plugs. Watering by overhead sprinklers follows, with generally no feeding until two or three weeks after transplanting, depending on soil type, crop, and location.

Transplanting vegetable or cut flower plugs into a field is very similar (fig. 17.5). The beds must be worked up properly to get the right texture, with a minimum of large clods. Soil fumigation may be necessary, depending on the crop planted and any crop rotation used. The soil should have already been tested for pH and soluble salts, with any pH adjustments made during bed preparation. Plastic mulch can be laid over the beds, with burned or punched holes through which the transplants will be placed. Some initial moisture is needed during this process, particularly when using plastic mulch. In many cases, a starter fertilizer will have already been placed under the mulch. Sometimes though, the starter fertilizer and water are injected into the holes where the transplants have been placed. Tomato and pepper plugs can be buried past the cotyledons to speed up rooting, especially when the transplants are tall (fig. 17.6). Watering-in of the recently transplanted field should be done the same day, either with sprinklers or furrow irrigation.

ROBOTIC TRANSPLANTERS

In recent years, fully robotic transplanters have come onto the market for transplanting plugs into finished bedding plant containers. There are also a few robotic transplanters for planting vegetable plugs into the field. With labor becoming more expensive and less available—and with the growing demand for plugs, whether vegetables or ornamentals—robotic transplanters

FIGURE 17.5 Tomato seedlings transplanted into plastic mulch beds. Courtesy Charles Vavrina, University of Florida.

FIGURE 17.6 Growth of tomato seedlings transplanted to different depths. Plant on left was transplanted the deepest. Courtesy Charles Vavrina, University of Florida.

will become more readily available and able to do more.

Transplanters run the range from inexpensive models designed for smaller producers all the way to top-of-the-line, heavy-duty models designed to plant 100,000 or more bedding plant flats annually (fig. 17.7). Each model requires at least one operator; some larger units need two or three workers to sort out trays and patch empty cells. Prices range from $20,000 to $130,000. Appendix 4 lists many of the robotic transplanters available on the market. This list can change yearly, as companies get into and out of the market. Also, there are transplanters available from Europe not on this list. Before you invest in a transplanter, ask yourself these questions:

- Can I increase my production volume enough to pay back the cost of a transplanter?

- Can I decrease my labor costs or reorganize my labor force with the machine?

FIGURE 17.7 Harrison (above) and Flier (below) robotic transplanters. Courtesy Blackmore Company Inc. and Flier USA Inc.

- Can the transplanter accommodate the plug tray sizes I prefer?

- Does it require additional parts?

- Will speed decrease when I use different tray sizes?

- How heavily does the machine rely on plug quality? Does the number of misses increase with overgrown or rootbound plugs?

- Does the machine grade to ensure 100% full-finished flats?

- Can my operation keep up with the machine? What other equipment will I need to purchase, and what work-flow adjustments will I need to make, to optimize the transplanter?

- Do I have the staff expertise to maintain and repair it? How well will the company service its product? What about training?

- Can the machine be adapted to transplant pots and hanging baskets?

- Does the machine effectively transplant the plug without damaging it?

As you can see, you need to ask more than just what the transplanter can do, how fast, and how much it costs. Talk with your neighbors or other growers who have been using the type of transplanter you are interested in, and ask if they would buy the same one again. If not, why not?

Understanding the limitations of any particular transplanter is just as important as understanding its positive attributes. A transplanter is a complicated piece of equipment run by computer programs. You need someone on staff who can handle problems with the equipment, and it may not be your normal maintenance person. Flexibility in handling different plug sizes going into different sizes of finished flats may be great, but at what cost? The ease of changing over may be very critical to you. Always try to see the transplanter in action on the types of crops you grow. Notice how well it handles plugs of different heights or levels of rooting. Transplanters that have sensors installed for detecting empty cells or nonusable seedlings will run slower than those without sensors. Reusing plug trays does not work well with a robot. The cracked edges do not allow the trays to move well through the machine, and the plug cells do not hold up to the abuse of pushing or picking up the plugs out of the tray.

Perhaps the biggest limitation to deal with is what kind of service you will get from the company when something goes wrong with the machine, as it inevitably will. Does the company have a customer service with someone technical on the other end who can walk you through problems? Does the company have trained staff who can get out to your place quickly (within 24 to 48 hours)? Are parts readily available from the company, and how hard is it to install them yourself? Finally, what backup plans do you have in case your transplanter breaks down during the peak season? Do you want to buy another machine and have it ready, in case? Do you keep your old manual transplanting line and have some labor to operate it?

The cost-payback analysis of your operation's robotic transplanters should also include how much you want to use the transplanter during the season. Many growers have had to change how they transplant to include a second shift and even a third shift to maximize transplanter use. This brings a grower closer to running a true manufacturing operation. Setting up additional shifts will take a lot of thought and supervision, as additional people will be needed, and product must be staged properly in the greenhouse for additional people to work effectively.

CRITICAL FIRST WEEK AFTER TRANSPLANTING

Newly transplanted seedlings should be placed in the proper environmental conditions to achieve optimum growth and finished quality. Temperature, water, nutrition, light, pesticides, and growth regulators are all important factors in producing quality finished plants from plugs.

Temperature. Initially, transplants should be allowed to become established at 65 to 70F (18 to 21C) soil temperature. Once established (in three or four days), the soil temperature can be lowered to 60 to 65F (15 to 18C) nights. Day temperatures should be 10F (6C) higher on cloudy days, 10 to 15F (6 to 8C) higher on sunny days, to promote plant growth. Maintaining constant day and night temperatures (zero DIF), or cooler day than night temperatures (–DIF), will produce more compact plant growth. A grower should use caution at temperatures of 50 to 55F (10 to 13C), as plant stunting and flower delay can occur on plants with warm temperature requirements. Similarly, temperatures over 75 to 80F (24 to 27C) may cause excessive stretching and blasting of the flowers. When measuring and controlling temperature, remember that the difference between air and soil temperature can be as great as 5 to 10F (3 to 6C), depending on the light levels and plant canopy cover. This difference gets bigger when the flats are laid on an unheated floor to grow. Always measure the soil temperature with a non-mercury thermometer or probe.

Water. Moisture can be applied manually or by automatic systems. The water amount must be enough to thoroughly saturate the media and allow leaching of 10 to 15%, particularly when you're dealing with less-than-desirable water quality. The media should then be allowed to dry down between watering for good root growth (fig. 17.8). Water quality is important. Keep alkalinity less than 120 ppm (with acid injection, if necessary), EC less than 1.0 mmhos, Ca greater than 50 ppm, Mg greater than 25 ppm, Na less than 40 ppm, and Cl less than 80 ppm.

Nutrition. After roots have become established, nutrients may be supplemented with liquid fertilizer. The type of fertilizer, rates, and frequency depend on the crop, cultivar, growing conditions, growing media, and the type of finished crop desired. Feed levels generally range from 100 to 300 ppm N. When using a slow-release fertilizer in the growing media, supplemental feeding may be needed, depending on how much water goes through the containers.

FIGURE 17.8 Drying of media in 4-inch pot for recently transplanted plugs.

Some crops are considered light feeders (100 to 150 ppm N), or salt-sensitive, whereas other crops are known as heavy feeders (250 to 300 ppm N), or salt-tolerant. Use caution with heavy feeding to prevent soluble salts from building up in the growing media. Impatiens, pansy, vinca, and salvia are relatively sensitive to soluble salts. Calendula, petunia, and geranium are relatively tolerant of soluble salts (except the latter and NH_4).

Low NH_4 fertilizers should be used if the average soil temperature is lower than 65F (18C). Soil bacteria are needed to convert the NH_4 to NO_3 which the plant can then use. Such bacteria are not as active when the temperature is consistently below 65F (18C), which slows the NH_4 conversion process. Ammonia toxicity may result, causing various forms of damage to the plants.

At low temperatures, plants do not grow as quickly and do not require water or fertilizer as often as at warmer temperatures. When the temperature is 70 to 80F (21 to 26C), plants grow more vigorously, are watered more often, and may need to be fertilized more frequently. However, high rates of fertilizer, particularly those containing more NH_4, will cause lush growth and excessive stretch and may delay flowering.

Finished bedding plants can be toned better with fertilizers higher in NO_3. Removing fertilizer one or two weeks before shipping, or at least decreasing feed levels, will help condition or tone the plants and increase their shelf-life expectancy.

Light. Daily fertilization at lower concentrations (75 to 100 ppm N) may be necessary to maintain vigorous plant growth under high light (greater than 4,000 fc, 43,000 lux). Generally, more NH_4 will be needed by plants growing under high light levels. Fertilizing under different light conditions is not necessarily dependent on frequency of watering. More nutrients (frequency, ppm, NH_4) are required under higher light conditions to support growth. Under low light conditions, the slow plant growth will require fertilizer less frequently and with more NO_3.

Pesticides. After roots have become established in the growing media (roots are growing out of the plug root ball), pesticides to treat specific diseases or insects may be applied to susceptible crops.

Growth regulators. Plant growth can be controlled by manipulating water, nutrition, temperature, and light. When additional control is needed, chemical growth regulators may be necessary. Apply chemical growth regulators after roots are out to the sides of the containers (usually after one week). Use slightly higher rates on finished crops than what is recommended for plugs.

COMMON PLUG PROBLEMS

Regardless of whether you grow your own plugs, buy plugs in, or do some combination of grow and buy, you will encounter some problems now and then with the quality or performance of some plugs. These difficulties can occur either before or after transplanting.

Before transplanting, you may notice plugs that are too tall, too small and not well-rooted, with yellow or twisted leaves, or already budded or flowering. Probably the most common pretransplanting plug problem, tall plugs have been experienced by every grower, especially if the plugs have been held due to delays in transplanting. Spraying a chemical growth regulator on tall plugs at this stage is like "locking the barn after the horse is gone"—*It's too late!* As long as the root systems are still active and not overly rootbound, transplant the plugs immediately at the appropriate depth.

Many crops cannot and should not be planted deeper than the plug depth. Sensitive crops, such as vinca and celosia, are very susceptible to *Rhizoctonia* stem rot when planted deeper than they should be. Other crops have leaves coming from a crown or rosette-type growth, such as begonia, lisianthus, primula, and pansy; if this crown is planted below the surface, it becomes more susceptible to *Rhizoctonia* and other rots. Cyclamen should be planted with the corm on the surface to avoid problems with *Fusarium;* otherwise, the net result is a loss of plants or uneven growth after transplanting. Some crops, such as pepper, tomato, and marigold, can be planted deeper with no problems. In fact, field growers would do better to plant tomato and pepper plugs deeper, past the cotyledons, in order to promote faster rooting.

Sometimes plugs are too small and with poorly developed root systems when the production schedule says they should be ready to transplant. When this happens, it is best to grow them on in the plug tray for a few more days to allow them to become transplantable. Feed them with 150 to 200 ppm N from 20-10-20, alternated with 14-0-14 or similar Ca fertilizer. Provide temperatures around 70F (21C) and light levels around 2,500 fc (27,000 lux) to promote shoot and root growth. Allow the media to dry between thorough waterings. The problem could be due to too much growth regulator, in which case these techniques may get the plants to grow out of it, or it could be from too little crop time. Either way, try not to transplant them for about a week, and pump them up to get some more size and roots on them.

When plugs are shipped in cardboard boxes for several days, they may emerge with yellow or twisted leaves. Impatiens (Color plate 58) and geraniums are probably the most common sufferers of this problem, which is due to ethylene production from the plants themselves during shipping. Stress during shipping (too cool, too warm, too wet) will increase ethylene in the box. Unbox the trays immediately and place them in a well-ventilated area of your greenhouse. The plants should grow out of the problem within two to four days. Use clear water when needed, but allow the trays to dry thoroughly between waterings.

For some crops, premature budding or flowering can be a major obstacle to getting uniform vegetative growth after transplanting. Crops that have a central stem and single flower are most likely to have difficulties growing out after transplanting, instead putting all their energy into making sure that first flower comes out. The result is no energy left for side branches to develop until after that flower is finished. Crops susceptible to premature flowering include celosia, French marigold, pansy, petunia, cut lisianthus, larkspur, and aster. Crops with multiple branches and multiple flowers (impatiens, alyssum, and begonia) will have no problem growing out. To get transplanted plugs to grow out when they have buds or blooms already showing, you need to increase the feeding with NH_4 fertilizers. You may need to double the rate you would normally use and feed with more 20-10-20 until vegetative growth resumes. Some growers pinch the flowers off, but this is very laborious. Reduce light levels, increase temperature, and keep media more moist (not drying it out between waterings) for the first two weeks, then readjust the environmental and cultural conditions to what you would normally have for finishing bedding plants. However, be careful of promoting root rot with these treatments. Apply a fungicide drench of Banrot or Cleary's 3336/Subdue for best protection.

After transplanting, you may find plugs not rooting out, foliage that is hard and won't grow, stunted growth with gnarled new leaves and no growing point, and yellow upper or lower leaves. The most common problem with plugs after transplanting is their not rooting out within 10 to 14 days. Normally, plugs with active root systems transplanted into good growing media and watered with high-quality water will start rooting out within three days (fig. 17.9). The soil temperature needs to be 65 to 70F (18 to 21C) for best success.

However, if your plugs are not rooting out, determine the possible causes before trying to correct the problem. First, low soil temperature right after transplanting will inhibit roots from coming out. Keep soil temperature at 65 to 70F (18 to 21C) for the first three or four days, then lower it to your normal growing temperature. The problem could also be from high soluble salts level in the media from overfertilization or too much starter charge. Test the EC level and keep it less than 1.5 mmhos (2:1 extraction) for the first week. Do not fertilize transplants until after roots start to come out!

The media may be holding too much moisture. This could be due to low air porosity in the mix, overwatering, or no drain holes in the containers. Reduce the watering frequency to allow the media to dry more between waterings. Remember, a plug's roots are in the top fourth or third of the container for the

FIGURE 17.9 Rooting-out of pansy plug after three days.

first week, and they need some air to grow. Also check your water quality for high alkalinity, high EC, high Na, or high Cl. Reduce alkalinity to 120 ppm bicarbonates with acid injection, if needed, keep EC lower than 1.0 mmhos, and Na less than 40 ppm, and Cl less than 80 ppm for best root growth. Finally, check the root systems of the plugs before transplanting. If damaged or diseased, then they are more than likely to get worse after transplanting.

A good example of a crop having problems rooting out for many growers is vinca. This crop needs to be grown warm, dry, at a low growing media pH, at a low EC level, and fed with more NO_3 fertilizer. Pietsch and Carlson [1], having conducted research on different methods of producing vinca, give the following tips:

- Water vinca flats sparingly, and let them dry out before watering again. This practice allows the roots to develop properly and prevents damage from root rot.

- Place vinca flats in the warmest part of the warmest greenhouse. Keep the flats above 68F (20C) at all times; temperatures below this will severely stunt growth.

- Keep the growing medium pH around 5.5 to 5.8, definitely below 6.5. Vinca is sensitive to iron deficiency and *Thielaviopsis,* both of which are more prevalent when pH is above 6.5.

- Allow the plants to get established before applying fertilizers, then apply them at low rates. Vinca is not tolerant of high soluble salts, and high fertilizer levels will damage roots, stunting growth when the plants are first transplanted. Vinca does best when fed 100 ppm N from a fertilizer high in NO_3. Be cautious of the effect that NH_4 can have on vinca roots.

Sometimes, plug foliage is hard, and the shoots just do not want to grow well after transplanting. Root growth may be excellent, but shoot growth lags behind or is nonuniform. Causes of this problem include high light levels, no NH_4 in the feed program, temperature lower than 65F (18C), or excessive growth regulator applications. Keep light levels between 2,500 to 4,000 fc (27,000 to 43,000 lux) for most crops after transplanting. Some crops, such as begonias (both fibrous and tuberous), primula, ranunculus, and impatiens, may need lower light levels for the first week, with increasing levels thereafter. If the feed program utilizes high NO_3 fertilizers, then some crops may not have enough food for rapid leaf expansion, particularly under high light and high temperature conditions. Increase the NH_4 levels to 40% of the total N applied, especially for begonias (both fibrous and tuberous), ranunculus, petunia, lisianthus, and gerbera. Make sure soil temperatures are greater than 60F (15C) for best shoot and root growth. If the plants will still not respond to these treatments, then an overapplication of chemical growth regulator during the plug stage or right after transplanting may have caused the problem. Do not apply Bonzi, Sumagic, or A-Rest when holding plugs or immediately after transplanting. Allow the roots to grow out to the sides of the container first, before applying any growth regulator. Check your records about any growth regulators applied to the plugs you grew and what the weather conditions were like at the time they were applied. Check with your plug supplier or broker if the plugs were brought in from another source.

During late spring through fall, it is not uncommon to have petunia or pansy transplants show stunted growth with tip abortion and the newest leaves looking gnarled, thickened, or puckered. This problem is due to B deficiency. Symptoms on pansy and petunia include stunting; newest leaves that are strapped, hardened, distorted, or mottled; proliferation of side shoots; and terminal bud abortion. Boron deficiency can be caused by B leaching out of the media in hot, sunny weather, when growers must water the plants more often. Usually, fertilization is reduced to prevent plant stretch in this type of weather; thus, not enough B is available to the plant. Overwatering also activates limestone in the growing media quicker, thereby raising soil pH above 6.5. Calcium may then be in excess and tie up B.

To control B deficiency, test your growing media and water regularly. Keep soil pH lower than 6.5 for both petunia and pansy. Monitor Ca and B levels in growing media, water, and the plant itself. During periods of warm weather and frequent watering, use Solubor at one-fourth oz per 100 gal or Borax at one-half oz per 100 gal as a drench about one or two weeks after transplant to provide supplemental B. Repeat in two or three weeks, if needed.

Yellow leaves showing up after transplanting can be a symptom of many things. First, look to see whether the yellowing is occurring mainly on the upper or lower leaves. If upper leaves are turning yellow first, check the roots and the media pH. If the roots show no signs of root rots, then it may be a symptom of Fe deficiency. Media pH greater than 6.5 for many crops will tie up Fe. Lower the media pH with an iron sulfate drench at 1 to 2 lb per 100 gal and rinse the plants off with clear water *immediately* afterward. Media pH can also be lowered by using more acid in the water or by using more acid fertilizer, such as 20-20-20 or 21-7-7. Cool, wet media will also prevent the roots from taking up Fe. If media pH is within proper levels, then dry the soil out and warm up the crop. The problem should go away within three days if the roots are still healthy. Sometimes high Mn levels, due to the micronutrient package added to the soilless mix, will tie up Fe. Send a media sample to a reputable testing lab for a complete analysis.

If the lower leaves are turning yellow first, check the media EC level to make sure there is enough fertilizer available to the plant. When plants are grown under high light levels and high temperature, they will need to be fertilized more often and with more NH_4. Check the root system and look for signs of *Pythium* or *Thielaviopsis*. Use a drench of Banrot or Cleary's 3336/Subdue if disease is present. Dry out the media thoroughly between waterings to improve root growth, making sure the media EC level is not greater than 1.5 mmhos (2:1 extraction) for most crops.

KEY POINTS TO REMEMBER

- Tone (harden) your own plugs or acclimate bought-in plugs before transplanting.

- Use a dibbler to make consistent holes in the moist, filled containers before transplanting the plugs, and use a plug extractor to remove the plugs from the tray.

- Ask the right questions before purchasing a robotic transplanter.

- Maintain proper media pH, soluble salt, and air porosity levels in the finished containers for best rooting-out of the plugs.

- Keep the soil temperature at 65 to 70F (18 to 21C) for the first three days after transplanting for best rooting-out. Temperature can then be lowered to 60 to 65F (15 to 18C) for growing-on.

- After roots emerge from the root ball, proceed with applications of fertilizer, fungicides, and water. For best rooting, allow the media to dry down between thorough waterings.

- Use recommended growth regulators, as needed, once plugs root out to the sides of the containers (usually after one week).

REFERENCES

[1] Pietsch, G.M., and W.H. Carlson. 1994. High temperatures/low water are the keys to producing quality vinca. *PPGA News* 25(3):2–4.

GROWER CHECKLIST FOR PLUG CROP PRODUCTION

T The following checklists have been collated from many years of experience consulting with growers and looking at crops worldwide, along with evaluating published scientific evidence. The checklist for each crop simply defines the key environmental and cultural factors that seem to affect the particular crop. These factors should be regularly checked to avoid common problems and improve the chances of growing a high-quality crop.

Every crop has unique requirements, and the best growers will use a checklist for each crop covering the critical factors of light, media, water, nutrients, and temperature. The four plug growth stages referred to in these checklists are:

Stage 1—Germination of the seed and emergence of the root
Stage 2—Emergence and opening of the cotyledons
Stage 3—Development of true leaves
Stage 4—Hardening and toning of the plug crop

BEGONIA CHECKLIST

- The pH of the growing media should be 5.5 to 5.8.

- Light is needed during the germination stage (10 to 100 fc, 108 to 1080 lux).

- The EC of the growing media should be 0.7 for Stage 1, and 1.0 to 1.5 for Stage 2. Seedlings in Stage 2 should not be watered in with fertilizer having an EC greater than 1.5.

- The requirement therefore is low, constant feeding. Ammonium fertilizer is beneficial throughout.

- The growing media should be uniformly moist throughout Stages 1, 2, and early 3 until the first true leaf is half expanded. At that time, the roots are going deeper into the cell, and moisture levels can be reduced to allow the soil surface to dry out before watering again.

- For pelleted seed, the pellets should be moist at all times until the radicle emerges, but the substrate should not be saturated.

- The soil temperature requirement throughout Stages 1 through 3 is 72 to 75F (22 to 24C) soil temperature without lights or 70F (21C) with lights. Warmer temperatures can cause poor uniformity.

- The calcium-to-magnesium ratio should be 2:1. Poor root development and growth structure can develop if calcium is deficient.

CELOSIA CHECKLIST

- The pH of the growing media should be 5.8 to 6.2.

- Damping-off at the soil line needs treatment with preventative fungicide, reduction in moisture, or better air movement.

- Feed at Stages 3 and 4 to maintain a soluble salt level of 1.0.

- Minimize stress on the plug to prevent premature flowering by
  - not allowing growing medium to dry out
  - using some ammonium fertilizer
  - avoiding high light levels (> 2,500 fc/27,000 lux)
  - not holding plugs past transplant date

DUSTY MILLER CHECKLIST

- The pH of the growing medium should be 5.8 to 6.2.

- Poor germination usually caused by damping-off. Preventative fungicides should be used.

- Sodium levels > 40 ppm can give stunted growth in Stages 2 to 4.

- Brown to black irregular spotting on the leaves is likely to be *Alternaria.* Dry off leaves and apply proper fungicide.

GERANIUM CHECKLIST

■ Keep Stage 1 soil temperature 70 to 75F (21 to 24C), no higher, as thermodormancy will occur. Soil temperature during all stages should not be less than 65F (18C), as this will inhibit the growth and development of young seedlings.

■ Supplemental lighting can be applied to young seedlings for two to four weeks after Stage 1. Light levels should be approximately 300 to 500 footcandles (3,200 to 5,400 lux) for 16 to 18 hours per day. Geraniums are light accumulators, meaning that the more light you give them, the faster they grow and flower.

■ The pH of the media during the entire growth of the plant should be 6.2 to 6.5 to avoid phytotoxicity of micronutrients.

■ Geraniums will produce the best root to shoot ratio when grown in a well-aerated growing medium with 10 to 20% air porosity.

■ The fertilizer program should consist mainly of potassium and calcium nitrate. Phosphorus can be applied to enhance growth at approximately 10 to 20 ppm.

■ Geraniums are sensitive to ammonium and should be provided no more than 10 ppm of this nutrient. In warmer growing regions with higher light levels, 20-10-20 may need to be utilized for leaf expansion and color.

■ Chlorine when applied at concentrations greater than 1 ppm may cause phytotoxicity on the cotyledons and immature leaves, particularly in fog zones or when using Cycocel early in seedling growth. Phytotoxicity is usually observed as chlorosis and areas of bleaching.

■ Geranium roots are sensitive to *Pythium* root rot, especially when grown too wet, too dry, or at too high salt levels. Use Subdue at low rate for best control.

■ Avoid excessive drying of the growing medium, as this will accumulate salts around the root system and cause burning of the roots. Symptoms of excessive drying include lower leaves turning reddish to yellow, and root tip dieback.

■ Control *Botrytis* with good air movement, good moisture control, dehumidification cycles in the greenhouse, and fungicides.

IMPATIENS CHECKLIST

- The pH of the growing media should be 6.2 to 6.5 from sowing the seed to selling the plants.

- Light is beneficial for days 1 and 2 of germination (10 to 100 fc, 108 to 1,080 lux).

- Maintain uniformly moist conditions for Stage 1. Reduce moisture levels during Stage 2 to allow the root to penetrate into the soil. Maintain a soil temperature of 73F (23C) for both stages.

- Oversaturation of the growing media in Stage 2 will reduce oxygen levels and damage root hairs.

- The growing media should have low EC of 0.4 to 0.8.

- Malformed leaves and stunted seedlings can form if EC, moisture, temperature, or pH are incorrect or the seed has poor vigor.

- Shoot tip abortion can occur if

  - growing media EC is too high (1.2 to 1.5)

  - shoot tips are left wet for more than four hours (the growing point drowns due to lack of oxygen; watering early in the day is important)

  - a cold (lower than 65F/18C), saturated growing media causes a toxic buildup of ethylene within the plant

  - low pH causes sodium toxicity

- Feeding calcium and reducing ammonium will produce a harder plant.

- Supplementary light for more than two weeks during Stages 2 and 3 can result in bleaching or yellowing of leaves (photooxidation).

- Leaf tip decaying quickly over a 12-hour period indicates *Pseudomonas* infection. Removal of plants is essential.

- Reddish leaf spots indicate *Alternaria*. Have a sample positively identified by a lab or clinic.

MARIGOLDS CHECKLIST

- The pH of the growing media should be 6.2 to 6.5.

- If lower leaves are showing yellowing (chlorosis) or marginal browning or burning (necrosis), the cause is likely to be iron, manganese, or sodium toxicity, caused by the pH having dropped to 5.5 to 6.0.

- Minimize stress on French marigolds to prevent premature flowering by
  - not allowing media to get too dry
  - feeding with both ammonium and calcium fertilizers
  - avoiding high light levels (greater than 2,500 fc, 27,000 lux)
  - not holding plugs past the transplanting date
- Bud abortion and lack of flower development is generally caused by
  - allowing the media to get too dry
  - a lack of calcium
  - too much ammonium fertilizer
  - excessive chemical growth regulation
- Soil calcium levels should be around 120 to 175 ppm.
- Excessive leafy growth is usually caused by the growing media being too moist and having too high an ammonium level.

PANSY CHECKLIST

- The pH of the growing media should be 5.8 to 6.0.
- Nonuniform germination will occur if the growing media is too dry in Stage 1 or too wet in stage 2.
- The EC of the growing media should be less than 0.5 for Stage 1 and less than 0.75 for Stage 2.
- Ammonium concentration of more than 5 ppm will cause seedlings to stretch.
- If the whole plant is getting leggy, the total nitrogen concentration, especially ammonium, in the growing media is too high, or the media is staying too moist too long.
- Average daily temperature for good growth is 68F (20C).
- Tip abortion or blindness can be caused by boron levels lower than 0.5 to 0.7 ppm in the soil or lower than 50 to 60 ppm in the tissue.
- Low calcium levels in the tissue (less than 1.75%) will produce malformed, puckered leaves. Calcium nitrate can be used as a feed, and calcium sulfate could be added to the growing media before sowing. The leaf symptoms may also represent the early stages of boron deficiency.
- Malformed, hard, leathery leaves develop with too high of a chemical growth regulator application (B-Nine at 5,000 ppm), especially at high temperatures (greater than 90F/32C).

- *Thielaviopsis* (black root rot) may develop as black lesions on the root when the pH is greater than 6.5. Preventative fungicidal treatment would be advisable. The disease spores can be spread in dust. Stressed plants grown under high temperatures are affected the most.

- You could try growing Tropicana vinca as an indicator plant in the same growing media alongside the pansies. At a pH of 7.0, it will quickly turn yellow to warn you of a problem.

PETUNIA GRANDIFLORA AND MULTIFLORA CHECKLIST

- The pH of the growing media should be 5.8 to 6.2.
- Light is needed during the germination stage (10 to 100 fc, 108 to 1,080 lux).
- Nonuniform germination and early seedling growth can be caused by saturated growing media in Stage 2. A presowing addition of 25 to 50 ppm potassium nitrate may enhance germination.
- Germination temperature should be between 72 and 76F (22 and 24C), no higher than 78F (25C).
- Boron concentration should be 0.5 to 0.7 in the soil and 40 to 60 ppm in the tissue to prevent tip abortion and blindness.
- Strapped new leaves indicate a calcium deficiency. This can be improved by a foliar feed of 100 to 150 ppm calcium nitrate. This symptom could also be an early sign of boron deficiency.
- Elongation of the leaf petiole usually indicates excess ammonium or too-moist conditions.
- Yellow upper leaves are usually caused by a high pH (greater than 6.6), which inhibits iron uptake.
- To initiate flowering, soil temperature above 60F (15C) and 13.5 hours of light per day are both needed. Without these conditions, flowering will be delayed.

PETUNIA FANTASY CHECKLIST

This differs from grandiflora and multiflora petunia culture in several ways:
- Due to slower root growth, it may need one week longer crop time in plugs and packs. It will do better in a larger plug cell.

- Sodium levels need to be lower than 20 ppm, calcium levels need to be 80 to 100 ppm, and phosphorus levels need to be 8 to 12 ppm in the soil for best root growth.

- No chemical growth regulators are needed.

- Do not use supplementary lighting for more than 10 to 12 hours per day, to prevent premature flowering.

- Feed with more ammonium fertilizer in Stages 3 and 4.

- Fantasy will flower early, but a good-sized plant needs to be established prior to flowering. Avoid stressing crop during its growing-on period.

SALVIA CHECKLIST

- The pH of the growing media should be 6.0.

- Poor germination is usually caused by too much wetness in Stage 2.

- Growing media EC greater than 1.5 in Stages 1, 2, and possibly 3 will cause stunted growth. Feeding should be in the later stages of development.

- Ammonium concentrations greater than 5 ppm can be toxic. Symptoms show as a gray cast or browning on immature leaves in Stages 2 and 3.

- Interveinal chlorosis with veins starting to yellow on mature leaves indicates a lack of magnesium.

- Downward cupping of the leaves indicates
    - the medium is too dry
    - the EC level is too high
    - the temperature is too cool

- Salvia can be grown alongside other crops as an indicator of too high a concentration of salts in the growing media.

SNAPDRAGON CHECKLIST

- The pH of the growing media should be 5.8 to 6.0. A pH above 6.5 could cause iron deficiency, showing as interveinal chlorosis on immature leaves.

- Keep growing media EC lower than 0.5 to improve germination, control growth, and prevent some diseases.

- Tip abortion or blindness can be caused by

  - high moisture on the meristem combined with cool temperature or high light

  - fertilizer with EC > 1.0

- Spotting on the upper leaves could be either downy or powdery mildew.

- Less than 13 hours of day length will promote vegetative growth and delay flowering for garden snapdragon varieties only.

VINCA CHECKLIST

- The pH of the growing media should be 5.8 to 6.0.

- Darkness is needed during the germination stage.

- The soil temperature should be 78F (25C) during Stage 1 and 72F (22C) throughout the rest of the crop cycle until they are sold.

- Use a preventative fungicide against *Thielaviopsis* (black root rot) and continue to inspect roots for black lesions.

- Damping-off at the surface of the soil is usually caused by *Rhizoctonia.*

- Keep the media EC less than 1.0 throughout all stages, and allow the media to dry out between waterings for best control of growth and diseases.

- Upward cupping of the leaves would indicate the growing media is too dry and light levels are too high in Stages 2 and 3.

- Downward cupping of the leaves would indicate the temperature is too cool or the DIF is too negative.

- Roots not actively growing after transplanting could be caused by

  - too low a soil temperature

  - *Thielaviopsis*

  - too high a salt concentration in the growing media (EC should be less than 1.5)

  - too high an ammonium level (keep less than 10 ppm)

- Interveinal chlorosis on younger leaves would indicate the pH is too high (greater than 6.5).

- Tropicana vinca will quickly show chlorosis at high pH and can be used as an indicator plant for other crops.

DETERMINING PERCENTAGES OF WATER-HOLDING CAPACITY AND AERATION IN GROWING MEDIA

T his method will show you how to test the relative differences between the percentage of water-holding capacity and that of aeration in growing media. Four-inch pots are used here, but the procedure should be conducted with the size of container that your plant will be grown in. If you are using premixed commercial media, these percentages should be available from the media manufacturer.

MATERIALS

Measuring cup or graduated cylinder
Masking tape
4-inch round pot (or other size of container)
Growing media
Beaker or small bucket
Pencil or marking pen
Water

PROCEDURE

1. Measure the volume of the container. Do this by first taping over the container's holes. Fill the container with water to a level where your typical soil line would be. Mark the line with a pencil or marking pen. Carefully pour the water back into the measuring cup or graduated cylinder. Record the volume on line A in Results.

2. Determine the total porosity of the medium. Dry the inside of the pot, then pack it with dry growing medium to the pencil line. Tap the pot lightly several times on the table to firm the medium. Using a graduated cylinder or measuring cup, add water slowly to the medium in the taped container until the water level is just even with that of the medium. You may have to wait a few minutes for the medium to become completely saturated. Record the amount of water added on line B in Results. This measures the total porosity (air and water) of the medium.

3. Determine the air porosity of the medium. Do this by holding the saturated pot above a beaker or small bucket. Carefully remove the tape from one hole in the bottom of the pot. Allow the pot to drain until no more water comes out. Record the amount of drained water on line C in Results. This volume of drained water is equivalent to the air pore space.

4. Determine the percentage of water-holding capacity of the medium. Note that not as much water drained from the medium as was applied. The difference between the amount of water applied and the amount drained is the medium's water-holding capacity.

RESULTS

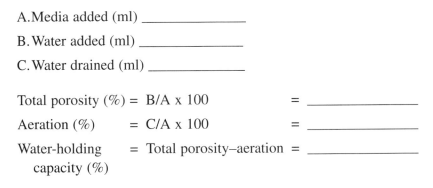

A. Media added (ml) _____

B. Water added (ml) _____

C. Water drained (ml) _____

Total porosity (%) = B/A x 100   = _____

Aeration (%)   = C/A x 100   = _____

Water-holding   = Total porosity–aeration = _____
   capacity (%)

SAMPLE PLUG NUTRITIONAL PROBLEMS

CASE HISTORY 1

SYMPTOMS

1. Plants nearly stop growing.

2. From a distance, the flat of plants appears totally chlorotic.

3. Up close, the younger tissue is the most chlorotic.

4. Roots are short and thickened.

WATER ANALYSIS

pH	7.0	Phosphorus (ppm)	1.0
EC (mmhos)	0.5	Potassium (ppm)	1.5
Alkalinity (me)[a]	1.0	Calcium (ppm)	40.0
NO_3 (ppm)	2.0	Magnesium (ppm)	12.0
NH_4 (ppm)	0.5		

SUBSTRATE ANALYSIS (SATURATED PASTE METHOD)

pH	5.9	Phosphorus (ppm)	5
EC (mmhos)	0.75	Potassium (ppm)	100
NH_4 (ppm)	5.0	Calcium (ppm)	80
NO_3 (ppm)	50.0	Magnesium (ppm)	135

Tissue analysis

Nitrogen (%)	4.0	Iron (ppm)	100
Phosphorus (%)	0.4	Manganese (ppm)	50
Potassium (%)	4.0	Zinc (ppm)	30
Calcium (%)	0.5	Copper (ppm)	10
Magnesium (%)	1.2	Boron (ppm)	35
Sulfur (%)	0.25	Molybdenum (ppm)	1

The nutrient disorder is   _____

The cause is   _____

Correction and prevention are   _____

[a] 50 ppm calcium carbonate = 1 milliequivalent (me); 61 ppm bicarbonate = 1 me

Case history 2

Symptoms

1. Plants stop growing.

2. Shoots abort.

3. Random chlorosis, more toward plant tops.

4. Young leaves are crinkled, twisted, thickened, and sometimes with corking.

5. Internodes are short.

Water analysis

pH	7.6	Phosphorus (ppm)	1.5
EC (mmhos)	1.1	Potassium (ppm)	2.1
Alkalinity (me)[a]	2.8	Calcium (ppm)	130.0
NO_3 (ppm)	1.7	Magnesium (ppm)	14.0
NH_4 (ppm)	0.3		

Substrate analysis (saturated paste method)

pH	6.7	Phosphorus (ppm)	3
EC (mmhos)	1.3	Potassium (ppm)	121
NH_4 (ppm)	4.0	Calcium (ppm)	360
NO_3 (ppm)	67.0	Magnesium (ppm)	48

Tissue analysis

Nitrogen (%)	3.9	Iron (ppm)	225
Phosphorus (%)	0.35	Manganese (ppm)	95
Potassium (%)	4.1	Zinc (ppm)	37
Calcium (%)	2.9	Copper (ppm)	21
Magnesium (%)	0.4	Boron (ppm)	17
Sulfur (%)	0.3	Molybdenum (ppm)	2

The nutrient disorder is _____

The cause is _____

Correction and prevention are _____

[a] 50 ppm calcium carbonate = 1 milliequivalent (me); 61 ppm bicarbonate = 1 me

---

Case history 3

Symptoms

1. Plant growth is moderately slow.

2. Interveinal chlorosis of young leaves.

3. In severe cases, young leaves turn yellow-white.

Water analysis

pH	5.5	Phosphorus (ppm)	1.0
EC (mmhos)	0.4	Potassium (ppm)	1.5
Alkalinity (me)[a]	1.0	Calcium (ppm)	25.0
NO_3 (ppm)	1.7	Magnesium (ppm)	7.0
NH_4 (ppm)	0.3		

Substrate analysis (saturated paste method)

pH	5.5	Phosphorus (ppm)	4
EC (mmhos)	1.3	Potassium (ppm)	110
NH_4 (ppm)	3	Calcium (ppm)	145
NO_3 (ppm)	60	Magnesium (ppm)	52

TISSUE ANALYSIS

Nitrogen (%)	4.2	Iron (ppm)	24
Phosphorus (%)	0.45	Manganese (ppm)	480
Potassium (%)	4.1	Zinc (ppm)	78
Calcium (%)	1.9	Copper (ppm)	30
Magnesium (%)	0.51	Boron (ppm)	57
Sulfur (%)	0.22	Molybdenum (ppm)	1.5

The nutrient disorder is _____

The cause is _____

Correction and prevention are _____

[a] 50 ppm calcium carbonate = 1 milliequivalent (me); 61 ppm bicarbonate = 1 me

CASE HISTORY 4

SYMPTOMS

1. Plant growth is heavily reduced.

2. Leaves curl at margins (up or down, depending on species).

3. Plants are chlorotic, more so on the older leaves.

4. Older leaves are necrotic.

5. Roots are dying from the tips back.

WATER ANALYSIS

pH	6.9	Phosphorus (ppm)	1.3
EC (mmhos)	0.45	Potassium (ppm)	1.1
Alkalinity (me)[a]	1.0	Calcium (ppm)	21.0
NO_3 (ppm)	1.9	Magnesium (ppm)	12.0
NH_4 (ppm)	0.4		

SUBSTRATE ANALYSIS (SATURATED PASTE METHOD)

pH	5.2	Phosphorus (ppm)	4.7
EC (mmhos)	1.2	Potassium (ppm)	106
NH_4 (ppm)	41.0	Calcium (ppm)	148
NO_3 (ppm)	52.0	Magnesium (ppm)	47

TISSUE ANALYSIS

Nitrogen (%)	4.1	Iron (ppm)	129
Phosphorus (%)	0.43	Manganese (ppm)	71
Potassium (%)	3.95	Zinc (ppm)	30
Calcium (%)	1.94	Copper (ppm)	12
Magnesium (%)	0.42	Boron (ppm)	38
Sulfur (%)	0.27	Molybdenum (ppm)	2

The nutrient disorder is _____

The cause is _____

Correction and prevention are _____

[a] 50 ppm calcium carbonate = 1 milliequivalent (me); 61 ppm bicarbonate = 1 me

REFERENCE FOR YOUR CALCULATIONS

- For water quality guidelines, see table 6.3, p. 91.
- For media nutrient guidelines, see table 7.11, p. 119.
- For tissue analysis guidelines, see table 11.10, p. 223.

SOME NORTH AMERICAN SOURCES FOR EQUIPMENT AND SUPPLIES

ANALYTICAL LABORATORIES FOR TESTING GREENHOUSE IRRIGATION WATER AND SOILLESS MEDIA

A & L Analytical Lab [a]
411 North Third St.
Memphis, TN 38105
Phone 901/527-2780
Fax   901/526-1031

Fafard Analytical Services
183 Paradise Blvd., Ste. 106
Athens, GA 30607
Phone 800/457-3301
Fax   706/354-0086

Fisons Analytical Lab
177 Sanfordville Rd.
Warwick, NY 10990
Phone 800/682-6667
Fax   914/870-6667

OARDC-REAL
1680 Madison Ave.
Wooster, OH 44691
Phone 216/263-3760
Fax   216/263-3660

Scotts Testing Laboratory
6656 Grant Way
Allentown, PA 18106
Phone 800/743-4769
          610/395-7104
Fax   610/391-1337

Soil & Plant Laboratories Inc.[a]
1594 North Maine St.
P.O. Box 6566
Orange, CA 92613
Phone 714/282-8777
Fax   714/282-8575

[a] Several laboratories at different locations.

BOOM IRRIGATORS

Andpro, Ltd.
P.O. Box 399
Waterford, ON, Canada N0E 1Y0
Phone   519/443-4411
Fax   519/443-8861

Canaan Industries Inc.
1369 Headland Ave.
P.O. Box 8097
Dothan, AL 36303
Phone   800/633-7560
Fax   800/581-0846

Cherry Creek Systems
11901 E. Palmer Divide Ave.
Larkspur, CO 80118
Phone   303/660-1196
Fax   303/660-1338

Growing Systems Inc.
2950 N. Weil St.
Milwaukee, WI 53212
Phone   414/263-3131
Fax   414/263-2454

ITS-McConkey Co.
P.O. Box 1690
Sumner, WA 98390
Phone   800/426-8124
           206/863-8111
Fax   206/863-5833

Transplant Systems
P.O. Box 983
Kinston, NC 28501
Phone   919/523-0970
Fax   919/523-4966

ENVIRONMENTAL CONTROL COMPUTERS

**Argus Control/Growth Zone
Systems**
1735 Cedardale Rd.
Mount Vernon, WA 98273
Phone   800/932-2214
Fax   360/428-4676

Priva Computers Inc.
3468 S. Service Rd.
Vineland Station, ON, Canada
L0R 2E0
Phone   905/562-7351
Fax   905/562-7717

Q-Com Corp.
17782 Cowan Ave., Ste. A
Irvine, CA 92714
Phone   800/833-9123
           714/833-1000
Fax   714/833-1116

Wadsworth Control Systems
5541 Marshall St.
Arvada, CO 80002
Phone   800/821-5829
           303/424-4461
Fax   303/424-6012

FERTILIZER INJECTORS

H.E. Anderson Co.
P.O. Box 1006
2100 Anderson Dr.
Muskogee, OK 74402
Phone 800/331-9620
918/687-4426
Fax 918/682-3342

Dosatron International Inc.
2090 Sunnydale Blvd.
Clearwater, FL 34625
Phone 800/523-8499
813/443-5404
Fax 813/447-0591

Dosmatic USA
1230 Crowley Cir.
Carrollton, TX 75006
Phone 800/344-6767
214/245-9765
Fax 214/245-9000

Smith Precision Products
1299 Lawrence Dr.
Newbury Park, CA 91320
Phone 805/498-6616
Fax 805/499-2867

HID LIGHTS

Diamond Lights
628 Lindaro St.
San Rafael, CA 94901
Phone 800/331-3994
415/459-3994
Fax 415/453-8311

GE Lighting Systems
Spartanburg Hwy.
Hendersonville, NC 28739
Phone 704/693-2198
Fax 704/693-2103

GTE Sylvania/Sylvania Lighting Division—U.S.
100 Endicott St.
Danvers, MA 01923
Phone 800/544-4828
508/777-1900
Fax 716/668-6254

Hamilton Technology Corp.
14902 S. Figueroa St.
Gardena, CA 90248
Phone 800/458-7474
310/217-0036
Fax 310/217-8821

Hydrofarm
3135 Kerner Blvd.
San Rafael, CA 94901
Phone 800/634-9999
415/459-7898
Fax 415/459-3710

P.L. Light Systems Canada Inc.
P.O. Box 206
183 South Service Rd., Unit 2
Grimsby, ON, Canada L3M 4G3
Phone 800/263-0213
905/945-4133
Fax 905/945-0444

NOZZLES

Dramm Corp.
P.O. Box 1960
Manitowoc, WI 54221
Phone   800/258-0848
          414/684-0227
Fax   414/684-4499

E.C. Geiger Inc.
Rt. 63, Box 285
Harleysville, PA 19438
Phone   800/443-4437
          215/256-6511
Fax   800/432-9434

Fogg-It Nozzle Co. Inc.
P.O. Box 16053
San Francisco, CA 94116
Phone   415/665-1212
Fax   415/665-7387

A.H. Hummert Seed Co.
2746 Chouteau Ave.
St. Louis, MO 63103
Phone   800/325-3055

Waldo & Associates Inc.
28214 Glenwood Rd.
Perrysburg, OH 43551
Phone   800/468-4011
          419/666-3662
Fax 419/666-2079

Note: Gardena Nozzles are available retail only at any hardware or garden center. Check with your local greenhouse supplies company for further nozzle information.

pH AND EC METERS

Cole-Parmer Instrument Co.
625 E. Bunker Ct.
Vernon Hills, IL 60061
Phone   800/323-4340
Fax   847/549-7676

Engineered Systems & Designs Inc.
119A Sandy Dr.
Newark, DE 19713
Phone   800/328-0516
          302/456-0046
Fax   302/456-0441

Extech Instruments Corp.
150 Bear Hill Rd.
Waltham, MA 02154
Phone   617/890-7440

Myron L Company
6115 Corte del Cedro
Carlsbad, CA 92009
Phone   619/438-2021
Fax   800/869-7668

Spectrum Technologies Inc.
23839 W. Andrew Rd.
Plainfield, IL 60544
Phone   800/248-8873
Fax   815/436-4460

Your local greenhouse supplies company

PLUG DISLODGERS (POPPERS)

Blackmore Company
10800 Blackmore Ave.
Belleville, MI 48111
Phone   800/874-8660
           313/483-8661
Fax   313/483-5454

Growing Systems Inc.
2950 N. Weil St.
Milwaukee, WI 53212
Phone   414/263-3131
Fax   414/263-2454

Seed E-Z Seeder Inc.
E11290 Hwy. 12
Prairie du Sac, WI 53578
Phone   800/448-9371
           608/643-4122
Fax   608/643-4289

Your local greenhouse supply company

PLUG FLAT FILLERS

Bouldin & Lawson Inc.
P.O. Box 7177
McMinnville, TN 37110
Phone   800/443-6398
           615/668-4090
Fax   615/668-3209

Flier USA Inc.
300 Artino Drive
Oberlin, OH 44074
Phone   800/354-3750
           216/774-2981
Fax   216/775-2104

Gleason Equipment by Measured Marketing
395 N. Schuyler Ave.
Kankakee, IL 60901
Phone   815/939-9746
Fax   815/939-9751

Javo USA Inc.
1900 Albritton Dr., Stes. G & H
Kennesaw, GA 30144
Phone 770/428-4491

K W Engineering Pty. Ltd.
P.O. Box 121
Palmwoods, Queensland 4555
Australia
Phone   61-74-459-549
Fax   61-74-450-499
(Distributed in U.S. by Flier USA)

PLUG MEDIA

ASB Greenworld Inc.
P.O. Box 1728
Valdosta, GA 31603
Phone   912/247-6218
Fax   912/247-4247

Ball Seed Company
622 Town Rd.
West Chicago, IL 60185
Phone   800/879-BALL
            630/231-3500

Blackmore Company
10800 Blackmore Ave.
Belleville, MI 48111
Phone   800/874-8660
            313/483-8661
Fax   313/483-5454

Conrad Fafard Inc.
P.O. Box 790
Agawam, MA 01001
Phone   800/874-8660
            413/786-4343
Fax   413/789-3425

J-M Trading Corp. (Heco)
241 Frontage Rd., Ste. 47
Burr Ridge, IL 60521
Phone   800/323-7638
            630/655-3305

Michigan Peat Company
P.O. Box 980129
Houston, TX 77098
Phone   800/324-PEAT
            713/522-0711
Fax   713/522-9060

Premier Horticulture
326 Main St.
Red Hill, PA 18076
Phone   800/525-2553
            215/679-5921
Fax   215/679-4119

The Scotts Company
14111 Scottslawn Rd.
Marysville, OH 43041
Phone   800/543-0006
            513/644-0011
Fax   513/644-7308

Sun Gro Horticulture Inc.
110–110th Ave. NE, Ste. 490
Bellevue, WA 98004
Phone   800/665-4525
            206/450-9379
Fax   800/665-4526

PLUG TRAY AND LINERS

Blackmore Company Inc.
10800 Blackmore Ave.
Belleville, MI 48111
Phone   800/874-8660
            313/483-8661
Fax   313/483-5454

East Jordan Plastics Inc.
P.O. Box 575
East Jordan, MI 49727
Phone   616/536-2243
Fax   616/536-7090

Growing Systems Inc.
2950 N. Weil St.
Milwaukee, WI 53212
Phone   414/263-3131
Fax   414/263-2454

Landmark Plastic Corp.
1331 Kelly Ave.
P.O. Box 7646
Akron, OH 44310
Phone   330/785-2200
Fax   330/785-9200

TLC Polyform Inc.
13055 15th Ave. N.
Plymouth, MN 55441
Phone   612/542-2240
Fax   612/542-1709

ROBOTIC TRANSPLANTERS

Company	Price range	Capacity (plugs/hr)	Plug tray sizes handled
Blackmore Company 10800 Blackmore Ave. Belleville, MI 48111 Phone 800/874-8660 313/483-8661 Fax 313/483-5454	$68,000 (16 head)	19,200 (512 trays)	288–648
Bouldin & Lawson Inc. P.O. Box 7177 McMinnville, TN 37110 Phone 800/443-6398 615/668-4090 Fax 615/668-3209	$59,000–75,000	12,000–17,000	Any
Flier USA Inc. 300 Artino Dr. Oberlin, OH 44074 Phone 800/354-3750 216/774-2981 Fax 216/775-2104	$68,600–130,000	16,000–30,000 (512 trays)	Any
MetroPlanter USA Inc. **(Hawe)** 16400 Huntersville-Concord Rd. Huntersville, NC 28078 Phone 800/222-2905 704/875-1371 Fax 704/875-6741	$64,000–118,000	12,240–43,200	288
Rapid Automated **Systems, LLC** 2445 Port Sheldon Rd. Jenison, MI 49428 Phone 616/662-0954 Fax 616/669-1260	$20,000–41,500 (512 trays)	10,800–20,570	288–512

ROBOTIC TRANSPLANTERS CONTINUED

Company	Price range	Capacity (plugs/hr)	Plug tray sizes handled
Robotic Solutions 395 N. Schuyler Ave. Kankakee, IL 60901 Phone 815/939-9746 Fax 815/939-9751	$43,000	3,600	Any
Seed E-Z Seeder Inc. E11290 Hwy. 12 Prairie du Sac, WI 53578 Phone 800/448-9371 608/643-4122 Fax 608/643-4289	$28,000	10,800	512 or smaller

SEEDERS

Company	Types offered	Options
Blackmore Company Inc. 10800 Blackmore Ave. Belleville, MI 48111 Phone 800/874-8660 313/483-8661 Fax 313/483-5454	Vacuum tip Vacuum needle Vacuum cylinder	Dibbler Top coater
Bouldin & Lawson Inc. P.O. Box 7177 McMinnville, TN 37110 Phone 800/443-6398 615/668-4090 Fax 615/668-3209	Vacuum needle Vacuum drum	Dibbler Top coater
Flier USA Inc. 300 Artino Dr. Oberlin, OH 44074 Phone 800/354-3750 216/774-2981 Fax 216/775-2104	Vacuum drum	Dibbler
Gleason Equipment by Measured Marketing 395 N. Schuyler Ave. Kankakee, IL 60901 Phone 815/939-9746 Fax 815/939-9751	Vacuum template Vacuum drum	Dibbler Top coater
Growing Systems Inc. 2950 N. Weil St. Milwaukee, WI 53212 Phone 414/263-3131 Fax 414/263-2454	Vacuum template (Vandana seeder)	None

SEEDERS CONTINUED

Company	Types offered	Options
T.W. Hamilton Design Ltd. Queen's Lodge, Cliveden Rd. Burnham, Bucks, SL1 8NX England Phone 0628-661362 Fax 0628-604284 Distributed in U.S. by BFG Supply Co. 14500 Kinsman Rd. P.O. Box 479 Burton, OH 44021 Phone 800/883-0234 216/834-1883 Fax 216/834-1885	Vacuum tip Vacuum cylinder	Dibbler Top coater
K W Engineering Pty. Ltd. P.O. Box 121 Palmwoods, Queensland 4555 Australia Phone 61-74-459-549 Fax 61-74-450-499 (Distributed in U.S. by Flier USA)	Vacuum needle	Dibbler Top coater
The Old Mill Co. 12011 Guilford Rd. #102 Annapolis Junction, MD 20701 Phone 301/725-8181 Fax 301/725-5762	Electronic eye	Top coater
Seed E-Z Seeder Inc. E11290 Hwy. 12 Prairie du Sac, WI 53578 Phone 800/448-9371 608/643-4122 Fax 608/643-4289	Vacuum template	Dibbler

SEEDERS CONTINUED

Company	Types offered	Options
Speedy Seeder/Division of Carolina Greenhouses P.O. Box 1140 Kinston, NC 28503	Vacuum template	None
Phone	800/635-4532 919/527-9700	
Fax	919/523-3691	

WATERING TUNNELS

Blackmore Company Inc.
10800 Blackmore Ave.
Belleville, MI 48111
Phone   800/874-8660
        313/483-8661
Fax   313/483-5454

Bouldin & Lawson Inc.
P.O. Box 7177
McMinnville, TN 37110
Phone   800/443-6398
        615/668-4090
Fax   615/668-3209

Flier USA Inc.
300 Artino Dr.
Oberlin, OH 44074
Phone   800/354-3750
        216/774-2981
Fax   216/775-2104

Gleason Equipment by Measured Marketing
395 N. Schuyler Ave.
Kankakee, IL 60901
Phone   815/939-9746
Fax   815/939-9751

K W Engineering Pty. Ltd.
P.O. Box 121
Palmwoods, Queensland 4555
Australia
Phone   61-74-459-549
Fax   61-74-450-499
(Distributed in U.S. by Flier USA)

WATER-SOLUBLE GREENHOUSE FERTILIZERS

GreenCare Fertilizers
5410 W. Roosevelt Rd.
Chicago, IL 60650
Phone 312/261-1088
Fax 312/261-1090
(Distributed through Blackmore,
J.M.Trading, and McConkey)

Grow More Inc.
15600 New Century Dr.
Gardena, CA 90248
Phone 310/515-1700
Fax 310/515-4937

Masterblend Fertilizer Co.
7401 S. Pulaski Rd.
Chicago, IL 60629
Phone 800/495-3783
Fax 312/735-6022

Peters Fertilizers
The Scotts Company
14111 Scottslawn Rd.
Marysville, OH 43041
Phone 800/543-0006
       513/644-0011
Fax 513/644-7308

Plantex Fertilizers
Plantco Inc.
314 Orenda Rd.
Brampton, ON, Canada L6T 1G1
Phone 905/793-8000
Fax 905/793-9157

Plant Marvel Laboratories Inc.
371 E. 16th
Chicago Heights, IL 60411
Phone 708/757-7500
Fax 708/757-5224

Technigro Fertilizers
Sun Gro Horticulture Inc.
110–110th Ave. NE, #490
Bellevue, WA 98004
Phone 800/665-4525
       206/450-9379
Fax 800/665-4526

Note: Contact your local distributor of greenhouse supplies, as many of these fertilizers
are sold through distributors. Some of them
are also sold outside of North America.

GLOSSARY

acclimate—to adapt to a new temperature, climate, or environment.

acid-head injector—a device attached to the irrigation line to inject a small amount of concentrated acid into the water stream to yield a dilute concentration of acid in the irrigation water. Proportioning can be fixed or adjustable. Also, a fertilizer injector with a specialized head resistant to the corrosion of concentrated acid.

active absorption—uptake of water by roots of plants that are slowly transpiring or losing water through the leaves. This uptake is slow with the roots behaving as osmometers.

aggregates—components added to peat moss providing different particle sizes that improve drainage and aeration (vermiculite, perlite, calcined clay).

Agribrom—bromine-containing compound dissolved in water and used for controlling algae, cleaning evaporative cooling pads, and disinfecting greenhouse floors and benches.

air porosity (AP)—the percent volume of growing media that is filled with air when irrigating media to container capacity. The air in media is primarily in the large macropores (noncapillary pore spaces).

alkalinity—a measure of water's capacity to neutralize acids. Generally expressed as the sum of the bicarbonates and carbonates (total carbonates) in the water. Consider it to be like lime in the water, meaning the higher the alkalinity level, the more it will raise the media pH.

ammoniacal-nitrogen—an inorganic fertilizer containing ammonia or ammonium (NH_4-N), such as ammonium nitrate or ammonium monophosphate.

ammonium—NH_4^+ ion.

anion—a negatively charged ion.

available water—water available to the plant. It is calculated by determining the container capacity, then subtracting the unavailable water (PWP).

average daily temperature (ADT)—the sum of the day temperature times hours of day and the night temperature times hours of night divided by 24. Important in determining leaf-unfolding rate and other growth parameters of plants.

base temperature—the temperature below which no plant growth occurs for that particular plant species.

buffering capacity—the ability to minimize pH fluctuations using carbonates and bicarbonates in the irrigation water. Another definition for water alkalinity.

calcined clay—an inorganic growing media component made from clay that is fired (calcined) to harden it, then crushed and screened to size.

calcitic lime—a lime composed of calcium carbonate ($CaCO_3$) derived from calcite. Pure calcitic lime contains 40% Ca.

capillary action—absorption and movement of water through capillary pore spaces (micropores) due to forces of capillary attraction.

capillary mats—a moistened mat or absorbent material from which water moves into or out of the container by capillary action.

capillary pore spaces—small pores between particles in growing media that retain water against gravity.

carbohydrates—sugars that plants produce through photosynthesis and use for energy, building blocks, and other essential compounds for growth.

cation—a positively charged ion.

cation exchange capacity (CEC)—a measure of the nutrient-holding capacity of a growing media or the magnitude of fixed negative electrical charge of the particles in the growing media. Generally expressed as millequivalents per 100 cm^3 of dry media.

chelates—A large organic molecule, called a chelating agent, that contains one of the micronutrient heavy metals (Fe, Mn, Zn, Cu) held in the center by ligand bonds. Used as micronutrient fertilizers in growing media high in pH to keep these micronutrients soluble.

chlamydospores—dark, thick-walled resting spores produced by some fungi such as *Thielaviopsis.*

chlorosis—the yellowing of foliage due to loss or breakdown of chlorophyll. Common symptom of certain nutrient deficiencies.

coated seed—seed that have a thin application of a clay-type material with a binder to increase the flowability of odd-shaped seed in mechanical seeders. The coating usually contains a dye, will not change the shape of seed, and will not readily wash off after watering.

container capacity—the percent volume of growing media filled with water after it has been saturated and allowed to drain. Also called water-holding capacity (WHC).

containerized benching—individual benches of pallet size that can be moved from one area to another via a system of wheels on posts and hydraulic or pneumatic lifters. The system is designed for optimum movement of individual benches from zone to zone, with stacking possible when benches are not needed.

cotyledons—the seed leaves, generally the first green leaves seen on most plug seedlings after germination.

damping-off—disease of seedlings caused by several fungi, including *Pythium, Rhizoctonia,* and *Botrytis.*

day-neutral—plants that are not responsive to changes in the day length (or length of night) for flowering.

defuzzed seed—seed that have had the fuzz mechanically removed for easier sowing, such as tomato and anemone.

dehumidification cycle—a period of ventilating out the warm, humid air inside the greenhouse, usually with an increase in the heat and opening of top vents. This cycle helps to lower the humidity of the greenhouse and prevent disease outbreaks.

desiccant—silica gel that absorbs moisture from the air. May or may not have an indicator dye to determine when hydrated.

de-tailed seed—seed that have had the tails mechanically removed for easier coating or seeding, such as marigold.

dewinged seed—seed that have had some appendages mechanically removed for easier coating, pelleting, or seeding, such as ageratum.

dibbling—the process of making an indentation in a filled plug tray to improve seed placement or of making a hole in a filled finished container to transplant the plug at the proper depth.

DIF—the difference between day temperature and night temperature. A positive DIF means the day temperature is greater than the night temperature, and internode length is promoted. Zero or negative DIF will keep seedlings more compact by reducing internode length.

dolomitic lime—a lime composed of calcium and magnesium carbonates.

dormancy—the period of inactivity in seeds when germination stops. Some changes in environment or internally in the seed are usually required before germination can resume.

ebb-and-flow system—a subirrigation growing system where containerized plants or trays are placed in watertight benches or molded concrete floors that are flooded when needed with nutrient solution, then drained. The nutrient solution can be collected and recirculated.

electroconductivity (EC)—the ability of a solution to conduct electricity due to dissolved or suspended ionic solutes. Used as a measure of soluble salts in water or a growing media extract. Generally expressed as mmhos/cm or mS/cm.

EPDM tubing—flexible tubing used for root-zone heating through which hot water can be passed. Generally attached just underneath expanded metal on benches.

ethylene—a natural plant hormone or a by-product of incomplete combustion that can cause yellowing or senescence of leaves and flowers, or promote branching by inhibiting flowering.

evaporation—loss of water from the soil and other surfaces into the air by conversion into water vapor.

fin pipe—type of piping with greater surface area than round piping, used under the bench for root-zone heating.

Foggit nozzle—brand of misting nozzle that has three holes for better uniformity and distribution of mist by hand.

fog system—a device that dispenses fine droplets of water (about 10 microns in size) that stay suspended in the air. Used for temperature and humidity control in greenhouses and germination chambers.

free-standing greenhouse—individual greenhouse not connected with other greenhouses at the gutter.

fritted—a slow-release fertilizer with the nutrients impregnated into powdered glass. Most commonly used for micronutrients.

germination—the process of sprouting of seeds, starting with the uptake of water (imbibition) and concluding with the emergence of the radicle or the establishment of a healthy seedling.

germination chamber—a room in which temperature, humidity, and light are controlled in order to germinate seeds in plug trays.

gibberellins—chemical compounds used to break flower bud dormancy, seed dormancy, or stimulate shoot elongation.

gutter-connected greenhouses—individual greenhouses that are connected together at the gutters to form one large greenhouse.

gypsum—calcium sulfate ($CaSO_4$). Used primarily as a calcium fertilizer, but it also supplies sulfur. Slow-releasing form of calcium used in growing media when increasing the media pH is not desired.

halo effect—the yellowing around the leaf margins from damage to the chloroplasts in the leaves, a phytotoxic reaction caused by high rates of Cycocel.

hardening-off—stoppage of growth and thickening of leaves and stems due to certain environmental and cultural conditions (Stage 4) that allow the seedlings to withstand holding, shipping, or harsh conditions after transplanting.

high-intensity-discharge lights (HID)—compact, high-output, supplemental light sources that are efficient producers of photosynthetically active radiation (PAR). The two most common types of HID lights are metal halide and high-pressure sodium (HPS).

high-pressure sodium lamps (HPS)—very high output lamps that provide light mostly in the yellow-orange part of the spectrum. Light is produced by passing an electric current through vaporized sodium under pressure at high temperature.

horizontal air flow (HAF)—continuous movement of internal air in the greenhouse with a series of small fans inside the greenhouse.

horticultural-grade—chemicals free of most all contaminants that may damage plants. Higher purity than agricultural-grade.

hydrated lime—lime composed of calcium hydroxide [$Ca(OH)_2$]. Hydrated lime is used to raise the media pH quickly.

hydroponic roots—long, thin, pale roots with no root hairs evident, such as may occur when grown directly in water. Result of overwatering and poor air porosity in the growing media.

hypnum peat—type of peat moss with a pH range of 5.2 to 5.5 and containing more nutrients initially than sphagnum peat.

hypocotyl—the initial stem of the emerging seedling.

imbibition—the physical process of water uptake by a dry seed.

infra-red—wavelengths of light (750 to 800 nm) beyond the red and far-red wavelengths. Source of radiant heat that plants can sense and use, but which does not heat the air first.

internode length—distance between nodes of a plant determined by cell extension and controlled by DIF.

leach—removal of nutrients, salts, pesticides, and other water soluble compounds from growing media with water.

leaching percentage—the percent of water applied during each irrigation that passes through the root zone and out the bottom of the container.

leaf-unfolding rate—speed at which the plant puts out new leaves (growth rate) and controlled by average daily temperature (ADT).

light-saturated—excess of 3,000 footcandles (32,280 lux) on the leaf surface by which photosynthesis requirements for light are satisfied. Excess light produces radiant heat on the leaf surface.

light accumulators—plants such as geranium and dianthus that need total amounts of light (not photoperiod) to initiate flowering.

long-night plant—plants that initiate flowering under long nights (or short days).

macronutrients—one of the six essential elements required by plants in larger quantities (N, K, P, Ca, Mg, S).

manifold vacuum seeders—seeders that use vacuum tips or needles to pick up seeds and drop them into plug trays through drop tubes.

metal halide lamps—type of supplemental HID light that uses iodides and mercury to produce light more in the blue-violet part of the spectrum. These lamps are not as efficient as HPS lamps, but provide a better light spectrum.

microenvironment—the environment directly around a germinating seed or growing plant.

micronutrients—one of the six essential elements required by plants in smaller quantities (Fe, Mn, B, Zn, Cu, Mo).

moisture stress—the drying of the growing media in the plug cell to the extent of some wilting of plants before water is added.

necrosis—brown, scorched, or dead areas on leaves. A common symptom of many nutrient deficiencies and diseases.

nitrate-nitrogen—an inorganic nitrogen fertilizer (NO_3-N). Most readily available form of nitrogen for uptake by plant roots.

noncapillary pore spaces—large pores between particles from which water drains rapidly due to gravity and air then fills the spaces.

nutrient sink—part of the plant that places the highest priority on usage of carbohydrates produced by photosynthesis.

optimal temperature—the temperature that maximizes the growth rate of a particular plant species.

passive absorption—uptake of water by roots of plants that are rapidly transpiring or losing water through their leaves. This uptake is rapid, with roots acting as absorbing surfaces.

peat humus—the most highly decomposed of the peats derived from hypnum peat moss or reed sedge peat. Not desirable for a plug-growing media.

peat moss—the least decomposed of the peats and formed from sphagnum or hypnum peat moss. Most commonly used in plug-growing media.

pelleted seed—small or irregular-shaped seed that have several layers of a clay-type material with a binder to build up the seed size and make it rounder, thereby making it easier for mechanical seeders to sow.

perlite—an inorganic growing media component made from alumino silicate volcanic rock that is mined, crushed, screened to size, then is heated to 1,800F (982C), which causes it to expand into a light-weight, white aggregate.

permanent wilting point (PWP)—the water content in a growing media at which the plant permanently wilts and will not recover unless additional water is added to the growing media.

petioles—the slender stems that connect the leaves to the main stems in some plants.

pH—negative logarithm of the hydrogen ion concentration. Describes the acidity or basicity of a solution. Below pH 7 is acid, pH 7 is neutral, and above pH 7 is basic.

phloem—the part of a plant's vascular system that transports carbohydrates and nutrients to other parts of the plant.

photodormancy—inability of some seeds to germinate due to total lack of light.

photomorphogenesis—plant morphology or height and shape of the plant.

photoperiodism—the flowering response of a plant to light duration (or night period).

photosynthesis—the process in a plant where sunlight, carbon dioxide, and water are combined to form carbohydrates or sugars for the plant to utilize. This process generally takes place in the plant's green leaves and stems.

photosynthetically-active radiation (PAR)—the part of the light spectrum needed for photosynthesis in plants.

phytochrome—plant pigment that utilizes red or far-red wavelengths to determine the plant morphology.

phytotoxicity—injury to plants from a chemical application.

plug—containerized transplant.

porosity—the amount of pore spaces in a growing media.

porous plastic—plastic coverings for germination that have punched holes or are spun-fabric allowing water and air to pass through, but helping to retain heat and humidity.

potential acidity—the pounds of calcium carbonate ($CaCO_3$) estimated to be required to neutralize the acidity caused by adding 1 ton of an acid-forming fertilizer to growing media. The higher the potential acidity of a fertilizer, the more likely it will cause the growing media pH to decrease over time.

potential basicity—the pounds of calcium carbonate ($CaCO_3$) estimated to be equal to the addition of 1 ton of a base-forming fertilizer to the growing media. The higher the potential basicity of a fertilizer, the more likely it will cause the growing media pH to increase over time.

pregerminated seed—seed that has been allowed to germinate to the beginning of radicle emergence, but then stopped. Dead seeds can then be separated from live seeds. When pregerminated seeds are sown, stand establishment is higher and much faster.

premature flowering—flowering in the plug tray or too soon after transplanting, resulting in poorly developed plants or flowers.

primed seed—seed that have started the germination process under controlled hydration, but stopped before radicle emergence and dried back to original moisture content. Once sown, the germination process proceeds much faster with better performance under a wider range of germination conditions.

pull-and-pack plugs—plugs or transplants pulled out of the trays and packed together into a box for cheaper shipping costs.

quarternary ammonium salts—chemicals such as Physan 20 and Greenshield that can be used as disinfectants in the greenhouse.

radiant heat—heat from excess light energy on leaves of plants.

radicle—the initial root emerging from a germinating seed.

reed-sedge peat—formed from swamp plants, more decomposed than peat moss, and with a poorer structure than peat moss. The pH level varies from 4.0 to 7.5.

reefer—truck trailer with a refrigeration unit.

refined seed—seed that have been mechanically separated by density, size, shape, or weight to improve vigor.

respiration—the process of breaking down carbohydrates or sugars to release energy for other plant processes.

retention pond—collection area for excess water from inside and outside the greenhouse.

retractable roof—type of greenhouse where the roof is made of saran-like shade cloth, which can be opened or closed as needed for more light and air movement.

reverse osmosis (R/O)—a water purification system where water is forced under high pressure through a semipermeable membrane that filters out dissolved solutes.

robotic transplanter—machine that automatically transplants plugs into finished containers.

root hairs—very small branches of roots that increase root surface area and improve uptake of water and nutrients from the growing media.

root-zone heating—heating below the bench that maintains soil temperature, not air temperature.

R-value—thermal resistance or insulation factor.

saturated media extract (SME)—a method of growing media extraction where the growing medium is mixed with just enough water to make a paste, and then some of the water is vacuumed out or squeezed out for testing.

seed quality—combination of viability and vigor.

shading response—sensing of far-red light by the leaves and the resultant stretching of the plant to receive more light than its neighbors.

short-night plants—plants that initiate flowering under short nights (long days).

slow-release fertilizers—a fertilizer that is not immediately soluble and available to plants because the nutrients are released over time, from weeks to months. Release is based on either low solubility, biological breakdown, or a semipermeable coating.

sodium absorption ratio (SAR)—a mathematical term used to estimate the sodium hazard in irrigation water. It is an equation that takes into account the sodium content of water in relation to the calcium and magnesium content. The higher the ratio, the greater the risk from sodium.

soluble salts—any salt that is soluble in water. Salts include most inorganic fertilizers (NH_4, NO_3, K, SO_4) and mineral salts (Na, Cl, HCO_3) dissolved in irrigation water.

source-sink relationship—priority of different plant parts for carbohydrates from photosynthesis. In seedlings, leaves have priority over roots. Once a flower forms, the flower has first priority, then leaves, then roots.

sphagnum peat moss—type of peat moss with lowest pH (3.0 to 4.5) and best characteristics for growing media. Preferred peat moss for plug mixes.

square foot weeks—method of determining production costs based on how much space a container takes up in the greenhouse and for how long.

squeeze method—a technique for quickly testing the pH and EC of a growing media.

Stage 0—the preparation stage including flat-filling, seeding, covering, and watering in.

starter charge—amount of fertilizer added to the growing media before seeding or transplanting.

stomates—openings in the leaves for taking in CO_2, letting out O_2, and letting out moisture (transpiration).

stratification—the process of using cool, moist conditions (sometimes warm and moist) to improve seed germination of dormant seeds.

superphosphate—a granular phosphorus fertilizer derived by dissolving raw rock phosphate with acid. Use of sulfuric acid produces single superphosphate (0-20-0 + gypsum), and use of phosphoric acid produces treble (or triple) superphosphate (0-45-0). An amendment commonly added to growing media before using to supply P.

supplemental lighting—additional lighting besides natural light to increase plant growth.

synergistic effect—greater effect when two chemicals are combined than when either is used separately.

tempered water—heated water for irrigation.

thermal curtain—blanket or curtain made of plastic and aluminum strips designed to retain heat in the greenhouse when the curtain is closed.

thermodormancy—inability of some seeds to germinate due to high temperature.

tip abortion—loss of the main growing point of the plant, probably due to nutrient imbalances.

toning—see hardening-off.

topcoater—machine for covering plug trays with media, vermiculite, or other loose coverings.

transpiration—the loss of water from the plant by water vapor moving out through the stomates. Process helps to cool the plant.

turgor pressure—the maintenance of water potential within plant cells.

turns—turning over of a greenhouse crop (shipping and selling it) and replacing it with another one.

ultraviolet—wavelengths of light in the 300 to 400 nm range that help keep plants shorter.

unavailable water—the percent volume of growing media occupied by water that is unavailable to the plant. It is also called the permanent wilting point (see definition).

urea-nitrogen—an organic nitrogen fertilizer [$CO(NH_2)_2$]. In the growing media, urea-nitrogen needs to be broken down to ammonium and then to nitrate, which is readily taken up by the plant roots. Urea-nitrogen is thus grouped with ammonical-nitrogen.

vacuum cylinder/drum seeders—type of high-speed mechanical seeders that use drums or cylinders with vacuum pick-up of seeds.

vacuum template seeder—type of hand seeder that uses vacuum template with holes in it to pick up seed.

vapor pressure deficit (VPD)—the difference between the actual water vapor pressure of the air and the saturation water vapor pressure of the evaporating surface of the media and seed.

vermiculite—an inorganic growing media component made from a mica-like ore of aluminum-iron magnesium silicate that is fired (heated) to cause the layers to expand into an accordion-like structure.

vernalization—cold, moist treatment applied to a plant to induce or hasten the development of the capacity for flowering.

viability—ability of a live seed to germinate under optimum conditions.

vigor—ability of a live seed to germinate under a range of conditions and still produce a usable seedling.

water-holding capacity (WHC)—container capacity or the ability of the growing media to hold water.

water-soluble fertilizers—fertilizers that are completely soluble in water and are dispensed through fertilizer injectors.

watering boom—a self-propelled pipe with several nozzles that is held above the bench or floor to water the crop.

watering tunnel—a conveyor with a series of nozzles to water in plug trays after seeding and finished containers after transplanting.

wetting agent—a compound that breaks up the surface tension of peat-based soilless mixes and allows the peat moss to absorb water easily.

xylem—the part of the vascular system of plants that transports water and nutrients from the roots to other parts of the plant.

INDEX